ISLAND PEOPLE FINDING OUR WAY

HENRY R. DANIELSON

PAGE PUBLISHING, INC.
New York, NY

First originally published by Page Publishing, Inc. 2017

ISBN 978-1-64138-199-4 (Paperback)
ISBN 978-1-64138-200-7 (Digital)

Printed in the United States of America

CONTENTS

INTRODUCTION

So there I was in school, and the girl who sat in front of me in eighth grade arithmetic, the cute little girl with brown hair, the one who graded my paper when we passed them to the person in front of us, helped me. Oh, we didn't cheat; she just pointed out little careless errors that I had made before the teacher made us correct the papers. She cared. Then she went away. She was gone for months, having her back fused in eleven places, the result of polio when she was much younger. When she returned, she was in a steel brace. We were still friends. Imagine being in junior high school, wearing a brace that went from your shoulders to the base of your spine, holding you rigid. After months, the brace came off, and Julie and I began to date. We went to dances, to movies, to parties. We went to different colleges, but we dated when we were home. We fell in love. We got engaged and married.

This is the story of my lovely wife, whom no one thought would live very long, and me, island people who somehow conquered one difficult situation after another throughout our lives. Yes, we lived on an island in Africa, and we live on an island in Florida in our retirement. We visited islands, in the North Channel of Lake Huron, in the Bahamas, in the Caribbean. It is a book about caring, about foreigners, about the good things that others have to offer us. It is not a war story; it does not involve killing or violence or anger or rage. Well, maybe a little. There are many people from different cultures here, but you may not see them as being much different from you. There are some tense moments. We did have a green mamba, a very deadly snake, living in our house for ten days in Africa. We did live on an island, with no civil authority for two years in the Peace Corps. We swam in waters populated by crocodiles and hippos. We sailed our small sailboats through the Great Lakes to Bermuda and the Caribbean. Often, we found ourselves in situations where there was no help, no one to call in an emergency. We looked out for each other.

Were we rich? Hardly. We lived on teacher's salaries. We had a small house in Western New York, and we heated it with wood. All but one of our boats were secondhand, but we used them to the max to discover our world. Still, there is joy here. We found a beautiful world out there, and this is the first part of our story.

PART 1

GROWING AND GROWING

CHAPTER 1

Where I Came From

Closer to Chicago than New York City—that was where I was born, in Jamestown, New York, Chautauqua County, Western New York. It was near the end of the war, January 1945. Swedes, we were Swedes in a town of Swedes and Italians, mostly. It was winter, January. There was a huge snowstorm. We lived in nearby Lakewood, just five miles north of the city. My dad had a flat tire, taking Mom to the hospital. He fixed it in the driving snow on an icy road, and despite his extreme nervous anxiety, they made it in time. I was born at eight the following morning. Mom had to spend two weeks in the hospital, or Dr. Bowman "wouldn't be responsible for her afterlife."

That was the start of me.

The family was another story.

Dad sold furniture, Elite Furniture, from his father's factory in Jamestown. His father, my grandfather, had moved there from Sweden at seventeen.

Gustaf, my grandfather, was a cabinetmaker's son who, unhappy with limited opportunities in Sweden, moved to America and to Jamestown. My great-grandfather, whom I never met, taught Grandpa to build furniture and made sure he worked in the family shop in Stockholm six days each week. When one of his friends died, Gus, Grandpa, had to lie down so his dad could design the coffin. It was a cruel joke Grandpa never forgot. His dad was a drinker. He would work all week and overindulge on Saturday night and then insist his children go to church with him all day Sunday to repent. Grandpa decided there must be a better life. He left home, a lonely seventeen-year-old, and began the trek to America.

Soon after he got to the States, he married Sarah, another seventeen-year-old, from Yorkshire, England, who worked in the woolen trade. English was the language of the house. Grandpa worked at Maddox Table Company, in Jamestown, for a while, and after a few years, he and some friends found several financial backers and started the Elite Furniture Company. They made tables—pedestal tables, end tables, and coffee tables—along with other furniture. After a few years, they built their own factory, a four-story brick building on Allen Street. The factory thrived. Gus and Sarah had five kids. My dad was third born, the eldest son.

We still keep in touch with much of the family and even had a reunion in Western New York in 2014.

My dad, Benny, continued to work for Elite as a salesman. He learned the woodworking trade from his father and actually built furniture of his own, some of which is still being enjoyed at our cottage in Henderson Harbor, New York. Mostly, however, he sold furniture. Monday through Friday he was on the road throughout Western New York and Northwestern Pennsylvania, selling Elite tables and other lines as well until the company closed in 1954.

My mother was a Swede too. Her dad and mom, my grandparents on the Reed side, met in Rockford, Illinois, quite by accident. Harriet Nelson had come across at about ten. They were in *steerage*, the lowest class on the ship. Her mother and father and two brothers were all seasick. She was the only one well enough to clean up after the others. We still have the small trunk in which they had packed all their family belongings. It is thirty-three inches long, fifteen inches wide, and fifteen inches high, and it held all the worldly goods of the Nelson family of five. The label said GOTHENBURG TO NEW YORK and WHITE STAR LINES.

Once they were settled in Rockford, Grandma Harriet was skating on the Rock River in Rockford one cold winter's day when she fell through the ice. A young passerby saw her go down. Victor Reed rescued her. He pulled her from the icy water and took her to her home. Later, they fell in love and were married. Victor was the eldest son of the Reed family. He sold woodworking machinery, and he often traveled to Jamestown, where he sold his equipment to the many furniture factories there. Victor and Harriet had three children, Roland, Marguerite, and Helen, my mother. In 1919, he moved the family to Jamestown, New York.

Grandpa bought a house on North Main Street in Jamestown and, with his wife, Harriet, and their three kids, drove their 1919 Howard Lexington touring car all the way from Rockford to Jamestown without a flat tire! Unheard of!

Victor Reed's business selling woodworking machinery continued to flourish after the move to Jamestown. He purchased a lovely summer cottage at Stockholm, on Lake Chautauqua, where the family enjoyed summer on the sparkling lake.

His son, Roland, inherited the business from his father. Roland married Ellen Spetz. Much of the woodworking machinery in Jamestown, and other woodworking centers in the Northeast was sold by the Jamestown company his father had started. The Reeds were prominent members of the community for many years to come.

Marguerite, Vic and Harriet's elder daughter, married Leon Carlson, an athlete and local baseball star. Leon played minor league baseball and advanced to the major leagues as a spitball pitcher for the Washington Senators. Babe Ruth is said to have hit his longest home run off a pitch thrown by my Uncle Leon. In the off season, Leon fished for muskelunge from rowboats in Chautauqua Lake. He claimed his best nights for fishing were when his oars just tinkled the ice. As there were no limits on catches in those days, he sold his catch to area hotels. When the depression hit, his wife had a miscarriage and he was out of work. He claimed he had to borrow a hundred dollars from the milk man to survive.

Leon learned that there was a need for workers to insulate pipes in refineries in nearby Warren and Bradford, Pennsylvania. He gathered some of his old teammates and bid on the job. The rest is history. Within a year he was driving his first Cadillac. They built a lovely stone house on Lake Chautauqua. Laco Industries in

Jamestown did insulation and roofing and was a very profitable company for many years.

Helen, my mother, was the youngest Reed Daughter. She was second in her class at Jamestown High School, sang in the a'capella choir and was a fine student. Though qualified to go on to college, her father insisted if she went, it would be in Rockford, where she could live with Aunt Selma, his sister. Mother decided that living with her aunt was not the answer, so she found a job as secretary to the president of a local insurance firm instead. She married my dad, Vernette, (Benny) Danielson in 1940. They met at the wedding of a mutual friend. She was twenty-five, he was ten years her senior.

Each of the three Reed children had one son, Charlie, Bill, and me. Charlie, Leon and Marguerite's son, excelled in football in high school and college, and was the first to attend Grove City College. After graduation he took over his father's business. Both he and his wife passed away after the premature loss of two of their three children. Bill, son of Roland and Ellen, also attended Grove city. He and his wife, Joan have two married children with families of their own. Like his father, he continued to run the family business successfully until his retirement. He and Joan, like Julie and me, live in Western New York in the summer and Southwest Florida in the winter months.

CHAPTER 2

Trains, Boats, and Wonderful Woods

Though my dad, a furniture salesman, had other lines than Elite, his father's company was the main one. He was on the road Monday to Friday. Mom and I stayed home. Weekends, they went out to the Chautauqua Lake Yacht Club, or The Town Club, and other social events. I stayed home with a sitter, Mrs. Stewart, if I was lucky; otherwise, it was some girl or old lady. I was never much trouble. I didn't mind. My dad wasn't very happy. He wanted to eat at home weekends after having eaten in restaurants all week, but my mom, who ate at home all week, wanted to go out. My dad wanted to move to Florida, my mom wanted to stay in town with her family, but Dad made a good living. We made it work.

One of my early memories was waking in the night to noise downstairs. I got up and walked down the stairs only to be picked up and whisked back to bed by my mom. She and Dad were drinking beer with the Grangers, their best friends. Hank Granger had been a paving contractor in the army during the war and had been building Allied airfields in the Azores when I was born, toward the end of World War II. I was named after him. By then, 1949, I was about four. My dad had ordered a Lionel train for me, and I learned, years later, they had set it up on the living room floor and were giving it a test run. As it would be a Christmas present, I was not allowed to see. I remember, that fall, my dad spent weekend time in the basement. He was hammering and sawing, sanding and painting. When Christmas came, I got my train. We took the train downstairs, and there, on one side of the basement, was a *layout*, not on the floor, but on a huge table. It was the full length of the house, twenty-three feet on one side and half the length of the house on the other. There were two switches so I could divert the steam engine, with real smoke, from one line to the other. There was a station, where the train stopped automatically on each round, and on a separate track, accessed by a switch was a coal station, where a gondola could be pushed up a ramp to dump its load of coal into the coal loader below. Some of my friends had trains too, but theirs circled the Christmas tree and went away after the tree came down. Dad and I spent hours and hours in the basement with that train. He carved figures in balsa wood, Mickey Mouse, a man in a canoe, a lady with a big hat, even Felix the Cat. We, but he mostly, crumpled screen, made papier-mâché hills and tunnels, a stream with a fly fisherman, brooks, bridges, and rills. There was a town with streetlights and houses. That is what Dad and I did when he was home in winter.

Years went by. When I was about ten, my cousin Bill, son of my dad's older sister, about a year older than me, used to come down, and we would run those trains all day and into the night, with regular schedules, hour after hour. Years later, the layout moved to the other side of the cellar. Two more engines, along with a cattle and milk car, were added. We made up stories of chases, escapes, train wrecks…

* * *

Turn on the twist switch at the top of the stairs, and the naked bulb on the cellar ceiling would burst into glaring light. Descend those stairs and walk ahead and to the left around the furnace. Pull out the stool with the faded blue top and sit. Reach forward, over the transformer, to the light switch mounted on the table. Snap. The layout in front of you is illuminated with tiny streetlights from the village to your right. There is a buzzing sound from an oil derrick across the table. A passenger train is stopped at the station across the tracks from where you sit. On your right are mounted four-switch controls with red and green lights. Numerous labeled toggle switches adorn the panel, and just below them is the large two-handled transformer. On the right is a green light. Grasp the lever and push it forward. Slowly, the Santa Fe diesel locomotive, in three sections, and its load of passenger cars begin to move down the track and toward the village to the east. Push the lever beside the throttle and blow the horn. Pass through the village and round the bend as the train rises slowly through two tunnels, rounds more curves, and passes another train on the inner track—this one, stopped, unloading cattle and milk cars and taking on coal from the freight yard.

* * *

One spring day while I was in kindergarten, in 1950, my dad and I went to Bemus Point, on Chautauqua Lake. L-S Aero Marine sold boats and motors, and my dad took me inside and showed me a twelve-foot boat. It was Bermuda green, with a tomahawk painted on the bow. Varnished inside, it was a cedar strip boat, and it glowed. The rich, warm smell of fresh paint and varnish filled the air. Beside it, on a stand, was a light-green two-and-a-half-horsepower Johnson outboard motor. Dave Lawson, my dad's friend and hunting buddy, made the sale. We added a red gas can to the purchase, a pair of varnished oars, and a life jacket for me. The next day, after the boat soaked up overnight at the marina, we came back, climbed in, bailed it out, and motored the eight miles or so back to the foot of Southland Avenue in Lakewood. Best of all, I was at the helm. I couldn't start the motor then, but I quickly learned to move the tiller and adjust the speed. The sweet smell of exhaust from that little two-stroke engine thrilled me.

Back home in Lakewood, we ordered some inch lumber and some two-by-fours and built skids so we could pull the boat up on the rocky beach at the foot of Southland Avenue. For years, Dad and I would get up early, load the motor and spare gas into the wheelbarrow, and walk several hundred yards across Terrace Avenue to the lake, where we would launch the boat and troll for muskellunge for hours. We caught a couple of keepers over the years, but that was rare. Mostly, we just sat facing each other, me at the helm on the rear seat, with one hand on the tiller, and he in the middle seat, with the two rods mounted in rod holders. We watched the rods, their ends jiggling with the action of the lures, waiting for a strike. We talked about everything. We talked about boats and people and cars. Dad had read to me for years. Every night when he was home, he would read to me before I went to bed. Tom Sawyer, Huckleberry Finn, and other classics were mine when other kids were dealing with children's books. We even talked about books. He had never graduated from high school, but he was an avid reader.

On Mondays, I would walk my dad to the neighbor's garage, where he kept the Chevy, and watch him drive off to sell furniture across his New York and Pennsylvania territory. I would be waiting for him when he came back on Friday afternoon.

For my tenth birthday, my present was an eight-foot Clearwater Pram, upon which the Optimist dinghy, a popular sailboat used in modern-day sail schools, was based. Mine was an unfinished plywood sailboat, and I would learn to sail it at the Chautauqua Lake Yacht Club, where my dad had been a founding member many years before. We sanded and painted and varnished the boat in our basement that winter. We named her *Pop Over*. Like our other boat, she was Bermuda green on the outside, and the interior was clear varnish. I read everything I could on sailing that winter, and the next summer, I started sailing. Dad was in the rowboat, and I was in the pram. He would yell what I should do, and when I did, I quickly sailed away from him. I knew the basics: turn into the wind, not away from it; trim the sails going to weather, ease them going downwind. I caught on quickly. It was 1955, the first year of the junior program at the nearby Chautauqua Lake Yacht Club.

It was about that time when the trouble started. Elite, my grandfather's company, had gone out of business. Grandpa and his partners were just getting too old. My dad decided to give up his salesman's job. He was offered other lines but wasn't interested. I didn't understand the gravity of his decision at that time, but he wanted to quit selling furniture on the road and get a job in a factory so he could be home with Mom and me. Mother was furious. She cried when she typed his letter of resignation. They argued fiercely during the night, which terrified me. His pay would be greatly reduced. Their lifestyle would change. What about their friends? Both their families had always been on the management side of things. Would he join the union? Go on strike? That remained to be seen. In some important ways, however, our lives would change.

* * *

One Sunday in Lakewood, I remember hearing the fire siren. My mom had rules about the siren. "When you hear the siren, get as far off the road as you can." The volunteers would get in their cars, place blinking blue lights on the dashboards, and race for the fire station. Once there, they would board one of the large red fire trucks and dash off for the fire, red lights flashing and sirens screaming.

On that particular Sunday, I remember watching from the neighbor's porch as truck after truck raced down Terrace Avenue, lights flashing and sirens screaming, and then turned abruptly toward the lake. It was an overcast summer afternoon, but a great pall of smoke drifted from the neighborhood. We kids raced for the spot. Wow, a house fire! We watched as the firemen attached hoses to hydrants and even ran a line to the lake as thick, rich blue smoke poured from cracks in the siding and a few broken windows of a big old house on the lake. It went on for hours. The fire had gotten into the walls. The smell was horrible. The old woman who lived there alone had hundreds of cats, we were told. Most were lost in the fire. She wandered back and forth on the lawn, with tears running down her wrinkled cheeks. The firemen carried a smoldering couch from her house. She touched it and again burst into tears. Suddenly, it wasn't fun anymore. A sadness came over me that I couldn't quite contain. I didn't even know her, but I just wanted the fire to be over. I wanted to go home.

A few months later, in September, the little store right around the corner from the house that burned caught fire and was gutted as well. The smell, the broken glass, the ruined black interior of the store somehow sickened me. I became terrified of fire. I would wake in the night frightened and weak.

* * *

There had been a time when I was very young when we used to sit on the front porch on Sunday afternoons. Dad and Mom would read the *New York Times*, do the crossword, have a few drinks, and visit with friends as they walked by. However, front porches became rather old-fashioned, as people drove more and walked less. So Dad designed and built a garage out back with a porch on the side, facing Mom's flower garden. It was lovely and private and the place where they spent weekend afternoons and evenings in summer.

"Hey, Dad, can we go up to the yacht club?" I was ten. We still belonged to the club, but we didn't go there much as a family. We really couldn't afford to.

"Why don't you just put the motor on the boat and take yourself up?" my dad said.

I was shocked. "Really?"

The wheelbarrow was behind the garage, and I pulled it down and wheeled it around to the front and inside, near where the motor was. I grabbed the old quilt off the motor and laid it in the wheelbarrow and then picked up and lugged the heavy motor over to the wheelbarrow, where I carefully, under the watchful eye of my father, laid it in place. I lifted the wheelbarrow handles and headed down the driveway. I walked to the lake and on the rocky shore, unloaded the motor, and carried it to the stern of the boat. I put it on the transom and tightened the clamps as tight as I could, tilted the little motor up, and pushed the boat, with all my might, into the water. I put the oars in the oarlocks and dipped them into the water, turning the boat around and rowing out to deep water, near the end of Mr. Kettle's dock. Once there, I pulled the oars from the locks and laid them on the seat beside me. I loosened the vent knob on the top of the motor's gas tank then reached behind the left side of the motor (facing aft) and loosened the brass valve that allowed fuel to flow from the tank to the carburetor. I adjusted the choke, moved the throttle to the "start" position, then pulled the recoil starter handle. The engine started at once. I pushed in the choke, and off we went. About a hundred yards up the lake, there was a lurch and a splash, and suddenly, the boat was going in circles and in silence. What happened?

The motor had fallen off into the pea-green water. It was gone.

I stared into the water in vain. I saw no one onshore to help me. I put the oars into the oarlocks and rowed as fast as I could back to the skids, where I pulled the boat up partway, as far as I could, and raced home to tell my dad. Back home, I donned my trunks and grabbed my mask, but back at the spot of loss, try as we did, we could find nothing under the murky water. I hadn't taken careful bearings and wasn't really sure where I had lost it. We organized swimming search parties among neighborhood kids, dragged magnets, even hired a diver, but we had no luck.

The motor was gone.

* * *

I mowed lawns that summer and substituted for a neighbor delivering papers over the winter. The next year, 1956, I spent all my savings and bought a red five-and-a-half-horsepower Johnson outboard for the boat. I added a safety chain, as insurance against loss, and understood the importance of tightening the transom clamps.

My cousin Bill, my best friend and the closest thing I had to a brother, visited often, and in the summer, we would take the boat and go off on grand adventures. When we were little, we used to kneel by the bathtub for hours, floating toy boats in the half-filled tub. We created storms with our hands, causing our miniature vessels to fill and sink. There were battles and sea voyages. We could entertain ourselves for hours, stopping only when someone needed the bathroom for other purposes. So when I was old enough to take the boat out alone, eleven or twelve, Bill and I would get up at first light and wheel the motor down to the boat to fish for muskellunge. Mostly, we just caught weeds, but the fishing was supposed to be better farther north, in the upper lake. So one day, we just kept going. When we got home in midafternoon, and still empty-handed, my mother was very upset. She glared at us. "Where the hell have you been?" she yelled. She had called my father at work. She was ready to call the fire department to start a search. When Dad got home, there was a terrible row. Ugly. We promised to do better next time.

A few weeks later, Bill and I agreed to be on our best behavior if we could go fishing again. That time, we caught a beautiful big bass and a keeper, thirty-five-inch muskellunge, which we carefully scaled and cleaned, much to my mother's delight. When my father came home from work, he was ready for a fight. Disarmed by the cleaned, fresh fish ready to be cooked for dinner, he was a bit let down, but a few scales on the grass gave him something to rail about. In reality, he couldn't have been more pleased.

At our house, it was the lake and the trains that entertained Bill and me. When I stayed at Bill's, we had the woods. Uncle Harold, Bill's dad, was a dentist. They had a lovely home in the country, with twenty seven acres of land, much of it woods. There was a cabin Bill and his dad and our grandpa had built down in the woods, just a mile from the house. Using four trees as the uprights, it offered little protection from weather and none from cold, but on mild weekends, we would sometimes go down to the cabin and spend the night. We would build a fire in front and cook our dinner over the coals, telling ghost stories to one another until we crawled into our sleeping bags for the night. Rain was always a problem, as there was no place really dry inside, but we did fine. Owls would screech in the night, terrifying us, and we were always amazed at the footprints around the cabin in the mornings. Skunks, raccoons, opossum, and even deer would come by and leave their tracks.

One time in our preteens, we headed for the woods after a winter snowfall. We slogged our way down through the pasture into the woods. We followed deer tracks for a while and wandered aimlessly. Soon, we realized we were lost. We thought, if we went to the right, we would come to the road. We walked and walked, but nothing looked familiar. Soon we stumbled upon another pair of footprints. It appeared to be of two people. We knew they would take us out of the woods, so we followed them. Then, after a while, we could see where two other people had joined the first group. We seemed to be following a group of four. Somehow, it dawned on us, something from *Winnie the Pooh*. Sure enough, we were following our own footprints, going in big circles through the woods.

It was getting late in the day. We left the tracks and headed toward the west, where the light was strongest. There, ahead of us, was an opening in the woods. Beyond that opening, up the hill and over the pasture, was Bill's house.

So that was how I grew up. I learned to appreciate the water and the woods. I had a loving family that cared for me and did what they could. In sixth grade, I remember the teacher, Mrs. Peterson, had a copy of *Science and Mechanics* magazine in the room. I was thumbing through it one day when I came upon an article about a seventeen-foot cabin cruiser that could be built from plans. The boat was called *Sea Knight*, and the plans were offered by Glen L. Marine. The plan set would cost ten dollars. I asked my dad if we could build a boat like that. It would be a large commitment, and Mother didn't think we could afford it.

We sent away for the plans, and I remember Dad and me drawing patterns of the frames on the Ping-Pong table in the basement. Dad agreed to do the building, but I had to be there to work with him. If I went off to play ball, there would be no work done on the boat! He brought discarded crating lumber home from the factory where he worked, and we built a jig in the garage. We would use that to mount the frames on and hold them in place to build the rest of the inverted hull. There was a factory that made MFG boats in nearby Celeron, and we bought mahogany for the frames from them. We bought plywood and screws and glue, and we set to work. I had no idea what we had gotten ourselves into, but I learned fast to measure, cut and screw and sand, clean and measure, and cut again. Everything had to be just right. We started in the winter, expecting to be finished by July, but July passed, and in October, we moved the hull out of the garage and covered it for the winter. The following spring, we fiberglassed the hull, turned it over, and started work on the decks, cabin top, and interior. I saved all my paper route money and bought a used 1957 Johnson 35 outboard motor for the boat at a cost of $230. Fiberglass was a relatively new thing then, and my cousin Charlie was in the business. He got us materials at a discount. We covered the whole boat with fiberglass and named her *Polly Ester*.

It was July of 1961 when that boat was launched at the foot of Southland Avenue. I was sixteen. There was a little leak from a missing screw in the skeg, which caused much amusement in the neighborhood, but we promptly plugged the leak. She was beautiful with her black hull and off-white cabin. We spent countless hours cruising and fishing Chautauqua Lake on that boat. She was indeed our great source of pride.

School? I wasn't a very good student. I failed algebra twice but did all right in everything else. I never liked it much. A skinny kid with pimples and blond hair, I wasn't much of an athlete, and I had terrible, uneven handwriting. I had a flair for English, and I loved to read. I must have been fifteen, in tenth grade, when I brought home *A Tale of Two Cities*. I groaned about having to read it after dinner one night. "Story about a senile old man," I mumbled.

My dad heard me and put down his pipe. He crumpled the newspaper he was reading.

"It was the best of times, it was the worst of times," he quoted from memory and then went on to quote the rest of the poem opening the novel. "What do you mean you don't like the book? It's about Jerry Cruncher, the most dangerous man in the world to play leapfrog with. It is about sacrifice and grave robbing and love. It is about the razor that shaves close, the guillotine. It's one of the best books I ever read! Turn to the last page," he commanded.

I did as directed.

"It is a far, far better thing I do than I have ever done. It is a far, far better place I go than I have ever been," he recited, quoting the ending. I was simply amazed. He had never graduated from high school. How could he know this stuff?

"Now go upstairs and put your pajamas on," he said. "I'm going to read to you like I used to. You're going to love this book."

I did what he said, and he made that book come to life for me. I learned a new appreciation for literature. It was a personal thing, not a school thing, but something far greater. We shared that book, and somehow, English class and writing took on a whole new meaning for me. Perhaps that evening led to my teaching English for thirty-three years. I think so.

Fortunately for me, my grandparents and my aunt Marguerite had sent along a little money for my education every Christmas and birthday, and by the time I was ready to go to college, the money was there. No one in my immediate family had ever gone to college. My mom was second in her class at Jamestown High but never went on; my dad quit in his senior year of high school. Three of my cousins had gone to Grove City College, a small Presbyterian school in

Western Pennsylvania, so it seemed to me that college meant Grove City. I applied and got accepted. I struggled as a psychology major at first but soon switched to English, and things were better. I graduated after four years, in 1967.

Two weeks after graduation at our respective colleges, Julie and I were married. Julie? I met Julie in math class in eighth grade. She had been challenged by polio as a child but was cured of the terrible disease and, with heroic perseverance after fusion of one-third of her vertebrae, overcame her paralysis. We had things in common. We both liked to sail. We both liked to fish. We liked each other. Where I was weak, she was strong. She asked me to a sorority dance, and I took her to junior and senior proms. We were an item all through high school. She went on a scholarship to Brockport State, part of the State University of New York, a long way from Grove City, but before we knew it, we were writing and calling and getting together whenever we could. As seniors in our respective schools, we were engaged and then married, and in the summer of 1967, we started married life in Pittsburgh, of all places, a long way from open water. I worked at Joseph Horn Company, a large department store. I was assistant buyer for children's shoes. It didn't take long for me to realize that merchandising, as Dr. Kauffman, one of my English professors, had suggested, wasn't for me.

While we were living in Pittsburgh, Julie got a letter from the Peace Corps. She had been one of the first applicants when President Kennedy introduced the program earlier in the decade. They told her at that time to finish high school and college and do her service then. She was invited to an education program in Malawi, Central Africa. I took a test at a local post office, they used my draft physical, and I was included in the invitation. We would serve as a married couple.

CHAPTER 3

Peace Corps Training, Macon County, Alabama

That fall, I quit my job at Horns, we packed up our things, and moved them back to Chautauqua County, where our parents would store them for us. Then we were off to Montgomery, Alabama, for Peace Corps training. People asked what exactly it was that we would be doing. We wondered. Malawi?

From Montgomery, where we were introduced to our trainers and to other members of the program, we traveled to Atkins Camp, an old Boy Scouts camp in Macon County, Alabama, not far from Tuskegee Institute. Julie and I were one of four married couples in the program, which totaled about sixty individuals. They showed us a skeleton of a shed. That was to be our home. Tar paper, shingles, and nails were available, along with some scrap lumber. That was about it. Before long, we had enclosed the framework with tar paper and shingled the roof. We made a window and a door. Inside, we made a huge bed and a desk. That was about all. We were given a Coleman gasoline heater and lantern and a fire extinguisher. Our heater and our lantern and our shack provided heat, light, and shelter—that was all we would need. There was a *sitoro*, or store, for sundries and beer and a dining hall for meals. When we went to town, we traveled in the back of old pickup trucks. What kind of government program was this?

It was an experience! There were wonderful trainers there. They were people who had been in the Peace Corps in Africa. Energetic, enthusiastic people who had been there and who had fallen in love with those in other countries and who enjoyed working with people with different outlooks. They were black and white. In my high school in Lakewood, there had been one black boy. Sometimes, I had sat with him on the school bus. That was it. There was a black girl in our Peace Corps program too, but just one.

There were half a dozen native Malawian men there too. They would be our language instructors. We would teach in English but were expected to know the native language, Chinyanja (in our case, Chitumbuka, for those farther north). Our language classes met numerous times each day. It was all oral learning. There was no spelling or verb conjugation, just conversation and repetition. "Hello, sir, where are you going?" "I am going to the lake." Over and over we said it in the native tongue. Our instructors promised never to utter a word in English but to act out what they were saying and say it as they were doing it. "I am standing on my desk." "I am cleaning the window." "I am reading a book." We would repeat what they said, and they would correct our pronunciation and go on to the next phrase. We were encouraged to use our local Malawian language, especially during meals. To be fair, our instructors cheated a little. They would try to explain more complex ideas in English. We, too, reverted to English at the dining hall most of the time. The training worked. Little by little, we became fluent, or at least able to communicate in the native tongue, which, we were reminded, we were never to use at school in Malawi.

There was other instruction as well. There were regular classes in teaching. We would prepare a lesson and teach our peers. We learned classroom management and discipline skills, something, we were told, we wouldn't need much in Malawi. The main thrust of the program was in cultural sensitivity. What? How would we live with and teach these people without offending them? What would offend them?

There were hours of instruction about the culture of Central Africa. When one met and shook hands with a Malawian man, he might not let go. Really? Really! He might hold your right hand for much of the conversation that would follow your initial meeting. Holding hands was common courtesy, not as in America. About the left hand. If someone invited you for dinner, never touch a dish of food with your left hand. If you do, others might refuse to eat from that dish. Never touch anyone with your left hand. That would be very impolite. Remember, in Latin, *right* is *dexter*; *left* is *sinister.* Some of our students would be of the Islamic faith, but none of them, Muslim or not, would like to be touched, pointed at, or even be handed a sheet of paper with the left hand. Never pat a child on the head with your palm. Africans believed it would stunt his or her growth. If you indicated the height of a child in his absence, never hold your palm horizontal but raise your hand so the fingers pointed upward, indicating his height with the base of your palm; otherwise, they believed he might cease to grow.

"What if you are left -handed?" someone asked.

"You must be aware of the enormity of that problem."

What a lot to learn.

Real sensitivity training came in group sessions. One of us would have to role-play in front of the whole group.

One time, a black man was seated in the front of the room. It was explained to us that he was a local farmer and that grant money was available for farmers like him to help them expand production and earn more money in exchange for a public right-of-way to part of his land. There were forty-three of us seated in the room, and one was picked to talk with the farmer. She was dealing with a rural American farmer in Alabama. He was black, with graying hair, a prickly beard, torn jeans, and a flannel shirt. He was a bit hunched over under a straw hat.

Beverly introduced herself and began talking with the farmer and telling him what the government wanted and had to offer. Her presentation seemed reasonable to most of us. It took just a few minutes for her to introduce herself and learn a little about the farmer. She presented what information she had clearly. What could be wrong with that? When she was finished, we all breathed more easily. *There but for the grace of God go I,* we thought. Then our moderator picked another one of us. He used much the same approach, introducing himself and describing what he needed and what he had to offer in exchange. He tried to learn what the farmer needed most and explain how he could help him with that. He learned a bit about the work the old man did and then pointed out what his program could provide.

Finally, there was Michael. He was a Harvard man, and his grandfather had been a powerful Boston politician. Michael limped to the table, introduced himself, and just talked to the farmer about his sore ankle, about farming, about the weather, about his family, about his farm, about his children, about everything except the right-of-way or the grant he had to offer. He went on and on and on, engaging the farmer in conversation, listening, but never mentioning the grant. They would have another meeting.

Later, when the old man had his turn to speak, we heard his side. He turned out to be amazingly articulate. He might have been an actor or a professor—they never told us. He had been insulted by the first two, who assumed that he wasn't happy and successful on his farm and needed help. He liked Michael; he didn't trust the other two.

So what were we to learn from that? Should we plan to go to Africa and never bring up what we were there for?

It was a lesson about us. About the goal-oriented world that we Americans live in. We may assume that a poor black farmer in Alabama is unhappy and unsatisfied working on his farm, but that may not be true. He may be quite fulfilled working his land, feeding his family, and caring for his animals. He may not want government interference or more money. It was clearly something for us to think about. It was about teaching others without imposing our will on them. We would be there to give Malawians skills needed in today's world but not to impose our political or religious or any other beliefs on them.

Every day we were stimulated by amazing people. One day, there was a professor from Columbia University who could soak up language like a sponge. He joined some of our Malawian teachers during our lessons and, that evening, began talking with us in the Chinyanja he had learned during the day. He was amazing.

A professor from Berkeley talked about witchcraft and the role it played in African life, even in places where people had been converted to Christianity for generations. There were sociologists and educators and explorers. They all made amazing presentations and then would often hang around for casual discussion over a beer or two after dinner. It was an education unlike we had ever found in college. There were no written tests, but many conversations. There were psychological evaluations—we were constantly being assessed.

We lived in our tar paper shacks with our Coleman heaters and gas lanterns.

One night, one of our guest speakers set his cabin on fire. We all grabbed our fire extinguishers and ran to his aid. One by one we pointed our fire extinguishers at the fire and squeezed the handle. Virtually none of them worked. The fire devoured that cabin. Imagine that.

We read and wrote home, and we learned a great deal about ourselves and one another. It was wonderful.

CHAPTER 4

Student Teaching

Then we went student teaching.

We would teach in all black segregated schools in Macon County, Alabama. It was 1967, ten years after *Brown v. the Board of Education*, but "separate but equal" was still the law of the land in Macon County. We would live with a black rural family, ride the school bus to school, and practice teach under an established teacher in this all-black high school.

Ed, a tall black man who had served in Ghana, took Julie and me to meet our host family in one of the pickup trucks. This time, we were able to ride in the cab rather than in the back. When we arrived at the rustic farmhouse, we walked under the pecan tree in the front yard and onto the porch of Mrs. Whitloe's home. Ethylene, who met us at the door, was a large dark-skinned woman with a broad smile. Ed introduced us, and off he went. We followed her into the house, and she showed us our room. It was a comfortable bedroom right off the living room. There was a bed and a small desk and a chair, along with a fireplace. There was a closet for our teaching clothes. The house was oppressively warm. Even though the sun was shining outside and it was a warm fall day, the heat was on. It must have been over eighty in the living room.

We had been warned that the first thing we should do when we met our host family was to pay them. We were given between three and four hundred dollars each to give to Mrs. Whitloe for our room and board. It was suggested to us that we also try to see where our host put the money after we gave it to him or her. Often, rural Alabama black families had never seen so much money at one time, and they might, in their excitement, forget where they stashed it. Well, that was not a choice for us. Ethylene dashed from the room with the money after introducing us to her daughter, Doris. Doris would be one of our students. She was an articulate and attractive sixteen-year-old junior. She sensed our distress right away.

"Can I get you water or something?" she asked.

"It is warm in here," I replied. "Do you always keep it so warm?"

After a pause, she said, "We thought, with your money and all, you white folks would always keep the heat on. I'll turn it down if you'd like."

At that point, Ethylene and a much older man entered the room. "This is Noon," said Mrs. Whitloe.

Noon looked at Julie and me and didn't say anything.

And that was the beginning of our three weeks staying with Mrs. Whitloe, her daughter Doris, and Noon. It was three weeks I shall never forget.

We got a tour of the place after that. There was, of course, the living room and our bedroom and a dining room and a kitchen with a stove, sink, and refrigerator and several large freezers. There was a bathroom with a tub and a sink and pump, but no running water. There were other bedrooms, but we didn't go there. Out back, there was an outhouse and a fire pit with a huge iron pot for laundry. There was a pigsty raised above the ground, with pigs inside, and chickens running around everywhere. There was also a henhouse and a small barn.

After the tour, we sat down for dinner. We had delicious pork chops with potatoes and gravy and grits. We drank water and passed around a towel for a napkin. Ethylene, Doris, Julie, and I sat at a large table. Noon sat at a separate table on the side. When I asked him about that, he explained he never wanted to sit at the same table with a white man.

That was the end of that.

After supper, we watched a little television, got acquainted with Doris, and retired early in the double bed. There was a big orange light in the backyard lighting the way to the outhouse. "Not a good idea to go in the middle of the night, snakes and things," said Ethylene.

The next morning, we were up early in time for a wonderful breakfast of eggs and fried chicken and grits and coffee. It was a huge meal, but there was no lunch at school, so it had to last throughout the day.

We waited out front for the school bus. I was dressed in jacket and tie, as teachers dressed in those days, and Julie wore a skirt and a sweater. We bumped along country roads in that bus filled with black students until we came to the school. Doris showed us where our respective rooms were. For the first few days, I would just observe, then I would begin teaching. I can't remember her name, but my supervising teacher worked hard with the kids, and they respected her. She was difficult for me to understand with her strong Southern accent and a bit of what I thought was a speech defect. She called me Mr. Danielsair. It didn't sound much like Danielson, but I lived with it. We worked with a grammar book and taught parts of speech. The kids behaved well, I thought, and they were respectful and cooperative. One girl wore a sign around her neck. "I am stupid," it said. Apparently, she had gotten in a fight with another girl the previous week, and wearing the sign was her punishment. She was quiet and very well-behaved in class. The teacher I worked with thought it would be well if I could teach these kids to speak more like I spoke. Perhaps I could, in my two weeks of student teaching, get them to sound like a person from Western New York, lose their Southern drawl, so they could more easily find a good job. We did some drills, and we practiced some sounds, but I'm afraid I failed miserably in that part of my student teaching.

Shortly after I started working in school, it was announced that there would be a PTA meeting, and teachers were encouraged to attend. The Peace Corps had suggested we do some little project during our student teaching time, something that might be helpful to the community. I decided that I could introduce Julie and myself and tell those in attendance a little about us and our Peace

Corps mission to teach in Africa. I asked the principal if I could have just five minutes or so to address the parents. The principal thought it was a wonderful idea and immediately called the preacher, who was supposed to talk, and told him that a student teacher wanted to speak instead. Of course, he didn't tell me that.

The night of the meeting, we all gathered in a meeting room of the school. Julie and I were in the second row with our supervising teachers and other members of the community scattered about. The preacher was there to conduct the meeting. He opened with a prayer, and then he said, "Let's begin this special night by having each and every one of us recite a psalm from the Bible. We'll start here in the front row."

I had been thinking about the little talk I was going to make when, suddenly, I felt a wave of nausea wash over me. A psalm from the Bible? There was a very large dark-skinned woman sitting next to me, and she saw my face. She leaned over toward me, took my arm in her large hand, and in a deep voice, said quietly, "Jesus wept."

It was the shortest psalm in the Bible.

With that, my confidence returned. Immediately, it seemed, it was my turn.

"For God so loved the world that he gave his only begotten son that whosoever believeth in him should not perish, but have everlasting life."

I had won a pencil for memorizing that in religious instruction class in grade school. Whew. It just came to me. It wasn't from the book of Psalms, but it was fine. Julie recited another verse, and the rest of the audience took their turn. There were a few who mumbled, "Jesus wept," but most people knew a psalm and recited it.

Then the minister introduced me as the guest speaker.

I was shocked. I just wanted a minute. I hardly thought of myself as a speaker at all. But there I was. I told them about where Julie and I had come from, and I told them we were going to Africa to teach in African schools in the Peace Corps and that we were doing our practice teaching in their schools. Exactly how teaching in English to English-speaking American black students would prepare us for teaching non-English-speaking Africans from a totally different culture did not come up. That was a good thing, because I was not sure I knew other than we needed to practice teaching and we were not used to associating with African Americans.

Everybody clapped when I finished. I'm not sure why other than that I was brief and finished. The preacher went ahead with his talk about sin, we went home, and I began to think about whether I had done anything worthwhile or had just stuck my nose where it didn't belong.

We heard from Ed that he would pick us up on Friday night and take us out for a little dancin' and drinkin'. He came by in his pickup truck and took us to a local nightclub, where we danced and met some local young people. Of course, we were the only white people there, as we were the only white people in school, but everyone was really gracious and kind. I had never seen people dance like they did. Wonderful! We drank a few beers. It was great fun. Julie and I danced with each other and with other people in the crowd. What a night! When Ed dropped us off, the house was dark. After I knocked on the door, I heard the locks click open, and there was Ethylene in her nightdress, grasping a double-barrel shotgun. She opened the door, let us pass, but never said a word.

One day, when I came home from school, I got off the bus all dressed up in a suit, and there was Noon in the yard beside the house, trying to get ahold of a pig that had gotten out of the sty. He had him by the hind legs, but the pig was jerking him around.

I asked him what I could do.

He said, "Grab him."

I tried to grab him by the front legs.

"Not that way," he said. "He'll bite you. Grab him by the ears."

I had never touched a pig before, but I did as instructed, and we muscled the animal, squealing and kicking, into the elevated sty. We threw him in and locked the door.

After that, Noon began to talk to me. He told me about his life in Mobile as a young man. He told me how he was athletic and white men would put him up to things so they could bet on him. One time, he and seven others were made to swim across the mouth of Mobile harbor in a hurricane. White men bet on who would make it back. He and three others did. The rest drowned. He told me about climbing greased poles at fairs and about prize fights. This had all happened during the aftermath of Reconstruction. He said it was a terrible time. He had never been able to forgive the white folks for it.

He still wouldn't eat at the table with us, but at least he was civil in conversation. Noon spoke in a quiet voice, with a strong Southern accent. He was difficult to understand sometimes. There was no question about his past, his anger, and his distrust of whites in general.

We would have two weekends at Mrs. Whitloe's house. One Saturday, we visited a sugar shack, where they were boiling sugarcane. The men sat around, adding wood to the fire, and I remember one man who had a wonderful, deep voice began to lead the men in song. He would sing a phrase, and they would respond. It was powerful and wonderful. They passed a bottle around from time to time. We were mesmerized. They enjoyed life.

On Sunday, there would be church. Doris pulled us aside. She told us how the minister worked everyone up into a kind of frenzy, and sometimes people passed out right in the service. It was often warm in the church, and they didn't open the windows. The heat raised the passions. She assured us it would be long but that we would be okay and not have to worry. I thought it was really unusual for a sixteen-year-old to be saying things like this; after all, it was just church, but she seemed concerned.

Dressed in a suit and tie and a white shirt that Mrs. Whitlow had washed in a huge iron pot over a fire in the backyard, and then pressed to perfection, I, with Julie by my side, descended from Mr. Young's truck that Sunday morning as he dropped us off in front of the church. We got there early so he could go back for a second load. The Whitloes didn't have a vehicle, so we always had to beg a ride. Mr. Young was the neighbor. There were groups of people chatting in the yard of the little white church. Some of them nodded, but no one said anything, so we went inside. We were the first ones there. Julie and I walked down the left side of the nave and sat down in the third pew. There were two large calendars on the walls facing the congregation, both carrying religious pictures and each sponsored by a competing funeral home. We smiled at that. After a while, we became aware that though it was nearly nine and time for the services to begin, we were still the only ones in the church. People had come up and looked in the door, but they didn't enter. Was it because we were white? Then, finally, a stylishly dressed young couple came in and sat behind us. After that, people streamed into the church. At first, I didn't notice, but then it was plain. All the men sat on the right side of the church and all the women sat on the left.

The choir filed in, taking their places behind the altar, and the minister made his appearance. Unlike the ministers I had grown accustomed to up north, this one didn't speak in quiet tones. He was spirited, loud, and emphatic. I can't tell you much about the prayers or the sermon except that there was great enthusiasm by the minister. The congregation responded with "Amens" at each point he made. There was no going to sleep in this service. The choir sang beautifully. There were no hymnals on the backs of the pews, but the same man who had sung the day before at the "sugaring off" would sing a line of a hymn and the congregation would repeat it. I got goose bumps. It was beautiful.

The first real surprise came when the plate was passed for the collection. Julie and I put a dollar on the plate as it passed by. There were quarters and nickels and dimes but, it seemed, not many dollars going into the plate. When the money was collected and the plates were returned to the front of the church, the minister asked, "Who needs change?" Hands went up, and the ushers returned to the crowd, making change for the parishioners. When the plates finally came back, the choir sang a hymn and the ushers were busy counting the money. When the hymn was over, the minister announced the total. "That's not enough!" he said. "We can't build a church on that paltry sum. We need a new roof. Payments are due. Pass the plate again!"

And the ushers passed the plates around the second time.

"Charlie Johnson, wasn't it your birthday this Wednesday? Come on, Charlie. Pass the plate back to Charlie and see what he can add to it. And, Freda Jones, didn't you come into some money when your brother passed away last month? Mr. and Mrs. Chumway, it was just a year ago that we had a wedding for you right here in this church. Couldn't you find a little more for us? Pass those plates around. This is our church. Eleanor Morris, your baby was Christened just a week ago. Dig in, Eleanor. Help us out."

And the plate was passed around again, and finally the preacher said, "There. That'll do."

The sermon was long. People stood up and confessed to having seen Jesus. It was hot in the church. Some folks cried. It was very moving. The windows remained closed. It was well past noon when we finally got out.

Afterward, there was a picnic. There were potato salad and fried chicken on paper plates. There were coffee and tea, and there were wonderful desserts. What I remember most, though, is that parents of both Julie's and my students bought dinners for us while we waited in line. We were so moved we could hardly speak. The children, dressed in their Sunday best, brought them to us. We couldn't say no, but how could we eat all that wonderful food?

Here we, the ones trained in sensitivity, had come, white people to a black church, blundered our way in, and sat together rather than apart, as was the custom. It was the African Americans who accepted us, even showed compassion for us afterward. And it was Doris who understood that we might be surprised by the church experience and tried to prepare us for it. Remember the PTA and the fat lady who told me the psalm?

Maybe it was the African Americans who should be teaching us about sensitivity. Maybe that was the whole idea. They were teaching us to live in a foreign culture in ways we never would have imagined. They were teaching us by example.

Back at the farm, things were falling into a rhythm. Pork chops for breakfast, chicken for dinner. Chicken for breakfast, pork chops for dinner. Two meals a day. One night, it was especially cold, and we were awakened by Ethylene lighting a fire in our bedroom fireplace. What a caring woman! It was still dark outside, and she was preparing to go out to pick cotton in the field. It seemed she was always working. "Every year, I plants more cotton, and every year, I gets less money," she would say and shake her head. She would come in before we got up and cook us a hot breakfast. While we were gone during the day, she washed our clothes and did other chores around the farm.

One night, after dinner, while Julie and I were preparing for school the next day, we heard a loud noise outside. Noon opened the front door and looked out then closed the door and locked it. It got louder and louder, an animal noise, like dogs barking and howling. Suddenly, we could hear them close—they were in the yard. Chickens scurried to their roosts as the pack of dogs chased one another in a mad rush. Then they were under the house, crashing into the foundation and bumping the floorboards underfoot. The racket was unnerving. I glanced outside, wondering about the outhouse in the backyard. Not tonight, I thought. But then the noise diminished and the pack moved away, still howling, but more faintly, until it was gone. The outhouse was there, the dust had settled, and it was quiet again.

Our last weekend with Mrs. Whitlow brought another surprise. Her son and his wife arrived from up north, where he worked in a factory in Detroit. They pulled up in a 1956 Chevy that had been lowered and partly customized. It was a beautiful car, and out of it came a young man with the biggest Afro I had ever seen. His wife had her long hair straightened. They wore flashy clothes, and frankly, they shocked us. We had never seen anything like them. Their arrival caused quite a stir in the household as well. Ethylene wanted to make a special dinner for them, but they had other plans. They didn't pay much attention to us, not that they should have. They went out with their friends that night. I remember, the next morning, there was a big breakfast, and Ethylene wanted to go to church with her children. She cooked breakfast and then started scrubbing her legs. It was time to go, and she wasn't dressed for church. Doris, Julie, and I climbed into the back seat of the Chevy, and it roared out of the yard, leaving Ethylene behind with tears running from her sad eyes. The kids dropped us off at church and were on their way to other adventures. There was no culture shock this time, just a long morning in church.

Toward the end of our student teaching experience, we moved schools. The Supreme Court had long before struck down "separate but equal," but Macon County had built a new school for black children anyway. It was a fine building not far from the old one, and it was our job to help move in. We carried books and supplies, and the transition was effortless.

Our last night was on a Friday. There was a dance in the gym. Julie and I went, and the kids were so kind to us. We were really pleased. I guess our whole experience with Mrs. Whitlow was one of gracious kindness. The students and the community had accepted us and our goal to teach in Africa with the Peace Corps. The white community, on the other hand, was much less warm.

I can remember stopping in a local store in Tuskegee and picking out a few toiletry items. When I went to the counter to pay, the white clerk pretended I wasn't there. She looked through me and refused to see me until all the local people in the place had left. I had never seen or felt anything like it.

During the time we were there, Mrs. Whitlow had been sewing a quilt. She cut patches, bits of worn-out garments from the farm. There were blue denim, brown corduroy, and bits of flannel. An American flag graced the front. The patches were filled with cotton freshly picked from her fields. I asked her if I could buy it, and she agreed to sell it to me for a few dollars. What a lovely memento of our stay in Macon County!

Back at Atkins Camp, we got our student teaching evaluations and continued working on language. We would have to rate 1+ on the Federal Service Institute exam, an oral test, to be able to qualify for the program. Finally, those few who were deselected, as they said, left the camp, and the rest of us prepared for our departure for Malawi, with one exception. Jim had been drafted. He and his wife, after being trained to teach in Malawi, would have to give it all up so he could go to war in Vietnam. There was no such thing as a deferment for the Peace Corps.

We would go home for a few days between Christmas and New Year's, and our flight would depart from New York at 9:00 p.m. on New Year's Day 1968.

CHAPTER 5

Travel to Malawi

Preparation for two years in a third world country like Malawi was not to be taken lightly. We would need clothes suitable for the tropical climate, toiletries, and other things we wanted to take with us. We each had a large *trunk* that would go with us. We could fill it with clothing, teaching aids, whatever we thought we would need. We were warned that, though we could buy many things in Malawi, we might not be able to buy the kinds of things we were used to. For that reason, we had been given a generous allowance for our needs. Of course, the night before our departure was New Year's Eve, and my parents saw us off with a rather lavish New Year's Eve party complete with cocktails and a fine dinner. Everything was packed, our papers were in order, and at 4:00 a.m., shortly after we had retired, the alarm went off and we loaded our bags in my dad's Chevy Corvair, and Mom and Dad and Julie and I headed some seventy miles for the Buffalo airport, where we said goodbye and climbed aboard a plane for New York City.

In New York, we visited Julie's maiden aunt Grace, who lived with her friend, Lenox. The two women had been schoolteachers, had traveled the world together, and were eager to see us off. Rather than enjoy New York, as they had planned, we had a long snooze in their guest bedroom and boarded our KLM flight, after a two-hour delay, at 11:00 p.m. Our first stop was Amsterdam, and there, at Duty Free, we picked out a Schaub Lorenz shortwave radio. It had a beautiful wood case and used D batteries, eight of them. We were excited to find such a fine radio, and when I reached for my wallet in the inside pocket of my sport coat, I had another surprise. Pull as I did, the wallet would not come out.

It seemed my mother, during the hour or two we had slept on New Year's Eve, had come into our bedroom and safety-pinned my wallet in place in my jacket. No pickpocket would take our adjustment allowance!

I tugged and tugged and finally pulled the wallet and pocket out so I could at least extract a little money, much to the amusement of those around us. In the end, we got our radio, but my face was red.

On the way south, we stopped at Entebbe in Uganda. It was a short stop, but I remember, when the doors of the plane were opened, the smell of fresh gardenia wafting in. The tropical night reached out and grabbed us.

In Nairobi, Kenya, we visited a game park and had our first look at the Great Rift Valley. Finally, we boarded an Air Malawi flight for Blantyre-Limbe, the biggest city in Malawi. There were receptions and speeches and more training. We observed classes at Saint Andrews School, a large private school, and soon we were on our way to Likoma Island, which would be our home for the next two years.

CHAPTER 6

Likoma Island

Likoma Island is a story in itself. About five miles long and two and a half miles wide, it is located midway up Lake Malawi, on the Portuguese East Africa, Mozambique, side of the lake. The island, located just twelve degrees south of the equator, is desertlike in appearance. There are some palms, but mostly cactus. Locals grow cassava, which they eat, generally with fish, which is netted in the lake. There are mango trees and baobabs, but little else. Most of the trees have been taken for making canoes or just for firewood, which is scarce. The island is home of the United Missions for Central Africa. That is the religious group that sent Dr. Livingston and Dr. Stanley to explore Central Africa. Hence, there are three churches and a proper cathedral there, albeit a cathedral of stone and mud and with a tin (but originally grass) roof. The story of how the church came to Likoma is a long one that involves the church's moving from the mosquito-and-malaria-infested Monkey Bay on the southern end of the lake to the healthier, breezy Likoma Island. The island is the home of the Likoma Day Secondary School, where we would teach. When we arrived, there were five thousand Africans on the island, along with an English Anglican priest who had been exiled there and a young English physician who was a lay missionary.

Peace Corps had never fared well at Likoma, perhaps because it was so isolated from other Peace Corps volunteers or because it was so isolated, period. The first volunteers to serve there had been married in training, and the island was given to them as a kind of wedding present. Another volunteer lived there alone and succumbed to the temptation of abundant marijuana. The island was held out as a kind of threat during training: "If you don't behave, we'll send you to Likoma Island." But Julie and I made it known that we loved the water and had always wanted to live on an island. So we got our wish.

From Blantyre, we boarded an Air Malawi DC-3, a twin-engine, propeller-driven World War II–era relic, and flew to Nkhata Bay, north of the island, where experienced fellow volunteers introduced us to the local market. We shopped for canned goods in local stores and bought meat and vegetables at the market.

While Julie shopped for veggies, I headed for the place where beef was sold. In one corner there was a tent, inside of which a recently slaughtered beef carcass hung from a hook. Flies were thick as a large African man stepped from the tent. He was covered in gore, dripping with blood. I was taken aback, but I remembered what I was told to say. "Two kilos fillet," I said, pointing to my midsection, just in case he didn't understand. The man turned, bloody machete in hand, and pushed aside the flap of the tent, where he began whacking away at the carcass. Soon he emerged with a huge hunk of meat that he placed on the scale. Flies were buzzing everywhere. I paid him, and then to my utter amazement, he picked up the huge hunk of quivering, bloody meat and handed it to me. Blood ran between my fingers, and I took it in both hands. What would I…?

It was then I began to hear the tittering of laughter behind me.

There was Julie with a basket and newspapers to wrap the meat. There were no grocery bags here or wax paper, but our Peace Corps friends from Nkhata Bay had gotten the necessary materials for us. It was a lesson well learned. From there we headed to a local bar, where, for a few beers, the bartender would keep the meat in his kerosene fridge until later that night, when we would pick it up and board the ship for the island. It was there in the bar we saw African men grab large insects that buzzed around the pressurized kerosene lamps hung from the rafters and eat them, followed by a swallow of beer. "They're really not too bad," said our friends.

We learned a lot about living in Africa that trip. We had joined a food co-op in Blantyre. They would ship our order to the island each month. Stork margarine came in a can. Malawi Gin was 40 proof, cheap, and much easier to carry over the three miles of rocky path to our house than a case of beer. We would be able to get fresh fish and chicken on the island. We owned some chickens, which were large and white and ran free with the other poultry, scurrying among the bushes, eating insects. We could pay a kid to catch one, and we would kill it and clean it ourselves. There were goats too, and occasionally, a cow would be killed and beef would be available. We hired a butcher from Nkhata Bay to send us a few pounds of beef each week. It would come on the ship Wednesday mornings, where I would pick it up before school.

That night, we boarded the ship. Several hundred feet long, the *Ilala* was a modern diesel-powered ship with a dozen or so first-class cabins, a room with perhaps two dozen bunk beds for second class, and deck passage for uncountable numbers in third class. Because Peace Corps had gotten first-class tickets for us, dinner was with the captain that evening in the officers' dining room. We "dressed" for dinner and enjoyed a fine meal with the captain and crew. Below us on the lower deck, perhaps a thousand people lay on the steel deck, their heads on their belongings, which were stuffed into sacks. Men, women nursing babies, and boys and girls all spread out, some propped against the walls, others lying on the floor. It was a mass of humanity unlike anything we had seen before. The smell of diesel mixed with the smell of raw humanity was almost overpowering at first. We were glad we had a cabin reserved for us. The cabin was small. It had two beds, a dresser, and a sink. That was it. Toilets down the hall. There was a porthole and electric lights.

The ship rolled through the waves on the huge freshwater lake as it headed from Nkhata Bay toward Likoma. When we awoke, we were pulling into the harbor, a protected space between a small island, really a huge rock, and Likoma Island itself. Our friends from Nkhata Bay were with us.

After breakfast, we descended to the lower deck and then the ladder onto the lifeboat tied to the side of the ship. We carried a small bag with personal belongings as we stepped onto the metal seats of the lifeboat. When it was fully loaded, an African man opened the hatch on the small engine compartment, reached inside, and lifted several levers on top of the engine. He then spun a crank and closed the levers as the engine roared to life. After a short run, the faded white lifeboat crunched on the sandy shore next to a boarding plat-form. We stepped out on the beach of what was to be our island-home for the next two years.

Waiting for us on the sandy shore, among a throng of Africans, were two white men. The first, a middle-aged Englishman, Ron Tovy, who was an Anglican priest, and the second, a younger Englishman named Paul Auklund, who was introduced to us as a physician. We walked together to a large open building with a thatched roof several hundred yards beyond the beach. There we sat with Father Tovy and Paul and had coffee. An African woman served us the coffee. She was deferential and quiet in her long skirt and bare feet as she set the full cups in front of us, then she stood by the door to the kitchen, as if waiting for further instructions.

Father Tovy did his best to make us comfortable. He talked a bit about the cathedral we could see in the distance and about the school, our house, and life on the island. All the while, people walked by, looking at the new teachers.

Before long, our trunks had arrived at the *Mezanni*, as the open-air porch was called, and it was time to leave and walk to our house. It would be a two-and-a-half-mile walk along a gravel path punctuated with rocks. Several African women wearing dresses, but barefoot, were there, whom we could hire to carry the trunks. They found men to lift the hundred-plus-pound trunks high enough, and they quickly stooped under them and balanced them on a ring of grass on their heads. A little adjustment, and they were off.

I could hardly believe my eyes!

We fell into a line behind them, walking along the narrow trail. Of course, in addition to the trunks, we had food, our suitcases, and other things we had acquired along the way.

We walked up a hill overlooking the bay the *Ilala* had sailed into. Down the road, ahead of us, was a fig tree, considered to have been cursed by the locals, as several people had been "mysteriously" assaulted while under it. Farther along was a huge rock that, when viewed from behind, appeared to be a woman in a long dress bowing her head, with a baby in her arms. It was believed to be a miracle: Jesus in the arms of Mary. Finally, we descended the hill, and there before us was a sign: "Likoma Day Secondary School, Likoma Island, Malawi." To our right was the school. There were two modern cement block buildings, painted white, with metal roofs. One contained two large well-lighted classrooms; the other was a small office complex. There was also a stone-and-mud building with an old steel roof. That, we were told, was the library. Ahead of us were three ranch-style houses made of cement block, with metal roofs. As the story goes, when the Americans agreed to build schools for the Malawi government and staff them with Peace Corps volunteers, the Malawians thought the least they could do was build American-style houses for the volunteers. So we would be living in the middle of Africa in a modern *American* home.

CHAPTER 7

Home

When we first entered our home, we went through the back door into the kitchen. There was a sink on our right, cupboards on the walls, and a wooden counter along the right wall. Ahead of us, across the room, was a large enameled woodstove / water heater, which was rather useless, as wood was scarce on the island. Beside it, a counter-high refrigerator. There was also a large propane tank in the kitchen with a two-burner stove and an oven that could be placed on top of the stove for baking. There was a large pantry with shelves lining the walls for food storage.

To the left of the kitchen was a comfortable dining room with table and six chairs lighted by a large window and, across from that, a living room with windows looking out on the lake. On the interior wall was a fireplace on a raised hearth, our only source of heat. Ironically, there was high demand for wood as cooking fuel on the island, and very few trees were left, so we would seldom, if ever, be able to use the stove or fireplace. There was a couch, coffee table, and several upholstered chairs in the living room along with a buffet, on top of which was the Peace Corps book locker. The book locker was simply a cardboard container with hundreds of titles of paperback books inside. There was everything from Chaucer, Shakespeare, and English poetry to Hawthorne, Melville, and American verse, up to and including some contemporary fiction. There was a dictionary, a small encyclopedia, nonfiction, and even cookbooks. We learned to live on *Fanny Farmer* and her cook-until-done recipes. Put together by university professors, the book locker was a treasure we were encouraged to use and to leave behind for those who followed us.

There were three bedrooms, two equipped with twin beds and mosquito nets dangling from frames above. The metal casement windows opened nicely and had screens to keep the bugs out. The third bedroom was our office. It had two desks, a lampstand, and chairs, just what we would need to prepare our lessons. The floors throughout were concrete, the walls painted gray. Of course, there was no electricity. For light, we had Aladdin lamps. They were clean-burning kerosene lamps that used a mantel to cast a bright white light and a great deal of heat into the room. We had two, and they, on lampstands, would be our only source of light, excepting, of course, flashlights, essential for any outdoor movement at night. Flashlights would keep away snakes, we were told. I almost forgot, the house had bathrooms too. Well, bathrooms? There were actually two rooms off the hall by the office. One room had just a toilet, the other, a sink and a tub. I guess you could say we had one bathroom in two rooms.

Our guest Peace Corps volunteers, those who traveled with us from Nkhata Bay, helped us move in and familiarized us with the fridge and stoves. Our refrigerator was an Electrolux, which, ironically, ran on kerosene and had to be filled regularly, lit, and maintained. It made two trays of ice cubes each day and kept our water and food cool. The Achilles' heel of the fridge was the small glass chimney at the back of the removable fuel tank. It directed the heat of the flame to the heat exchanger, it was blue glass, and from time to time, it would break. One knew when it was broken, because the food quickly warmed. A spare was an essential, but they were available only in major cities, days' travel away, so we kept several on hand.

Our propane stove was convenient, but propane was expensive and difficult to transport, so we relied on small portable kerosene stoves for cooking. It took a bit of learning to light one. First, after filling the reservoir with kerosene, or paraffin, one would pump up a little pressure in the stove and then pour mentholated spirit into the cup under the burner. After lighting the spirit, he or she would use a pricker and clean the nozzle with a pin on the end of a handle. When the spirit fire went out, he or she would light a match and open the burner. If the kerosene had vaporized, the fumes would roar to life and the burner was lit and would continue burning. If, however, one had skimped on the spirit, clear kerosene would hit the hot burner and very flammable black smoke would fill the room. Nasty. These little stoves came with one of two kinds of burners, silent or noisy. The silent were quiet, and the noisy, a little easier to light, roared to life and kept roaring.

In addition to stove and fridge, the third essential to a kitchen is water. We had water. We would hire women to fill four-gallon tubs from the lake a few hundred yards from the house, and they would place them on their heads and carry them back up to the house, where they would pour them into a buried fifty-gallon tank. If the tank was empty, it would take a dozen trips. Later, I would, by hand, pump the water up into a tank next to the chimney, on the roof. There was a hand pump attached to a pipe from the underground tank to the roof tank. From there, the water would flow through the plumbing to sinks, tub, and toilet. We had hot water too! Well, not really. The *hot* water would flow through the woodstove, but as there was no wood available for the woodstove, the hot water, like the cold, was always cold. Once we drew water from the tap, we would carry it to a filter. The filter was a large double-walled porcelain urn with a ceramic filter. We kept it on the counter in the kitchen, and it took out all solid particles from the water. Filtration was a slow process. The water would then be drawn from the filter, placed on the kerosene stove, and boiled. That meant brought to a rolling boil and boiled for five minutes by the clock. Then it would be cooled and refrigerated. Several times, while we lived on the island, we found ourselves without filtered, boiled water to drink. When we tried drinking just a little water that hadn't been processed, without fail, we got sick.

Our first dinner that night was memorable. We had been able to bring fresh vegetables form the mainland, and of course, we had some meat. Salad? Forget it. All our food had to be cooked to well-done. We generally ground our meat and then boiled it and then fried it before mixing it with spaghetti sauce or curry. We would then serve it over rice or pasta. We had bread too, and butter from a can. There might have been pudding for dessert.

Sometimes we would have mangoes, and often, papaya was available. Papaya could be served cooked like a vegetable, green, or fresh when ripe. Women would come by selling hen's eggs, which we would buy as long as they passed the test. The price was two for a penny, and we would always float the egg in a glass of water before buying. If the egg floated, it was spoiled inside. If it sank, it was okay. Why were they so cheap? Everyone there knew that eating eggs made one sterile. How did they keep them without refrigeration? Of course, eggs don't have to be refrigerated and can be kept for up to six weeks without. Europeans have known that for years; only we Americans insist on refrigerated eggs.

We spent the next few days familiarizing ourselves with the island and the people who lived there. Our friends left for home the following Saturday morning, and by then, we felt we had a handle on things. Because the island had been home to the United Missions for Central Africa for years, most people knew a little English. Besides, Father Tovy and Paul were just a few miles away, should we need help. We were all set, or so we thought.

It was on our first night alone that things got interesting. We had arranged with Stevenson, one of our students-to-be, to help us around the house in exchange for payment of his school fees. He was a student from the mainland who would rent a house with several other young men and attend our day secondary school as a boarding student. The school had nothing to do with the boarding arrangements; they were made entirely by the students. Although the school was intended for students from the island, because classes were not full, extra seats were filled by young people from other districts who could make their own boarding arrangements.

As school would begin the following Monday, by Saturday, the young people were beginning to arrive, many of them on the *Ilala*. Often, several students would get together and rent a house. That was the case this time. The house was simply a mud-brick building consisting usually of two rooms covered by a grass roof. There would be a *chimbuzi*, or outhouse, out back.

On this particular evening, several of the boys arrived earlier in the day, and when the last one came, from the neighboring island of Chizamulu, the trouble started. Alfred was much littler than the other boys and was rather timid. When he showed up, those who had agreed to share a house with him laughed at him and told him to go find another place to live. Alfred disappeared. Everything was fine until someone found out that on Chizamulu, Alfred's home, his father was a witch doctor. That was frightening information, indeed. The boys reasoned that if Alfred could get word of his mistreatment to his father, they would be cursed and might die. They searched for him, but to no avail. Boats sailed between the islands daily. What to do? That night, three young African men knocked on the door of the new teachers' house, looking for an answer.

Imagine a twenty-two-year-old couple from Western New York spending their first night alone on an island deep in tropical Africa. Now imagine three teenage African boys appearing at their door, obviously distraught, with tears filling their eyes and sometimes trickling down their faces. The boys were sure that Alfred would get word to his father and have them cursed and killed. I tried to reason with them, but to no avail. They were terrified. "Were they not Christians?" I asked. They insisted that though they were, indeed, good Christians, a curse would still kill them. There was no place they could hide. Julie and I thought they might be putting us on, but no one could fake such tears. It was totally dark outside by the time we persuaded them to return to their rented house. As it turned out, Alfred was there when they got back. They made up, and soon the incident was forgotten. No curses, no more fears—at least that was what we were led to believe.

That night, as we snuggled in our warm bed, we heard the sound of drums and saw flickers of yellow light over the water.

We wondered what it meant.

CHAPTER 8

The Neighborhood

The location of our house was special. It was on the school campus, one of three identical homes. One belonged to the principal, one to us, and one to the Malawi Young Pioneer (more on that later). The houses were located on a little peninsula, with water on two sides. To the east was the village of Maculaui, in a little bay with a beach in calm water, protected from the winds. To the west was Mtoo, another village, this one on the windward side, where we would swim. Breaking waves there greatly lessened the threat of bilharzia, an often-lethal disease carried by snails living in calm water. Each of the villages had just a few houses, where families raised their children. There were chickens running about, and there were raised platforms where fish dried in the sun. Women worked gardens, where they grew a few crops, mostly cassava. They would hoe and weed and work constantly in the heat of the day, often with babies on their backs. The men seemed to sit around and play games as the women worked. At night, the men would board dugout canoes and drive small fish into nets by banging on the sides of their canoes and lighting fires of grass as they paddled toward the nets. That was the sound of drums and the flickering light we had heard and seen the previous night. The fish and cassava, along with a little chicken, made up most of the food these people ate. We would walk through Mtoo on the way to the lake every afternoon for the next two years as we went for a swim and a wash.

The beach at Mtoo was delightful. Tall grasses separated it from the village, so it was private. The sand was coarse, but it was firm and easy to walk on. On the south end, to our right as we faced the water, was a huge pile of boulders. We were warned that some people used it as a *chim* (toilet), so it was best not to swim there. Still, naked African boys, none older than six or seven, loved to run over the rocks and dive and jump into the warm, clear water. They would laugh and shout and play tag, jumping from rock to rock.

There, too, by that huge pile of rocks, were tropical fish. Thousands of them swam in schools, darting through the water among the rocks. They were red and blue and green and yellow, colorful, beautiful, as they darted or rested in the water lifted and lowered by the waves as they swam near the rocks. The beach was a beautiful place, a magical place that we visited each afternoon between two, after school let out, and four, when there was no more swimming for us. You see, the Peace Corps didn't have many rules, but there were three that mattered. Number one: no drugs. Two: no monkeys as pets. Monkeys carry rabies but don't get it. We couldn't keep monkeys as pets. Rule three was no swimming before ten in the morning or after four in the afternoon. From 4:00 p.m. to 10:00 a.m. was when crocodiles fed. As there were many crocs on the island, and especially as people were still being taken and eaten by them, rule three was especially important. Oh, the African kids would laugh at us when we told them about crocs. "Bodza!" they would say. "Crocodiles don't eat white people!"

"But that's because white people don't swim after four or before ten."

And all that was true.

Usually, it was women doing breakfast dishes in the breaking waves that were knocked down and dragged away by those green monsters. There was one man on the island who was locally famous because he claimed he had been caught and taken to a crocodile nest as a child while swimming and left for dead. He came to and escaped before the croc returned.

So there were endearing attractions at the beach and a menace as well. We always took soap and shampoo with us, and we always wore our bathing suits. The Africans left us alone when we swam those afternoons. It was a beautiful reprieve from the busy pace of the school and the island. We were fortunate to enjoy the warm waters of a tropical beach on a tropical island. Sound like paradise? It was beautiful, really.

CHAPTER 9

School

School started on Monday. There were two classrooms, and Julie and I were the two teachers. There was a Malawi Young Pioneer, who taught a kind of physical education, more like soldiering, and the headmaster, Mr. Kayawa, who taught Chinyanja, the local language. I taught English nine times each week to each of the two forms (grades). At first, some of the students were sure they couldn't understand a word I said, but after a while, they got used to my American English. They had been taught by local African teachers in primary school, but they had been taught English with a strong British accent.

The classes were like something I had never seen. There were twenty double desks in the classroom, each with a bench big enough for two students. Therefore, forty thirteen-year-olds, roughly speaking, would be in front of me each period. At the beginning of the day, the school "clark," or clerk, would take attendance by calling out each child's name. Responses were crisp and clear. He would also make announcements regarding school business. When either Julie or I entered, the students would stand and say, "Good morning, sir/madam." I would then answer, "Good morning, class. You may sit down." The class would begin. There were no—and I mean *no*—discipline problems. The kids were all there because they had qualified and because someone had paid their fees. They liked school, and it showed. If someone misbehaved, he was gone, and that was all there was to it. Girls wore dresses and boys wore shorts. Most were barefoot, but some young people wore Bata plastic shoes in bright colors. They would carry their shoes on their heads, girls especially, when they came to school over the rocky path so as not to wear them out. The kids were clean. They bathed regularly, and their clothes, though often tattered, were washed regularly. I dreaded to think that they most likely washed themselves and their clothes in the lake early in the morning, putting themselves at risk, but we never lost anyone while we were there. About a fifth of the class were girls—that was all. The room was painted white and brightly lighted with opening windows on both sides. When it rained, seldom in the school year, the noise of rain on the aluminum roof would bring the class to a halt. It was not unusual for goats or chickens to wander through the open doors into the classroom, and no one paid much attention when they did.

I had a regular text for English. The lessons were progressive and helped the kids develop their language. These young people were amazingly talented at memorizing. Sometimes I would write an essay on the blackboard that might cover two or three panels. I would then call on a student to read it and erase one of the words that we were studying. He would call on another student to read the passage and erase more words. We would continue that until the board was blank. Then I would ask the students to write the passage in their copybooks as best as they could remember. I was simply amazed at how many of them could write the entire passage exactly as it had been written, all from memory.

History class had no text. The curriculum guide simply listed what was to be covered. It might say, "Egypt, the Fertile Crescent, Greece, Rome, Ancient African History, European Colonization of Africa, World Wars I and II." It was up to the teacher how much of each area of history he or she wished to cover.

I had studied ancient history in college and found a copy of James Henry Breasted's *The History of the Ancient World* in the school's library. I based much of my history class on that book, one that Dr. Harker at Grove City College had referred to often. The students would be tested on history on their junior certificate exam.

This test would determine who could go on in school and whose education would end. How I presented history was up to me, but it was vitally important that these students be well grounded. I would relate information and write it on the board, and they would copy it in their copybooks and memorize it. I would never experience students more motivated in my thirty-odd-year teaching career. Every day there was something new.

I taught the first year of physics with chemistry, which was new for me as well as for the kids. The curriculum was clearly written, and it was delightful. Much of it dealt with things easily understood by American children but very much of a mystery to these Malawians. Most of our students had never left the island, and though they had seen ships and planes, they had never ridden in or even seen a car or bus. There were no roads wide enough to accommodate such vehicles on the island. One of the lessons I had to teach was how an internal combustion engine works. When I tried to explain it, the kids laughed. *Ofiti wa chizungu*, or "white man's magic," was what it was to them, and there was simply no explaining it. I remember bringing my Honda 90 motorbike into the room, removing and explaining the function of the spark plug and having each student look into the little hole as I moved the starter, causing the piston to rise into view and fall away. We burned, but never exploded, gasoline, and I carefully explained how the burning gas would expand and force the piston down, causing the crankshaft to turn and, in turn, cause the transmission to turn and move the chain, which would move the wheel. I screwed the spark plug back in, connected the wire to it, kicked the starter, and the bike roared to life. The class wrote it all down and learned it, but it was still "white man's magic," just as the airplane, the elevator (or *lift*), and this thing called television were, something they couldn't even imagine. "Bodza!" they would say. "That cannot be so!"

One of my early lessons with chemistry dealt with the states of matter, solid, liquid, and gas. I took water, which we all were familiar with, boiled it, and turned it to steam, then condensed the steam back to water. They understood that.

"But what about the solid part?" someone asked.

"Tomorrow," I said. "Tomorrow we will deal with the solid part."

The next day, I came to class with a tray of ice cubes carefully wrapped in newspaper. The class had heard of ice but, of course, had never experienced it. They weren't convinced it really existed at all. I told them I had forgotten something at the house and that I would be right back. "But first," I said, "I want to pass these out. I want you to hold them carefully and pass them back in your row so everyone has a chance to hold one and examine it and then pass them all back to the front. I will collect them when I return. There are eight. I expect eight when I get back, one for each section of this little tray." I left the tray on the desk in front of the class and then passed them out and left the room. I watched what happened from outside. The kids would touch the ice and exclaim that it burned. They would pass the cubes back and sometimes drop them because they were slippery. They noticed that their hands got wet when they handled them and that, somehow, they were getting smaller. They tasted them and noticed they were indeed made of water. When I returned a few minutes later, the class was silent and there were no smiles.

"Pass them up," I said. "I want the ice cubes now, please. There should be eight of them, one for each slot of this little tray."

Silence. Finally, Juliet, a tall slender young lady who was unusually verbal for an African girl, said, "But, sir, we did as you said. We passed them around, we touched them, they became wet, and they went away. We did not take them, sir, but they are gone."

"So where do you think they went?"

"They just went to water and were gone."

With that, I unwrapped the second tray of ice cubes I had brought from home. The class was all smiles. They understood. They had never seen ice, and believed in it as much as American students might believe in witchcraft, but now it all made sense. Water really did come in a solid state. Solid, liquid, and gas. That was it. We passed more ice cubes around again, and the class was delighted. We melted some and then boiled it and watched it turn to steam. There was the innocent glee that goes with really understanding something. What a joy it was to share what I had experienced all my life with these delightful young people who had grown up in a tropical land where ice does not exist.

Of course, life at school was not all successful teaching. Sometimes there were clashes of culture that seemed overwhelming. One of our little disagreements had to do with eggs. If you remember, we talked before about buying eggs, two for a penny, and floating them to be sure they were good. Why were they so cheap? Africans firmly believed that eating eggs would make one, man or woman, sterile. Consequently, the eater of eggs would not be able to bear children. Julie worked tirelessly in her biology classes to explain that hen's eggs are a healthy, inexpensive source of food. Rich in protein, they are good for you. We pointed out that we bought all the eggs that were available and that we ate them. In Malawi, as in other parts of Africa, it was illegal to teach about or supply information about birth control. There was a widespread belief that birth control was "a white man's ploy to keep down the blacks." Naturally, Peace Corps volunteers were not in a place to raise children, so especially for married volunteers, birth control was required. If a pregnancy occurred, the couple would be sent home. That was that.

Of course, our students knew about birth control, but not the details, and it was absolutely forbidden for us to fill in those details. The Malawi Young Pioneer, the gym teacher, was also there to keep an eye on us. If we ever breached the subject with the kids and he found out, it would be the end of us. Hence, one can understand why our students, even after we assured them that eggs were safe, refused to consume them. Even after two years, on our last day of classes, when we asked if they felt there was anything we had taught them that wasn't true, they brought up the idea of eggs and becoming sterile. "You and Mrs. Danielson," said Stevenson, "have lived together for two years, and you eat all the eggs you can get, and you are one of the few couples we know who have had no children."

That was a hard argument to refute.

On the windowsill of the form 2 classroom was a large brass bell with a wooden handle. After fifty minutes of class, the *clark* would come out of his office, walk to the window, and ring the bell for classes to end. It was orderly and reasonable procedure. Then, of course, there was Mary.

Mary was a middle-aged woman who wandered the island freely but, let us say, was not quite right mentally. She dressed nicely, was very quiet, but when one saw her, he or she never knew quite what to expect. More than once, she entered the classroom, bowed respectfully to me, smiled at the class, turned, and left. Occasionally, too, she would be seen outside, staring silently at the bell on the windowsill. She would move closer and closer and suddenly pick up that bell and ring it with all her might, put it down on the windowsill, and walk away. It was a small disruption, but that was all.

CHAPTER 10

The Doctor

Paul was the physician in residence when we came to the island. An Englishman, he was about our age, and he lived on the other end of the island, at the mission. Technically, he was a lay missionary, and he minded the hospital there.

One of the things we inherited with the house was a motorcycle. We had bought bicycles in Blantyre, but when they arrived, it was obvious that their narrow tires weren't suitable for the rocky gravel paths on the island. The motorcycle, along with an old wooden boat with a British Seagull outboard motor, had been a gift to placate previous lonely volunteers and help persuade them to stay on the island. Now they belonged to us. Trouble was, I had never learned to ride anything but a bike. Paul was the answer. He had a cycle and had ridden one in England for years. Ours was a Honda 90, and his a 150; they were the only two cycles, motor vehicles even, on the island. He was an expert, and he made it his job to teach me to ride. It took a little coordination. "The left-hand *brake* is the clutch, the right *brake* is the brake for the front wheel. The left foot shifts up and down and the right foot works the rear brake."

At first, I was wobbly, but before long, I was negotiating the hills and rocky gravel along the steep path to Chipyela with no trouble. With Julie on the back, we could cut the travel time to the *Mezanni* at the mission to ten minutes. We had a few close calls but never hurt ourselves enough to need professional attention. When the slow pace of the island got to us, we could ride to the landing strip on the other side of the island and zip over the grass at speeds up to forty miles per hour. We'd do that two or three times, and somehow it brought us back to the modern world. *Azungu* was the Yanja word for *white person*, also the word for *crazy*. After we rode up and down the landing strip a few times, local residents made a point of waving and calling out, "Azungu!" We were never quite certain how to take that.

One time, shortly after we got accustomed to riding, on a Saturday afternoon, as we rode near the cathedral, a police officer popped out from behind a bush and raised his hand for us to stop. We did. He was dressed in an official-looking uniform, with dark shorts, a shirt with epithets, a hat, and a badge. He asked me to turn on the headlight of the bike. I did so, but it was futile, as the headlight was broken. I had used the kickstand to support the bike on the sand one evening, and during the night, when it rained, the bike had fallen into a mango tree and the plastic headlight had taken the brunt of the fall against the tree. The light casing was shattered, and the light dangled from below the handlebars. The officer calmly wrote out a ticket for me and said I was to appear in Nkhata Bay the following Thursday. When I explained that would require closing the school for a few days so I could take the ship to Nkhata Bay and back, he didn't seem to care. Again, Paul came to the rescue. We carefully reassembled the headlight and taped it together with electrical tape so that it worked when turned on. We then telegraphed the justice of the peace at Nkhata Bay and told him the story in as few words as possible. He wrote back that as the light had been repaired, the case was dismissed and we need not appear.

It was learning how to ride that got Julie and me really acquainted with Paul. He was a motor head, as I was. We both loved reading about sports cars and road races. He had an Austin-Healey 3000 back in England, painted "letter box red". We would get together on Friday evenings for drinks and dinner at our house, and afterward, we would play cribbage. We had wonderful times those evenings. It was the only time we could discuss world and local events with someone accustomed to modern Western culture. We each had shortwave radios and were able to keep up with current events that way. We also were able to relate our experiences on the island and learn much more about the local culture by sharing. Several stories stood out.

CHAPTER 11

Varmints

While we were in training, we had been regularly cautioned about moving about at night in Malawi. We were warned that snakes might be on paths and that, if you carried a flashlight, it would scare them away, or at least let you see them as you approached. Venomous snakes were prevalent. Mambas, adders, and spitting cobras made the island their home. Malawians had a way of walking on their heels at night to alert the snakes. It was serious business.

On one of those Friday evenings, Paul related his experience of the previous evening. He had awakened in the middle of the night and had to go to the bathroom. Unfortunately, the old house he lived in at the mission had no indoor plumbing, so he had to go out back to the *chimbuzi*, or *chim*, which was Malawian for *outhouse*. He was frustrated because the batteries in his *torch*, or flashlight, were dead. He could just take a chance, or he could take the Tilley lantern down from the shelf, pour some mentholated spirit into the bowl under the mantel, light it, wait for it to heat up the heat exchanger to vaporize the kerosene, or paraffin, light it again, and then go to the chim. He looked out at the dark night, thought about it a moment, and then reached for the lantern and went through the long process of lighting it. When he got to the outhouse, there, coiled on the seat, was a puff adder, a deadly snake, ready to strike. He backed away from the door, and the large snake slithered off into the night.

His story that night sent a shiver through all three of us.

Years before, not far from the cathedral, several women missionaries had killed a spitting cobra, a snake that spits venom, blinding rather than poisoning the victim. None of us wanted to deal with poisonous snakes. The Africans thought of them as spirits, beings without bones, that haunted the night. We thought it best not to dwell on the subject.

There were other problems besides snakes, though not as dramatic, that made life on the island, shall we say, challenging. From time to time, after we moved in to the house, we would come upon a cockroach. When I opened a drawer in the bedroom, sometimes there would be a rustling sound, and occasionally, a huge brown roach would drop to the floor. They were a nuisance, and they were multiplying. Paul insisted that living in a house filled with roaches may not be healthful. He suggested using a sprayer from the hospital and spraying the house with a powerful insecticide to kill the insects. Coincidentally, we had received word that there would be a gathering of Peace Corps volunteers in Nkhata Bay the following weekend to celebrate our first month in the country. We might borrow the sprayer and chemical, spray the house on Saturday morning, and close all the windows and doors, sealing in the fumes to kill the pests. We would then leave on the ship on Saturday afternoon, to return on the following Wednesday in time for school. We would have to ask permission of the headmaster for us to be away for two days, but Mr. Kaiwa had been very gracious and we didn't see a problem with that.

Early Saturday morning, we cleaned out the dressers, and with the spraying equipment, we treated every bit of furniture in the house. Every niche and corner was sprayed until the place reeked with the sweet smell of poison. We closed up, locked the doors, and took our Air Malawi bag on our way to Nkhata Bay for the celebration. That morning, we waited with Father Tovy and Paul for the gray-and-white ship, *Ilala*, to arrive. There was coffee, and more coffee, but no sign of the ship. Paul took his Honda to the top of the hill, but when he looked to the south, there was no ship on the horizon.

Morning turned to noon. "Would you stay for lunch?" said the Anglican priest, Father Tovy. We stayed. Finally, the postmaster came by. He had gotten a telegram from the government. It said the ship would be in dry dock for four to six weeks. Routine maintenance. "Would you like a glass of wine?" asked Paul.

There would be no party for us, only a bumpy motorbike ride to our house filled with dead cockroaches and the sickening smell of poison.

That evening, when we returned to face our foul-smelling house, we heard what we thought was thunder. How unusual to hear thunder in the dry season. But it wasn't thunder; it was a raid on the military post on the Portuguese side of the lake at Cobue, just a few miles away. The Frelimo, a group fighting for Mozambique independence from Portugal, was the cause. We wondered whether the military action so close to the island had anything to do with the *Ilala* needing unannounced maintenance.

We swept up the dead insects scattered about on the floor, opened the windows, and were thankful that, at least here in Malawi, there was no war going on.

CHAPTER 12

Neighbors

Living on the island made us part of a community, and as part of the community, we had visitors. Many of them. One old man would knock on our door from time to time, and in his hand was a small ball of twine made tediously of strands of fiber from the baobab tree. He wanted to sell his string for a penny or two. He never said anything; he simply held up the string and looked at us. We always bought from him. Sometimes it was woven into rope, but still, we bought what he had made. He was old, crippled with arthritis, and we respected his efforts and paid him for what he had made.

More often, it was kids—*iwes*, they were called—who knocked. They would stand by the backyard and call out, "Bucketey, buanjay." That meant "Tin can, please." If we had an empty tin, we would give it to them, and they would use it for a toy. Often, they would get someone to punch a hole in the bottom, knot a piece of string and feed it through the hole, and then use the cans as kind of stilts, holding them on with the string rising between their toes and leading to their small hands. We had a garbage can that came with the house, and whenever we dropped an empty can or bottle into it, it was just a minute or two before we would hear someone lift the lid and help themselves.

Another issue was more bothersome. A lady would appear at the door and say, "*Ticki buanjay.*" That meant she wanted money, a *ticki*, or three cents, to be exact. We would buy things, eggs, meat, milk, chickens, but we didn't give money away. We knew that if we started doing that, there would be no end to it. A more troubling issue was when a woman came to the door with a cut or some other injury to herself or her child. She would beg for a *ticki* so she could go to the hospital or take her child to the hospital. Three cents were the cost to enter the hospital. It was a nominal amount that almost everyone could afford. We were happy to give a ticki so a woman or her child could have a cut treated.

On Friday nights, when Paul came over for dinner and we told him about our good deeds, he was concerned. He told us that those we had sponsored often had not shown up for treatment at the clinic. Some of the women had simply taken the money and dressed the wound themselves or, worse, had let it go untreated altogether. To remedy this, he suggested giving us some gentian violet antiseptic and some bandages. We would clean the injury, apply the antiseptic to the wound, and dress minor cuts and bruises for free. More serious injuries would have to go on to the clinic, but we would take care of the lesser ones ourselves. Even small cuts and abrasions could turn to ugly tropical ulcers in that steamy climate. We were providing a real service. It was a good idea. It would keep the women from carrying their children two and a half miles to the hospital, it would save them three cents, and it would relieve stress at the clinic, which was always a busy place. In addition, it allowed us to do something worthwhile for the community along with teaching school.

The idea caught on right away, and whether it was a child, a student at school, or an old woman, everyone knew they could come to our house to have their cuts and bruises treated and bandaged. "Si como," they would say. "Si como, Maie, si como." Thank you, madam, thank you. These kind people would say this to Julie when she finished dressing their wounds.

CHAPTER 13

Curses

One Friday, Paul came over, obviously depressed. He sat on the couch and sipped his beer.

"It has been a terrible week," he said. He looked drained, exhausted, really. "It started on Wednesday. I went to the little village of Yofu, and everyone was sitting around a fire. People were crying, moaning. It was terrible. There was a young man there who looked especially depressed. When I asked what was wrong, they told me that the young man had been cursed and was going to die."

Paul met my smile with a stern look.

"I took his temperature and his blood pressure. It was obvious he was under stress, but his temperature was normal, though slightly elevated. So was his blood pressure. I tried to assure everyone that he would be all right, but there was nothing but gloom. He had been cursed, and he would die. Then I did something very unusual. I asked him to climb on the back of the Honda. I was taking him to the hospital. You understand that here in Malawi, when people are so ill we feel they cannot recover, we send them home. We take only people who can get well to the hospital. By asking this young man to come with me to the hospital, I was saying I could save him.

"*He was terrified, but he climbed on the back of the bike, and with him wearing my helmet, we rode off toward the hospital. I put him in a room by himself and told the nurse in charge for the night to be sure he had a good dinner. I kept tabs on him for a while. He was still very frightened, but still healthy. We secured the room. The next morning, when the nurse checked in on him, he was dead. There was no sign of a security breach, no sign of disorder or any kind of violence. He was simply dead in his bed. I notified the family of the tragic outcome, and they were reserved. It was as if nothing unexpected had happened. I performed an autopsy, as much as I could do on the island, and there was simply no obvious cause of death. I'm sure there is nothing in Western medicine that can explain it. He, an adolescent Malawian, previously in good health, with an athletic build, had simply died. That was all there was to it. He died as the result of a curse."*

We tried to make light of it, to somehow relegate it to bad luck, but Paul assured us that wasn't so.

"No," he said. "It wasn't bad luck, it was a curse. Remember those boys you were telling me about who came 'round and were afraid of the kid whose father was a witch doctor? That's what we're dealing with. That, whatever it is, is what those boys were afraid of. I don't know what this young man did, but whatever it was, he ticked off the wrong person. Now he's dead."

Later in the school year, in history class, we were talking about the ancient raids of the Carthaginians on the Romans. The Africans from Carthage invaded continuously until the Romans had had enough and they attacked Carthage, burned the city, and plowed salt into the soil. That was what the book said, and that was what I told the kids in class.

Alfred was the one. He was the son of the witch doctor who had so frightened his classmates on that first night we spent alone on the island. "But, sir," he said, "how could they do that?"

"Well, Alfred," I said, trying to explain, "you know the Portuguese soldiers who occasionally land on the island to buy chickens and eggs? They have their gunboats and their guns and all. We on the island don't have any guns, or any soldiers, or any weapons to fight with. What if those soldiers decided to take this island. How would we stop them?"

Suddenly, the classroom was very quiet, and Alfred, still standing, said, "But, sir, we have our magic."

Nobody laughed.

That was a lesson for me. Witchcraft, which I was assured didn't work on white people, was very real here on this African island. We had been conditioned in America not to believe it could be real, but here on Likoma Island, it was different.

Paul had been a good friend. He was there to reestablish the hospital after the previous people in charge had put beer in the refrigerator and left drugs that needed to be kept cool on the shelf. There was a nurse practitioner on the way from the mainland to take over the hospital. Paul had done his job and would be reassigned elsewhere on the mainland. He had been wonderful company. We would miss him. That was for certain.

With Paul gone after just six weeks, we felt a bit alone. Father Tovy was still there, and we had delightful times with him at the Mezzani. On Saturday mornings, when the ship came in, we would meet with him for coffee. When he had guests, he would often invite us for dinner. He lent wonderful insights into the island. The details escape me, but he had been exiled there because of humanitarian deeds he had done for Africans during times of political turmoil in Malawi. He was a true hero.

CHAPTER 14

Cobue

Across Lake Malawi, on the Mozambique side—or in those days, the Portuguese East Africa side—was the town of Cobue. It had been an African village, but then the Portuguese military took it over and made it a military base. There was a war going on. In this case, it was a war between a group called the Frelimo and the Portuguese, who had colonized the country years before. Weekly, a boat, actually an Arab dhow, would sail from Likoma Island over to Cobue, a distance of about five miles, where locals would buy wine and radios and other things at discount prices through the post exchange at the Portuguese military base there. We had heard that the previous volunteers had gone there, so why shouldn't we?

One Sunday morning, we walked over to a little village from where the dhow would depart. I remember it was a beautiful day and the boat was pulled up on the beach. Men and women were climbing over the bow and lining the seats on the sides of the boat. Julie and I climbed in, and part of the crew pushed the boat aft away from the shore. As she sank to her lines, water began sprouting in through a hole near the bow. "Not to worry, sir," said one of the crew. He took a tired-looking board from the bow of the boat and four rusty nails from a bag. A hammer appeared, and still standing in the shallow water, he nailed the board over the leak. The leak slowed, but water still seeped into the boat from numerous places. Undaunted, the crew pushed the boat off and raised the lateen sail to reach across toward the port of Cobue. The boat had no centerboard, so it couldn't really point into the wind at all, but it could reach across the wind and waves, and that would bring it easily to Cobue. When we pushed off, one of the women picked up a four-gallon bucket, similar to those used to fill our reservoir at home, and began dipping it beneath the floorboards, where it would quickly fill with water. She would then lift it and dump it over the side. Constantly as we sailed, she bailed, four gallons at a time. It was a huge amount of work and a commentary on both the strength of African women and the leaky hull beneath us.

Perhaps even more alarming was the sail. There were many patched tears and holes, but most outstanding was at the tack, where the mast meets the boom, or gaff, in this case. There, a hole, possibly large enough for me to step through, was visible. The entire boat seemed terribly vulnerable.

We sailed into the port of Cobue several hours later. We climbed from the boat with the Africans and met several armed men in military uniform standing on the quay. They didn't speak much English but were obviously concerned about something. Of course, there were no formalities, but something was wrong. It was us. It was also my camera. Normally, when Europeans were coming to the base, they would send word ahead so that an officer could greet them. Sure enough, one of the men ran ahead, and before long, an English-speaking officer appeared to escort Julie and me to the officers mess and the post exchange, where there were all kinds of Western goods for sale. He took my camera and explained he would return it when we left. We had lunch with him and some of the men. We bought several bottles of wine for ourselves to take home and some other goods. Everyone was very kind to us.

Late in the afternoon, we received word that our dhow was about to head back. We walked to the landing where the boat had been partially beached. The Africans had loaded the boat with goods, flour, and millet and other things they had bought at the local market. The crew also had open jugs of wine, and they were drinking heartily. The boat slid off the beach with the heaving of the crew and seemed to leak even more rapidly with its extra weight. As we left the bay and headed for our island home, it was obvious the helmsman at the tiller was intoxicated. He was laughing and singing and not paying attention to where we were going. Before long, we were a bit downwind off where we should have been heading. The breeze was still adequate, but if we went farther downwind, we would certainly not be able to make it to the place where we left, and we might miss the island altogether.

I knew I had to do something. I asked the captain if I could take a turn at the helm. Could I steer? He immediately translated my request in to the local language, and a roar of laughter engulfed the boat. "Azungu wants to steer the boat." Everyone laughed, but the man at the helm moved over, patted me on the back, and placed the tiller in my hand. That was all I needed. I hauled in the large sail a bit and headed the boat up toward the village we came from. The laughter subsided, and they let me keep steering.

"How can a schoolteacher steer a boat?" someone asked. "It is not possible, he is a schoolteacher, not a sailor."

The boat heaved and gushed through the gentle waves, and several ladies took turns bailing as the sun began to set and we came to the little bay where we had left. The bow of the boat crunched on the sand just as the last glimmers of sunlight reflected off the lake. We were right at the spot from where we had started. Women climbed over the side and waded to shore, bags of flour and millet on their shoulders or their heads. We had made it.

Julie and I took our things and headed back to our house in the cool of the evening. "Amazing! The schoolteacher can sail a boat! Amazing!" I said to her as we walked along the path. "Thank God for sail school!"

We wondered what would have happened had they continued to fall off the wind and missed the island. Would we have kept going for twenty or thirty miles in those crocodile-and-hippo-filled waters until we reached mainland Malawi? Would the crew have used the oars to row upwind to our point of departure? Of course, they made the trip regularly and they didn't all perish on a regular basis. More likely, they were putting us on, having fun with us, trying to scare us. Did we really somehow save them? Certainly not. I'm sure they would have done fine without us. What if a storm had come up? What if the wind had increased? Those could have been issues, but they knew weather patterns on Lake Malawi far better than we did. There were a thousand questions, but we didn't think we would need to make the trip to Cobue a regular thing.

CHAPTER 15

Our Day

As time went on, our lives began to fit a regular schedule. Stevenson, our *houseboy*, would arrive early in the morning, do the dishes from the previous evening, and prepare our breakfast. He did that in exchange for our paying his school fees. We would rise and dress, eat breakfast, and walk the hundred yards or so to school, where we would teach our respective classes.

Wednesdays, however, were an exception. On Wednesdays, I would rise early and ride to the harbor to meet the ship. There, I would take a boat to the ship, where I would pick up our supply of beef, a pound or so, right from the refrigerator on board. I might also have coffee with the captain. I could get back just in time for breakfast and school.

At noon, there was a lunch break. We would come home, and Julie would make a light lunch. We would eat and then go to the living room, where we had an ongoing cribbage game. Back at school, we would continue to teach until around two, when school let out. We then changed to our bathing suits, grabbed soap and shampoo, and walked to the beach at Mtoo, where we would swim and bathe in the warm, clear water, sure to return home before the magic hour of four.

There would be cocktails and dinner in the evening, and then we would spend the rest of the night, until bedtime, under the Aladdin lamp in the office, preparing lessons. As I taught English nine times a week, geography, and history to both forms and physics with chemistry to form 1, preparation was no small thing. Especially since we didn't have regular texts to work from, I remember spending hours writing material on the history of the world that I drew from reference books in the library. Not only did I have to tell the story, but I also had to select salient points to write on the board for the students to write in their copybooks. Preparation was a huge job. Lesson plans, turned in every month, were mere outlines, but the devil was in the details.

Julie taught two levels of math, biology, and health and the second level of physics with chemistry. Her job was huge, and she was up to it.

CHAPTER 16

Dances

Occasionally, on a Friday night, there would be a dance at the school. The custodian would move the furniture to one side, and a kerosene-powered Tilly lamp would be suspended from the ceiling to provide light. There was a battery-powered record player and half a dozen 45 rpm records available for the dance. The kids were always excited about these affairs. From time to time, our parents would send us a care package from home, and one of the things we really appreciated was popcorn.

One night, when there was a dance, Julie lit our little kerosene stove and began popping popcorn with abandon until she filled a huge bowl. We carried it to the school, and the kids were simply delighted. They had never seen anything like it. They talked of people holding mealie cobs (corncobs) over a fire and chasing the occasional kernel that popped off, but they had never seen anything like this. I can still see them crowding around the bowl in the flickering light, some of them jumping up and down with excitement. Did they stuff their hungry mouths full, gorging themselves in selfish glee? Hardly. They took a few pieces and moved out of the way so everyone could share. They thanked us. To be sure, they ate it all and expressed their amazement at the few unpopped kernels at the bottom of the bowl. They were so truly appreciative. They were wonderful kids.

The dance would be over when the batteries in the record player ran down, and that didn't take long. The kids were graceful dancers.

Of course, as there was only one girl for every five boys enrolled in school, there wasn't a whole lot of coed dancing going on. It was quiet too; the louder the music, the less time for listening and dancing.

Julie and I would dance too.

Ever so slowly, we felt accepted.

We were increasingly a part of things.

CHAPTER 17

Green Mamba

One Saturday, just after lunch, James Chapola, a form 1 student, knocked on our living room door. I could see he was sort of scrunched down as he stood, waiting for me to open it.

"Hello, James," I said. "Here for a little help with your maths?"

"Yes, sir," he answered. "But, sir, there is a snake there on the porch."

I opened the door farther, and James scooted by me into the living room.

"Julie!" I called. "James is here for a little help."

My wife of less than a year appeared, and she and James went to the dining room table to work on some difficulties he had with solving the maths problems in his text. The *s* added to *math* is a British idea.

Meanwhile, I was left alone with the snake on the front porch. I could see it through the window. It was resting on a beam, with its head over the door. About five feet long, it was just above a clothes-line strung on the porch, where Stevenson, our helper, would hang laundry. It lay there, completely immobile, its beady eyes blinking occasionally, but that was all. What to do? Was it dangerous? There was a book on native wildlife in the book locker, and sure enough, it had a section on snakes. I turned to it and looked for long skinny green ones. There were two native to the area. One, the boomslang, was nonpoisonous. The inside of its mouth was red. The other, nearly identical, was the green mamba. It was described as being very fast and capable of catching birds in trees. It carried a neurotoxic venom that might kill a human in ninety seconds if he were so unlucky as to be bitten on the body core. The inside of its mouth was black. It was first cousin to the black mamba, an even more aggressive snake that had been known to attack and kill men on horseback.

So which was it? I sat on the couch and looked at the snake, wondering what to do. He calmly turned his head toward me and yawned. Black. We had a green mamba. He or she was apparently waiting above the clothesline for an unsuspecting bird to flutter by and light. Bang, it would be over in a second. The snake would strike, the bird would succumb instantly, and that would be that.

Before long, James was finished with his lesson, and I heard Julie escort him to the back door.

We needed a plan. I definitely didn't like the notion of a poisonous snake on the porch. Julie and I watched for a while, but it seemed obvious that the snake had no idea of moving. It was quite happy on its perch and not ready at all to leave. Of course, there were no real weapons we could use to kill it, but there was a hatchet for cutting wood. Perhaps if we tied the hatchet to the end of a clothespole and then sneaked up on the snake, I could whack it. I got the clothespole from the front porch and carried it into the house through the back way. Inside, we found the hatchet and some twine we had bought from the string man. While I held the two together, Julie tightly wound the twine around the handle of the hatchet and the end of the clothespole. We added more and more twine until the fit was snug and the two, hatchet and pole, moved as one.

I built up my courage as we devised our plan. First, Julie found a syringe and some snakebite medicine in the refrigerator. Of course the refrigerator was off when we arrived on the island, and heaven only knew how long the antivenom had been stored warm. We had it ready anyway. Then, as evening approached, I carried the weapon outside through the back door, around the house, to the front. Julie was behind me, keeping an eye on things. All the while, I was thinking of the snake lunging through trees to catch a bird. Would it lunge at me?

I carefully approached the porch and lifted the pole so the hatchet was poised over the snake. Then I pulled it down on him with all my might!

It was a glancing blow. The snake lifted its head, centered me in its gaze, and struck viciously as I dropped pole and hatchet and backed away. It then coiled upward and found a crack between the corrugated metal roof and the fascia and darted inside the attic of the house.

There we were outside our house in the heart of Africa as night fell, looking at our hatchet and clothespole lying on the porch, with the full knowledge that we had just driven a very deadly snake inside our house. Now we would have to go inside too.

It was not a pleasant moment.

Fortunately, I think, there was no access to the attic of the house from inside. One would have to take down part of the ceiling to get there. Going into a dark attic, hunting for a dangerous and now-angry snake was not my idea of a good time or a wise thing to do, anyway. Of course, we went into the house, we had a cocktail, and Julie prepared dinner. Sometimes I thought I could hear the snake moving about above me on the other side of the ceiling. It was a disturbing thought, as there were openings where the pipes descended from the water tank en route to sinks and tub and toilet. Normally, in Western homes, there are seals around pipes where they come through the wall or ceiling. Not here. There was just a plain space big enough for a snake to get through easily around each pipe.

Perhaps you have thought about what it would be like to live in the same house with a deadly snake. Probably not. So I will share some impressions.

First, there is a heightened awareness. One looks where one places his hand or where he sits. There is suddenly much more curiosity about out-of-the-way places, behind the stove, under the refrigerator, than there was before the snake. Sleep becomes more difficult. Little sounds tend to wake one from a sound sleep. The mere touch of the hand or leg of your lover makes you suddenly wide awake, ready to leap from the bed. There is nothing positive about the experience. One becomes short and unpleasant.

Look as we did, we didn't see the snake in the house at all that week. It was the following Saturday that James came back for more help with his maths. Again, he knocked on the front door, and again, he had that scrunched-down look.

"Please, sir, let me in quickly. The snake is back!"

I jumped out of the way, and James dashed into the room. Sure enough, the snake was back. He lay on the beam in much the same position as he was the previous week. James and Julie went to the dining room to tend to his lessons. Stevenson, our helper, was in the kitchen, cleaning up some dishes.

"Please, sir," said Stevenson, "let me tend to the snake. We Africans have no fear of snakes. I will take care of it, sir."

I knew Stevenson was lying. Africans have a natural fear of snakes. It is a preservation mechanism, simple as that. Stevenson wanted to impress us, as he always did, with his studies and his housework. He was a fine student and a hard worker.

He picked up the clothespole and pulled the hatchet off the end. "I will knock him down, and we will kill him with stones."

As there were numerous round rocks nearby, I gathered a few, and Stevenson, with the long pole in hand, went for the snake. We could see a bruise on his body where I had injured him the week before, but he was ready this time. Right away, he struck at Stevenson, who dropped the pole and fled. Instantly, the snake spun around and darted back through the same opening he had used the week before. He was back inside the house. Oh no! He was really mad now, and we had to live with him in that state for, well, maybe forever. Stevenson was gone. What now?

Back inside, we glanced at the openings around the pipes coming through the ceiling, Julie went back to work with James, and I picked up a book. Do you know how hard it is to concentrate with an angry, deadly viper just over your head? Very hard. Well, it was still early afternoon. Maybe we could go for a swim before the crocodiles fed. It was not a strong moment.

But life goes on. We pulled down the covers and checked the bed carefully before crawling in and looked under the bed. A careful check of the bathroom was essential—those pipes, you know. Of course, there was no light in the bathroom, unless we took a flashlight, which we did, always.

It was the following Wednesday, when I got up early to go to the *Ilala*, when things changed. Stevenson had returned on Monday, and things were almost back to normal. I climbed onto the motorcycle in the early light and sped off toward the mission. I took a boat to the ship, where I visited briefly with the captain and picked up our weekly meat supply. Then I headed home. I parked the Honda under the mango tree and walked toward the porch, where I noticed what at first appeared to be a clothesline dangling from the wall. Then the snake was swinging toward me, with mouth open wide. Startled, I backed away as the viper dropped just inches from my feet. Quickly I backed away, found a rock, and heaved it at the monster as it slithered through the grass and disappeared. I picked up another rock and began to chase it but then thought better of it.

Back inside, I sat down with Julie to relate the news.

We had a relaxed breakfast for a change and then headed off for school.

CHAPTER 18

Lake Flies

The Likoma Day Secondary School was located on a peninsula at the end of the island. Though we couldn't see the lake clearly from the school because of hills and vegetation, the lake was the dominant feature of the area. One day, our headmaster, Mr. Kaiawa, came to the classroom and announced that because of the insects, the school would be closed for the rest of the day.

What? Insects? Could this be real?

But everyone got up out of his or her seat, picked up their belongings, and left the classroom. Outside, there were swarms of bugs in the air. Over the lake, there was a dark cloud. *Insects* was the translation. Obviously.

We had read that clouds of insects on Lake Malawi would cause ships to change course, as they were so thick and dense as to pose a health hazard to the crew. Indeed, but we were not prepared for what we saw next.

Women from the villages, along with our female students, were holding baskets and even bits of clothing and swinging them in the air to try to catch the bugs. As the dark cloud approached, the excitement grew. We were amazed. The girls swung their baskets into the swarm and collected the bugs in whatever container they could find. They would wrap a scarf around their nose and mouth and dash about the school yard, or wherever, swinging their baskets in the air to catch the bugs. We went home to get away from the menace, but the bug cloud lasted most of the rest of the day.

The next day in school, we expressed our curiosity. The girls were quick to explain that they collected the lake flies to eat. They would mix them with water and cook them somehow so that they were cakes of bugs. Then they would be ready to eat. The kids assured us that they were delicious. *We should try some.*

I told them that in America, people didn't eat insects, and that began a conversation. "But you eat bottom-feeders," said one of our students.

"Bottom-feeders?" I questioned.

"Yes," said Mattia, "you eat clams and crabs and lobsters and things that crawl on the bottom of the sea. They are the lowest of beings. Things that eat the droppings of other fish. We don't eat those things."

"Right," I said, "we do eat those things. We think they are delicacies. Lobster is very expensive, as are clams. We think they are delicious."

"But we would never eat them. They are dirty," said Mattia. "They eat the soil on the bottom of the sea."

The class chuckled at his rather-forward statement.

"But these insects," he said, "they are born on the water. They are only one day old. They fly in great swarms from the water and wash over the island. They are clean and have never been exposed to the soil or to filth or the bottom of the lake. Of course we eat them. They are clean and pure and delicious."

I was not prepared for this line of reasoning, so I admitted that I had never thought about it that way and that they had a good point.

"Sir?" said Cotilda, a light-skinned girl in the front row. "Suppose that Beatrice and I bring some fly cakes to your house this afternoon. Will you try them?"

I was caught off guard. Me, Julie and me, eat insects?

"Sure," I said. "I think we have a tin of oysters or clams at home. Would you taste them?"

Beatrice scowled, but Cotilda allowed that she might.

We had a date.

Later that afternoon, Julie and I waited in the dining room for the girls to appear. Right on time, there was a knock on the door, and there they were with something carefully wrapped in paper. They came in, and we all sat down at the dining room table. Julie brought four plates and two tins from the pantry, which she had opened in the kitchen, one marked CLAMS, and the other OYSTERS.

Cotilda opened the package, and there were several "cakes" inside. They were dark brown in color and nondescript in appearance. We all grimaced a bit, but well, we agreed to go first.

I picked up a piece of one of the cakes and sniffed. It smelled a little like meat. I looked at it carefully, and there were little bodies of insects complete with wings all pressed together. Perhaps this wasn't the best idea. I took a bite and began to chew. To my surprise, my taste buds detected the flavor of lamb. The texture, somewhat crumbly, was not a texture I would ever associate with meat, but the flavor was lamb. It was, well, not delicious, but fine. Julie bit enthusiastically into her serving, and she agreed. We liked it. We smiled. The girls' eyes were bright. They were delighted; they couldn't help but giggle. Wonderful.

But now it was their turn. We placed a small serving of clams and oysters onto their plates. They took a tentative bite, very tiny, but then tried again. Before long, we had all sampled some. Another wall had come tumbling down. We ate and liked their lake flies, and they ate and liked our clams. Somehow, we had all won. They thanked us, we thanked them, we visited for a while, and they went back to relay their story to their friends.

The flies were gone. There were no clouds of them on the horizon. It had been a one-day experience, and from that we had learned a great deal about ourselves and about the wonderful Malawian children we had the good fortune of teaching.

CHAPTER 19

A Camera

Our lives on Likoma Island were so amazingly rich that, somehow, the Kodak Brownie camera we brought with us from home just didn't make it. Though, believe it or not, there were Kodak signs at stores on the island, and film was available, flashcubes were not. Besides, our friends seemed to have real SLR cameras that could take pictures in moderate light without relying heavily on flash. Good cameras were available mail order from Hong Kong. We borrowed a catalog and ordered an Asahi Pentax along with a 300-mm and a 28-mm lens with the 55-mm lens that came with the camera. We got a case of film and several filters at the same time. A few weeks later, we received a letter from the Malawi airport that a package had arrived for us, but we had to prove that its origin was not the Soviet Union.

There would be a school break coming up shortly, so we contacted our friends the Ryans in Nkhotakota to see whether they could put us up for a night so we could get a bus to the airport to pick up our new camera. We would then fly to Rhodesia to spend our Christmas holiday visiting that country. Michael had visited Likoma in his role as an architect for the mission. He and his wife, Ann, were lay missionaries stationed at Nkhotakota. Ann was a midwife. We contacted them and found that they, too, had business in Lilongwe and that we could ride together.

When the first break in the school year finally came, we took the *Ilala* to Nkhotakota and spent the evening with Ann and Michael.

Before dinner, a man at the mission prepared steaming baths for us. After that, we had a cocktail and a dinner of curried meat over rice. The meal was new to us. We hadn't known much about curry, but it was spicy and delicious.

Early the next morning, we departed for Lilongwe. Michael had borrowed a tiny Renault to take the four of us to town. Though it was small, it was quick, and we zoomed over the gravel roads on the left, of course, always careful of numerous bicycles, pedestrians, and even herds of animals wandering the roads. Naturally, there were other cars too, and large trucks, or lorries, lumbering over the unpaved narrow ways. The road was rough, and we got our first puncture about halfway to Lilongwe. We had a spare, so after some working in the dust, we got it fixed. A short time later, we got a second puncture. Michael took off the wheel, and with some difficulty, we removed the tire and managed to affix a patch over the leak in the tube and pump it back up. The tire was badly damaged. When we finally arrived in Lilongwe, we found a service station that would replace the tire and repair the other flat, but it wouldn't be ready until the following day. That meant that, like us, Michael and Ann would be spending the night in the Lilongwe Hotel.

We slowly drove to the airport to pick up the camera and signed the certificate of origin, and the deed was done. Then we drove on to the hotel. I had no idea. Here, in the middle of Malawi, was this lovely hotel. It was clean and light and open. One was expected to *dress* for dinner. That meant a coat and tie. Unfortunately, Michael, who had expected to drive back later that day, had neither. But the hotel was prepared. They found a jacket and tie for him in a closet. Ann's clothes were fine. No problem.

In the dining room, we found ourselves in a lovely setting. The waiters were Africans, barefoot, dressed in clean white clothing. The service, impeccable. The table was set with an array of knives and forks and spoons to boggle the American mind. On our right were several knives and spoons, on the left an equal array of forks. The waiter took our order, and soup came first. Easy. We picked up the soupspoon and ate our soup. Then came the fish. I reached across my plate to pick up the inside fork with my right hand and then picked up the inside knife on the right side with my left hand and began to cut the fish. Ann, across the table, began to laugh. She tried to cover it up, but she broke into a grin and covered her mouth.

"I'm so sorry," she said. "You Americans are so lovely, but you really must learn to eat more formally, especially in a place like this. Please, I don't mean to be rude, but normally, we pick up the outside fork in the left hand and the outside knife in the right. We invert the fork and push the fish onto the fork like this. Then the next course, we take the next knife and fork, beginning from the outside. That way, when dessert comes, we have just one knife and fork left. Perfect."

I had to admit that it was all new to me. "Having two forks was a lot at home," I admitted. "One for dinner, the other for salad."

But we had a delightful time with the Ryans that evening. When we had finished with the fish course, the waiter picked up Michael and Ann's plates right away, but ours were left in front of us.

"You have to signal the waiter that you are finished," said Michael. "Put your knife and fork side by side on the plate, and he will take it away."

We did so, and the plate vanished.

What a lesson it was! Not only did we have to learn a great deal from the Africans, we also had a lot to learn from the English. There was a whole world out there we never knew about.

Ann and Michael were about our age and were from Stony Stratford in England. We got along famously from the start. Ann's help showing us how to eat was something that only a true friend would offer. The lesson was indispensable. We laughed about our shortcomings and about the difference between the United States and England, two countries separated by a common language.

After dinner, we went to our room and played cribbage. We laughed and laughed and had a wonderful time.

"Why don't you come back and spend Christmas with us?" said Ann.

"Oh," said Julie, "we'd love to, but we'll be in Rhodesia. School doesn't start till after the first of the year. We'll be back before then, but I doubt Christmas."

"Well, think about it. You can stay with us. It would be wonderful to have you two spend Christmas with us. We'd love that. Please keep us in mind."

CHAPTER 20

Off to Rhodesia

Early the next morning, we boarded an Air Malawi DC-3 for Salisbury, Rhodesia. Today, Rhodesia is called Zimbabwe, but in the sixties, it was segregated and called Rhodesia. Peace Corps policy was that we would spend vacation time in the cultural area, which included Rhodesia. We did that at our peril, knowing that there was the risk that if we had Rhodesia stamped in our passport, it would not be accepted in other African countries where we hoped to travel. Those who had traveled before us had prepared us for how to deal with formalities. When we landed at the airport, there was a large white gentleman there who asked for our passports. We handed them to him, and we slipped pieces of paper into the page where the stamp would go. I asked him if he would stamp the paper instead of the book. He nodded. No problem. I heaved a sigh as he handed the book back to me. We spent a day in Salisbury and then boarded a train for Victoria Falls.

The train ride to Victoria Falls was magnificent. The locomotive was steam powered; it was delightful. I remember the passenger car we rode on had 1913, the year my mother was born, stamped onto part of the trucks. The train was different from what we were used to in Malawi. The conductor and engineer were white. The passengers in our car were white.

When we got to the falls, we found a campground where one could rent a tent for the night. There were regular beds, a little kitchen, and a sitting room in the tent. We walked through the park to the area where the waters of the mighty Zambezi tumbled over the falls. It was magnificent but so different from what we had experienced in America. There were walkways, but no fences. One could walk right up to the edge of the chasm on the slippery grass and gaze at the falls. The great green stream of water would plunge hundreds of feet onto the rocks below and explode in a mass of spray and mist. It was beautiful. "The smoke that thunders," it was called, and for good reason. There was a tropical rain forest nearby, and even a golf course had a hole overlooking the chasm.

That evening, there was a gathering of campers around a fire, and we were asked to join them for cocktails. Everyone introduced themselves and talked a little about where they were from. When it was our turn, we said that we taught school in Malawi. When someone asked where, I told them we taught on Likoma Island, in an African day secondary school. We were the only white people there. That was the end of the conversation for us. Suddenly, I noticed that everyone was visiting with one another but no one was talking with us. We said our goodbyes, but no one seemed to notice. We walked off to a restaurant for dinner. That night, we went to sleep to the roar of the falls and the roar of discrimination and intolerance. We didn't sleep well.

The following day, we had a boat ride on the Zambezi, above the falls. The river was alive with crocodiles and hippos, which the tour boat driver was quick to point out. He liked to entertain us with stories of waterskiing on the Zambezi. Somehow, I didn't envy him for that.

From there we tried to catch a bus to Zimbabwe, the ancient fort where stones had been so craftily cut and stacked that one couldn't slide a dollar bill between them. We raised our hand when the bus came, but it refused to stop. Finally, a man in a Rover stopped and told us that buses didn't pick up white people in Rhodesia. He was going our way and gave us a ride. The place was simply amazing. We looked at the beautiful walls and wondered at the people who called it home. Little is known about those people, except that they all left at the same time. There is no sign of a disaster, but it is known that the people there would trade gold for salt pound for pound. Obviously, the people left because of a pressing need of some kind. It was beautiful. We went from there to Bulawayo, a city designed with wide streets, so wide that a wagon and team of six horses could turn around without backing up. What an amazing city! It was there, at a Rhodes gallery, we bought a soapstone sculpture, which we paid to have packed and sent home to my parents. We had no idea anything could be so complicated. My parents worked for weeks to pick up the statue sent from Rhodesia, a country boycotted by the United States because of the policies of its apartheid government.

It was just outside Bulawayo that we found ourselves, one Sunday morning, beside a little white church with a steeple and open windows. Christmas hymns were bursting from those windows.

CHAPTER 21

Back toward Malawi

It was that morning that we looked at each other and decided that we would return to Nkhotakota to be with our friends the Ryans at Christmas. We had given up on buses, so we stuck our hands in the air and lowered them at the first car that came along. We hitchhiked, a perfectly respectable way to get around in Africa in those days. We got picked up by the first car that came by.

It wasn't a car, exactly. It was a Volkswagen bus. It stopped, and its enthusiastic white driver beckoned Julie and me to climb aboard. We squeezed into the seat beside him, and he shifted into first and we rolled. Right away, I began to regret my decision. The driver had a bottle of beer between his legs, and he swigged from it from time to time. He wasn't drunk, but it wasn't the first beer that day either. Also, it was just after eleven in the morning, early for drinking. His name was Bruno Depetro. He told us he was a contractor and he had finished a job building a large house on an agricultural estate. He had been paid, and he was bringing his crew back to Salisbury for the holidays. Sure enough, behind us, behind a canvas curtain, sat at least half a dozen African men jostling back and forth as the car sped over the rough road. They were his crew, he had said. He was going to Salisbury, and Salisbury was where we would catch our flight to Blantyre-Limbe. He would take us there. Some deal.

Right away, Bruno spotted the new Pentax camera dangling over my shoulder on its strap. "Where'd you get that camera?" he asked.

"Oh, my wife and I live in Malawi," I told him. "We bought it in Asia and had it shipped to Lilongwe. I just picked it up. Malawi is such a beautiful place. I really wanted a good camera to photograph it, so we saved our money and bought it. We're here in Rhodesia on holiday. We've taken rolls of film in Rhodesia too. Beautiful." I was beaming.

"What did you pay for it?" he asked.

I stuttered. "Pay for it? What do you mean?"

"Whatever you paid for it, I'll pay you twice. If that isn't enough, I'll pay what you ask."

"I don't want to sell the camera. It has taken months for us to get it, and it would take at least that long again, and we would run out of time."

"See that briefcase at your feet?" Bruno said. "Open it."

I reached down and unsnapped the briefcase and recoiled, as though it were filled with snakes. In fact, it was filled with money. Bundles of large-denomination Rhodesian bills. On top of it, lying casually on the heap of bills, was a semiautomatic pistol.

Bruno laughed. "Did you ever read any James Bond?" he asked.

A bit shell -shocked, I replied, "All of it."

"What do you remember about his gun?"

"Beretta, .25 caliber," I said.

"Exactly!" said Bruno. "And that is what I have here. Now, if you want some money for your camera, take it."

"You see, Bruno, I had to declare the camera when I left Malawi and when I entered Rhodesia. If I don't have it when I return, I'll be in trouble. I'm not allowed to sell it here. I have to have it to return," I lied.

He smiled and seemed to accept my reasoning.

"Please close the briefcase," he said. I closed the briefcase and heaved a sigh. "I have some pictures I want to show you," he said next. He reached inside his jacket and pulled a package of prints from his shirt pocket and handed them to me. I opened the envelope and pulled out the pictures. They were pictures of the moon in black-and-white. Some of them were blurry. They showed no detail. I knew right away that, with a tripod and my 300-mm lens, I could do much, much better.

"You Americans are going to the moon," he said. "I think that is so exciting. I look at the moon, and I try to photograph it, but these are pathetic, no? You are going to the moon!" That was when Bruno began to review the history of the Apollo moon program. The little bus sped along the road, rocking back and forth over the some-what-uneven pavement. Bruno, with his beer in his lap and a fortune at his feet, protected with the Beretta .25, was telling me about his love for the Apollo program as Julie and I held on for dear life and half a dozen African men mumbled quietly behind us.

It was miles and miles to Salisbury, but by late afternoon, we arrived in a residential section of town.

"Thanks, Bruno," I said. "We can find our hotel from here."

"Oh, but no," said Bruno, "you must meet my family. You must come for dinner and meet my family. Please, please! You will come to dinner."

A few minutes later, the bus pulled into a driveway in front of a two-story house on a residential street. We climbed out, and Bruno opened the rear door to let the Africans out. They drifted off, and we went up on the porch of the house. Suddenly, the door opened, and a large woman who had a family resemblance to Bruno appeared.

"Oh, Bruno!" she said and started to sob.

"Oh, Rosa!" Bruno said, and they hugged enthusiastically. "Rosa, this is Henry and Julie," said Bruno.

"Oh, Henry," said Rosa, and she wrapped her thick arms around me and squeezed me hard. "Oh, Julie," Rosa said, and Julie suffered the same greeting.

Inside there were greetings from other relatives and friends who had been invited for dinner. There was also beer, plenty of beer. Two more places were set at the table, and we ate. We ate and we ate. There were hors d'oeuvres, then salad and pasta, and meat and wine. Several bottles of wine. Finally, Bruno said, "Dessert!"

And Rosa said, "Spumoni!"

"Oh Rosa!" said Bruno.

"Oh, Bruno, we have spumoni!" said Rosa.

We ate bowls of spumoni.

Finally, Julie and I said we would have to leave to get a room at a hotel. We thanked everyone and headed for the door.

"Wait," said Bruno. I hesitated, but Bruno was in no condition to drive us anywhere. "Guido will take you," Bruno gasped.

We got our things from the microbus, and Bruno backed it into the street. A man in a dark suit with a small chauffer's cap, Guido, pushed open garage doors in the small garage at the top of the drive, and a black Peugeot limo slowly backed out next to us.

"Get in," said Bruno.

We said our thank-yous, and we got in the back seat of the large car. Guido turned to me, obviously annoyed.

"Where you go?" said Guido.

"The Florida Hotel," I said.

Guido scowled at me and lit a cigarette, and we headed off toward our destination. Obviously, the Florida Hotel was far beneath his dignity, being a cheap hotel in the Indian part of town. It was clean and inexpensive, a place where other volunteers had directed Julie and me. Guido pulled the limo up to the modest hotel and opened the door for us to get out. I'm sure we were the first Peace Corps volunteers to ever arrive at the Florida Hotel in a black limousine.

CHAPTER 22

A Bumpy Road

The night at the Florida Hotel was uneventful, as was the flight from Salisbury to Blantyre-Limbe the following day. For our exit, Rhodesian customs stamped the same piece of paper I had slipped in the passport upon arrival. Had one looked at our passports carefully, he would have seen that we had left Malawi for several weeks, gone nowhere, and returned. Still, no one seemed to notice or comment on the omission.

Things got interesting later that day on the bus to Lilongwe. We got our tickets right at the terminal, but when we saw the crowd waiting for the bus, it was obvious that there were a lot more people waiting than seats, or standing room, for that matter. People had live chickens, and one man had a goat on a rope. This was not your group of Englishmen in a queue. It was a horde, pushing toward the open door of the bus, with everyone squeezing and trying to get ahead of everyone else. Perhaps they treated me with a bit of deference, I don't know for sure, but we did manage to get aboard and even get a seat toward the back. It was a seat with a back, too, unlike the seat behind it, which had no cushion on the backrest, just a metal frame. We stored our bags on the rack above us. Heavy *katundu*, or baggage, was stored on the bus roof. We were off after a while, a bus loaded with African men and women with babies and children, and Julie and me. People had brought food, and they were eating. Everyone was talking.

The road, once we passed through the country's only traffic light and got out of the city, was rough. It was a dirt road, and as it was during the rainy season, it was muddy as well. We sped along without incident. Interestingly, the driver was sipping a beer, a Lion lager, if I remember correctly. After a while, on a lonely stretch of road, the bus stopped and everyone got out. Men on the right side, women on the left. It was a pit stop. We could do our thing and then climb back onto the bus.

As night fell, we found another diversion. The full moon rose out of a clear sky. As the bus sped along, weaving back and forth with the road, the moon appeared to shift from one side of the bus to the other, causing great laughter among the passengers, who might have never before traveled at night on a bus.

And then it happened. The headlights went out. The driver skillfully pulled the bus to a stop on the side of the road. "*Torche bwanje?*" he asked. Anyone have a flashlight? Everyone looked at us. Julie had a small flashlight in her bag, and we took it forward to the driver. "*Si como,*" he said.

In a few moments, he had gone outside and lifted a compartment in the front of the bus and replaced the fuse. We were off again, headlights beaming, bouncing through the night. A short time later, the bus pulled into a small town and stopped. Everyone cheered. It was pitch-black outside. What was everyone cheering about? Someone explained it to me as we all disembarked the bus. We were the first to arrive. It was kind of a race. The first bus to the town gets to go to the bar and drink beer, along with the driver, until the second bus arrives. Then the drivers switch buses, we all get back on our respective buses, and we continue our journey with our new driver, who drives back home to either Blantyre-Limbe or Lilongwe. Perhaps they were cheering because they knew the second driver wouldn't have a chance to drink much beer. At least that was why I was cheering.

Anyway, the second half of the trip was uneventful, and by the time we reached the Lilongwe Hotel and ordered a room, we fell into bed. We were exhausted.

The next morning, after a hearty breakfast, we went back to the bus station and found a bus to Nkhotakota. Again, there was a pit stop along the way, but this time, when the driver pulled over, the big bus slid off the road into the mud. He got stuck. It had rained during the night and was raining still, and the dual rear tires on the left, shoulder side, had sunk into the soft ground just off the road. All the men were instructed to go back and push. Well, I was a man, and so I walked behind the bus and leaned on the rear bumper with a dozen other souls. It was kind of dangerous work as the driver tried to rock the bus to get it out of the hole it had dug for itself. He would ease forward and then let it roll back and then gun the engine as we pushed for all we were worth. We were directed when to push by a man on the side who somehow got signals from the driver. When the driver lunged ahead, the rear wheels would spin and throw mud and gravel back at us. We finally got the bus out of the mudhole and climbed back aboard for the rest of the ride. I was plastered with mud on the front of my pants up to my chest.

Riding a bus in Malawi in 1968 was not always an easy thing to do.

Ann and Michael were so happy to see us on Christmas Eve when we arrived at their home in Nkhotakota. We had a bath before dinner—an English tradition, I believe, and a good idea, especially for me. What a wonderful evening!

It was the beginning of a fine friendship that lasted many years.

CHAPTER 23

Modzie

As I remember, it was one of the students who told us. He said that there was a litter of puppies under a bush near the house, weaned and ready to be adopted. Julie and I went over, and sure enough, covered with dirt and ticks, there was a little pup under a bush. He was beige in color, with white paws and a white chest. There was no bitch in sight. I reached down and picked him up. He looked weak, but otherwise, he was okay. We took him home and warmed some water that I then poured into the bathroom sink. After his bath, he looked a little better, but numerous fat ticks had bitten into him. We used a match to heat tweezers then applied the tweezers to the tick, causing it to let go and back out of our puppy. One by one they were gone.

Julie made a formula with powdered milk. He licked it from our fingers at first, but before long, he was lapping from a dish. We called him Modzie, which meant "one" in Chinyanja. In our training in Alabama, one of the instructors at Camp Atkins had had a dog named Atatoo. *Atatoo* meant "three." Modzie was to be our one and only; three was not an option!

Africans didn't seem to have the same relationship with dogs as we did. There were dogs around the villages, and when people approached, if the dogs barked, they might be dispersed by throwing stones at them. Dogs were considered very lowly creatures. One would never call anyone a dog—it was the ultimate insult. We never saw that dogs were domesticated in the sense we were used to.

Modzie didn't know that, however. We were amazed at how easy he was to housebreak. When he had an accident inside, we took him right to the door and put him outside. In no time, it seemed, he was trained. We fed him meals of cassava flour and water along with our table scraps. I contacted the Peace Corps, and they sent a syringe and rabies vaccine. I remember practicing on a piece of meat with an old syringe first, and then, while Julie held him still, I jabbed him with the needle and pushed the plunger home. He yelped, but that was it.

We really enjoyed teaching him. First, we got him to come when he was called. It worked, inside and out. He would eagerly run to us when we said his name. Next, it was "Sit." He would sit and stay until released. We used a little treat from time to time, but he loved to please, and the treat became optional. We taught him other things too. He could stand in the corner, for instance. He would run to the corner of the room, lean into the corner, and stand on his hind legs, facing outward. We tried to get him to just sit up, but he kept falling over. "In the corner" was all it took. He slept outside on a chair on the porch. Our African friends were surprised at his affable, friendly nature and, I think, a little surprised at how close we were to him.

He used to come with us to school, and he would lie at our feet while we taught. I remember, one day in English class, the kids were complaining about some confusing aspect of the language. Probably something like "shipping by air" or "cargo loaded aboard ships." There are many things about English that don't seem to make sense to a nonnative speaker. I remember someone saying, "This is just too hard, sir."

From time to time, I couldn't resist a little tease.

"Oh," I said, "it's not really that difficult. Modzie knows English."

"Bodza!" someone said. *Bodza* meaning nonsense. I heard it often from the class. They didn't believe me.

The students had made it clear that it was odd that we would give a dog a name and more so that we would name a dog a number.

"Modzie, come," I said. Our dog was immediately alert and walked over to me.

"Sit." He sat. "Shake hands." He lifted his right paw, and we shook hands. "In the corner," I said. He backed into the corner of the classroom and propped himself up.

The class was stunned. "A dog learn English! Impossible! Azungu! Crazy!"

But that was the way it went with him. He was gentle and easygoing, and he knew English. The kids really didn't know what to make of him. They weren't hostile—they were very accepting, in fact—but this was something outside their experience.

Of course, we tried to teach our curriculum and nothing else, but in this case, we had taught, quite inadvertently, our cultural bias toward dogs. It was eye-opening.

We had to teach him not to follow us when we went off on the motorcycle. He didn't like to stay home alone, but we left water and food and he would wait there for us to return. I tried to teach him to swim, but he hated the water. I carried him into the water while Julie and I were bathing, and he could swim just fine, but he would dog-paddle his way to the beach, walk out on the sand, shake wildly, and watch us continue our bath from a safe distance.

We weren't aware of it at that time, but many of the Africans feared him. He didn't run when people approached; he barked when people walking on the path approached the house late at night. He was a devoted pet.

Anytime we left the island, he became a concern. We didn't take him with us. It would be just too difficult to deal with him away from home. We found that Stevenson or, later, George, young men who helped us around the house, would take good care of him when we were gone. They came to the house and fed him. He was fine living outside and, really, besides food and water, needed little.

CHAPTER 24

Chisamulu

To the west of the island was a second island in the Likoma group. Called Chisamulu, it was a beautiful mountaintop rising from the lake. Think Bali Ha'i in the musical *South Pacific*. Perhaps not quite so dramatic, but the same idea. If you remember, Alfred lived there. His father was the witch doctor. Hensley, another student, a quiet, serious young man, was from that island as well, and one day, he invited Julie and me to come visit the island on a weekend and meet his family. We enthusiastically accepted his invitation and took a dhow on Saturday morning toward the island, perhaps half a dozen miles away. We left the dog with George, a student who helped around the house, and we were on our way. We climbed into the boat with Hensley and other passengers, this time in a much more seaworthy dhow. The crew raised sail, and we were off. There was little wind, and the boat sailed slowly away from the island.

Before long, we noticed splashing behind us. It was Modzie. He was dog-paddling with all his might, trying to catch the boat. We pulled away from him as the wind increased. We had been told he wouldn't be welcomed on Chisamulu; hence, there was no taking him with us. For a while, he continued to follow, paddling furiously, looking back from time to time at the shore. Finally, he gave up, turned around, and headed back for Likoma. Julie and I looked at each other and tried to smile. One of the passengers, a surly old man, told us he would never make it back to shore and that if he did, he might be stoned by the villagers. We were horrified at that prospect. The fate of our dog was out of our control.

We landed on the island and walked along narrow paths through dense vegetation to Hensley's house. It was a two-room house made of mud-dried brick, with several openings for windows but, of course, no glass. We were shown mats where we would sleep. We had a dinner of nsima and endewo, the former a mixture of cassava flour and water, the latter fish with sauce. It was a pleasant time. There was a flickering lantern on the table. Everyone tried very hard to speak, and they were generous and kind indeed. When it was time to use the bathroom before bed, Hensley explained that there were no chims on the island. One just "used the bush." We went into the total darkness to find a private place free from snakes or other menaces. It was a challenge we had not expected.

The next morning, after breakfast, we climbed the hill, the distinguishing feature of the island, visiting several villages along the way. No white woman and few white men had ever been on Chisamulu, so Julie and I were indeed curiosities. Women brought their children to see us. They wanted to touch Julie's soft long hair and have Julie hold their babies. Most kids screamed at the sight of us; we were something so out of their experience. Even adults were often unsure. They stared, obviously uncomfortable in our presence.

On Sunday afternoon, we reboarded the boat and headed back for Likoma. As we approached the island, we scanned the shore for some sign of our dog but saw nothing. Was he gone? Had he been stoned to death? Eaten by a crocodile?

But there he was on the porch, waiting for us, wagging his tail. All was well.

CHAPTER 25

Tiger Snake

It was a Wednesday morning, I remember, when I rose early to climb on the bike and head for the mission to catch the *Ilala*. Julie rolled over when I got up.

"Slept well?" I said into her tired eyes.

"I dreamed there was a snake in the house," she said in a groggy voice.

"Really?"

And that was that. I met the captain and got our meat ration, and when I came back, Julie was there at the dining room table, still in her nightdress. Usually, she would be dressed and ready to bounce off to school.

"What's the matter?" I said as I came in and slid the meat packet into the fridge. "Snake in the pantry?"

"No," said Julie. "There's a snake in the broom closet."

I stared at her in disbelief.

"I saw it coiled on top of the boxes there. It's a tiger snake," she said. "I looked it up. Go see for yourself."

Ever so cautiously, I opened the door to the broom closet next to the stove. Nothing. There was nothing there. Julie came over and stood beside me.

"Be careful," she said. "It has a small mouth, so small it could only bite you on the finger, but it is still deadly!"

I carefully removed bits of paper and kindling from the closet until the spotted shaft of the body became visible. It struggled, but I crushed its head with a blow from the baseball bat also in the cupboard. To my amazement, Julie picked up the body of the snake and put it in a bag. She was dressed in a moment and headed off to maths class. Immediately, she changed the schedule. It was biology.

With the students gathered around, she displayed the snake and announced that they would dissect it and view its internal organs.

This was a double whammy to our African students. They were carefully trained to follow rituals where school was concerned, and Julie had violated a sacred ritual. She changed maths class to biology. Never mind that they both met the same day and that she taught both classes. Secondly, many rural Africans believed that snakes were not animals at all but spirits. Their bite was deadly, but unlike other animals, they didn't have bones or organs or any of the things that make up the rest of us. They were simply spirits, otherworldly things that might cause your death or let you go. Nobody was ready for biology, and nobody was ready to see the dissection of a snake.

Nevertheless, Julie went ahead. She carefully began opening the body of the snake, revealing its inner parts. Amazingly, though its head had been smashed, its tiny four-chambered heart was still beating. She revealed the lungs and other parts of the snake to the kids. They all saw what they had come to believe was not so. It was an amazing teaching moment. When the dissection was finished, she placed the snake in a bottle of sodium hydroxide so the skin would be melted away and only the skeleton would remain.

"The students seemed to accept the lesson," she said, "but they still don't believe snakes have bones."

Sure enough, by the following day, the bottle held the coiled skeleton of the snake. Julie proudly passed it around for the class to examine in biology class. The kids looked skeptically at the bottle and somewhat reluctantly agreed that at least this snake had organs and bones. No doubt what Julie taught was contrary to what the kids believed, but it reinforced the curriculum and taught a lesson many of them would never forget.

CHAPTER 26

An Accident

There were many reasons for us to travel across the island from day to day. We had a fifty-gallon drum of kerosene, or paraffin, that we kept locked in a shed near the mission, for one thing. There were several little stores there, for another. You couldn't really buy much in the stores, but they did have flour and sugar and batteries and sundry other things.

One time, we wanted to buy a flashlight and batteries in a local store. When I pushed the switch, the flashlight didn't light. I asked about it, but the young man behind the counter dismissed me with a smile. "It only works at night," he said with a straight face. I thought about it a second and changed my mind about the purchase.

Anyway, it was on one of those routine trips across the island that it happened. I was riding the motorbike along the path when I slowed for a woman and some children who were also sharing the path. As I passed them, a little boy, perhaps five years old, frightened by the strange sight of the motorcycle, bolted from behind the woman's skirt right in front of the motorcycle. I hit him, but didn't run over him, and he fell onto the rocky ground. I stopped, of course, terrified that I had hurt the child. The woman, whom I thought was his mother, bent over him, and then he jumped to his feet and scrambled off into the bush. "*Pe Pane*," she said. I'm sorry. When I tried to ask her who the boy was, she shook her head. "*Iwe*," she said, meaning a little kid. She spoke no English. She just shrugged, smiled, and continued down the path. I tried to ask her name and where she was from, but she spoke rapidly, and as I had nothing to write with…

I knew I should report what had happened to someone. I immediately thought of the police and the man who had arrested me for riding with a defective headlight months before. I went to the building where the police had been, but the door was locked. There was no one there. Father Tovy would have been a good second choice, but like Dr. Paul, he, too, had left and probably returned to England. Finally, I found Father Meseka Wantu. He was the African bishop on the island. I told him the story, and he assured me that if the boy was not all right, he would hear about it and let me know. Word traveled fast on the island. Still, it was all very disturbing. I had had an accident, which I felt should be reported. But it was obvious that there was no one to report it to.

Finally, it dawned on me. Julie and I were truly alone on the island. It was us and five thousand Africans. There was no civil authority. There were tribal leaders, of course, but they were in the villages, and we didn't really even know who they were. Occasionally, a member of Peace Corps Malawi would visit, but seldom. We were an out-of-the-way post, requiring a ship voyage to reach. Things seemed to be going well for us. Why should they take the time?

One time, the Malawi English minister of education even visited. Stan Moss was a redheaded Englishman. He stayed in our house with us when he came to evaluate the work we were doing with the school. In fact, he was there on the first anniversary of our marriage. He was embarrassed about that, but he gave us a good report. He observed our teaching. He liked what we were doing with the school. He found we had a good rapport with the kids and the headmaster. He never came back.

So we were living on this island, and we were really on our own. The Malawians tolerated us and our strange behavior, and we grew to really like them. It was a symbiotic relationship; we liked and helped them, and they helped and seemed to like us. Somehow, we thought, that was the way things should be.

I worried about the little boy for a few days, but we never heard anything more about it. No one ever said anything to us. It seemed as if it had never happened. Though it was fifty years ago, I still remember it as if it were yesterday.

CHAPTER 27

Water What?

There were some really odd things that happened while we lived on the island. One afternoon, a Portuguese gunboat dropped anchor in the cove right behind our house. There was a knock on the door. A young naval officer was there. "Excuse me," he said. "Would you and the missus care to water-ski this afternoon? The captain has sent me to ask. If you would, you may join us down at Makulawe."

I was speechless at first. "Water-ski?" I heard myself say.

"Yes. You and the missus."

I looked at Julie, who burst into a smile. "We'll be right there," I said.

Was this a wise thing to do? I wondered. This was the calm side of the island. There could be bilharzia.

We had finished our teaching duties for the day. I supposed there was no reason we shouldn't. After all, we swam every day, just like everyone else. Why shouldn't we water-ski? We put on our bathing suits, and off we went.

There was an inflatable boat pulled up on the beach, with a young uniformed man standing nearby. He pushed the boat into shallow water and indicated for us to board. The boat had a large Mercury outboard motor on its transom, and in no time, we had motored out to the gunboat anchored in the bay. We climbed aboard and met the captain. He introduced himself and gestured to a table and chairs. There were snacks, wine, and other liquor on the bar. The captain, Mario, took a State Express 555 cigarette from a pack, and an enlisted man, who appeared to be his personal servant, immediately lit it for him. He offered us a smoke, and then we had a cocktail. We were seated on the aft deck of the boat, under an awning. We visited for a while. He told us he had been drafted from medical school in Portugal to serve in the navy. He was eager to get back to his studies. We talked about life on the island. It was a delightful time.

The captain went first. He got up on one ski as the rubber boat roared off, and then he did spins and jumps and simply amazed us, especially me. The driver of the boat would drive fast and turn hard near rocks, but Mario never minded. He skimmed over the shallows and rocky shoals and let go of the rope just when he could coast to the side of the ship.

My attempt was much more mundane. I needed two skis to get up and managed to finally drop one, but that was it for me. I could get outside the wake, and the pilot of the rubber boat made sure I had a fast ride, but there was nothing spectacular there.

Julie, on the other hand, had grown up on the water, skiing behind her family's boat. She could juggle three tennis balls on skis with the rope between her knees and could do one ski with class.

Our rides were long and exhausting, and when we were done, we went back to the boat for more cocktails and conversation. Mario, we learned, had water-skied all his life and was training for international competition. His family was owner of a large winery in Portugal.

Suddenly, they had to go. They took us to shore, in the inflatable boat, and we thanked them, and after returning to the ship, they hoisted anchor and motored off into the lake.

It was an old man who said it first. "*Bambo y Maie*, you walk on the water."

We all laughed. We had wondered how the Africans would take all this. They had indeed been entertained but seemed to hold no ill feelings. Some of our students, too, had seen us ski. It was again completely out of their experience. They laughed and asked about it. It seemed to be all some kind of magic to them.

A short time later, we heard that Mario, the captain of the gun-boat, had died of cerebral malaria. There were no details. What a sad day. That was it.

CHAPTER 28

A Party

We worked hard with our students. They were good kids and so cooperative and pleasant we truly enjoyed them. They studied diligently and made a real effort at understanding and memorizing what we were teaching. There were virtually no discipline problems, ever. There was a reason for that. One of our students had stolen a deck of cards from a previous teacher's open windowsill. He was arrested and sentenced to a year of hard labor. We could hardly believe Mattia had received such harsh punishment.

Toward the end of the first year, we decided we would have a party for the form 2 students who would be taking their exam and leaving. It would not be a big deal, but we would have some treats for them, with music and dancing at our house. It would be in the evening, after dinner. We wrote home and asked our families to send some goodies. Most of these kids had never tasted a Coke, but the logistics, not to mention the cost, of getting Coke to the island would be just too much. We had other ideas.

When the time came, the kids came to the house. Their eyes flashed as they entered the kitchen, as many of them had never been in a house built of cement blocks, as ours was. They looked around and went into the living room. We played some music using the school's record player and our batteries, but the students made the party. They were happy, smiling and joyful. Julie was in the kitchen, making popcorn. They had seen the popcorn when we brought it to dances, but they had never seen it popped.

Our little kerosene stove was roaring on the counter, and the popcorn was popping wildly in the pot. The kids were watching in disbelief as every kernel appeared to pop, so unlike anything they had ever seen. They loved to watch it, especially when Julie lifted the lid on the kettle and a late popper exploded, spilling overflow onto the counter. We poured it into bowls and served it along with another treat they had not experienced, Kool-Aid. They sipped the cool, colored drink, something else new for them, and ate the popcorn and smiled and laughed, and everyone seemed to be having a very good time.

Finally, the big surprise. Julie had made bowls of Jell-O, and we served it out of the fridge onto plates for the kids. To see them would have made the best commercial ever. They looked at it on their plate, wiggled it back and forth, and watched it jiggle. They smiled and looked through it as it wiggled. They tasted it and savored the flavor. You've heard the expression "You can't have your cake and eat it too"? Well, this was that expression come to life. One young man, Samuel, looked at me and said, "I know what this is, sir. It is ice cream." Indeed, ice cream was something Samuel had heard of but had never expected to taste. His smile was wide. More "white man's magic."

Indeed, our teaching was not in the curriculum, but we truly wanted these kids to experience something from outside their island. True, life here was simple and genuine, and in some ways, they were experiencing a kind of paradise. But they were bright and capable, but very poor, with limited opportunity, and we wanted them to strive for better things.

I remember one day in the classroom, when I talked with Charles about his future. He told me that after he finished his education (that would be when he could no longer pass the leaving examination and would not advance), he wanted to go to South Africa, where he would work in the mines.

We had watched men go to the mines. They would go to Blantyre-Limbe quite literally in rags. We saw men there standing at the airport, waiting for the plane. When the plane landed, young men in black suits and red cummerbunds would descend the steps onto the tarmac, waiting for their luggage, which was a bicycle and a transistor radio. These men had spent two years of their lives in the mines. They were stripped naked when they first arrived, issued work clothing, and made to work daily in the dangerous underground mines until their two-year stay was up. Then they would again be stripped to be sure they hadn't concealed any gold or diamonds, given a cheap black suit, and sent back to their homes. Money to keep their families alive had been sent home while they were away; they might make enough to buy a metal roof for their mud hut. Many of them didn't survive. I remember seeing some of them upon their return, departing the *Ilala*, all smiles, their new suits soaked through with sweat. They had earned a suit, a symbol of English business success, so inappropriate on a tropical island.

Why would anyone who could read and write English and have a basic understanding of math, history, and science subject himself to that? He could take a civil service test, at least. Still, these people had been so looked down upon by those who had come here—missionaries, explorers, and others—that they believed in their inferiority. They were truly humble.

Charles was a good example. How could we help him overcome this nagging self-doubt?

CHAPTER 29

Rocks

One morning, while Julie and I were at home, preparing for class, we had a frightening experience. The headmaster and the Malawi Young Pioneer were teaching their classes, and we had an hour to ourselves at home. Julie was in the bedroom, as I remember, and I was in the office. Suddenly, I heard a huge crash, decidedly like breaking glass. I ran to the living room to see a rock had flown through the dining room window and landed on the living room floor, surrounded by bits of broken glass. In a second, I saw another rock shatter the window in the door in the kitchen. A man was running toward the door. I, too, ran to the kitchen, turned the lock, and removed the key as another rock smashed a window over the sink. Outside, a young man, with an armful of rocks and fire in his eyes, was heaving them as fast as he could at the house. Glass smashed all around me. There was no place to hide. Shards of glass were everywhere. It seemed he had stashed piles of rocks all around the house, and he heaved them through the bedroom windows as well as the windows in the living room. I locked that living room door too, but he wasn't throwing at the house or the windows; he was throwing them at us! After a few moments, nearly every window had a jagged hole through it. Some were broken out completely. Our dog, Modzie, looked at us with terrified eyes. Neither he nor we had ever experienced anything like this.

What to do? We had no weapons, no way to defend ourselves, but perhaps with a ball bat. I saw him, but the rage on his face made him impossible to identify. We tried to plan a counteroffensive, and I was about to don my motorcycle helmet and charge when the stoning stopped and urgent voices came from behind the house.

Outside, in the yard, there was clearly a scuffle, and the area was full of people. I unlocked the back door, and we went out. The voices I had heard were of our students. They had heard the commotion, run from the classroom, and had subdued the man and were holding him on the ground. He was securely pinned, struggling and kicking, but unable to get up. George, our houseboy, was holding him down, aided by nearly everyone else.

"George tackled him and held him down," Juliet said. Juliet was tall, slender, and smart. Anywhere else, she could have been a model or a news reporter.

The headmaster appeared with the *clark*, who had a ball of twine. The boys took the twine and bound the man's wrists tightly and led him off.

Julie and I were simply overflowing with emotion. What was this?

"My class is over," said Mr. Manyongo, the new headmaster. "You teach in fifteen minutes."

Sure enough, minutes later, we walked up to the school, Julie in science and me in English.

I walked into the classroom and tried to discuss with the students what they had seen and what they thought it meant. I asked Beatrice first, but she was silent. Her eyes flashed from side to side. She didn't know what to say. Then I asked Alfred.

"We heard the crashes, and then several of the boys stood up and someone said, 'They are attacking the Danielsons,' and everyone ran out. And George tackled the man and held him down, and we all jumped on him. We might have killed him, but the headmaster came."

Outside the classroom, there was some commotion. We looked outside, and the clark and the headmaster had brought Mr. Maswanu to the school and were tying him to the mango tree in the courtyard, right outside our classroom window. He was jerking and tugging, but he seemed, for the moment, secure. This was more than I was prepared to use as a backdrop for teaching the novel we had been reading.

I handed out paper, and we all, individually, recounted what had happened just a short time before, as the perpetrator, finally resigned to his fate, reclined quietly against the mango tree in the school-yard. This might have been one of the best writing lessons I ever did. We wrote and read our various versions. The students worked hard to express precisely what they had seen. We discussed our different points of view. What I had seen was vastly different from what they had seen. The students corrected one another, and everyone finished his or her account. The finished papers were wonderful.

It was during our lunch break that day that I learned that Mr. Maswanu was a refugee from Portuguese East Africa, that his family had been killed by the white soldiers there, and that he blamed us, as white people, for the killing of his family. He wanted revenge against "the Egyptian woman," Julie, perhaps, so I would feel the agony he had felt. Some people said he wanted to marry the Egyptian woman or kill her. Neither reason sounded good to us. Suddenly, however, I felt a bit of compassion. How horrible would it be to have your family killed by foreign troops!

The headmaster assured me he would be dealt with by the tribal authorities as, he had been told, the police no longer had a presence on the island. He would surely be sent to Nkhata Bay, where his crime would be considered more formally by the justice of the peace there.

That was that. We never saw any more of Mr. Maswanu for the rest of the week. I talked to the bishop, who assured me he was being held securely. It wasn't until the following Saturday that we again saw the culprit. That day, the *Ilala* came to port as usual, and Julie and I took the first boat out to the ship. We liked to greet guests, if there were any, and talk to the captain. The first boat was reserved for out-going mail and official business, and for some reason, we qualified. We climbed aboard the lifeboat, and the African skipper turned the crank and closed the valves and started the little diesel engine as the boat surged away from the shore toward the huge ship. It only took us a minute to realize who the other two "guests" were aboard the boat. One was a uniformed Malawian policeman from Nkhata Bay, and the other was Mr. Maswanu, in handcuffs, who stared at me the whole time, his muscles flexing, his eyes meeting mine, wet with the mixed emotions of rage and fear.

When we got to the ship, I talked with the captain. He was aware of the situation, and he assured me the man had been held safely on the island and that he would be sternly dealt with by the authorities on the mainland. We would have nothing to worry about. The broken windows in our house, on the other hand, might pose a larger problem. It could be months before a work party and materials could be assembled to properly repair them.

Back on the island, I asked Father Meseka Wantu exactly how the man had been held. "Had they locked him inside a house? What house is there with no windows from which he could escape?" I had asked.

"No, Henry," he had said. "We had no place to keep him. The tribal elders met and talked with him, and he promised not to go to your end of the island again. That was it. We have no jail here." The good bishop laughed and asked Julie and me to come to the Mezzani for coffee. We did.

But that was just the half of it. Our house was wide-open to every angry or insane person on the island. What would we do?

One after another they came. Mostly it was the women. They would come to the house and say, "*Pe pane, pe pane.* So sorry, so sorry. You safe. You safe. No worry."

Even though the windows were broken out everywhere and the locks were useless, we never were bothered by anyone. People still came by to beg and have their wounds covered, but no one ever molested us in any way. We left the house daily when we were teaching or to visit the ship, once even for a weeklong visit to Nkhotakota, but nothing in the house was ever touched. Our shortwave radio, out of the question price-wise for these people, remained on the table. No one touched anything. Was this out of fear on their part or simple compassion for visitors from a foreign land? I think it was the latter, and I think it showed the kind of decent people they were. It showed a sense of community some of us in America might not understand. We had learned to have great respect for these rural Africans.

As it turned out, several months passed before a work party from the mainland arrived and the windows were repaired. But nothing was ever taken or damaged during that time.

CHAPTER 30

A Visit

Life on the island continued as the second year went by. We had a
new headmaster, Mr. Manyongo. He was more communicative than
our previous principal had been, but still, he seemed distant, though
he lived in the house next door.

One Saturday, we received a letter from my mother back
in Western New York. "Sit down before you read this!" it said in
large print across the top. The gist of the story was that my aunt
Marguerite, my mom's sister and the only wealthy person we knew,
had offered to fly mom and dad to Malawi to visit us. Julie and I
could hardly believe it. My mother and father had never crossed an
ocean, not to mention travel to Africa. Nevertheless, that was the
plan. They would fly to England first and visit my grandmother's
family in Yorkshire. From there they would fly south to Kenya and
on to Blantyre, take the train to Monkey Bay, and sail on the *Ilala* to
Likoma Island. From there, they would be with us for a week before
they would fly home.

Indeed, it was a shock to us. How would they deal with such
a different culture? Neither of my parents had gone to college, nor
had they done any world travel. My dad was very well-read and once
had been a supercargo on a ship laden with furniture from New York
to Florida. He liked to read the adventures of others who had traveled the world. He had been a traveling salesman for years, driving
regularly from our home in Western New York to the East Coast

and as far west as Chicago. Still, he had never flown in an airplane or ventured outside the United States beyond Canada. How would they manage?

We followed every step of their preparation in their weekly letters to us. It would, indeed, be an experience of a lifetime for them.

In the meantime, things kept evolving for us on the island. By now we had met many of the animals that lived there. There were the snakes, of course, and though we had not seen one, we knew about the crocodiles. There were birds and, of course, fish. Every few days, someone would come by with a fish for us to buy. Most often, they were M'buvu, a kind of catfish. Sometimes they were more like bass. We ate them regularly and enjoyed them. But there was one animal we had heard about but had never seen, the monkey.

We had been told from the start that monkeys were prevalent on the island, but it would likely be at least a year before we would see one. We found this hard to believe, but it was true that we never saw any monkeys for the first year or so, so we rather dismissed the idea altogether. Probably the sound of the motorbike had scared them off. We didn't know.

It was one day when we were walking back from the mission when all that changed. The island was covered with large gray rocks. If you remember, I mentioned one that looked like a woman holding a baby. It was near that place, while we were walking back from the ship, that it happened. I glanced to one side, and there was a small gray monkey with a black face and black eyes peering over a rock at us. We stopped and looked, and he watched us. We looked at him, and it was clear that he was looking at us. Then others appeared. There were several faces atop small gray bodies, looking at us from various rocks. It was eerie, strange. There was no panic; they were not blocking the path, but no one moved. Then they were gone. We went on our way. From that day on, we often saw the monkeys along the paths. Of course, we had been duly warned not to touch them or try to make pets of them because they could carry rabies, but that never entered our minds. Still, we had seen them; we had broken the curse. It had been a little more than a year, just as predicted.

Time went on, and there was a change of seasons. Folks say they like to live in the north of the United States because there is a change of seasons. In summer, it is warm, and then the green foliage explodes into riotous colors of red and orange and yellow and then the leaves fall and only the evergreens add their green glow to the naked forest. Snow falls, and in a few short months, the landscape changes completely. What was green and lush becomes cold and barren.

In Malawi, too, there was a change. The rains come, and the barren, dry land turns to lush green. It becomes warm and humid, and animals and insects abound. There is a summer school break during the wet season, and that was when we left the island and headed for the Nyika Plateau.

CHAPTER 31

Animal Census

There was to be a survey of native animals on the Nyika Plateau, and they desperately needed people to count and record the game. Julie and I volunteered. We took the ship to Nkhata Bay, to the north, and joined a crew in Land Rovers to head for the plateau. These English vehicles had four-wheel drive and four-cylinder engines, with manual transmissions, but they were rugged and carried us over the treacherous terrain to the park. The lodge there would be our headquarters, where we returned each evening and where we turned in our tallies. The lodge was made of wood, logs. It had a fireplace for heat, and so unlike Likoma, there was an abundance of wood in the area for fuel. There were wild animals there too. Numerous kinds of antelope, wildebeest, even lions and hyenas were found on the plain. There were warthogs and wild boars. It would be our job to survey the fields and identify the animals. We would determine the number of males and females we saw and record the place and time we saw them. Of course, we would have an African guide who would iden-tify and count the animals we saw. We would be with him and record what he saw, along with the time and numbers.

It all sounded rather dangerous to us. We had been on photo-graphic safaris before, but always in the security of a van or car. This time, it would be us, on foot, and them, with nothing between us.

For several days, we moved through the fields with our savvy African guide. He was a young man, fit and docile. He had sharp eyes that could scan a herd of animals and tell us how many were male, how many female, and how many were immature. We counted too, but we could never find fault with his numbers. We would crouch down and move through the bush quietly. He had been given an area to explore, knew his boundaries, and led us quietly as close to the herd as possible. He seemed to have no fear, moving us close to the animals he spotted. From time to time, we would come upon warthogs, wild hogs that ran with their tails straight up in the air. He would tell us to stand up when we were near a herd of them. They could slit us open if we were on the ground, so he insisted we stand and show ourselves and make ourselves appear as large as possible. Fortunately, we were never attacked. The purpose of the survey was to determine whether there was sufficient game in the area to harvest some to feed the local population.

In the evening, when we returned to the lodge, we would build a fire in the fireplace, as temperatures on this high plateau dropped when the sun went down. They would put kindling under the logs in the fireplace and then place a wooden cover over all but the bottom inch of the opening. When the kindling was lit, it would come to life, and the draft would roar as the kindling was quickly devoured. Soon, the logs would catch, and warmth would flood the cool room. We had delicious meals of meat and vegetables while we were there. There was beer and delightful conversation. We would share our tales of the day. It was a wonderful time.

One night, we heard the howl of hyenas, and our guide came to us and asked if we wanted to see them. We would need a torch, he explained. The hyenas would not attack a man with a light. We had been told that kills credited to lions were often the work of hyenas, which, after the kill, had been scared away by the big cats. The only flashlight we could find was very dim and would only light when whacked on the side with the palm of my hand. It was fine with our guide, but we decided, since our lives would depend on the light from the flashlight, we would forego the hyena experience.

Julie and I, together with our guide, counted hundreds of animals, all without incident, over the three-day adventure. One time, still on the Nyika, an English guide took us in his brand-new Land

Rover to the Vwaza marsh, where he was sure we would find some elephants. The car lunged and splashed through the wet terrain. We plunged through thick foliage and sunk into the soft earth as we moved through the dense jungle. Surely, we would find elephants. But though the gleaming white vehicle was covered with mud, there were no elephants, at least not where we looked.

On our last day, we were offered a chance to buy "the tooth of an elephant." On the floor of a shed next to the lodge were stacks of elephant tusks. They were from elephants taken by paid hunters (in reality, they were hunters who paid to take them), which had been marauding local gardens. The cost was a pound ($2.40) per pound in 1968. Several volunteers bought tusks and tied them on the roof of the Land Rover as we drove back to Nkhata Bay, where Julie and I would catch the ship to Likoma.

When we got home, it was time to prepare for my parents' visit. We made the beds in the guest bedroom, stocked up as much as we could on fresh food, and well, waited.

CHAPTER 32

The Visit

Finally, that Saturday arrived, and we stood on shore as the *Ilala*, gleaming gray and white, eased into the cove near the cathedral. I could see a man on the upper deck in a seersucker sports jacket. It had to be my father. Mother stood next to him. They were aboard the first boat to shore, and we greeted them with big hugs. Women bowed deferentially to my mother and father. Dressed in stylish Western clothes, they seemed somewhat out of place in this foreign land. We stopped at the Mezzani for coffee and then began the long walk to the house. It was a two-and-a-half-mile walk on a warm, eighty-something-degree day. My dad, in his sports coat, smoking a cigarette, and my mom, cigarette in hand, in her skirt and hose, and sneakers. Dad was in his midsixties; Mom, just ten years younger. They were reasonably fit, and as it turned out, the walk didn't bother them.

Back at the house, we heard their story. They were comforted when they saw the house. The thick, solid walls and metal roof gave them a sense of security they certainly wouldn't have found in a mud hut with a grass roof, which would describe most of the other dwellings on the island. They told of riding on the train at night through villages with no lights. "There was complete and utter darkness. We could see that there was a village, and there were people at the station, but it was so dark."

Dad had rented a car at the airport, thinking he would be able to drive on the left, shift gears, and navigate in a country with few street signs and only one traffic light. It was when he stopped for his first school bus, not a custom in Malawi, that he decided their guide could do the driving.

We had given them a short list of a few things they could pick up for us in Blantyre. A "noisy burner for a Hipolito stove" was one thing on the list, along with mantles for an Aladdin lamp and glass chimneys for our Electrolux refrigerator. They had no idea where to look, but their guide took them right to a shop that sold such items. They presented them to us with pride.

We had cocktails that night, made with 40-proof Malawi Gin. Julie made hors d'oeuvres, and we enjoyed a chicken dinner at the dining room table. Later, we played cribbage.

As the week went on, they adapted easily. Mother said she wanted to bring me a safari jacket but was unable to find one in Jamestown. I was very pleased about that. Thank goodness she couldn't find a pith helmet either! There were no snakes or crocodiles to threaten them while they were there, and though my dad had never been much of a swimmer, both he and Mom swam with us and the tropical fishes at the beach at Mtoo in Lake Malawi. They met our students, who were deferential and kind to them, but they never ventured to the school while we were teaching.

The week they were with us went quickly. They shared their adventures in Yorkshire, England, where they had been entertained by relatives, descendants of my grandmother on Dad's side. Their understanding of the African culture was weak, but they were eager to see and learn. They found themselves somewhat amazed that the culture of the people on this island was so primitive and, at the same time, that the people there, so dark and so different, were also very human and warm. It was so alien and yet so like home.

We went with them on the *Ilala* to Nkhata Bay when they left, and we watched them climb aboard an Air Malawi DC-3 en route to Blantyre and then on to France and back home to Lakewood.

Our students were fascinated with them. George, a very person-able young man who worked for us, confided, "They are not really your parents, sir, we students have decided, because Mr. and Mrs. Danielson are white, and you and Mrs. Danielson, you are…are…beige."

And that was that.

Explaining tanning was like explaining bones in a snake or the world being round. We did breach the subject, but…well, Agustus, he was the *dark* one, and Cotilda, she was the *light* one, and it didn't matter whether Agustus went in the sun or not—he was blue-black in color. Cotilda was light tan, and she spent as much time outside as everyone else. It was because of who they were and who their parents were and, well, those folks who came to visit, being so light skinned and all, they definitely were not my parents. That was that!

Not long after Mom and Dad left, Julie developed a rash on her face. We thought, at that time, it might have been a reaction to some perfumed soap my mother had brought with her and left for Julie at the house. We will never know for sure. At any rate, the rash got worse, and her face began to swell. She went to bed and slept most of the time. Her face swelled and swelled until her eyes began to be squeezed shut. I rode to the hospital, but the doctor had left, and the nurse who was stationed there was gone as well. At the post office, I was able to send a telegram to the Peace Corps headquarters, asking for advice. By then, Julie's eyes were squeezed shut. She could breathe, but her breathing was labored. Then, slowly, the swelling began to recede. Her eyes reopened, and she was on the mend.

What a frightening time!

CHAPTER 33

Replacements

It was late in the summer of 1968 when Mr. and Mrs. Frey came to stay with us. They would be our replacements when we left the island, as the end of our two-year tour was approaching. Unlike us, they would have the opportunity to stay with us, the current teachers, and learn some of our successful techniques and some of the pitfalls to watch out for. They were a likable and friendly couple. Of course, they were a bit intimidated by the remoteness of the post and the isolation of the island, but they were eager to teach, and that was what was important.

I remember one of my lessons in geography class that was somewhat puzzling to them at first but that illustrated the kinds of people with whom we worked. It was a lesson on maps and mapping. Of course, as Americans, we had grown up understanding maps. Many of our students, however, didn't understand maps, had never seen a map, and were unclear about their purpose. I had no text but did my best to explain what a map was. Then I handed out several old road maps that the kids looked at. Though they could read the names of the towns and cities on the maps, they had a great deal of trouble with relationships and distances.

We went outside. I had read about an exercise to explain mapping in a syllabus and decided to try it. We took two wooden stakes and pounded them in the ground just ten meters apart, in the middle of the campus. We then drew two dots on our paper representing the two stakes. That gave us a scale that represented ten meters. We then copied angles from each of the stakes to corners of buildings on the campus, the classrooms, the offices, the library, and the chims, or outdoor toilets. Students did the work in groups, sharing a clipboard and a sheet of paper. They became absorbed in the activity, and each group came back to the classroom with a scale drawing of the campus and all its buildings. We then went out and measured the distances from the stakes to the buildings and the sizes of the buildings and compared them to the drawings we had made. Of course, they were far from perfect, but there was an "Aha!" moment I had seldom seen in my teaching. The kids enjoyed the activity, and they really learned something while they were doing it. Maps were no longer so obscure.

Our replacement teachers enjoyed the students and the dog and the house, and they seemed somewhat enthusiastic. They were awed by the kids' ability and desire to memorize facts in history class and biology. They joined us in the classroom, and they seemed up to the job.

CHAPTER 34

Malaria

It was then that I began to feel dizzy. One day, I came home from school with a headache. I felt feverish and went to our bedroom to lie down. Julie took my temperature, and it was very high, well over 104 degrees Fahrenheit. I remember the chills. I was freezing cold, though the temperature in the house was over eighty. I climbed into a fur-lined sleeping bag and shivered. I fell into a deep sleep and awoke in a soggy mess. I had perspired through the bag and desperately needed to use the toilet. I struggled to free myself from the bag and was amazed at how weak I was. I fantasized that there was a line of people to use the bathroom. Of course, it was the middle of the night, and there was no line.

Julie thought I had malaria.

Perhaps I had missed one of the chloroquine tablets we were required to take—one on Wednesday and two on Sunday—to prevent the disease. That might have done it.

As there was no doctor available, she wired Peace Corps, Malawi, in Blantyre, from our post office, and in a return telegram, they agreed with her diagnosis. They prescribed I be given six chloroquine tablets at once to combat the disease, with a decreasing regimen. Fortunately, we had a good supply of pills on hand. I began taking them immediately. It was a little frightening, as one tablet can kill a baby. As an adult, tolerance is greater.

I responded quickly, and the first thing I remember as I began to wake from a coma-like sleep was listening to the first lunar landing on *Voice of America* with Julie on our Schaub Lorenz radio, the one we had bought on the way over in Amsterdam. There was such a sense of joy and fulfillment in that broadcast, for both me and the astronauts; it filled me with a sense of relief I shall never forget. Somehow, I had gotten through the disease and the lunar landing. For a few days, I was very weak, but I went back to teaching, and gradually, my strength returned.

Of course, our replacements, the Frys, were there with us. How it affected them, I don't know, but I am sure it was a terrifying experience to see a fellow Peace Corps volunteer become so ill so far from any kind of professional help. I was a little surprised they didn't take the first boat home, but they stayed on the full two weeks and left on schedule.

CHAPTER 35

Leaving Likoma

Our tour was nearing its end, and now we had to decide how we would return to America. Airline tickets would be provided, or we could take cash and see what we could negotiate for a ride home. We took the cash. We found a ship, the *Pacific*, a French liner that would take us from Mombasa in Kenya, to Bombay in India, to Colombo, Ceylon, Singapore, Hong Kong, and on to Yokohama in Japan. The trip would take a month, and we would fly from Japan to Hawaii then on to San Francisco. At that point, we figured $99 Greyhound bus tickets, good for a month, would easily carry us back to our home in Western New York. We booked the tickets. We would have to get a visa for Japan, but we learned we could stop at the Japanese consulate in Nairobi before we departed and that would take care of that. We would go home around the world. Wow!

Back on the island, there was so much to do. Of course, there was the final push to get the students ready for the JC, or junior certificate exam. That was everything to our kids. Their pass and level of pass would determine whether they could continue their education or find a government job. We did all we knew how to encourage them and motivate them on the test. We had another party. I remember so well the young people dancing in our living room. They moved easily and smoothly. Those get-togethers were very happy times. We knew we would miss these kids.

We had been warned that when we wanted to get rid of our stuff before we left, we should not give it away but have a sale. We had always done our best to refuse beggars on the island but to buy eggs or fish or chicken that was offered, so a sale sounded like a good idea to us. Our worn-out belongings were of no value to us, but as they were somewhat stylish and made in America, they had considerable value to those on the island. So we decided what things would go in our trunks to be shipped home, what would go with us on the ship, and what we would sell. The sale would be our last day on the island.

We moved the huge steamer trunks into our bedroom and began packing odds and ends and clothing in them. Over the two years, we had accrued a fair amount of stuff, and we emptied our drawers.

One night in the living room, Julie and I were playing cards, and we noticed something strange. Modzie, our dog, was missing. I went outside and called, but he didn't come. He was always around, a quiet friend. He went to school with us in the mornings and spent the evenings with us in the living room at home. We had arranged with the Frys to keep him when they came and took over our jobs and our house. That wouldn't be until the beginning of the next school year, however, and George, our houseboy, would take care of him until then. But where was he now? Julie went into the bedroom and called to me. When I got there, I gasped. There was Modzie, lying on top of our clothes in one of our trunks. He knew we were leaving, and he wanted to go home with us. He looked at us with sad eyes and put his head on his paws. He made no effort to get out of the trunk. Of course, it was hard to think of leaving this place, where we had spent most of the first two years of our married lives, but this made it even harder. I lifted him out of the trunk and closed the lid, and he curled up on the rug at the foot of the bed. How sad.

The sale went well. Villagers and students came and, for a few pennies, bought old T-shirts, some well-worn shoes, and other things we no longer had a use for. I especially remember our *clark*, the secretary in the principal's office, buying a Camp Seven Hills jacket. Julie had worked at a Girl Scout camp summers while she was in college, and this maroon jacket was a souvenir she no longer wanted.

The *clark* was so pleased with it he was beyond words. He put it on and moved about, showing it off to everyone. His smile was simply infectious.

The next morning, we locked the doors. Two women came by to help us move the trunks across the island. Most of our students had left, had gone back to their homes. George and I hoisted the hundred-pound trunks onto small rings of grass on the women's heads, and off they went in their bare feet across the stony path toward the harbor in the center of the island, where they would have to find helpers to lower the heavy trunks to the ground.

The motorcycle was where we had found it when we came, leaning against the mango tree in our backyard. Otherwise, little had changed.

We looked back at our first real home and then set out on foot toward the mission and the cathedral, where we would say our goodbyes to Likoma Island. Would we ever return? We wondered how we could leave the house, the beach, the school, the tropical fish, the birds, but mostly the warm, wonderful people. What about the delightful kids in school? Could we just walk away and never see them again? And what about Modzie, our dog? She walked with us on our last walk across the island, up the hill, away from the school, across the plain with the rock that looked like Virgin Mary and baby Jesus, under the magic fig tree, and down to the Mezzani and then to the landing, where the metal lifeboats would crunch their bows in the sand.

We had our overnight bags with us when we climbed aboard the first boat. There were lots of people there, perhaps to see us off, perhaps not. There were always people on the beach when the ship came in. We felt a kind of panic at that moment. George held our dog back, and we climbed aboard that boat, somehow torn between leaving this place that had so loved us and returning to a land embittered by war and the enmity toward foreigners that goes with it. We said our goodbyes, all too briefly, and the crew started the diesel engine of the small boat and pushed her off the shore as they jumped aboard.

In a few minutes, we were back aboard the *Ilala*, greeted by the captain and taken to our cabin on the upper deck. Of course, we had to wade through the mass of humanity on the lower deck first. That was the place we had often ridden when we paid for passage for the day trip to Nkhata Bay or Nkhotakota, there with the nursing mothers, small children, bags of rice and dried fish; there with men and women, scantily clad, sitting on the steel deck and leaning against the rail. That was where we usually rode. But this time, we would be first class, in a cabin on the upper deck, with the white people, the captain and the first mate. The Peace Corps bought us the tickets. It would be an overnight to Monkey Bay; why not take a cabin?

We loaded our bags into the cabin and went to the upper deck to watch the captain give commands and the huge windless raise the anchor as the *Ilala* eased out of the harbor. Then we walked to the stern of the ship, on the second deck, where our cabin was. The ship had gained speed, and we looked over the rail to watch our magic island slip into the distance. And there, there in our wake was a little brown head. It was Modzie, our friendly African dog, swimming frantically after the ship, to be with us wherever we were going, wanting, more than anything, not to be left behind. We were speechless as the ship accelerated and our loving dog and beautiful island slowly sank into the clear but menacing waters of Lake Malawi.

Before we left, we had looked briefly into the possibility of having Modzie shipped home, but we were quickly discouraged. An animal that had lived in tropical Africa, even though vaccinated against rabies, would have a very difficult time being imported to the United States, we were told. It might involve months of quarantine, even up to a year, the cost of which would have been prohibitive.

A bell rang. Lunch was served in the first-class dining room.

But neither of us was very hungry.

CHAPTER 36

Another African Adventure

There was a debriefing in Monkey Bay. There were questions about what went well in our experience, what went badly. What were our triumphs, our failures? But mostly, we shared our stories with the other volunteers, many of whom we had trained with but not seen much of over the years. It was a bittersweet time. Some of our friends had signed on for a third year. Some had been drafted from the Peace Corps into the military to serve in Vietnam. Others, for one reason or another, had gone home. We picked up our paperwork for travel home in Blantyre and were again reminded of our need for Japanese visas before we could board the ship in Mombasa. I remember departing from the airport outside Blantyre. When I lifted my foot to step onto the stair that led up to the old Air Malawi DC-3, I wondered whether I would ever again set foot on Malawi soil.

Our first stop on the way home was in Dar es Salaam in Tanzania. It is famous for African carvings. Perhaps we could find some and ship them home. We spent the day in that old city wandering and searching for some special souvenirs. We had some Malawian work, but well, we wanted more. Sure enough, not far from the waterfront, on a back street, we found Peeras. It was a shop filled with delightful Maconde carvings. They were deeply symbolic figures that communicated a thought along with a human figure. One of my favorites was a carving in ebony of a man sipping his beer, and on top of his head was the figure of a voluptuous African woman. We bought it. There was a chess set with all the pieces as African dancers. The pieces were beautifully carved. It would be our last chance.

We were having the items packed to be shipped when the clerk asked, "Do you know tanzanite?"

Of course we didn't.

He went on to explain that it was a gemstone first discovered in Tanzania. He quickly pulled a small tray of the beautifully cut small stones from one of the shelves under the glass counter and placed it on top under the light. The stones ranged from tiny to larger ones of several carats. Julie picked one up that she especially liked. It was brilliant blue with a tinge of red, and as she examined it, it slipped from between her fingers. It bounced on the glass cabinet top and then fell into the space between two cabinets. For a moment, it was very quiet, but then two men were summoned from somewhere in the store, and they lifted one of the heavy cabinets to the side. There, right where the two cabinets had met, where the floor should have been, was a furnace grate. There was no stone in sight. A screwdriver appeared, and one of the men took the face off the register, and there was the tiny sparkling stone nestled in the dust at the bottom of the duct. The staff of the store had been reassuring throughout the ordeal, and they insisted that, the stone found or not, it had been an accident and was not our fault. When things settled down, we asked for the price of the stone. We wanted to buy it, but as we would be leaving the following morning, we needed it mounted in a ring so Julie could wear it and so it could more easily be imported into the United States.

Mr. Peera, the owner of the store, appeared. He was a dignified Indian man in a brown suit. "I can have the stone mounted in a setting of your choice and can have it ready by ten this evening," he said. "If you come by the store at ten tonight, I will have the ring ready for you, and you can take it with you."

We agreed.

The deal was done. We would be back at ten to pick up Julie's tanzanite ring.

I don't remember much about what transpired that evening except that after dinner, we returned to our hotel and then set out for

Peera's. Of course, at night, the streets were dark. It was not like the bustling streets in the daytime. Oh, there were some streetlights, but it was shadowy and quiet, and though the crowds had gone, there were a few clusters of people nestled in the corners. We stood in front of Peera's store for a few minutes before a dark Mercedes pulled up. It was Mr. Peera. He looked relaxed in his gray suit and open-necked white shirt. He unlocked the door, and we followed him in. He produced a box from his pocket, and when I opened it, there was Julie's stone, beautifully mounted on a silver ring. We spent the next few minutes, in the darkened shop, signing traveler's checks. When the deal was done, we thanked him, and we left, walking quickly back to our hotel.

From Dar, we traveled to the island of Zanzibar, where, as part of a tour, we explored the rich island. Our guide took us to gardens where cloves and cinnamon were grown along with a myriad of other spices. There was a cacao plantation and a tea plantation as well. We enjoyed the rich aroma of the spices and toured a processing plant for tea. I noticed around the machines that ground the tea leaves there was a great deal of spillage on the floor. Barefoot men carrying bags of tea were walking through it. I asked one of the men working there what they did with all the tea on the floor and in the corners. He stopped what he was doing, looked at me, paused, and said with a British accent, "We sweep it up, put it in tea bags, and send it to America." And then he turned and went back to work. I guess I got my answer.

On the tour, there was a young man whose family owned a New York department store. He was our age, and we got acquainted with him as we went from place to place on the tour. When the tour was over, we stopped for a beer at a little café. We had a lively conversation, relating our various adventures. He told us that the government in Zanzibar was communist. "They are very suspect of foreigners," he said. "Did you notice we're being followed?" I looked at him in disbelief. "Sure," he said. "See that man over there?"

I looked at a table across the room, and there was an African man in shorts and a colorful shirt. He shifted his eyes to avoid my glance.

"He's been following us since we left the tour. Let's buy him a beer."

With that, Casey raised his hand, and a server approached the table. "See that man over there in the corner? Bring him a beer and put it on my tab."

With that, the three of us got up and, having paid for our drinks, walked out of the restaurant toward the terminal, where we would catch the ferry back to the mainland and then a bus for Mombasa in Kenya. Our tail smiled and gave us a friendly wave as he sipped his beer and we walked out the door.

In Mombasa, we found a hotel near the waterfront. But the first item of business was our visa for Japan. We had been told absolutely that we would not be allowed to board the ship without the visa stamped on our passport. We bought tickets for a bus ride to Nairobi, and early the following morning, we climbed on a shining large bus. What an experience! Unlike the buses in Malawi that we were accustomed to, this was a comfortable, air-conditioned coach. There were plenty of clean seats with backs and no goats or chickens in the aisles. We were truly being spoiled. But there were other passengers on the bus who were not so reinforcing. He was a Canadian VSO, Volunteer Service Overseas, and he sat across from me. "You need a visa for Japan," he repeated, "and your ship leaves in two days? Good luck! I know it takes at least two weeks to get a Japanese visa. Maybe things have changed, but I don't think so."

And with that not-so-very-good news, we rode the rest of the way to Nairobi, got off the bus, and found our way to the Japanese consulate. We walked to the office where visas were issued and spoke to the lady at the desk. We explained that we would need our visas right away as we would be leaving on a ship from Mombasa in two days. She asked to see our tickets for the passage. We laid down our passports and our tickets, and with a wry smile, she picked them all up and disappeared into a back room. If there is one thing we had been warned before we left Malawi, it was never to let our passports out of our sight. What could we do? We sat and waited. Half an hour passed. People came and went. The lady at the desk returned but paid no attention to us. Then, after what seemed like an interminable time, a man in a colorful robe came through the door, bowed respectfully to us, and gave us our tickets and our passports, stamped with a Japanese visa.

We thanked him, he smiled, and we were done.

We left the consulate, heaved a sigh of relief, and returned to the hotel. Success.

That night, we took the overnight bus back to Mombasa.

CHAPTER 37

Pacific

The *Pacific* was the ship we would sail home on. She was a beautiful French liner of the Messagerie Maritimes Company, on her last run around the world. I remember the first time we saw her in Mombasa that lovely September morning. She was gleaming white, and cranes were busy loading her with cargo as passengers embarked and disembarked on long gangways. All was not well, however. There were groups of Indians, men in suits, women in saris, and they were protesting vehemently around the ship. From what we could tell, the Indians, many of whom ran successful businesses in Kenya, were being forced out. They wanted transportation to India for them and for their belongings. There was a Mercedes-Benz on the docks, and the crew refused to load it onto the ship. We were told that the ship would not depart until late in the afternoon. Negotiations were continuing.

Meanwhile, a prominent Mombasa resident and member of the Mombasa Yacht Club suggested that several of us accompany him to the club for lunch. We were quick to snap up the invitation, left the ship, and walked a short distance to the club, where we enjoyed a hearty lunch from a second-story dining room overlooking the busy harbor.

Back on board, later in the afternoon, Indian women would not leave the gangways, bravely clinging to the rails as cranes tried to lift them so the ship could leave port. It was a desperate time, but somehow, it was resolved, and the *Pacific* eased away from the pier as long streamers of colorful crepe paper connected those on the pier with those on deck until the ship finally broke free.

The ship was fascinating. There were three classes of passengers on board. In the lower decks were the economy class. They were completely isolated from the rest of the ship, had their own dining room and bar, and even had a small pool visible to us from the bridge.

We were tourist class. We had our own dining room, but we shared the bar below the bridge with the first-class passengers. We also could use the same pool as first class, and we had access to deck tennis as well. The bar would close for us at nine unless there were first-class passengers drinking. As long as there were first-class passengers present, the bar would stay open until they called it quits. There was recorded music and a dance floor. Our dining room was a movie theater during the afternoon, and French and English films were regular fare.

The food was wonderful, as was the wine. Every table at lunch and dinner came with two bottles of wine, a red and a white. Drink one halfway down, and it was replaced with a full one. This was something we were not accustomed to, but the other passengers seemed to take it in stride, and we rather liked it ourselves.

Pacific was not a cruise liner; she was a passenger ship. Originally named *Vietnam*, she had had her name changed after the unfortunate war in that country. There were several couples our age, Canadian VSOs, and an English couple, heading home from their service overseas. We had a wonderful time together. We were the youngest people on the ship, and we took advantage of all she had to offer.

There was a very attractive woman who was traveling first class. She mentioned that she was a princess from Latin America. We enjoyed her company, and she made it clear to us that anytime we wanted to stay up late and party at the bar, she would be there and keep the place open as long as we wanted.

I can remember one night in particular. It was rough on the ocean, and the ship, without stabilizers, rolled and rolled in the waves. Julie and I and some of our Canadian and British friends took advantage of the situation, unlike most of the passengers, who were seasick, and we went up on deck to dance at the bar. We danced from one side of the ballroom to the other as the ship rolled from side to side. Our friend the princess kept the bar open and the music playing.

What a memorable night! What a lovely lady!

CHAPTER 38

Bombay

Today, it is the city of Mumbai, but then it was Bombay. Of course, we were supposed to have stopped in Karachi, Pakistan, but local tensions, even in 1969, changed our plans. I remember the water in the toilets on the ship, using seawater to flush, turned muddy brown as we approached the subcontinent and the city of Bombay.

The ship docked in early evening, and Julie and I and two Canadian couples decided we would go for a walk along the waterfront. What harm could that be? We were all experienced travelers. It was dark and hot as we strolled from the ship and onto the streets of that famous city. The rich odor of filth came on the breeze. We stepped over people sleeping on the sidewalks, covered only by newspapers. Prostitutes called to us from windows. A man in rags came to us clutching a lovely small pedestal table of teak beautifully inlaid with ivory. "Five dollar, five dollar!" he exclaimed. Obviously, it was stolen, worth much more than five dollars, and the person caught holding it might find himself in an Indian jail. It was not a bargain. We tried to ignore him, but he was persistent, following us along the street.

A double-decker bus roared around a corner nearby, careening dangerously. We passed a large home with a doorman staring straight ahead outside a large double door at the top of a long flight of stairs. A Rolls-Royce was parked in front. Ahead of us, we heard a commotion. There was a noisy crowd in the street. Suddenly, a man in rags spread his arms and stepped in front of us. "No, no, please, do not go that way. It is very dangerous for you. Please go home."

With that warning, we turned and headed for the ship. The man with the table followed us, and back at the ship, he tried to sell his table at the ship's entrance but was quickly shooed away by the crew. This was definitely not Africa. Here was a much more aggressive culture filled with extremes of poverty and wealth coexisting very near one another—the free market taken to the extreme.

The next morning, we boarded a tour bus for an inexpensive tour of the city. In front of the Taj Hotel, snake charmers carried cobras in wicker baskets on their hips, releasing them on the pavement as a crowd gathered. Then, with an ebony flute, he would charm the snake, getting closer and closer to the weaving viper. The crowd of tourists threw money, and the snake weaved back and forth, just inches from the man with the flute. There were horse-drawn carriages and taxis in that huge plaza. Rickshaws and trikshas passed us by. The man with the flute and the snake, now back in the round woven container on his hip, begged the crowd for more money. With a few rupees, I bought his flute.

We toured the city's jammed streets and stopped at several spots. One that, I particularly remember, was a kind of temple. It had a very tall tower, and hundreds of huge birds circled it constantly. Members of the congregation, when they died, had their bodies carried to the tower, where the vultures tore them apart and ate them. The details of the religion escape me, but their treatment of the deceased was dramatic indeed.

CHAPTER 39

Ceylon: A Drive up the Coast

Back aboard the ship, we were headed for Ceylon, the island-nation to the south of India, now Sri Lanka. The tour offered by the ship was to Kandy, home of the Temple of the Tooth, an edifice built around the tooth of Buddha. Unfortunately, it was far inland, near the center of the island, and because of the long bus ride involved, it was expensive. We decided against it. What to do?

At about that time, we met a couple who was a bit older than us, from England originally but who lived in Ceylon. Because he was a poor student at school, his father had sent him to Ceylon to "plant tea." That was what wealthy people did with their kids who were not ready for business in the competitive United Kingdom. His wife was very attractive and friendly. "Why don't you come stay with us for a few weeks? We'd love to have you," she offered.

But there was no way we could just leave the ship. It would only be in Colombo one day, and we would still have to find our way home.

"I'll tell you," said Steve, "soon as you get off the ship, grab a taxi and tell the driver you want to go, say, thirty-five miles up the coast. It is one of the most spectacular coastlines you'll ever see." He went on to talk about the beautiful, sandy beaches, the fishing villages, etc.

So when the ship landed, we found a taxi with an open door and tried to explain to the driver what we wanted. There was a language problem right away, and the price seemed excessive. Just then, Steve came by. He smiled at our fumbling attempt. Then he turned to the driver. "What's your name?"

"Siddy Water," said the driver of a dilapidated Volkswagen Beetle with TAXI hand-lettered on the sides.

"These people would like to see our beautiful coastline. Could you drive them about seventy kilometers up the coast and then bring them back here?"

Siddy's eyes lit up. "Is that all?"

"Yes, and could you do it for thirty-five baht?"

"Get in," said Siddy.

We paid him his fee, and off we went.

"You thirsty?" said Siddy.

We had to admit that we were a little thirsty. Our driver then diverted from the coastal road and pulled up in front of a small thatched cottage. A barefoot man came out to greet him, and after a bit of conversation, he amazed us by climbing to the top of a beautiful nearby coconut palm and coming down with three green coconuts. With his knife, a machete, he cut off the tops and gave us straws.

"You drink," said Siddy.

I could hardly believe it. The milk was sweet and clear and almost reminded me somehow of 7 Up. It was refreshing. *Wonderful!* We returned to the road and enjoyed the wide beach and the beautiful sea. The day was glorious, sunny and mild. Siddy was relaxed. He stopped at a fishing village, where we saw a man on a bicycle with a huge shark draped over the support over the rear fender. He had caught it and was bringing it home for his family. Fishing boats, pulled up on the sand, were long and narrow and were sewn together with some kind of heavy twine rather than being nailed or screwed. I took pictures. Some were multihulled, with masts and sails. It was all magnificent.

"You like coconut milk?" said Siddy.

"Yes, it was delicious," I said.

"You like toddy" was his reply.

We stopped along the way at a restaurant, where we took an outside table. Siddy went inside and came out a few moments later with three mugs of foamy liquid. "This is toddy," he said. "It's beer made from coconut milk."

We enjoyed the beer. It was tangy and delicious.

"What do we owe you?" Siddy just smiled.

Back on the road, we noticed old men hauling large barrels on wheels. Sometimes they were being pulled by donkeys, but the rig was the same. "They are barrels of arrack," said Siddy. "It is a brandy made from coconut milk. It is very strong. I will not buy you arrack. If you want some, you must buy it yourself. I do not drink."

Julie and I agreed that stopping for a taste of arrack was fine. Siddy was willing to stop at the next tavern so we could sample some. "It is fine liquor," he said. "It is shipped all over the world. You must drink it without ice, straight up."

We both had a shot of arrack, and as Siddy had said, it was very much like brandy. We paid our tab and headed for the car.

The Volkswagen rumbled on, stopping here and there at a fishing village or a wonderful vista, and before long, we were back in Colombo, the capital of Ceylon. He took us to the tower in the center of town. "It is the only city clock tower in the world that also serves as the lighthouse for the harbor," he said.

After that, we went to the Mt. Airy Hotel, where we parked. Mount Airy wasn't a mountain at all, just the highest point at that part of the island.

Siddy turned to us and said, "Do you like curry?"

We laughed and told him how Julie and a friend in Malawi used to compete to see who could make the hottest and best-tasting curry. Siddy excused himself, leaving us in the car. A few minutes later, he returned with takeaway boxes filled with delicious curried chicken dinners. We ate them in the Volkswagen, and afterward, he took us back to the ship. I offered him a tip, but he pushed it away. "You paid me much more than I ever expected to make on this day. Thank you." And with a friendly wave, he put the little VW in first gear and accelerated out of the parking area.

Julie and I looked at each other, amazed at this fine man's generosity and kindness. Our friends on board, returning from Kandy, talked of a tedious bus ride, another Buddhist temple, and mediocre food. Nobody could quite comprehend our good fortune finding Siddy Water and having a ride to be remembered, all for a meager thirty-five baht, a fraction of what they had paid.

We were sad to leave Ceylon.

CHAPTER 40

Adventure in Thailand

The ship visited Singapore, where we rode in trickshas, bicycle-powered rickshaws. We enjoyed the city and the shopping. We bought a few souvenirs and marveled at the busy harbor and then went on to Thailand.

Pacific, our glistening white home, snaked up the river to the city of Bangkok. Small boats with VW-like engines, balanced on their transoms with long propeller shafts, raced about as the huge ship moved upriver to her mooring.

Ashore, we visited the Grand Palace, the place where the story for the musical *The King and I* was set. There were Buddhist temples all about, with a Buddha encased in gold, sitting Buddhas, reclining Buddhas, even an emerald Buddha. We enjoyed them all. We removed our shoes at each entrance and tried to understand the love and compassion expressed by followers of this faith. Tours of the temples were inexpensive and occupied our day. I took pictures there I used in my classroom as I taught *The King and I* years later.

The evening of the second day, there was a Thai dinner offered. Again, it was expensive. The tour included bus transportation to and from the restaurant, along with the price of the dinner and tip. There would be Thai dancing afterward. It was a "must do," we were told, but Julie had found an advert in a guidebook that offered a Thai dinner and Thai dancing at a much more reasonable cost. It was nearer where the ship was docked, and we might be able to find public transportation, a cab or a bus, that made it a much better deal.

We were on our own when we left the ship that night. Most everyone else had subscribed to the tour. We walked through the waterfront. It wasn't the best part of town by a long shot. A Volkswagen was wrapped around a utility pole and abandoned. It looked as though it might have been there for days. A car had run into the rear of a motorcycle, and the two drivers were having an emotional chat. We had been told that we would have to walk a few blocks to find a bus. Finally, a man in a small car stopped and asked if he could help us. We asked about the restaurant, and he told us to jump in. We rode for about fifteen minutes, and there we were. Inside we removed our shoes and walked on thick red carpet until we were seated on the floor at a low table. We ordered our dinner, some wine and enjoyed a spicy, rich, and flavorful meal. The staff was warm and welcoming. We were thrilled. Later, there was Thai dancing. Gold costumes clad the dancers. It was beautiful, romantic, moving. Then it was over.

We ventured outside into the warm night. Across the street, there was a bus stop. On the corner, a policeman, with a look of concern, tried to answer our questions. He knew no English, but he tried to find someone to help. Meanwhile, I jumped on each bus that stopped and said to the driver, "Harbor? to the harbor?"

Each time, the answer was the same. The driver looked at me and shrugged. Other passengers shook their heads and smiled. Nobody knew what I wanted. English was not their language. In the meantime, Julie had found someone to translate. *Buck Namm*, she said to me, means, "harbor." "Say *Buck Namm*, and the driver should say yes or no."

It was a very busy stop, and though drivers shook their heads the first few times, finally, one man's eyes lit up, and he said, "Buck Namm, Buck Namm." We boarded the crowded bus and paid our fee, and Julie found a seat next to a young man while I stood in the rear. I watched her take the map from her purse and try to locate our position. Suddenly, she was engaged in conversation with the young man next to her. She pointed to one place on the map, and he pointed to another. Suddenly, she stood up and came to me. "We have to get off this bus!" she said. "It is the harbor bus, but it is going the wrong way. It has come from the harbor and is going to the bus garage. Bus service ends at eleven. It's almost eleven now."

We got off the bus.

By then, we were miles from the harbor, in a totally unfamiliar city. There was a bar with people around it outside on the sidewalk. A rather drab taxi was there as well. I had just a few dollars of local cash left. I went up to the cabbie, opened my wallet, and asked him if he could take us to the ship for the money I had left. He pretended he didn't understand at first, but then someone from the crowd came over to help. It was noisy, and people began surrounding the car. I thought at first I might have started some kind of disturbance. There was shouting. But then it dawned on me, after I heard *American* a few times in the conversation, that this might be a bar that US servicemen on leave from the war in Vietnam frequented. Were these people on our side? Someone opened the door, and we got in. The taxi zoomed off into the night. I hoped the driver understood where we wanted to go, but everything was unfamiliar. Where would he take us through these dark streets? The ship was leaving early the next morning. Whatever would we do if we didn't make it back?

But then I saw that crumpled Volkswagen, still wrapped around a pole, and I knew we were on the right track. Our driver, silent until then, looked at me and said, "We're almost there," in English. A few minutes later, I emptied my wallet into his hands. He thanked me and drove off into the night as we ascended the gangplank onto *Pacific*.

As had happened so often in our experience, others, whether they be African Americans, Africans, or in this case, Thailanders, had come to our rescue. We had been recruited as Americans, sent to other lands to help others, yet repeatedly, it seemed, it was those we visited who ended up helping us.

It was late when we turned out the light in our little cave of a stateroom with no window. We were completely in the dark.

CHAPTER 41

Vietnam

As we left Thailand, we rounded the cape and headed north along the coast of Vietnam. Winds increased from the north, and *Pacific* plunged through the huge waves. Early on in the voyage, Julie and I ventured to the bow of the ship, where she plunged up and down through the ever-increasing seas. Before long, the captain ordered us off the foredeck. We retreated to a companionway below the bridge and descended to the passageway on our way to the dining room. Lunch was being served, and we were ready. There were few others there, however. Eating was the last thing on the minds of most passengers as the ship rolled and plunged through heavy seas.

On our port side was the country of Vietnam, the place after which our ship had been originally named. There, American military men were fighting and dying by the thousands. No doubt, the people they were shooting at were the same kinds of people who had so often come to our rescue in our travels. They had been drafted, as many of our men had, by a government bent on domination of others. They were moms and dads, sons and daughters. They might have had nothing to do with the politics of their nation, but they were there to fight for it.

How had I ever escaped that fate? I had registered, as required, for the Selective Service at eighteen and watched my status change after college from "student" to "eligible." I was immediately called for a draft physical. When Julie and I accepted our Peace Corps invitation, there was no change in status. Others in our group were drafted right from training. I just never got the call. My brother-in-law was drafted from Peace Corps service in Colombia. Somehow, I had escaped. Again, I was in the dark.

Our ship was stopped that night by American forces. The small boat alongside was there for a while before we were allowed to go on. There was never an official explanation. Perhaps we were too near the shore. As I remember, it was raining and very, very dark.

The ship anchored in Hong Kong, that beautiful city now under the control of the Chinese. Julie and I walked the wide sidewalks and saw smartly dressed businesswomen enjoying lunch in fine restaurants. We marveled at the view and bought good watches at moderate prices. We dined at a floating restaurant, and before we knew it, we were on our way to Japan, where we would land at Yokohama and disembark *Pacific* for the last time. Indeed, it would be the last time. Our lovely ship was having its final voyage. Air travel had made passenger ships obsolete. She would be reconfigured into a freighter or cut up for scrap. How sad, but how lucky for us that we had the opportunity to enjoy her.

CHAPTER 42

Japan and Home

We arrived in Yokohama, Japan, a modern city. It was clean and mechanized. In a department store, we found ourselves viewing a display of American goods available in Japan. We ate Ritz Crackers, Campbell's Soup, and Hershey's chocolate. We saw American products on display and realized we were ready to return home. It had been our idea to rent a car and drive through rural Japan, but we were discouraged by others who said that English was not available at all in the countryside, and with us having no background in Japanese, it might not be wise.

We traveled to Kobe and Kyoto and saw magnificent gates and gardens. A golden pavilion was reflected in a clear pool, and there was a nightingale floor surrounding a palace. It squeaked whenever anyone walked on it, alerting guards and those inside to an unseen presence. We rode the bullet train to Tokyo, our first high-speed train experience. It was all wonderful, all very programmed and safe. We made flight reservations from Tokyo to Hawaii and on to San Francisco.

One day during our stay in Tokyo, there were anti-American demonstrations, and Americans were warned not to venture into the streets. We went for meals, as always, viewing the numbered displays of artificial food in restaurant windows and then holding up the appropriate number of fingers when the waiter came by. We ate with chopsticks. There was no anti-American sentiment that we could find.

Landing in Honolulu, we found an inexpensive hotel just a block back from the huge towers that lined the beach. It came with a breakfast buffet, a real deal. Suddenly, everyone spoke English. We saw SeaWorld, where dolphins performed for us. We walked Waikiki Beach and looked up at Diamond Head. We swam in warm waters, saw powerboats, and sailboats. We were finally home.

I called friends of my parents who had belonged to our old yacht club in Lakewood, and they invited us to their Hawaii home for a sail and a meal. Their boat was an Islander sloop, about thirty feet. It was our first time to sail on the ocean. Julie and I put the jib on upside down, I remember, but we quickly remedied that. He had a little battery-powered television in the cabin, and he kept track of the action in the NFL as we sailed. Winds were light, we motored back, but it was our first time in a keelboat. *A sail to remember.*

We went to dinner one night at one of the large beachfront hotels. They wouldn't serve Julie a glass of wine unless she could prove she was over twenty-one. As she was twenty-four at that time, it should have been a compliment, but we had to walk back to the hotel to get her passport. We were indeed back in the USA. We enjoyed the beach and the easy access to our bargain hotel. We decided to stay another week.

When I went to a travel agent to change our flights from Honolulu to San Francisco and then on to Los Angeles, where Julie and I would stay a few days with her aunt and uncle before continuing on home, the agent discovered we had so many miles already from Japan to Hawaii and then to San Francisco and LA that we could add a flight to Cleveland for a really nominal cost. We wouldn't have to take the bus, after all.

So that was what we did. We wired the LA relatives about our later arrival, enjoyed the beach a few more days, knowing that November in Western New York would not be so mild, and flew to San Francisco, then to LA, where we were surprised to find Julie's aunt Grace and her friend Lenox there to greet us at the airport. They were the last family to see us when we left New York City and the first to greet us upon our return. Of course, our extra week in Hawaii had cramped their plans a bit, but that's how it goes with surprises.

Southern California offered the hospitality of Julie's aunt and uncle, who took us to Disneyland and a drive-in church where the pastor was collecting money to build a crystal cathedral. Universal Studios provided a glimpse at how movies were made. We viewed the Rose Bowl stadium. Then it was off to Cleveland.

Our descent to the Cleveland Airport was rough. The plane flew into thick snow and broke through just over the parking lot. "One more try, and then we go to Pittsburgh," said the pilot. But the second time was the charm. We found the runway and met my parents at the terminal. We drove home in their new Chevy Nova, stopped for dinner at the William Peacock Inn in Mayville, and were sleeping soundly in my old bed in Lakewood by midnight.

Two days later, thanks to the efforts of Julie's mother, a junior high English teacher, I was interviewed for a possible long-term substitute position at Jamestown High School, teaching English. An elderly teacher had become ill, and the school needed a replacement until June. I observed classes on a Friday, to see if I thought I could do it, and began teaching on Tuesday, the day after Veterans Day in 1969.

JHS was where I would work for the next thirty-one years. That, however, is another story.

Part 2

At Work And Play

CHAPTER 43

Back Home, a Job

Julie's mother, Eleanor Coulter, was a teacher at Lincoln Junior High School in Jamestown, and she had learned of the opening at the high school and mentioned my name. I had attended Southwestern, a neighborhood school, and as a local boy, I got the appointment.

Was I qualified? I suppose. I had graduated from Grove City as an English major but had never taken an education course there. My training came from working with students in Macon County, Alabama, and from teaching in Africa. My teaching degree was from the University of Wisconsin at Tuskegee Institute. Few people knew there was such a place.

I got the job. There were few African American students at JHS, but they needed an English teacher, and I was one. I started out teaching tenth and eleventh grades at both the Regents and basic levels. In those days in New York State, schools were segregated by ability levels. Very bright students took advanced placement classes. They were taught by a few very well-qualified teachers. Students fortunate enough to be accepted got high school credit, and sometimes college credit, if they passed an AP exam. Students of average or slightly above average ability took Regents classes. These were guided by New York State curriculum and evaluated by a Regents exam at some point. Students who didn't pass the Regents failed the course. A Regents diploma was awarded to those who passed all the Regents courses they took. It was key to college in New York State. I never did well in math. I didn't have a Regents diploma. I managed to get into Grove City, an out-of-state school, in spite of that.

Non-Regents students were just below the Regents level. They did much of the same course work, but with lower expectations. Less was demanded of them. They were often discipline problems in class. Basic students just came to school and did enough to show basic competence in reading and writing. Homework was not expected of them. They did poorly on tests. Often, they came from broken homes and very poor families. Their home life was sometimes so challenging that school was merely a safe place, where a good lunch was available.

What did I do as an English teacher? At first, not much. There was a literature text and a grammar text, a spelling list, and a vocabulary program. I would assign a story to read and then go over the questions at the end. I would occasionally give pop quizzes on the work and always a unit test at the end of a unit. There were twenty spelling words to be tested on Friday, and on Wednesday, there was always a vocabulary test. There were about twenty English teachers in the department, and we would get together twice each year, by grade, to write an exam for our students. Everyone in the same grade and level took the same test. It kept us all honest. The exam grade would be averaged in with classwork grades and determine passing or failing. Students from Jamestown were successful at colleges and universities all over the country. The system worked.

Several times in the first few months of employment, my department head or principal would slip into the room and observe. It was never a problem. The kids were well-behaved, and we were on task.

CHAPTER 44

Fulton Street

We lived with our parents for the first week or two, but we knew right away that couldn't go on. We looked for an apartment, and we found one, on Fulton Street, in Jamestown, just three blocks from JHS. It was a one-bedroom second-floor walk-up in an old house that had been converted to three apartments. Mr. Klinck was our landlord, and he appeared regularly the first of each month to collect his seventy-dollar rent, which included utilities. There was a gas space heater in the living room and a small kitchen. To say it was shabby is an understatement, but it was affordable, near where I worked, and there was a place out back to keep a car.

I remember our parents came with paintbrushes and rollers and helped us paint the inside walls before we moved in. It was partially furnished, and we brought what little furniture we had. One thing we did have was a car. I had an old Volvo 544 coupe that I had stored in my uncle's barn when we went away. It was black with red interior, but two years in a barn had not been kind to it. Julie, who had earned her NYS Teacher Certification at SUNY Brockport, signed up as a substitute teacher at area schools, and she would use the car to drive to work, as I could walk to the high school.

To complicate things, even though I was a permanent substitute, I had to have New York State Certification to work in New York schools. I had provisional certification only. That meant I would have to get a master's degree. Normally, educators in New

York were expected to acquire their master's within five years of graduation. Two years had passed already, and neither of us had any idea about a master's. We met with an administrator at the local Board of Cooperative Educational Services center, and he arranged to forgive those two years. We would, however, need our master's by the spring of 1975.

The State University of New York at Fredonia was thirty miles away. We applied and were accepted into the master's program. We would begin classes in January. I would work on a master of arts in English, and Julie would begin her master of science in chemistry. As each of us was enrolled in two classes, it would require driving to Fredonia four nights each week after school. We took none of the same classes but always drove together. While she was in class, I would do library research. While I was in class, she would do lab work. It made for a grueling time. We would teach all day, drive thirty miles, often in snowstorms, sit in classes for several hours and then drive home, grab a bite to eat, and do lessons until midnight to prepare for the next day at school. Weekends were filled with writing papers and doing college classwork. It was not an easy life.

The apartment became more colorful too. The people downstairs, a young couple with two little boys, would occasionally have disagreements. He would come home at about one in the morning and be greeted by his wife with "Where the hell have you been? You're drunk again, aren't you?" and he would say something, and the yelling would continue until both the little boys started crying. Finally, they would get things quieted down, and sometimes we could fall asleep.

Along with the apartment, downstairs, there was a one-room apartment next to our bedroom. An attractive young woman lived there. She kept to herself, always dressed neatly, and we almost never saw her. We didn't even know her name.

She had a lover. He would visit in the middle of the night. He had a deep voice that carried nicely through the paper-thin walls of the flat. Obviously, their relationship was clandestine. He might have been married and worked a night shift—who knows? All we knew was that their lovemaking, or whatever, was another disturbance clawing at our desperate need for sleep. These things, along with the whir of spinning tires on the steep, slippery bricks of Fulton Street on snowy nights, made living in our inexpensive apartment a bit of a challenge.

Were we the perfect tenants? Well, for our first Christmas, Julie surprised me with a ping-pong table. She cajoled the people downstairs to leave it in their hallway until she could surprise me with it on Christmas Eve. We could seat a dozen people there for dinner in the living room then take off the tablecloth and entertain ourselves with thrilling games of Ping-Pong through the evening. I don't suppose that made any noise downstairs, do you? Then there was the Fisher. Fisher made stereo equipment, and 1970 was the day of the stereo. I remember we drove to Erie one Saturday and bought a Fisher stereo-turntable combination with XP-66 speakers. We balanced all three on TV trays at one end of the living room, beside the twelve-inch television. The sound was wonderful. Certainly, those in the other apartments couldn't hear our music, do you think?

So we had a routine. We would teach, drive to Fredonia for our grad school classes, prepare, and try to rest. We got a new car, too, at Valentine's. It wasn't really new; it was a used 1967 Volvo P1800 S sports car, red with black leather. It didn't make our daily sixty-mile round trip any shorter, but it did make it a lot more pleasant.

By spring, we had successfully completed our first classes and had begun the summer session. June was a nightmare, nothing less. We had papers due for grad school, and our students had to review and take exams. We had to grade all our exams, average our grades, make reports, mark report cards, and on and on. It seemed this would never end. I remember, one night, there was a party, and we were at a friend's house in Bemus Point. Music was playing, people were laughing and talking, and Julie was sitting up on the couch, sound asleep. Still, we made it. I was hired permanently for the following year, and Julie was hired as a full-time chemistry teacher at Southwestern, the school where we both had graduated.

CHAPTER 45

Why Not a Yacht?

Finally, graduate school ended for the year, and the school year was over. It was summer. Julie's family had a summer cottage on Lake Ontario at Henderson Harbor, New York. So after a short trip to New England, we came back to the cottage, where we moved in and enjoyed some time at the lake. On previous visits, we had looked at the sailboats plying back and forth in the harbor and venturing out into the lake. Often, one would anchor for the night in front of the cottage. With both of us working, we figured we could afford a boat, so decided to look. We had sailed on that Islander 30 in Hawaii, and we had always been intrigued with the Pearson Triton, a twenty-eight-footer, but we knew they were both out of range financially.

We began our search. Near Sodus, New York, we found a Columbia 22, which was what we thought we were looking for. The salesman, however, was busy visiting with friends and didn't pay much attention to us. He obviously thought the boat was out of our range. "You two kids come back sometime when I'm not so busy, and maybe I'll take you for a sail," he said. We found an Irwin 23 in Chaumont, but the boat was brand-new and was not set up to sail at all, having no winches or even an outboard motor. By the time it was properly fitted out, we would not have been able to afford it.

Finally, a friend suggested we drive to Rochester, where there was a much larger used-boat market.

We drove to Shumway Marine in Rochester, New York, where we found her. She was a Pearson 22, a Dick Shaw design. She had dark-blue topsides and gray decks and cabin. She was called *Mary K.* A six-horsepower Johnson outboard graced her stern. We made an offer, fifty-five hundred dollars, and it was accepted. All we had to do was get the money, and she was ours.

The credit union at Jamestown High School gave us a loan for half the cost, we took the rest from our savings, and the boat was ours. Julie's mom drove us to Rochester in her little white Saab and dropped us off for the cruise back to Henderson. It would be a three-day sail with stops in Sodus and Oswego. We were very excited.

The boat came well equipped with a compass, life jackets, a horn, and a fire extinguisher to make her legal. She had no radio, but she did have a storage battery and lights, along with small winches. There were four berths, a sink, and a head, or toilet. We thought of her as a real world cruiser. We bought charts, parallel rules, and dividers. After having taken numerous United States Power Squadron courses over the years, I felt well qualified to navigate her back to the cottage. The next morning, we bought supplies at a grocery store across the street and finally motored out of Rochester Harbor into the big lake. Winds were light out of the southwest, but to be on the safe side, we put up the smaller of the two jibs along with the mainsail. There was no speedometer on the boat, no depth gauge. We planned to go as far as Sodus that night, about thirty miles, but we weren't really confident just how long that would take, as we didn't know our speed. We had both sailed small boats, prams, before, so we knew the basics of sail trim, but neither of us had ever navigated open water. Fortunately, all we would have to do was follow the shoreline to the east, and we would come to Sodus. Ever so slowly we glided along. The afternoon turned to evening, and Julie made sandwiches. There was pop in the cooler. Then it was dark.

An offshore wind sprung up, and we glided along. Soon, the light at Sodus appeared in the distance. Finally, we rounded the wall, dropped the sails, started the motor, and headed into Sodus Bay. We could see on the chart there was a small island just to the left of the harbor entrance, with a cove on its back side. We thought that would be a good place to drop anchor for the night. We slipped into the cove, and *bang*, the keel struck a rock. We were going slowly, so we didn't think there was any damage, but it startled us. On closer examination, there were stars on the chart. That meant rocks—not a good place to anchor. We moved around until we found a safe place, dropped anchor, and then lifted the floorboards to check the bilge. Fortunately, the bilge was bone dry. We washed hands and faces and brushed our teeth in the little plastic sink on the port side of the boat and crawled in bed. It had been our first successful day of cruising.

Early the next morning, we arose, ate some cereal and milk, and got ready for another day of sailing. Before we raised anchor, however, I lifted the floorboards. There was a half-inch or so of milky water moving back and forth as the boat rocked. Where had it come from? Had we damaged the keel after all? Were we slowly sinking? Unlike wood, fiberglass has no natural floatation. With our thousand-pound keel, we would sink like a stone if we filled with water.

After a little search, we found the problem. Our sink, the one with the built-in water tank, drained directly into the bilge.

We raised anchor, motored out of our protected anchorage, and headed again into Lake Ontario. We picked up landmarks as we sailed along, kept much better track of our progress than the previous day, and pulled into Oswego Harbor well before sunset. Rather than go into the busy marina there, we thought we would just tie to the wall at the mouth of the Oswego Canal for the night. There was a ship there tied to the wall just forward of us. We felt good about ourselves, finding a place to tie up without paying dockage fees. We learned our lesson a short time later.

When the canal lock opened and the ship moored forward of us began to move into the canal, her huge prop created a wild swirl of water around our new boat. The force of the moving water ripped the tiller from my hand and pushed the boat hard into the wall. We bobbed up and down, flattening our fenders, scraping our rail on the rough stone wall. Definitely, this was not a good place. I started the motor, and we powered into the marina, where, for ten cents per foot, two dollars and twenty-two cents, we would indeed have a safe place to stay overnight.

The third day, we rose and walked to a little restaurant for breakfast before venturing out onto the lake. We would head north some forty miles from Oswego, along the treacherous eastern shore of Lake Ontario to Stoney Point, Association Island, and Henderson. Before we left, we checked the forecast in the marina, which said winds should be favorable and the weather, fair. So we set out into the lake. We set our course halfway between Stoney Point on the mainland and Stoney Island out in the lake. It was a beautiful reach. First, the island came into view, then the point and its distinctive lighthouse. We continued up the shore, past Association Island, past Dulles Island, and finally, after Six Town Island, we turned south, leaving Lime Barrel Shoal on our port side, and headed into Henderson Bay. Home at last, we cast the navy anchor off the bow and, with seventy feet of rode, considered ourselves safely anchored right in front of the cottage. We had succeeded on our first cruise, but we had definitely learned some lessons the hard way.

It was mid-August when we anchored the boat in front of the cottage. We sailed every day. We sailed in light wind; we even practiced sailing in heavier wind, but we didn't do that so much. The boat didn't have reefing, a method of shortening sail, so we limited ourselves to sailing in moderate breezes.

I remember one windy day, sailing with the family aboard. Hugh, Julie's father, was lying on the leeward berth as the boat heeled far over. He didn't seem very happy. We loved the boat. Julie and I would go out after dinner, drop our lines, and sail into the night in the beautiful harbor. Everyone thought there would be no wind, but there was always a delightful breeze. We would fairly gush along in the calm water.

Then, one day, we had a forecast of a northeaster. Henderson Bay is protected from all directions but the northeast. What to do? There was a brigantine, *Saint Lawrence II*, anchored in the harbor across from where we were. She was a square-rigged Canadian training ship, a brigantine, a beautifully restored relic from an earlier time. We thought it best to be on board our boat when the weather hit. We went out in Julie's eight-foot dinghy, *Apache*, and climbed aboard.

Naturally, it was difficult to sleep in a small boat when the wind kicked up, rolling and pitching in the waves, but we were jolted during the night by the boat moving aft and crashing into her dinghy. Indeed, the anchor was dragging. Wind howled through the rigging. Rain pounded on deck. Julie, in her pajamas, ran to the foredeck and hauled on the anchor as I moved aft and started the little outboard. The dinghy painter immediately fouled itself in the prop. The boat turned sideways and rocked wildly. We were getting closer and closer to shore. I pulled up the motor, Julie got me a knife from the galley, and I cut the line, letting the dinghy go free. I started the motor and got us moving again just before we touched bottom. We anchored a second time and let out all the line we had. This time, the anchor had a better set and we held. The dinghy washed up on shore, all but undamaged.

Shortly after sunrise, Julie's sister, Carolyn, rowed out to bring us to shore.

Our summer was over.

We drove to Chaumont, a nearby harbor, where George Castle agreed to haul and store our boat inside in a shed for the winter. Graduate school started the first of September, and our school began the day after Labor Day.

We were back at it.

CHAPTER 46

Grad School

The course was something about teaching writing. It was an English education course, and I expected talks about topic sentences and supporting sentences and effective conclusions. I got to class early and took a seat at a conference table. There was a guy next to me with a full brown beard and a thick head of long hair. He wore an open shirt and a casual sport coat. I assumed he was a fellow teacher. "Know anything about this guy?" I said, referring to the professor who taught the course.

He looked at me, shook his head, and said, "Not much. Hear he gives homework, pages of homework."

I shuddered at the thought of not only keeping ahead of my students at school but doing this man's homework as well.

Meanwhile, other students filed into the room and took their places at the table. Most were obviously about my age, but there were several older people. Then that man next to me, the one with the full beard, began to speak.

"Good afternoon. I'm Dr. Pat Courts. You can call me Pat."

He went on to tell a little bit about his background and his teaching experience. He talked about his beard and his long hair. He talked about writing and teaching writing. He thought one learned to write by writing, and so he told us to go home and introduce ourselves to the class. He asked each of us to write a biographical piece about ourselves. We would type it up, run off a copy for each person in the class, about a dozen of us, and bring it to class the following week. That was it. Goodbye. No topic sentences, no supporting sentences. We got out an hour early. Was I getting my money's worth? I wasn't sure I had made a very good first impression on this professor.

It would be a while before Julie got out of her class, so I went to the library to begin writing my piece.

I had never thought much about writing about myself.

I had never thought about sharing a piece I wrote with fellow students and teachers. Some of those people appeared to be more experienced older teachers. What would they say about me, my writing, about my going to the Peace Corps in time of war, about our buying a boat before a house? So it was with some trepidation that I sat in the library that night and began to tell my story. It would be limited to a single-spaced typed page, so I would have to make important choices. My spelling and word choice, not to mention punctuation, would have to be perfect. That old lady at the end of the table with the spectacles and the frown—what would she say?

The next Tuesday, we returned to the classroom. I had a dozen copies of my piece carefully clipped in my notebook. I was a little uneasy.

The professor came in and sat down and began the class by passing out his own one page bio. He read it to us, and then he asked for comments. It was beautifully written, really, but he didn't want to hear that. He wanted criticism. He wanted to know how he could say it better. What was this? I thought the professor was supposed to tell us.

Each of us passed out our bios and then waited for the group to read them and comment. The old English teacher, the lady with the specs and white hair, made a few comments about comma faults and a run-on sentence, but that wasn't received very well by the group. Slowly we began to make constructive comments on how each of us might make our work a little better, more convincing, more clear. There was a math teacher who was very frustrated and dropped the class. There was a foreign student whose writing seemed shallow and insincere. She lined up perfect sentences that didn't seem to say anything. The class thought what I wrote about sail school in my childhood was pretentious. They liked most of the rest of what I said.

That was all there was. Week after week, we would find something that interested us and present it to the class. Papers were about relationships, current events, classroom activities at school, anything. We picked the topic, but we had to write every week.

The prof would give written comments on our writing, suggestions on how it might be improved, or his reaction to it. Everyone else would say something about our paper, and we would leave, and that would be it. We took no notes. There were no lectures about comma splices or topic sentences. What was this?

Something changed. I was the world's worst procrastinator normally, but I found myself composing the next week's paper in the car, driving home. When I got home, I went right to the typewriter and did a first draft. I was driven.

The old lady wrote papers that were grammatically perfect but didn't say anything. When someone mentioned that, she was obviously uncomfortable. As time went on, things began to develop. We knew one another better. We understood one another's weaknesses, and our writing became more personal, more meaningful.

It was the foreign student who broke it. One week she read her paper about her college graduation. She was from Latin America and had earned scholarships to college. Her mother was a widow, and she saved her money, and as a surprise, she came to Fredonia to see her daughter graduate from college. Mother and daughter had dinner together the night before, and then she, the girl in our class, had gone out to celebrate with her friends. She overslept, she missed a bus, there were a series of unfortunate coincidences, but when her name was called to receive her diploma, she wasn't there. Her mother, in the audience, was heartbroken. Tears streamed from this woman's face as she read her story. There wasn't a dry eye in class. There was nothing trite, nothing simple, nothing wrong with what she had written. It was moving and powerful, and we had all learned a lesson. For the writer to write well, the subject matter has to be meaningful to him or her. The audience has to be real and important to the writer as well.

The good doctor had not told us any of this, but we had learned it by doing it. We had written each week, and we knew we would have to share what we wrote with our peers. We would read to them, and they would react to us. Our writing changed. It became important. It became much, much better.

It dawned on me that reading a story and answering the questions at the end of the chapter was not a good way to teach anything. How could I ever get twenty-five students to type a paper and make a copy for everyone else in the class? We would never have time to read all of them in the forty-five-minute period. The paper. It would take tons of paper and hours at the copy machine. Other teachers waiting in line would be furious with me. How could I ever apply this to English 10?

CHAPTER 47

Talk to Grandma

So that year, I still assigned compositions about "my summer vacation" or some other trite topic suggested in the grammar book, and I corrected them for spelling and punctuation and proper usage. Nobody liked it much. There was so much to cover in the curriculum. How could I make this more meaningful to the kids, more tolerable for me?

I don't remember where I got the idea. It might have been something I read in the *English Journal.*

Around Thanksgiving, I asked sophomore students to interview an older person about something important that had happened to them in the past. As many of them were second- or third-generation Americans, I suggested, for example, asking a grandparent to tell about coming to America. I explained that I didn't want anything embarrassing or any family secrets. I just wanted a simple story about something that had happened to them long ago. The students were to write it up in a paper of not fewer than five pages, typed and double spaced. It would be due at the end of the first week in January. That would give everyone Thanksgiving and Christmas, two holidays where they might be with and have a chance to interview their older relatives.

There were groans. "Nobody else has to do this," said one boy.

It was true; no other tenth graders had such an assignment.

"My dad says it's none of your business," said another.

"I'm not asking for family secrets" was my reply.

As students do, however, the kids wrote down the assignment and took it home with them, and for the most part, I didn't hear anything more from them.

One day, an African American student came to me after school. "Nobody in my family never did nothing worth writing about," he said, looking down.

"Have you asked anyone?"

"Well, I was gonna ask my grandma, but she's old and just sits in the chair all day. She never did nothin'."

"Well, Vince," I said, "I suggest you go home and ask your grandma to tell you a story. If you try and you don't get any response and you can't find anyone else, you can come and interview me. I will tell you a story about something that happened to me, and I will evaluate you on how well you tell my story and how well you recount the details."

I could tell right away Grandma would get a second chance.

I got a few calls from parents. For some reason, they were sure I was digging for embarrassing stories about illegitimate children or some kind of illegal behavior. I insisted such was not the case. I wanted them to learn something important about someone they cared about, write it up, and hand it in. That was it.

The end of the first week in January came, and I had a pile of papers on my desk. They were neatly typed, and some of them were in covers. I took some of them home and began to read and evaluate them. They were interesting, and they were, for the most part, well-told stories of things that had happened to local people. There was a difference, however, from the work I had received in the past. There were far fewer spelling errors. Punctuation was better. There was seldom a run-on sentence or a fragment. I was very pleased.

When I came in to school on Monday morning, a girl was waiting for me at the door. I no longer remember her name, but I do remember her question.

"Read my paper yet?" she asked.

I had not read it, but I could take a hint.

That night, I fished through the rest of the papers and found hers. It was the story of a woman who lived in Northern England. In the early part of the twentieth century, she decided she wanted to come to America. She had worked in a worsted mill in Yorkshire, and she heard they needed mill workers in Jamestown. She made her way across the Atlantic and found her way to Jamestown, where she was immediately hired. Her plan was to work till fall and then return home. She saved her money and bought a return ticket to England. Two days before she was to leave, a man with whom she worked asked her out on a date on a Saturday night. They had a good time, and he asked her to go out again on Sunday. That was when he asked her to marry him. She had to decide whether to forfeit her ticket and marry the man or return to England. They got married a short time later. The paper ended with saying that the writer's mother still had the ticket for return passage and that, if I would like to see it, her mother would be happy to bring it in and show it to me.

On Tuesday, the girl, again, met me at the door. I told her I had read her paper and was eager to see the ticket. Mom and daughter showed up Wednesday morning with the family scrapbook in hand. On my desk, they opened the heavy book, and there, taped to the page, was a ticket for the fateful voyage of the *Lusitania*. The sinking of that ship by a German submarine had cost thousands of lives and had brought the United States into World War I.

The three of us looked at one another and could hardly hold back the tears. "She didn't really know the story," the girl's mother said, "until she got this assignment and sat down and really talked with her grandma."

I was floored. I had no idea.

The kids had done with their families much of what we had done in that writing class. They had gotten the story, but other family members wanted to see what they had written. They reacted to it and looked it over, and when the paper was finally done, it was often better than anything they had done before.

Of course, this was an exception. Over the years, there were hundreds of moving stories, some of them humorous, some of them frightening, many of them terribly sad. There was the woman in Italy who was kept in a cave with other women and forced to cook for Nazi soldiers who occupied Italy during World War II. There was a family who came from Sweden with next to nothing and managed to buy a farm and eke out a living. There was a woman who, on her first airplane ride, a flight back to Italy to visit her dying father, went into the restroom when they dimmed the lights and put on her pajamas then returned to her seat to sleep comfortably, much to the amusement of fellow passengers.

I remember a young Italian boy's story about his father, who lived in Italy in the 1920s. They were terribly poor, but he met, fell in love with, and married a beautiful girl. Shortly after his marriage, he learned that in Jamestown, in America, they were looking for workers to build the street railway. He left his home and his pregnant wife and came to Jamestown. His plan was to bring his young family to America when he could. He saved his money, but the Depression hit and he lost his job. World War II happened, and he was drafted. He hoped he would be sent to Italy, but that was not to be. Finally, after the war, more than twenty years after leaving home, he was able to bring his wife and his adult daughter, whom he had never seen before, to America. They had more children and continued to live happily in Jamestown.

And about Vince, the boy whose relatives had never done anything good and didn't have any stories. His grandma ended up telling him an amazing story about living in the South when the house they lived in caught fire and burned down. She got her brother and sister out and went back in to try to rouse her parents. After a heroic struggle, she managed to pull both her parents out of the burning building, saving their lives.

I used that assignment for the rest of my career. It is one of the things I am most proud of, because it involved students in meaningful writing. They wrote, rewrote, listened to criticism, from family members mostly, and produced things to really be proud of. I got no complaints. Moms told me in some cases it was the first time the kids had ever really talked to their grandparents. Even the parents learned things they had never known before.

One time, a young man wrote of his grandfather coming from Sweden, getting a job at Jamestown Lounge Company, and working on leather pieces, each of which he signed. We had an old red leather Jamestown Lounge chair in our living room. Sure enough, I picked up the seat cushion, and under it was a label, signed by the young man's grandfather. I carefully cut it out and included it with my comments when I returned the paper. I asked my students to keep those papers to show their children and their grandchildren. I just wished I had had the wit to ask my grandparents to tell me a story about their childhood.

CHAPTER 48

Skiing

Winter in Western New York is not easy. In my family, on Sunday afternoons, we would sit at home, have a few cocktails, and watch football. In Julie's family, Julie and her father went skiing after church on Sunday. After we were married and had been living in Jamestown, I tried going skiing with Hugh and Julie, but it was a miserable experience for me. They would take the chairlift and head for the big hill, zooming back and forth across the hills, riding the moguls, while I mostly took the rope tow and fell down the bunny slope. It was not something that made me happy. Maybe football and cocktails?

But Julie had read about Nordic skiing, and she wondered if that might interest me. I agreed to try, so we went to a local sporting goods store in Jamestown, where a high school classmate of ours, Les Johnson, sold us skis and boots and poles and a wineskin. We bought waxes and klisters and cross-country ski clothing, and we agreed to give it a try. The first time or two were a bit dismal. I fell down a lot and worked up a considerable sweat trying to get up the hills. Les offered to take us to a place in the country where we could really enjoy the sport. We took the Volvo, he took his 1960 Chevy convertible, and off we went. We found our way to a remote country road, where we parked and skied on trails that had been packed down by other skiers. We found a steep hill, and suddenly, I learned I could enjoy the downward run. I could even get back up the hill without overheating. The snow was falling, and the pines were majestic. I was beginning to really like this skiing thing. By late afternoon, when we returned to the cars, a fair amount of snow had fallen. So much so that the Volvo would ride up on it and get stuck. We were on what was officially called an unplowed road. That meant that no snow-plow would come to our rescue. Les took off in his Chevy, which was just able to get through, and found a farmer who came back with a tractor to pull Julie and me in the Volvo to roads we could drive on. It was a miserable, embarrassing experience, enough to turn most people off to skiing altogether, but in spite of the hardship, I managed to smile. It had been a good day, far better than anything in front of the TV.

So Julie and I were cross-country skiers. We would sometimes ski at Allegany State Park, sometimes ski on the thick ice on Chautauqua Lake, but when conditions were right, in the winter, we went skiing. Julie beamed, her face flushing with the cold. She was so strong, and she loved that she and I could enjoy this new sport together.

CHAPTER 49

Confession

On Monday mornings, we would always be back in school, teaching and working with our students. We might have been tired from the weekend's exertion, but we were there, teaching our kids.

On one such Monday, a student asked to see me after school. She was not an attractive girl, pudgy and plain. She was obviously from a poor family and was not a good student. I assumed she felt she needed help with some aspect of what I was trying to teach.

She came in the room after school and closed the door. She pulled a chair up to my desk. "I have to talk to you," she said. She was pale and appeared frightened.

"What is it?" I answered.

"I'm pregnant," she said as the tears began to roll from her eyes. "If I tell my dad, he will disown me. If I tell my mom, she'll kill me. I hate my counselor. You are the only person I think I can trust. Please help me."

With that, she began to sob.

Why me, God? was all I could think. Of course, I had nothing to do with her condition. I hardly knew her, but I knew I had to do something. She needed a hug, but the last thing a teacher can ever do is hug a student. Tenured or not, touching is forbidden.

"I have a friend who might be able help you," I said. "I will talk with him tonight and see what he has to say. We will find a way to break this to your parents and keep you safe. Come back tomorrow afternoon, and I will let you know what I found out."

Her face was puffy and red. It was obvious that she had been sobbing, but she turned and left the room. Fortunately, no one had interrupted us, but I hated to see her go into the hallway with such an unhappy face. What might people think?

That night, I called my friend who was a counselor at the high school. I told him the situation, and he agreed to contact Social Services so that he and other professionals could be present when the girl broke the news to her parents. It would protect her from her parents' wrath and give her an opportunity to get help with her pregnancy and, later, with her baby.

Until then, I had no idea of the immense responsibility that might go along with the teaching of high school English.

It opened my eyes to what it must be like to be unloved and poor and in that fix. How would she ever support herself, not to mention a child? Would her parents be loving and understanding and help her and her baby? What about the baby's father? He wasn't even part of the conversation.

That was the last time I ever saw her in school. She just went away.

CHAPTER 50

Serious Sailing

We finished that school year living in the same noisy apartment. My evaluations were positive, and school was going well. Both of our master's programs were on track for us to get a degree within the five years allowed. We wouldn't need to attend graduate school in the summer.

As the weather warmed up, we could hardly wait to get out of our stuffy apartment. Over the summer, we went to the cottage and sailed regularly. We renamed our boat *Twiga*, which means "giraffe" in Swahili. It seemed fitting to name our boat after those long-necked graceful creatures we had loved to watch roam the woodlands in the bush. We joined a local yacht club in Henderson Harbor and began to race. Everyone was supportive and wanted to help. We didn't win many races, but we tried hard, and every week we did a little better. Races were held on Sundays in Henderson Bay, and we found ourselves truly enjoying the sport. We even bought a spinnaker, a large red-yellow-and-blue downwind sail. Though neither of us had even been on a boat with a spinnaker, we watched how others did it, and after a little practice and a few mistakes, we found we truly loved gushing through the water under the large colorful sail.

There was more to sailing than weekend racing, however. Our club had the Duck Island Race, a race from Henderson Harbor around Duck Island in Canada and back to the club. It was often plagued by light winds, which made it difficult for small boats like

188

ours to finish the whole race. Julie and I signed up and sailed our best. We ended up with a hand-carved trophy, the back half of a duck. We were last to finish.

There was a race from a neighboring yacht club, however, that intrigued us. It was the Crescent Cup, sponsored by Crescent Yacht Club in nearby Chaumont, New York. Chaumont was where we stored our boat. The race was sailed on the Saturday night in August closest to the full moon. People talked of sailing into the lake on calm water, with a gentle offshore pushing the boats along. We would sail around Stoney and Galloo Islands, to a boat marked with a strobe light, and then return to the club. It was an all-night race. There would be a dinner before and a breakfast after. Julie and I loved sailing at night. What an adventure! So we signed up.

The day of the race was cloudy. There was almost no wind, but it was warm and humid. We sailed and motored the boat to Chaumont, enjoyed the dinner before the race, and pushed off. The boats floated in mirror-calm water at the start as guns went off, marking ten minutes, five minutes, and the start. It was amusing to see this fleet of sailboats standing almost still at the start of an all-night race. But ever so slowly, we all began to move as a gentle breeze urged us out into the lake. The gray day darkened, and running lights came on as we drifted away from shore toward the distant lonely islands. Before long, the gurgle of water at the bow was audible, the sails pulled harder, and we were off indeed. We had carefully plotted our course and were sailing by the compass. Thoughts of the spinnaker came and went as strong gusts pulled at our sails and heeled us over. Julie went below and got our thin orange foul-weather gear as drops of rain were mixed with the wind. I pulled the belt from my pants and wrapped it around the boom and, with a short line, attached it to a block on the deck. We needed to vang the main, pull it down to flatten it, and make it more efficient.

After a few minutes, there was a *bang*, and the belt parted—the boat rounded into the wind.

We thought we should take down the large jib and replace it with the working jib, but in the dark, in these ever-building waves, everything was different. The wind was whistling through the rigging. Suddenly, it was pouring rain. The boat began to turn and twist as she ran before the wind. The big jib was in the shadow of the main, so most of the time, it flogged but wouldn't fill. We knew we should take it down, but we had never sailed in such wind before. What if one of us was thrown overboard? How would the other ever be able to get back to him or her?

We were soaked and cold.

The boom flew across the boat as we jibed accidentally. Several times, we were near to capsizing, but *Twiga's* heavy keel always righted her.

Ahead of us was the strobe light on the marker boat at the head of Stoney Island. We were amazed to see the thirty-three-foot Chris Craft cruiser strain at her anchor and bury her bow in the huge waves. The race committee shined a light on our sail as we sped by. We passed the head of Galloo Island and then turned to head into the wind and home to Chaumont. We hauled in our sails as *Twiga* heeled far over and crashed into the waves, enshrouding us in heavy spray. We had been sailing for hours, over canvased and totally unprepared, mentally or in any other way, for the weather we were experiencing. What ever happened to a moonlit night with gentle zephyrs?

As we worked our way back to Chaumont, we were hit again by squalls. There was limited visibility. Wind-driven rain and spray hit the mainsail and rolled down on us. Lightning flashed and thunder roared from the sky. Julie used her flashlight to try to illuminate the chart, but the light was so bright that it was blinding. From time to time, in the most vicious gusts, the boat would be spun around and tipped far over, and water would gush into the cockpit. We kept the companionway board in place and the slide closed. We really didn't want to swamp the boat in case of a serious knockdown. We luffed the sails in the wildest gusts. The rocky cliffs of Galloo Island were not far away. We knew we didn't want to mess with those.

We knew we must be near the foot of Galloo Island. Unfortunately for us, the compass was gyrating, so as we plunged through the waves and we were knocked about by the wind, we weren't sure just where we were. There was a flashing light ahead, and we headed for that. When we got there, we saw it carried the number 2. We tried to search for it on the chart, but with our too-bright light, we couldn't find a 2 anywhere. Had we washed up toward the Saint Lawrence River? We tried to head for what we thought was Chaumont, but then the sound of waves crashing on shore caused us to come about and head back out into the lake. Land was near, but no opening, no friendly harbor. A red light shone in the distance, and we went for it. It was steady and quickly grew brighter. Julie shone the powerful flashlight ahead, and there was the bow of a lake freighter, most likely heading out of Sacket's Harbor. Again, we came about, but this time, we headed downwind, out into the lake. Trying to find our way to shore in this wild weather was crazy. We would sail into the lake until sunrise and then, when we could get our bearings, go home. We could see the lights on Galloo and Main Duck Islands, and we headed for the deep water between them.

Before long, there was light in the eastern sky. The winds abated a bit, and we turned *Twiga* toward the Lime Barrel Shoal and Henderson Bay. We were exhausted, soaked, and cold. We had installed a proper mooring in front of the cottage that summer, and when we picked up the painter attached to the buoy, made it fast, and then lowered the sails, we were ready for bed. Julie's sister, Carolyn, rowed out to pick us up. There had been a phone call. We had been one of three boats reported missing to the coast guard. When I got into the cottage, I called Crescent Yacht Club and told them that Julie and I were safe. They told me other boats were missing as well. It had been a terrible night. We dried off, climbed the steps to our bedroom, and fell into a sound sleep.

At noon, Julie's mother called us for a hot lunch. She was not very sympathetic to our ordeal as she had often said she didn't believe in sailing at night. I began to understand what she meant.

The news on the radio was not good. Two of the three missing boats, ours and one other, had been accounted for, but a third was still missing. A search was underway.

The missing boat was among the smaller boats in the race. It was just a foot shorter than ours. It belonged to the husband of a friend of Julie's mom, Eleanor. He was an enthusiastic sailor and had sponsored Julie and me for membership at Henderson Harbor Yacht

Club. The cottage where we were staying had belonged to his wife's family before Eleanor's family bought it in 1922. He, Bob, was missing with his brother and his brother's son. We listened to the radio that day for updates. Finally, late in the afternoon, we heard that the boat had washed up in Canada, with the brother and his son aboard, but not Bob.

Apparently, in the wild wind, they had decided to seek shelter at Gill Harbor, near the coast guard station on Galloo Island. They hit the rocks, Bob was thrown overboard, and the boat sailed off by itself toward Canada. The brother and his son were not sailors and could not control the boat.

Later in the week, a diver found Bob's body right where they had struck the rocks. There was a great deal of sadness. There was a funeral. It was a very hard time.

We knew we had to reevaluate this sailing thing. What did we do wrong? What did we do right? Were we fit to sail a boat like this by ourselves in a great lake? We had plenty of learning to do. We read, we talked to people, and we learned a great deal.

If you remember, when we bought the boat, the previous owner insisted he had not paid the extra money for a reefing system for the boat. He only sailed in fair weather.

It was a friend of ours at the yacht club who showed me. "You simply pull the boom aft and twist it, and by releasing the halyard, the mainsail can be rolled up on the boom," he said. The boat did, indeed, have roller reefing. We were shocked.

"It was so rough that, after a while, even if we had known we had roller reefing, we couldn't safely venture to the cabin top to put in the reef," I said.

"You reef the first time you think of it!" was his emphatic reply. "You remove your big jib then, too, not after it is blowing too hard. At night, especially, shorten down early! That's the rule!" He looked at me and tilted his head. "Did you know sailboats sail faster in heavy air if their sails are appropriately shortened?" I told him I didn't know that. "They are much more manageable. The boat heels less and is less prone to rounding up into the gusts. Also, there is much less strain on the rig. You are just lucky, being so overpowered as you were, that nothing broke. Imagine losing a mast in those conditions. What would you have done, then?"

I shuddered to think what the answer might be, but Julie and I agreed that we enjoyed sailing and racing our sailboat, and we were going to learn to do it right.

CHAPTER 51

A Challenging Year

In September of 1972, I was still an untenured teacher. I was beginning classes for the third time in Jamestown, and I was comfortable with what I was doing. I was being evaluated by the principal, formally and informally as he walked by the open door of my classroom, by my department head, and even by an assistant superintendent one time. There were two kinds of evaluations, formal and drop-in. The formal evaluations were your basic dog-and-pony show. I was given a few days' notice before the evaluation took place. Of course, I was ready. I made sure my lesson plans were up-to-date and reflected exactly what we were doing in class that day. I would be sure my shoes were shined and my tie was straight, as "professional appearance" was one of the categories. My presentation would be clear and well-structured, with ample class participation as part of the lesson. When I think about it, "dog-and-pony show" is an apt description. I never had a bad time when I was being formally evaluated. Everything went much as planned. The observer liked that.

I had never really given it much thought, but there was a lot more going on during those evaluations than them watching me do my thing. What the evaluator was doing was watching the kids and how they reacted to a supervisor being in the room. Everybody knew I was being evaluated, so the success of my evaluation depended on how the kids reacted. Fortunately, I had good rapport with the students, and they always made me look good. They would often go out of their way to ask questions and give thoughtful answers to my inquiries. On the other hand, had my little show been significantly different from what we had usually done in class, had we been coasting all year and all of a sudden I tried to put on a show, the kids would have crucified me. People don't seem to realize that about teachers. They are evaluated every day by smart, capable young people. If you as the teacher don't deliver, they will make life difficult for you.

One time, our English department chair was in the room while I was giving a spelling test. The door was open, and she slipped in quietly while the kids were hard at work. After the test, we collected the papers, graded them in class, and then went on with our work. At the end, Ms. Jacques came up to me and said, "Mr. Danielson, did you realize that girl sitting in front of me was cheating on her spelling test?"

"I missed it," I said.

"She had the spelling list on her lap, and I saw her looking at it. You need to deal with that. Keep your eye on her. Speak to her about it. Don't ever let that happen again."

That girl happened to be the daughter of a member of the board of education. I asked her to stay after class the following day and told her our department head had seen her cheating and that I would give her a zero on the test and to never try to do it again. She frowned and said she was sorry. For a moment, I thought she would burst into tears, but she sucked it up and repeated her apology. Then she asked me if I would tell her mother.

I was thoughtful. After all, I hadn't caught her cheating—my supervisor had. I began to realize the magnitude of the situation for both of us. Her mother, an influential member of the community, obviously put great pressure on her daughter to do well in class and make her proud. Should she be caught cheating in a nontenured English teacher's class, it would reflect poorly on not only the child but also her mother. Her mother might be very angry and even vindictive, punishing or even abusing the child. At the same time, if I insisted on making a big deal of all this, calling the mother and embarrassing the family, the mother could vote to deny me tenure and end my career at Jamestown. I doubted she would, but why would I chance it?

On the other hand, what if it had been a poor black student Ms. Jacques had caught cheating? What then? How would I treat that child?

I decided at that moment. "Priscilla," I said, "I've been thinking about this. I gave you a zero because someone else said you were cheating in my class. If you wish to do some extra credit to make up for that, you may. Tell me what you will do, and if we agree it is suitable, I will be willing to average that grade in with your other grades to help compensate for that zero on the test. Is that fair? What do you think?"

"Oh, thank you so much! Perhaps I could do a written report on a book I have been reading. Would that be okay?"

"I think a book report is a fine idea," I said.

It was then I realized the pressure that many students are under to perform well in class. Like a beginning teacher whose career depends on how he or she does and how he or she is perceived by others, students, too, depend on their evaluations to determine future success in college, in the workplace, and in life. Here was a girl, in a way, under the gun to do well. Her mother would be devastated if she found out. Would Ms. Jacques speak to the mother? That was out of my control. I felt I had treated her much the same as I would have treated anyone else.

Teaching English was indeed a big deal. I was working with human beings, young ones who had growing up to do, but I was dealing with real people, and what I did, I felt, was very important.

CHAPTER 52

On Strike

One of the questions posed to a struggling new teacher was whether to join the union. It was voluntary. At the same time, almost everyone did. It was the bargaining unit, and the union represented the teachers in contract negotiations and labor issues. It was a good idea to join, and I did.

Joining the union, however, was not simple. One had to join the National Education Association, the American Federation of Teachers, New York State United Teachers, and the Jamestown Teachers Association. It wasn't cheap, but everyone insisted it was important. The year in question, 1972, our teacher's contract was up for renewal. There were several issues at play. The first was merit pay. Student performance was to be factored into the teacher's pay scale. The union was against it. There were also pay issues, class size, and other things.

It was early in October, and negotiations were going poorly. It was against New York State law for public employees to go on strike. What would we do? We knew the penalty for a work stoppage was the loss of two days' pay for each day out. The Jamestown Teachers Association took a vote. I got the call on a Sunday night. There was a telephone tree set up to deliver important messages. The teachers would strike. I was to report to the high school for the first shift on Monday morning. I would be picketing the high school. Me, a non-tenured teacher, walking the picket lines. *Whew!*

I can remember walking from the apartment on Fulton Street to the school. The school was closed. There were no students milling about, just a big empty building. There were no teachers in sight either. Would I be the only one? As usual, I was professionally dressed, suit and tie. It was a cloudy day. I think I wore a raincoat. I could imagine myself parading back and forth in front of that huge building, holding a picket sign, all alone, knowing that I would lose my job for my audacious, illegal action. On the other hand, I could just open the door and announce that I was reporting for work as usual on a Monday morning. That would not garner the respect of my fellow teachers, perhaps, but it was the safer alternative, especially as far as keeping my job was concerned.

I rounded the corner near the parking lot, and there was a small knot of people by the side door. I saw that they were fellow teachers and a few union representatives I didn't know. They were getting ready to picket. Horrors! There were signs. We would walk back and forth in front of the high school until relieved, several hours. A schedule had been prepared. Negotiations had broken down.

I remember getting a pep talk from the union man. "Walk back and forth, no more than two in a group. This is serious business. You are standing up for better education in Jamestown."

We walked. People driving by on Second Street honked their horns, gave us the finger, or saluted. There were unkind derisive shouts from parents about our being lawbreakers, unfit to teach their kids. There were news reporters who wanted us to comment. There were pictures in the paper every night. It was not fun. A few teachers did not participate. They came to work every day even though the school was closed and there were no kids to teach. There were hard feelings. There were unkind words. There were teachers supporting families who needed food stamps. Because Julie was teaching in another district, money was not a factor for the two of us, but other people were hurting.

The strike went on for two weeks. We walked in the rain, in the wind, and in the cold. We walked and walked. On beautiful, sunny days with autumn leaves falling, we walked. An administrator, a former teacher, took pictures of us from behind bushes and trees as we carried our signs in front of the school. We all chipped in and sent him forty dimes, forty pieces of silver, in the mail. An unhappy memory.

At Halloween, it ended.

There was an agreement. We got no merit pay, a limit on class size, and a pay increase. Of course, we wouldn't get a paycheck for another month, but the strike was over. We could go back to work, and we did.

I felt we had stood up for a principle. It was important to us that teachers should be able to own a home, raise a family, and send their kids to college. More than that, however, it was important that our students, rich or poor, have access to a first-class education. If we had to break a law to make that happen, so be it. We did what we had to do. We paid our fines, and we prevailed.

CHAPTER 53

Science Fiction

Shortly after the teachers' strike, there was an English department meeting that I will long remember. We had a new interim department head, and he wanted to institute an elective program at the high school. Students would have to take English 10, 11, and 12 for half the year, but they could choose an elective for the other half. Each teacher could choose an elective he or she wanted to teach then prepare the course and teach it. Each student would get to choose the courses he or she wanted.

It seemed everyone but me was aware of the program and had submitted an idea. There were courses on American novels, English novels, creative writing, Bible as literature, and on and on. At the end of the meeting, our chairman looked at me. "Mr. Danielson," he said, "one of the courses I'd like to see taught is a course in science fiction. I wonder if you would be willing to prepare such a course."

I was caught a bit off guard. I knew nothing about science fiction; it wasn't covered in any of my college. "Well, I…I suppose. Yes, I could do that," I said.

"Good. See me right after this meeting. I have an idea."

So right after the meeting, I walked to the front of the room to speak to our department chair.

"Henry, as you probably know, there is an English teachers' conference going on as we speak in Rochester. I've been told they have books available for numerous elective programs. Would you be willing to drive to Rochester tomorrow, go to the conference, and perhaps pick up some materials that you might be able to use in your science fiction class?" He squinted at me and frowned.

"Tomorrow?"

"Yes, tomorrow. I've spoken to Mr. Levin, the assistant principal, and he said he could take your classes tomorrow. It's about a hundred and fifty miles each way. You would come back tomorrow night. I can't afford to have you out two days and pay your hotel bills and all, but we can give you money for lunch and pay for your gas. What do you say?"

"Of course" was all I could say.

I headed for my room. I had lesson plans—that was essential—but they were hardly fit for the assistant principal. My heart was in my throat. What could I do? We were in the middle of a novel in the Regents classes. He would have to have the class fill him in on what was going on in the book. There was vocabulary and grammar to deal with in the basic classes. I added a little detail but left the plans for Thursday as they were. I would be back on Friday.

It was much later than usual when I picked up Julie that night at Southwestern. I told her what had happened. We decided, as we had only one car, I would drop her off at work the next morning before I headed for Rochester. She would have to find her own way home after school.

That night, I planned my route. I wondered how I would ever know what materials to pick. Were there textbooks for science fiction? I had no choice. I would do what I could.

I fired up the bright-red Volvo the next morning, and I dropped Julie off as planned, and by ten, I was in a huge downtown Rochester parking ramp. The hotel where the conference was being held was across the street. I signed in for the conference and found a panel discussion on electives. Several teachers discussed their opinions and experiences teaching various electives. They didn't seem overly enthusiastic. At another presentation, a teacher extolled the virtues of his public speaking class. He talked about stage fright and teaching playacting and debate and oration. He was wonderful.

After lunch, I found the book displays. I had never read any of the books there, but the salespeople were giving free samples, and I loaded my briefcase. There were the paperback novels *The Andromeda Strain* by Michael Crichton, *Childhood's End* by Arthur C. Clarke, *Fantastic Voyage* by Isaac Asimov, and others. There was a collection called *The Greatest Science Fiction Stories of All Time*, another called simply *Science Fiction*, another *Science Fact/Fiction*. By the time I was ready to leave, I must have had a dozen free samples, upon which I hoped to build my course. Most of what I had picked out were not textbooks; they were just paperbacks. There were no questions at the ends of stories. Were these stories even acceptable for use in the classroom? I had a great deal of reading to do.

It was cold when I returned to the car. I was excited and eager to start the long drive home. I stuck the key in the ignition and twisted it hard to the right. The key stuck for a second and then broke off right in my hand. I was in my car, the ignition was on, the warning lights on the dash were lit, but the engine hadn't started and the key was broken off inside the lock. I tried to twist the bit of the key that stuck out, but it wouldn't move. What would I do?

I glanced in the rearview mirror as a little white Saab drove by. Eleanor! Julie's mother. She was at the conference too! That was Eleanor, I thought. But she was gone. What now?

I got out of the car and began to walk toward the elevator when that Saab again came around the corner. I signaled, and she stopped.

"Oh, thank God!" she said.

"What's the matter?" I responded. "I'm so glad to see you!"

"You're glad! I'm so happy to see you! I don't have enough cash to get out of the parking ramp," said Eleanor. "They won't take my out-of-town check!"

"Well, the key broke off in my car. I can't start it." I held up the stub of my broken key. "I've got to get back to teach tomorrow. What'll I do?"

Eleanor dug through her purse and found a paper clip and a hairpin. "Will these help?"

I went back to my beautiful but useless vehicle and opened the door. With my mother-in-law looking on, I managed to twist the ignition off and, finally, remove the broken part of the key. By then, it was completely dark outside.

Eleanor and I drove to a hardware store that was still open, and they managed to make several copies of the damaged key. The man there did the best he could, clamping the broken key in the grinder, but he admitted he couldn't guarantee the results. We returned to the parking garage, and I, after much manipulation, managed to get the car started.

"Come to my brother Dick's house with me," said Eleanor. "You can spend the night at their house and call in from there."

"Call in!" I said.

"Of course. You can't drive that car home tonight. What if you need gas? You have to shut off the car to get gas. Even if you got home, how would you get it started in the morning to go to school? It would be too late to call in. You stay with us at Dick's tonight. Go to the Volvo dealer in the morning and see if they can fix it. Julie can find a ride to work."

I did as suggested. I managed to get the car started the next morning, but the Volvo dealer didn't have the switch I needed. I filled the tank with the motor running and made it home without further problems.

School had gone well. Mr. Levine had taken my classes again and had no complaints. A man who specialized in Volvo repair in the nearby village of Busti rewired the ignition and installed a starter button. The car was fine.

That summer, the board paid me for two additional weeks' work to write the curriculum for my science fiction course. It seemed so trivial to me until I began to read some of the stories by people like Isaac Asimov and Arthur C. Clarke. What was *science fiction*, anyway? Asimov said it was "human reaction to advances in science and technology." The point was that it was *human reaction*. It was not about space travel or monsters or aliens. It was about people. Like all other literature, it was about people and the way they would react to new things. What a wake-up call for me! That was how I would structure the course. How might people react to time travel? How might people react to aliens? How might people react to robots?

Could people fall in love with robots? What if advanced robots were humanoid and were made very beautiful? Could humans make love with them? How would others feel about that? If a woman fell in love with a Martian, what would her family think? Could we relate that to the world we live in? What if a white man fell in love with a black woman? What if a Catholic fell in love with a Jew? Do men fall in love with their cars?

But this was an English class. We would have our own vocabulary; we would discuss, imagine, write. We would create. I had no idea just how this would turn out, but I was excited. I had read hundreds of stories, and my imagination ran wild. The possibilities seemed endless!

It was the middle of August when I got my first shock of reality regarding this science fiction stuff. All my classes the following year, both semesters, would be science fiction. The student population had reacted very positively to the elective, and it would fill my schedule. They asked me to develop both a Regents and a non-Regents level. I would be evaluated for tenure on my classes teaching the course I wrote. If it all worked out as I hoped, it would be good. If it was a flop, I was finished.

Graduate school was interesting that year, too. The focus was on classroom independence. Less on teacher guidance, more student-guided activity. How could kids learn anything if it wasn't presented? The professor asked us to read a story and, in groups, do a project related to it. He suggested drawings, plays, poetry, various ways to represent what the story said. I remember bringing one of the science fiction stories I planned to teach—"The Good Provider," it was called, about a man who tinkered in his garage to build a time machine. He sent his wife back to the Depression to buy expensive pieces of meat at prices he could afford. We, all experienced teachers, dramatized the story, wrote a script, and recorded our work on tape to be played for the class. Our hearts were in our throats when we switched on that tape recorder and played the material to the graduate-level English class. It mattered. That was what it was all about. When it matters, people try hard. What more can we do?

But old habits die hard. I started out my science fiction classes by asking everyone to read a story so we could discuss it the following day. I generally led the discussion, and the class went on from there. There was a great deal the students didn't know.

We talked about the speed of light and Einstein and how, if one approached and then exceeded the speed of light, time would slow down, stop, and then flow backward. We talked about the distance of stars from Earth and how long it might take to get there. We figured out how many miles there are in a light-year. We talked about the number of stars in the visible universe. Think about the number of grains of sand on all the beaches of the world. We had discussions and discussions. Sometimes I had a quiz on the reading, and the class generally did well on it. They were engaged. But they had a surprise for me.

After doing a number of short stories, I assigned Michael Crichton's *The Andromeda Strain.* I had been teaching long enough to know that twenty to thirty pages were enough to ask high school students to read in a night. So I subdivided the book in sections for discussion, as I might have with, say, *Silas Marner* or some other classic. The first day, the discussion was robust, and after that, the kids seemed to have lost interest. It wasn't that they didn't know the answers, but many of them had already finished the book! They wanted to discuss the whole thing. I had never seen anything like it in my teaching career. I knew there was really something here, and I had to get ahold of it.

A thick book, *Science Fiction Hall of Fame*, was an anthology of science fiction stories, many of which were more than a hundred pages in length. At first, I was concerned the length of the selections would be a turn off. We started with shorter stories, but the strong students, especially, hungered for more. "A Martian Odyssey" described exotic creatures who lived on Mars, but the first story to really grab their attention was called "First Contact" by Murray Leinster. It's about an American spaceship that contacts an alien ship in deep space. The two ships, in juxtaposition, are frozen in place, neither daring to head home for fear that the other would follow and destroy the home planet. The story, written shortly after World War

II, shows the paranoia that came with the introduction of the nuclear age, along with the nuclear standoff, better known as the cold war. In another anthology, "The Cold Equations" deals with a young woman who stows away in a space capsule. The captain understands that her additional weight added to the weight of the capsule will lead to the mathematical certainty of the destruction of the ship. The only salvation is for her, lovely as she is, to be jettisoned into space and her certain death. As others try to lend encouragement by radio, it is the perfect opportunity for a hero to save the day, but there is no hero. No one can save her from mathematical certainty.

Ray Bradbury's *The Martian Chronicles* was about the settlement of Mars by humans. First, they had to defeat the native inhabitants, then they developed the place. Earth became a distant planet. There was a war on earth. Some powerful attraction had made them go back home to fight the war. They had come to Mars to escape war, but they went back. There was no one left on Mars when man finally, we assume, destroyed himself with a nuclear war on Earth.

When the students realized that *The Martian Chronicles* was really an allegory, they were surprised. It was the story of Europeans coming to America, conquering the natives, settling the place, and building a kind of utopia, only to heed the call of war drums from Europe, which eventually led to the atomic age and possible nuclear destruction.

And then there was "One Love Have I." In a corrupt futuristic state, a man is convicted of political meddling and sentenced to a hundred years in a frozen state of suspended animation. His lover, a younger woman, finds a job on a spaceship going to another solar system light-years away. As the ship approaches light speed, time for her slows down and all but stops, as Einstein described in his theory of relativity. During the time she is on that distant planet, she ages normally, but as she speeds back toward Earth, time again slows so that when she returns, a hundred years have passed on Earth but only about ten for her. When her lover is thawed, revitalized, and released, she is there to greet him, still youthful and lovely, but now about his age.

The kids loved these stories that so graphically described physical theories they might have never had a reason to understand and think about.

Somehow, a test on the content of what we had studied seemed terribly shallow. Of course, we had to have grades, so we used quiz grades and test grades, but that wasn't meaningful. In graduate school, our professors had encouraged us to let our students go. Let them find ways to express themselves about the literature we were reading. So that was what we did.

I asked the class to pick a story and represent what they saw or learned from that story in some other medium. It could be a play, a poem, even a painting, a picture, or a technical drawing. The response was overwhelming. I had no idea that my students were so creative. One young man would make illustrations from the stories and books we read. The results had to be posted for the rest of the class to see, and I regularly posted his drawings and paintings. Often, when my back was turned, they were stolen. It was a terrible disappointment to me but, in a way, a real compliment to him and his creative talents.

The work these young people did mattered to them. In one instance, I hadn't understood the technical research a young man had done to create a drawing of a device to generate electricity using differences in air pressure. I didn't give him what, in his mind, was a fair grade. The point is that he had actually looked into the idea, thought about it, and from a very abstract description, created a literal drawing of it. Had he done a great deal of writing? No. But he had done very careful reading, some research, and had created an excellent interpretation of what he learned. Then he came to me after school and defended his idea. He thought he deserved more than I had awarded him. His defense was appropriate and his argument, sound. I raised his grade.

Radio plays were another device often used to interpret what we had read. Sometimes they would be news reports, sometimes a narrative from one of the characters in a story telling what went on from a different viewpoint. Sometimes they were dramatizations of selections. I had no idea what I was getting into when I started. I explained to the students that they would write a short play about some aspect of one of the stories we had read. They would work with a group to read their play into a tape recorder, complete with sound effects, and we would play it back to the class.

There were issues, however. Where could these young people prepare and produce these plays? They could write them in groups in class, but where could they find a quiet space to produce them without various groups interrupting one another? I mentioned the problem to several teachers along the hallway, and they agreed they would leave their doors unlocked during their free periods so my kids could use their rooms while they were vacant. Of course, the doors had to be left open while they were working in the classroom, and I would walk from room to room to be sure they remained on task.

The students had great fun with the project. Everyone had to contribute. They especially enjoyed the sound effects part. They brought in music for background and made quite believable sound effects. They began criticizing one another's writing. They reworded passages others had written to make them sound more believable. They did exactly what a writer had to do before his work is ready for the public eye. Creating believable images is difficult work, but they used their imaginations and pulled it off. How did I know that? I found that there was seldom a problem when these kids were left alone with their projects. Teachers who came back to their rooms while the groups were working passed along little but praise for their effort and enthusiasm. When we regrouped to listen to and evaluate the presentations, there was tension in the air. The work mattered, and that made it very worthwhile.

Over the more than ten years that we did radio plays, I did have one problem. A teacher reported to me that money had been taken from his desk. It turned out his son, a student in one of my classes, who was using his room for a project, had taken it. That was between them.

The thing I remember most, though, was a young man in one of my classes. He had an Italian name. He was not a strong English student, but he was filled with enthusiasm. I remember he was with a group doing an interpretation of "The Survivor," a story about a young man who was placed in an arena with modern weapons, a shoot-out to quench our appetite for war, which had become so destructive due to nuclear weapons it threatened the world. He and his group did their project, and his booming voice portraying the protagonist was very popular among his classmates. Years later, he got a job as a custodian at Southwestern, the school where Julie taught chemistry. He told her the one thing he remembered about my class was making that tape. When she came home and told me about it, I rummaged through the old tapes in my desk drawer, and there it was. I had used it for years as a good example of what could be done using radio plays. I brought it to Southwestern, and in Julie's classroom, I was excited to play it for him. He just beamed. I was pleased to be able to give it to him after all those years. The significance of it to me was that the activity of working with others to produce worthwhile interpretation of literature had made a lasting impression on him.

The experience was a positive one for us all. I even wrote an article for *The English Journal* called "Radio Plays in the Classroom: Another Way to Teach Writing." It was published in October of 1981, my first publication. It made me very proud.

I remember, at parents' night, one time a father was indignant that his son was reading stories he believed had no substance rather than the classics like Dickens and Shakespeare. He wanted to know why his son wasn't studying grammar, diagraming sentences, and writing book reports, as he had done when he was in school. My answer to him was my own justification for the class. True, we didn't study grammar. There is little evidence that the study of formal grammar leads to improvement in the end product of writing. We did study classical literature, including Shakespeare and Dickens, during the other half of the English year. In science fiction, students had an opportunity to create literature on their own. It might not have been great literature, but it was an interpretation of literature that included several worthwhile activities. There was group discussion leading to a creative idea. The idea was developed and written into play format. The play was read dramatically into a microphone and produced a tape that was evaluated by an audience.

Did everyone come up with the idea? No. Did everyone write the play? Probably not. Everyone did, however, contribute to or at least learn from the contributions of others about writing a play. They were involved in the production, and their voices were heard on the tape. It took language learning to a much higher level, in my view, than simply answering questions after having read a "classic." More than that, weaker students were able to see how stronger students put words together, cooperated, and together created something worthwhile. The enthusiasm generated in the groups brought out the best in everyone. It was fun. That is exactly what language learning should be.

Of course, there was a final exam for the course, and performance on that test counted two times as much as any semester grade. There were objective, multiple-choice questions about the many stories and several novels we had read during the class. Students were expected to be familiar with titles, authors, character names, and themes. There was also an essay where we compared or contrasted works, themes, or ideas dealt with during the class.

The class was so successful that it was taught on both the Regents and non-Regents levels from 1973 until the mid-1980's. It consumed most of my teaching time during that time. There was another English teacher, a history teacher, and a foreign-language teacher who helped out by each teaching a section or two. I was even asked to write a "research science fiction" class to be offered as an advanced elective. Some students became so interested in the ideas of time travel and other themes in science fiction that they asked for a course where they could explore further the science behind the literature. It was a very open class, where most of our work was done in the library. We soon discovered that resources in the high school library were insufficient to do justice to the subject, but we did give it a try.

CHAPTER 54

A House

Life in the apartment was more and more of a challenge as time went on. The people downstairs, who used to scream at each other, moved out, and a woman with two teenage sons moved in. That was fine for a while, until the boys decided to start a rock band. They practiced at night when the mother was working. There were drums and an amplified guitar. It was not music, just noise, as far as we were concerned. At midnight, I would have to pound on their door to get them to quit.

The girl in front, the one with the deep-voiced, late-night lover, moved out as well. She was replaced with a large high school boy who brought various girlfriends home to his room. Teaching high school, doing graduate work, and living on Fulton Street were simply no longer compatible. We had to find another place to live. I was warned that buying a house before one had tenure was not wise, but something had to change.

It was during Christmas break in 1972 that we started the hunt. We called a realtor and placed ourselves at his mercy. We drove around and looked at houses in the city and around the countryside. Finally, the realtor drove up a long steep driveway to a little two-bedroom house with a huge garage. It was on two acres and overlooked Chautauqua Lake. The price was right. We made the plunge.

The house was interesting and especially attractive to a young couple. It had a partial view of the lake. There were woods out back and a long sweeping front yard. The driveway was paved up to the parking area in front of the two-car garage. As it was December, we were a little surprised that there was no snow on its almost-flat roof, but there were huge pillar-like icicles drooping from the eaves. There was a large fireplace in the living room. It had oil heat, a well, and a septic system. The kitchen was tiny, and there was only one bathroom, but compared to the apartment, it was paradise. There was a little porch on the south side, covered by an awning in summer.

We actually called the realtor and made the commitment to buy on New Year's Day 1973. We would take possession on February 15 of that year. On Valentine's Day, we had an early thaw, and friends asked us to go on a winter picnic with them. On the way home, we drove by the house. Gene pulled into the driveway, which was bare, and drove up to the house so we could all have a look. The owners were just leaving.

"Gosh, we just left the keys on the kitchen counter and locked the doors," the previous owner said. He thought a minute. "The utility room window isn't locked. I can push little Jimmy through, and he can unlock the front door, and you can have the house tonight. How would that be?"

"Wow!" I said. "That would be great!"

Dad dangled the little boy through the window, carefully lowering him to the floor. He walked to the front door and opened it. We were home. The old owners got in their car and drove off. That was it. The house was ours.

Our friend Ted turned on the electric burner on the stove and touched it. "Ouch!" he said. The stove worked! The huge fireplace in the living room was filled with old newspapers and magazines. "Let's have a fire," said Gene, another friend with us on the picnic. He leaned down to light the papers.

"Wait!" I said as I groped inside the chimney for the damper. Smoke began to billow into the room but quickly disappeared when I got the damper open. The fire roared on the hearth, lighting the living room in the waning afternoon light. After a few minutes, the fire burned down. We had no food, no furniture, not even a chair.

We all piled into Gene's Suburban and headed for our old apartment on Fulton, where our friends let us off.

"You can borrow the Suburban anytime to move your stuff," said Gene. We thanked him, said our goodbyes, and climbed the steps to our apartment. We grabbed sleeping bags, some pots and pans, and plates and our silverware, packed what food we had into our Coleman cooler, and loaded it all into the Volvo for the first of many trips to our new home. There was firewood in the garage, so we built a fire in the living room and ate dinner on the floor. Later, we looked over our lessons planned for the next day, spread our sleeping bags on the living room carpet in front of the fireplace, and drifted off into a deep, uninterrupted sleep. In the morning, we ate our cereal and drank our coffee from our spot on the floor and headed for school. What a joy it was to lift the garage door and back our car out of the garage clean and ready to go. Later that day, it snowed. When we came home that night with another load of stuff from the apartment, we learned our Volvo, even with snow tires, couldn't make it up the driveway without it first being plowed.

We knew we would have to buy a refrigerator, and we had put money aside for that. But what about a snowblower? The driveway was three hundred feet long, the length of a football field, far too long to shovel. So we headed for a shop that sold lawn mowers and snowblowers and picked out an Ariens walk behind tractor with both mower and snowblower attachments. It took all our refrigerator money and more to pay for it, but the owner of the shop dropped it off on his way home that evening, full of gas and ready to go. Before dinner that night, I had plowed the driveway and gotten the Volvo into the garage. Who needs a refrigerator? There were plenty of icicles dangling from the roof. We could put them in the Coleman cooler and use that for a refrigerator, at least until the next payday. By the following weekend, we had borrowed Gene's suburban, and with a few friends' help, we moved our humble belongings into our new home.

We learned a little about the house as well. The story we learned from the neighbors was that there was a woman who used to ride horseback on a trail through the area, and she stopped to admire the view of the lake where the house was. It was shortly after WWII. She thought it would be the perfect place for a cabin. She bought the land and, with used lumber, built a small house with one bedroom, a bath, a tiny kitchen, and a living room with a large fireplace. She lived there for a while but then abandoned the house. Young people in the neighborhood used it for a hangout for a while until someone else bought it and added the master bedroom, utility room, side porch, and garage. It was sold again, and those people added carpeting and tastefully redecorated the inside.

It wasn't long, however, before we learned the house had real issues. In the far corner of the master bedroom, the floor was *springy*. The flooring was loose and the joists beneath, rotten. That wasn't good. Also, there were roof leaks after heavy snow. Because there was so little insulation, the snow on the roof would melt and run down the shallow sloped roof to refreeze when it reached the eaves. The ice dams would hold water, which would then back up through the shingles and leak into the house, dripping onto the windows and floor from the inside. There was, however, a remedy. I could simply lean our aluminum ladder against the roof, take a hatchet, and chop through the ice dam and remove a chunk of ice, whereupon gallons and gallons of icy water would cascade over me. It was not pleasant.

In April, my parents came home from Florida. I'm sure they were shocked at our purchase, but they were kind about it. My dad came up while we were in school and began ripping out the bedroom floor. He found the joists were very rotted and replaced them with treated ones. As time went on, we had a basement dug under the house and added insulation and a whole new roof structure. We replaced the steel windows with thermal pane and replaced the fireplace with a woodstove. During the oil crisis in the seventies, we added a solar wall heater to the south side. When the sun was shining on a zero-degree day, the house would hold at seventy degrees with no other heat. The house was warm, comfortable, and affordable, and we really enjoyed it. I could walk out the back door and hunt grouse or turkey, and we could ski on the back hill. It was a great place for a dog. True, it had some drawbacks, but overall, it suited Julie and me just fine.

About that time, our good friend Bill Sharp got a new toy. It was a Commodore computer. There was a program on it that allowed one to compute how much money he or she would pay on a loan at various interest rates over specified times. When we plugged the numbers about our house into his computer, we were surprised by the answer. The result was that over the twenty years of our mortgage, we would pay as much in interest as we paid for the house. We grew from that lesson. Right away, we started doubling up on our house payments. Extra money came right off the principal with no penalty. We bore down and paid for our house in five years.

CHAPTER 55

Tenure

Once I was granted tenure, after three years, I needed only permanent certification to keep my job. That meant the master's degree. We kept up the frightful pace of driving the thirty miles to Fredonia and back three or four times each week during the school year until we finished our degree work in 1975. I remember only that there was a terrible April snowstorm the morning I was scheduled to write my final paper to qualify me for the master of arts in English degree. The roads were covered with snow and ice. But we made it over and back—it all worked out. There had been "reduction in force" agreements each year I was employed, but though others lost their jobs, at least temporarily, I never did.

When I got tenure, I was asked to become a "building rep" for the union. It was an important position as it allowed me to be part of a team to discuss issues with the administration representing the teachers. We would have meetings regularly, which, though seldom contentious, enabled us to share our side of things with the principals. Often, we found ways to resolve issues without having to go through official channels. There were no more strikes. Even major issues between the teachers' association and the board were resolved more amicably. Jamestown High School, where my mother and father had attended with Lucille Ball and Roger Tory Peterson, where Walter Washington, the first African American mayor of Washington, DC, had graduated, was, indeed, a delightful place to work.

CHAPTER 56

Twiga's End

We sailed and raced *Twiga*, our Pearson 22, each summer from 1970 to 1975. We learned to sail her in all weather. We could fly a spinnaker, reef her sails, or ghost along in the gentlest of winds. There were no more close calls for us after the all-night Crescent Cup, where we were truly tested, though another boat from our club sank during a spring race and a man died before he could be rescued. We learned to be careful.

We enjoyed the river ice in our icebox, collected and sold the old-fashioned way from the Saint Lawrence, where we explored as far east as the Thousand Islands, Alexandrea Bay, and Clayton, New York. Often, we took one of Julie's sisters along or even her mother. The romance of sailing on the Great Lakes is alluring, but the act of doing it is sometimes more than it seems at first. One memorable evening, after a long sail in the hot August sun, Julie's Mom, who had joined us, complained she was "too tired to eat and too hungry to sleep." That says volumes about life on a small boat.

For several years, we went to Canada, where we would have to enter at Kingston. Customs there was a challenge. Our little twenty-two-footer was a world cruiser to us, but the customs agents there were used to working on much bigger, more stable boats.

After we checked in, the agent would often come to the dock to "inspect" the yacht. For some reason, when we went to Kingston, it was always windy. Waves washed into the concrete slips at customs, both from the wind and from passing ferries and ships. The waves didn't affect bigger boats much, but *Twiga* rolled and sloshed about a great deal.

I remember, one young customs agent came out to the boat with us. His face wore a big frown as he watched our boat toss about. He had hard-sole black leather shoes on, and he paused, hesitating several times to step on the bobbing boat. That was when Julie grabbed his arm and pulled him aboard. "Been assigned to bridges?" asked my wife, noting his inappropriate footwear. That was all it took. I knew we were in for it.

"Got any booze or tobacco?" asked the young man.

There were several bottles of bourbon in a small locker below, and Julie pulled out a bottle or two. "For personal consumption, ship's stores," she said.

"You sleep on this thing?" asked customs.

Julie climbed below and produced her nighty. "Every night," she said. The customs officer, embarrassed, looked around to see if any of his compatriots were watching. He definitely wasn't ready for that. Meanwhile, the boat sloshed and rolled in the slip.

"Do you have any more booze?" the young man asked.

"Yes," I answered. "There is some crème de menthe here, a little gin for gin and tonic…"

"Look," he said, "I can't fine you for all that. I just have to dump it. You're only allowed a bottle each. Please buy your booze in Canada. Those are just little American bottles. They don't amount to much. Enjoy your stay."

He turned around, looking a bit green, and leaped for the dock.

We did enjoy our stay in Canada. We sailed on the Bay of Quinte and had memorable nights in little coves in that protected, inland sea, visiting towns like Picton, Bellville, and Trenton. On the way home the first time, we ventured to Cape Vincent to check in to American customs. We had detailed instructions on how to find the place, and when we got there, we found the customs house to be a smoking ruin. It had been destroyed by fire the night before. The fire trucks were still there, and the head officer, who had been up all night, was surly.

"What do you have to declare?" he all but shouted at me.

"Nothing," I replied.

"Then what are you bothering me for? Come to customs when you have something to declare. Otherwise, keep out of my hair."

We never went to US Customs in that boat again!

Our last trip to Canada, in 1975, again took us to the Bay of Quinte. Rather than pay hefty docking fees during our overnight, we tied to an "under construction" ferry terminal. We had a wonderful dinner in town and slipped away in the morning before work on the terminal resumed. A few days later, in a blow, one of the turnbuckles on the port upper shroud parted, and the mast came crashing to the deck. We did what we could to salvage the mast, lashing it to the deck, started our outboard motor, and moved on to Trenton, where we contacted our insurance company. We had heard there was a boat-building company there that might be able to replace the rig. The surveyor there said that it looked as if somehow the boat had surged up against the turnbuckle and sheared it nearly off. The heavy weather finished the job. So much for our cheap night at the unfinished dock in Kingston.

We waited to leave the following morning so we would make the swing bridge at Belville's nine o'clock opening. Of course, without the mast, we could slip right under the bridge without an opening. We needn't have waited. We were so flustered we could hardly think. We filled our tanks and headed back toward Henderson Harbor. The plan was to cross the lake at night, when it was forecast to be calm. As we pulled into a little harbor to again replenish our fuel supply, the attendant noted the bent and broken rig on deck.

"Second one of those I've seen last few days," he said.

"Really?" I said.

"Two couples on a thirty-three-footer charted out of Toronto. Got becalmed out there, one of those quiet nights when the low fog settles in. Know what I mean?"

I nodded.

"Used up all their fuel. Just sittin' there, bobbin' up and down, and got into the booze. It was around three when one of the men found the flare kit. Set off the flares to amuse themselves. Passin' freighter seen it. Came 'round to search and picked up the dark yacht on the port anchor 'tween the forestay and mainmast. Dragged the boat for near a mile before they ripped out the mast and nearly sunk the boat. Rescued the folks, who had been asleep below. Came in here in a lifeboat, survivors did, towin' what was left of the yacht. They called for a taxi from Toronto. Wouldn't even get back on that boat to fetch their belongings. Ugly scene."

So back in the States, after collecting our insurance and having repairs made, we put *Twiga* up for sale and began to look for a larger boat. This time, we would have an inboard engine and wheel steering. *A proper yacht!*

CHAPTER 57

Dogs

There were no children in our lives, outside of school, but we did have dogs. Our first—well, second, if you count Modzie, who we sadly left in Malawi, was Buff. Buff was a mutt, born by accident to our Ashville neighbors' bitch. The pups were allowed to roam free and were being run down mercilessly in the highway in front of our house. One wandered our way, and we adopted him. He looked much like Modzie, with four white feet, a white chest, and a soft brown coat, but there the resemblance stopped. He was hard to housebreak and train. He loved to run to pastures up the hill behind the house and roll in manure. He hated baths, much as we disliked giving them to him. We made him a run, simply a nylon line between two trees, where he could get a little exercise during the day. Often, when we got home, he had wrapped himself around and around one of the trees but was not smart enough to unwrap himself; he just pulled harder and harder and wound himself up until his little head was smack against the tree and he was unable even to lie down. Julie worked with him for hours, training him to stay away from the road, but it was all in vain. Like the rest of his family, he was eventually hit and killed.

A short time later, around Presidents' Day, we started a dog search. We looked at liters of pugs and springer spaniels, and then we found another litter of springers in Rochester. We didn't pick the dog; he picked us. We named him Troy. He was a thoroughbred with papers, and we paid around a hundred dollars for him. He was sweet and cuddly and loving. He learned to come when called, and he was housebroken almost immediately after we got him home. We left him in the house all day when we were teaching, and he never damaged anything or made a mess. He was a little devious, but not in a harmful way. He stayed on the lawn and kept away from the road. He learned to sit and speak and roll over on command. He loved visitors too. I often thought, had an intruder forced his way into our house, Troy would have surely knocked him down and licked him to death. Oh, he kept off the furniture too. Well…

We had a wicker dining room table overlooking the lake and the driveway out front. Troy was never allowed on any of the furniture, but we noticed, from time to time, if we left, say, salt and pepper on the table, it might be on the floor when we got home from work in the afternoon. Of course, one couldn't punish a dog for something he hadn't seen happen, and we never actually caught him on the table. We were sure the dog sometimes waited for us on the top of the dining room table so he could better see us driving up the long driveway, but he never got caught.

One winter's night, the neighbors called and asked us if we wanted to come over to play bridge with them. We heated the house with a woodstove we had installed to replace the huge old fireplace. The house was warm and comfortable. We put our hats and coats and boots on and left our friend curled up in front of the warm stove. We came back a few hours later, but of course, we had walked, not taken the car, so approaching the house quietly, when we peeked in the window, we found Troy lying on his back, sound asleep, with his favorite toy, on the couch! I unlocked the front door, and by the time we had passed through the vestibule, there was our dog, just waking up on the floor in front of the stove, wagging his stump of a tail, looking innocent as could be.

He was always a good dog—well, usually. He traveled easily in the car and in the boat. He got along with other dogs well. He never barked or caused a fuss. I say *never*, but there was a time or two. At Henderson Harbor, there was a Great Dane mix that lived next door. His name was Modred, named for the illegitimate son of King

Arthur. He was an easygoing large dog who didn't much like the water and simply couldn't understand why Troy would race off the dock, diving headfirst into the lake just to fetch a stick. Modred was visibly upset, wagging his tail and prancing in circles as Troy again and again fetched the stick and dropped it at my feet, hoping with bright eyes I would throw one more time. So on Saturday nights, when the family served steak, Troy would get the bone. Would he settle down and munch on it? No. He would take the bone out the door and go find Modred, drop the juicy tidbit in front of him, and dare him to pick it up. Modred would, of course, do as expected, and there would be a nasty snarling match. It was the last thing anyone wanted on a Saturday night. Fortunately, there was never a fight. We would separate the dogs, and that would be that.

One time, years later, while cruising on Lake Michigan, we came upon an antique wooden sailboat show. With Troy on lead, we paid our admission and walked the docks, admiring the sleek and beautiful sailing yachts of the past. There was another couple at the show with a dog. It was a Great Dane and looked remarkably like Modred. Troy was impossible. He growled and snarled at that dog. He strained on the leash, and his feet slipped on the dock as he tried to break free. Fortunately, the other dog was much better behaved. I was frustrated and embarrassed with Troy's aggressive behavior as I held him tight on the short end of a long leash. So I simply let go. He dashed toward the other dog, but when he realized I was no longer holding him back, he quickly skidded to a stop and dashed behind us, looking at Julie and me as if to say, "Don't you realize I could have been killed?" Troy was aggressive only when he knew we were there to rescue him.

It was a cold, snowy Friday night when I picked Julie up after school and we went shopping for an electric typewriter. We were excited about the purchase and decided to go to dinner with friends at a nearby restaurant to round out the evening. On the way home, before dinner, we stopped at a pet shop and bought a dog bed for Troy. It was foam filled and soft, with a red cover. When we got to Ashville, we gave him his gift, and he seemed thrilled. He lay down on it right away, wagging his tail. We opened our typewriter, plugged it in, and gave it a try. Great. We let the dog out for a few minutes, and when he came back in, we gave him his dinner and headed out for a dinner of our own.

When we got home later that night, the dog bed was in shreds. There was foam all over the living room, and the red cover was in tatters. Troy looked at us sadly. "Cheap trick," he seemed to say. "You think you can leave me home alone all day and then give me that bed and leave me alone at night too? I don't think so!" Troy, 1; us, 0.

My favorite Troy story happened while we were sailing in Toronto. We had taken the boat to a remote island in the harbor, anchored, and then gone ashore with the dog in our dinghy. The area was nearly deserted. As we walked along, I noticed splashing a couple of hundred feet from the beach. It was a duck struggling in the water. Troy immediately jumped in and started swimming toward the disturbance. A large lady in a black bathing suit began screaming. "That dog! That dog is killing that duck. Police! Police! Help! That dog is killing that duck!" Her face was red, and her voice made it sound as if the dog were killing *her*.

In the meantime, Troy had reached the struggling animal, had grabbed it, and was swimming back to the beach. Helplessly, we watched as our dog carried the wounded duck to shore and laid it at Julie's feet. My wife and I bent down and grasped the flapping bird firmly, and Julie removed a hook from its beak. We then began untangling the line wrapped around its feet and wings.

Just as we were finishing, a police officer came running, blowing his whistle.

The lady who started the commotion had one hand over her mouth, the other pointing at the dog, her eyes bulging.

"What's going on here?" said the officer.

"This mallard was tangled in fishline with a hook in its beak," said Julie. "It was struggling right out there. Our dog brought it ashore. I removed the hook and untangled the line. I think it'll be okay." With that, Julie released the duck, which dashed for the water and swam out of reach into the lake.

"What a good dog!" said the officer. "Soft mouth." He smiled, looked at the woman standing nearby, and shook his head. "I guess there's no reason for alarm, then," he said and went on his way.

Troy had learned the value of a soft mouth by retrieving water balloons kids had thrown in the lake. He broke the first one but always brought the rest to shore intact.

Our first sailboat had been *Twiga*. She was such a fine little yacht. We really liked her. Troy, our springer, was such a loving dog that we decided to start a tradition. We would begin the names of our boats and dogs with *T*. It seemed lucky for us.

For the next thirty years, we had dogs, and they came with us almost everywhere we went.

CHAPTER 58

Temerity

We found her at the Erie Yacht Club. She had been "boat of the year" for the racing honors she had won the year before. She was a Morgan 27, five feet bigger than *Twiga*, but a Charlie Morgan designed MORC (Midget Ocean Racing Cup) boat that had won top honors at Erie, Pennsylvania, near our Western New York home the previous year. She didn't have wheel steering or an inboard but had a tiller and a 7.5 Mercury outboard. She was not the quiet, reserved, safe girl next door, but a sexy blond knockout. Her sleek lines, swept-back keel, and streamlined cabin were striking and beautiful.

We fell in love.

Her spinnaker was simply huge, with every color in the rainbow, and she gushed through the water like no boat we had ever experienced. Her name had been *Fat Cat*. She was wide and carried a bustle, or bulge, on each side of her hull to help keep her upright and glide through the waves in a blow. We were not cat people, however, so we renamed her *Temerity*. The word means "arrogant courage." It is not a nice word, but it is a bit obscure and most people don't understand its denotation. "Oh, *Temerity*, timid and merry, I guess." They couldn't have been more wrong. But it was fitting, indeed.

We bought her at the Erie Yacht Club, and they launched her for us.

"I christen thee *Temerity*. May you always take us to sea and always bring us back."

With that, Julie smashed a bottle of champagne over her bow, and she was lowered into the water.

It happened to be Memorial Day weekend when we launched her, and while we were busy doing final preparations for our sail to Barcelona, New York, along the Lake Erie shore, they had a ceremony at the yacht club honoring fallen heroes. Of course, we were polite and attentive as the officers surrounded the flagpole and made short speeches ending with a fusillade of gunfire. Our dog, Troy, on the other hand, an English springer spaniel, a mediocre but enthusiastic hunter, leaped from the boat and made a mad dash down the dock toward the assembled dignitaries, searching the water furtively for the fallen duck. The crowd loved it, but unfortunately, it somewhat tainted the dignity of the occasion.

Our first cruise on *Temerity* was to be from the marina at Barcelona to the cottage at Henderson Harbor. It would involve transit of the Welland Canal, the huge Canadian lock system that allows ships and boats to travel back and forth from Lake Ontario to Lake Erie, avoiding Niagara Falls.

It was a beautiful morning when we set out in our new-to-us boat, but a midafternoon thunderstorm proved to be an omen of what was in store. We shortened sail, but gusty winds hammered us. At Port Colborne, we called into customs, and as we had no radio, we used the *blue phone*, a phone on a utility pole with a blue light over it, to call the lockmaster. He told us three persons were required to take a boat through the locks. He could make an exception as we were going down. We were to stand by until he called us back. It was a bit of a walk from the phone to the boat, and we could hardly hear the ring with all the background noise of the port.

The following morning, we got the call, the giant doors of the lock opened in front of us, and we started our seven-and-a-half-horsepower outboard, casting off the lines and gliding into the vast basin of the lock. We each took a line, one on the bow, the other on the stern, and held on as the boat descended. "Be sure to carry a knife and never tie a line," the lockmaster had told us, sensing this was something new to us. Indeed, once started, it is very hard to reverse the flow of water from a lock. A snagged line can cause a small yacht to be suspended in the air as the water is drained away beneath it. This was serious business. Still, going down a set of locks is relatively easy. In a few hours, we found ourselves on the southern shore of Lake Ontario, ready to embark on our eastward journey. We tied alongside the canal walls in Port Weller and slept soundly.

Southwesterly winds pushed us up the shore past the Niagara River to Wilson, New York, where we pulled in for our second night. There had been some rain during the day, but no thunderstorms. The weather was manageable. No big deal. We even carried the spinnaker for a while. At Wilson, we discovered a forward lower shroud had lost its cotter pin and loosened. We carefully adjusted the turnbuckle and replaced the pin. We rechecked the rig, and the next morning, we headed for Rochester. There were more thunderstorms in the forecast, but we felt we were in control.

This time, it was different. The rain came in sheets with roaring wind, lightning, and thunder, and then rather than dying out, it swung around to the northeast and beat against us with clearing winds. We shortened sail, and Julie went forward to put up our smallest jib. We beat into headwinds for hours before we finally came to the harbor mouth at Rochester. We docked at the Rochester Yacht Club that night, and after a dinner at the club, we slept soundly.

It was the next morning when things got sticky. Winds had come up from the southwest overnight, and we discovered something we had already realized about our little seven-and-a-half Mercury outboard. When placed in reverse, it simply would not stop the boat. Because the exhaust exited through a vent in the center of the propeller, the exhaust gasses would keep the prop from getting a good hold on the water. It would cavitate and produce next to no reverse thrust.

Julie pushed us out of the slip as I tried in vain to move the boat backward against the wind. Our faithful springer spaniel, Troy, saw her effort and leaped ashore to give her some help. Of course, he couldn't do that, and by the time Julie got the boat moving and the motor finally took hold, I was on my own at the helm, powering the boat ahead, with my wife and dog still on the dock. Not good! I moved the boat out of the yacht club and signaled Julie to move to the dock at the river's edge. I thought, if I kept the boat moving and passed close to the dock, Julie could easily swing aboard, and Troy would follow. It was a good idea, but that was when a policeman came by and tried to help. He grabbed the moving boat and, with all his might, stopped it so my wife could step aboard. Big mistake. The boat swung broadside to the wind and crashed sideways into a cement piling, causing a six-inch gash in the side of our prize boat.

By the time we got her swung around and the crew aboard, it was obvious we couldn't go out into that tumultuous lake with a gash in our side. So we moved the boat back to Shumway Marine, the place where we had bought our first boat, *Twiga*, some six years before. The repairs manager there, a man named Wes, looked at the angry scar deeply cut into the side of the boat. He decided the damage was largely superficial, as it did not penetrate the hull, and that it could be repaired with several layers of properly applied fiberglass resin and mat. As time was important, he suggested covering the gash with several layers of heavy duct tape to keep dirt and water from getting into and corrupting the fiberglass. We could have final repairs done in Henderson. The job was done in minutes, and before long, we were on our way.

We rigged a small jib and reefed the main, and once out of the harbor entrance at Rochester, we fell off the wind, let out the sails, and set a course for Sodus. Winds were strong, in the twenty-five- to thirty-knot range, but the boat simply flew. She lifted her bow out of the water as she sped over the top of one wave and plunged down the leading edge of the next. Occasionally, she would round up, heeling far over until her sails flapped wildly and then falling back down again, racing through whitecaps. We had only one set of reef points. Julie struggled forward and released the main halyard, I rounded the boat into the wind, and we clawed the mainsail down. Julie lashed the sail around the boom, and I found I could steer much more easily with just the small jib. Still, we gushed through the waves at over six knots. Rain showers pelted us from time to time. It was a wild day. Julie made sandwiches. Troy wagged his stub of a tail from the cabin below. We held on.

After a while, we overtook another sailboat. It was a Cape Dory 28, just the kind of boat we had been looking for when we bought

Temerity. She was a sweet girl with a long keel, wheel steering, and an inboard diesel. Her crew, too, had dropped their main, but they had a large jib up that was obviously causing them some difficulty. The boat rounded up again and again into the wind. As we got nearer, with the binoculars, we could see they had something new, roller furling, a device intended to roll the jib onto the forestay. A man on the bow was trying to work with it, but there was obviously a problem. Then, in a huge gust of wind, they rounded up, and the boat knocked down to the point where the spreaders on the mast were in the water. We watched in horror as the man on the bow clung to the deck until the boat finally righted and headed into the wind and the sail was, with great difficulty, wound up.

The wind screamed at us. Our single small sail slammed and whipped in the gusts until Julie struggled forward and took it down. Still, *Temerity* made four knots through the water with nothing but the American flag flapping and whipping wildly from its pole on the stern. Before long, the wall at Sodus appeared ahead. Waves were crashing over that wall, sending spray high into the air. I first lowered then started our little outboard, and we powered through the spray between the walls of the harbor entrance into the relative safety of Sodus Bay. We motored to the Sodus Bay Yacht Club and took a place at the end of the pier, right behind the Cape Dory that had entered the harbor just ahead of us.

We made the boat fast to the dock and headed for the clubhouse to sign in. Our Henderson Harbor Yacht Club membership guaranteed us a free night. Troy relished his moment onshore but was ready to return with us in the pelting rain. On the way to the boat, a head appeared from the companionway of the Cape Dory. "Come for a drink, please," said the man, and then he ducked below, out of the rain. We took Troy back to the boat, fed and watered him, and ventured over to the neighboring boat.

Two men greeted us and offered strong drink and a comfortable seat inside their beautiful, new boat. We shared our tales of woe for the day. They were on their second day out from Toronto when the storm hit.

"You wouldn't have believed it if you had seen it. I pulled and pulled on the line to roll up the genoa, but it just wouldn't come. At one point, the wind speed meter read sixty-five knots!" The line just ripped out of my hand, and the sail was all the way out. A huge gust of wind came, and we knocked down, and Ralph was on the bow. He hung on for dear life. The cockpit half-filled with water! I started the engine and put it in gear, and we rounded into the wind. We put the line on a winch, released the sheet, and finally managed to roll the jib up. Oh my god, scared to death!"

I sipped a strong bourbon Manhattan.

"We know a guy," said Tom, "who lives right here in Sodus. Good guy, but he lost his wife recently in an ugly divorce. He has a little cruiser, and he offered to take us to dinner. You two want to join us? Club's dead tonight, but there are neat little nightclubs around the bay. Why don't you join us? He'll pick us up in about half an hour. Said he'd be here at seven. What do you say?"

"Sounds good," I said.

We went back to *Temerity* to change into clean clothes and then put our foul-weather jackets back on. We told Troy to be a good dog and not bark, snapped a lock on the companionway, and walked toward a Marionette 27 that was moored ahead of the Cape Dory, its engine still running. Inside, we met Will. He introduced us to Colleen, a fetching young blonde in low heels, somehow a bit delicate and out of place on this boat on a wild and stormy June night.

With that, Ralph released the lines, and Will accelerated the little cruiser into the gloom. Half an hour or so later, we tied to a dock and, huddled under umbrellas, walked into a restaurant. There was a band. People were dancing. The music was way too loud, but we found a table big enough for the six of us. Our friends on the Dory turned out to be Canadian cigarette salesmen with free samples. Smoking wasn't our thing, but it was the thing in the seventies and the cigarettes were free, so…Of course, there was a drink and another drink and "Let me buy a round" until everyone had more than enough. There was dinner, a fish fry, and then beer. We danced. Fatigue and alcohol owned the night.

That was when we noticed that Colleen was no longer among us. And neither was Will. Julie looked in the women's restroom, but no Colleen. Ralph insisted he had seen this coming and held up the boat keys. At least they hadn't deserted us in the pouring rain and taken the boat. Still, we could hardly abandon them. The night, like the day, was turning into an ugly snarl. Before long, Ralph appeared. It seemed Colleen had called her brother to pick her up as she didn't feel Will was fit to take her home in the boat.

With that, we all went back to the Marionette and had a very subdued ride across the gusty, rainy, lumpy bay to the yacht club, where we were greeted with the mournful howl of our dog, Troy, who met us with mixed emotions.

We took the dog for a short walk in the rain, and back aboard, we quickly undressed, brushed, and flushed and snuggled into the V berth forward, with the sound of rain pounding on the deck over-head. Troy waited until he thought we were asleep and then flopped down between us on the bed. We were so tired even a wet dog couldn't keep us awake.

In the morning, it was strangely quiet. Fog enshrouded the bay. It was still gloomy, but the wind had abated, and it was wonderfully still.

I walked the dog as Julie made a pot of coffee and scrambled up some eggs. The little engine started on the first pull, and we headed out through the gloom into Lake Ontario, where we were met with leftover seas and light southwesterly breezes. We shut off the engine and raised sail. How disappointing. The previous day, the sails had been filled until they were hard as steel, and the boat had flown over the waves. We had sailed where few powerboats dared to venture. Today, the sails hardly filled. We rocked back and forth in huge waves and made little progress.

"Let's try the spinnaker," said Julie.

As the wind, what little there was of it, was on the port quarter, it sounded reasonable. Julie went forward and set the lines, and with the tiller between my legs, I raised the spinnaker pole to an appropri-ate height, set it, and adjusted it for the wind direction. I pulled for all I was worth on the spinnaker halyard, and before long, we were moving through the waves at about four knots. In ten hours or so, before dark, we hoped, we should be home in Henderson Harbor.

But that was not to be. Suddenly, just for a moment, the wind abated and the boat slowed, and then the huge chute began gyrating, wrapping itself round and round the forestay. The boat stopped and rocked and rocked, and with each gyration, the spinnaker wrapped itself again around the forestay. We struggled to take it down, but it was wrapped fast and tight. It wouldn't come down. The pole was close to the forestay, and though we released it and unclipped the sheet, there was no unwrapping the tangle. With a ten-foot spinnaker bubble, filled backward, we motored toward Sodus, the port we had just left, as dark clouds again appeared on the western horizon. Winds like yesterday would surely do us in with the uncontrolled spinnaker in this state. Fortunately, we made it to Sill's Marina, where, with the aid of a gin pole and a boswan's chair, I was hoisted to the masthead and able to untangle the ripstop nylon mess. With that, we filled all our fuel tanks and again headed into the lake. It would be a long, slow motor run as the boat continued to roll with the huge seas across Mexico Bay, a Lake Ontario ship's graveyard, past Stoney Point and into Henderson Bay, where, at eleven that night, in pitch-dark, we dropped anchor in front of the cottage.

The lights were dim on the boat but bright in the cottage.

"I think they're here," said someone inside the warmly lighted building. At that moment, there was an impossibly loud crash, some groaning, and then quiet.

Julie's sister, Carolyn, came alongside in *Appache*, Julie's old dinghy, a few minutes later.

"What happened?" I asked right away.

"Oh, Daddy bumped those shelves on the dresser, the ones with the paint cans and nails and stuff. It fell. Big mess. He wasn't hurt or anything. That's all."

It was a fitting end to a terrible cruise that had begun with a thunderstorm and truly ended with a bang!

That summer, we raced *Temerity* at the yacht club with Julie's cousin Dwight and Janet, his wife. We had fun and were often first across the finish line, but with her thoroughbred handicap, *Temerity* rarely finished among the top boats on corrected time.

We borrowed George Castle's brand-new Chevrolet dump truck and drove back to Erie, where, after much discussion with the dockmaster, we picked up *Temerity*'s iron cradle and moved it four hundred miles to Chaumont.

During our tumultuous cruise and subsequent races, we learned that *Temerity*'s chain plates, mounted in the deck, caused the deck to flex in strong winds. We had Sill's Marina at Sodus reinforce them and anchor them in the woodwork below. She was our boat, and we were determined to make her a winner. Maybe next year.

CHAPTER 59

Trent Severn

The second year of life with our racy broad, *Temerity*, was not altogether easy either. If you remember, our little Mercury 7.5 could not stop the boat very well. That meant that without careful planning, one might crash seven thousand pounds of fiberglass and lead into the dock, causing possible damage to both the boat and the dock. What could we do? I went to our friendly Mercury dealer and explained the problem to him. When I told him that I had a twenty-seven-foot sailboat with a seven-and-a-half outboard, he immediately understood that I needed a bigger motor, much bigger. He obviously was not familiar with keel sailboats. As we had not bought the motor from him and did not rise to his suggestion that we go bigger, he wasn't very interested in our problem.

"I think I saw a bulletin about just that problem, Henry," he said to me. "You can look through that book over there, and maybe you can find it."

Julie and I began pawing through a huge loose-leafed book on the man's desk until we came upon a bulletin about reversing. It explained what we knew to be the problem, which was exhaust gasses being sucked in by the motor's propeller, greatly reducing its efficiency in reverse. It had a two-part solution. First, one would use the template provided and drill two holes, one on each side, in the lower unit of the motor. As this would greatly increase the power of the engine in reverse, one needed to also buy a small fitting that would reinforce the tilt lock so the locking device could keep the motor, with its newfound power, from popping out of the water in reverse. Our dealer happily made a copy of the template for the holes we had to drill and let me fill out a form to order the part we needed. He said he would call us when the part arrived. It would cost seventy-five cents for the part, and it would be delivered with his next order. He would call us when it came in.

I remember laying the motor on its side in the driveway, doing careful measurements, and placing the template in the exact position indicated in the instructions. I used a center punch to mark the center of where the half-inch hole should be drilled and then drilled through the aluminum. We flopped the motor over and did the same thing on the other side. We waited several weeks but didn't hear from the Mercury dealer, so we went back.

"Hmm. Never saw an order for you," he said. "Let's try again." I again filled out the form, but again, we never heard from the dealer. Another visit, another order. What could be going on?

By then, it was May 1977. We wanted to launch our boat. We had decided we would take the boat on an ambitious cruise that summer. We would sail to the Bay of Quinte in Canadian waters, in Northern Lake Ontario, have the mast lowered at Belleville, and then enter the Trent Severn Waterway at Trenton and motor to Perry Sound in the Georgian Bay of Lake Huron. We would then raise the mast and sail through the Georgian Bay and the North Channel of Lake Huron before heading south and sailing down the main lake to the Saint Clair and Detroit Rivers to Lake Erie and back to Dunkirk, near our Western New York home in Chautauqua County.

Our motor would have to be working perfectly for the trip. It would have to not only go forward for hundreds of miles but would also have to be able to stop the boat hundreds of times for every lock and every dockage.

However, the part simply did not arrive. We had ordered it over and over. I was very frustrated. I phoned the distribution center in Buffalo and explained my problem, but they suggested going back to the dealer and ordering it again. Finally, totally frustrated, I called again and asked to speak to the chief executive. Surprisingly, he came on the phone. I explained my problem, our intended cruise, and my frustration.

"Listen," he said, "I have your part in stock. I don't know what is going on, but I'm going to send a rep from my office with that part in his hand to your dealer. He'll get there Saturday morning at about ten. They'll call you from the marina, and you can come down and pick it up in person. How would that be?"

"Thank you," I said. "I'll be waiting for your call."

Sure enough, on Saturday morning, I got a call from the dealer, and an anxious voice suggested I should come to the marina at once. When Julie and I got there, a rather red-faced mechanic was standing next to a man dressed in suit and tie.

"Mr. Danielson," said the man in the suit, "I believe you have tried without success to order this part. Here it is. Please accept it at no charge. We thank you for your business."

I thanked him, and he got back in his car for the two-hour drive back to Buffalo. The mechanic turned to me. "Let me see that part," he said, and I handed it to him.

"This is what you've been fussin' about? Hell, I got half a dozen of these things floatin' around the shop. They seem to come with every order. Don't know what they're for."

So that was that. We had our part. We took it home, and in half an hour, it was installed on the motor. We were ready to go.

We drove to Chaumont and installed the motor on the boat. We stayed at the cottage nights and cooked on our little grill on the porch. It was a wonderful time. The boat was launched, the motor worked beautifully, and for the first time, she would stop on a dime. As soon as school was finished, we were off. We went to Kingston and checked in with customs with nothing to write home about. Then we sailed up the Bay of Quinte to Bellville, Ontario, where we lowered the mast and secured it on deck for the short run to Trenton, where we would enter the Trent Severn Waterway and go cross-country to the southern end of Lake Huron in Georgian Bay. Perry Sound, it was called, and there we would descend an amazing marine railway, where our girl would be carried hundreds of feet down to the Lake Huron waters.

We snaked our way through lovely Canadian towns, crossed Lake Simcoe, and finally arrived at our destination. The news was not good. They told us they had lowered the water in Perry Sound for construction of the new railway that could handle boats of up to six-foot draft. Therefore, there was a question about getting our four-foot, six-inch draft Morgan off the car at the bottom. Other years, it would have been no problem, but with the low water, it could be an issue. They assured us they would try anyway, but it didn't look good. We motored the boat into the marine railway car, and ever so slowly, our girl was moved down the hillside until she entered the water at Perry Sound.

Sure enough, at the end of the railway, when the car hit the bumper at the end of the track, *Temerity's* waterline was still six inches at least above the level of the water.

"Used to have a man here who would haul her halfway up and let her go," said the man in charge. "Got fired for damaging too many boats. Don't do that now."

That was it. There was nothing we could do but have her hauled back up to the top of the escarpment and floated off to buy another pass and head back to Lake Ontario.

"So sorry, don't ya know."

So that was what we did. We started our little Mercury and headed south from just a few hundred yards short of our destination. It was quiet time on board. There was nothing funny about it. We would have to suck up to all our friends and admit that our first cruise on *Temerity* had been a failure.

Temperatures rose. It was thirty-three degrees centigrade, over ninety degrees Fahrenheit, when we got back to Lake Simcoe several days later. We filled our tanks in late afternoon and decided to cross before dark.

We marked our course carefully on the chart and headed out into the lake. But there was something strange. The sky to the west was blue, like everywhere else, but it was a dark blue. Then all hell broke loose. Suddenly, the lake was a mass of dark water, waves formed, and the tops of the waves blew off in gusting winds. Rain pummeled us from above first, then horizontally. Troy, our faithful springer spaniel, darted for the cabin and leaped onto our bed in the bow. Julie clutched the chart in her secure hand, but the wind tore it free, and it followed the dog into the bow of the boat. Whitecaps were everywhere. Waves built and built, and we found ourselves hanging on desperately as the boat rocked and surged in the wind. The little seven-and-a-half Merc roared, then screamed, as its prop was lifted clear on large waves. Worst of all, we found ourselves clinging to a forty-seven-foot aluminum mast tied on deck that began surging fore and aft as the boat plunged into seas and slowed then accelerated as the boat went down the other side. Lightning and thunder punctuated the afternoon. We had been careful to drag one of the shrouds in the water. Would that protect us from this viscous lightning? We hoped.

I remember Julie's scream. "Oh no!" The anchor, so carefully secured to the bow pulpit, broke free when we slammed into an especially large wave. Fastened to the boat by its rode, it was banging against the bottom of the boat. That same wave swept one of the sawhorses that supported the mast into the water. I worked my way forward and hauled on the anchor rode, pulling the little Danforth anchor back on deck and securing it. That was when I noticed another problem. Not only was my weight on the bow lifting the motor out of the water more frequently, the surging of the mast was also literally tearing the bow pulpit, to which the long and heavy mast was secured, off the boat. I did what I could to secure it using the anchor rode. On my knees on the plunging bow, waves breaking over me, I wrapped the line around the pulpit, which had sheared several set screws, and lashed it as tight as I could to the forward mooring cleats. This did not look good. Julie, in the meantime, was hanging on to the mast as it surged forward and aft, tugging at the stern pulpit, which also was breaking free. We literally exhausted ourselves in our attempt to secure the mast, all the while steering the boat, doing our best to keep her on course.

Then, as suddenly as it had begun, the storm abated. It was nearly dark as we pulled into the southern port, where the canal would take us back to Belleville. We tied to a dock there, aligned the mast, did our best to refasten the pulpits, tightened set screws, and thankful that we had survived, enjoyed a hearty dinner.

Passersby mentioned the afternoon squall but seemed to have no idea of its intensity. We slept soundly.

Back on Lake Ontario at Belleville, we waited our turn to raise our mast. A friendly Canadian offered his help. His name was John. He and his wife had a CS-27, and after I related our tale of woe, he invited Julie and me to his boat for drinks. He simply could not imagine what we had been through. But he suggested that rather than simply giving up on our summer, we should follow him to Toronto, where he would show us a good time. We accepted his kind invitation. Several days later, we pulled into Ontario Place, where John was sure we could find a place to moor the boat in for a few days. No problem.

After dinner aboard at Ontario Place, Julie took Troy for a little walk. Things looked better all of a sudden. The huge CN Tower shone in the distance as the city of Toronto illuminated the night. Ontario Place, a huge park, was a great place for a dog to romp. Troy ran and jumped and played and panted and then…then he became fascinated with a particular little area with a few thick bushes. He was sniffing and sniffing, and there was some commotion. It seemed he had interrupted a little tryst, a private moment between two young lovers. They didn't see humor in the situation. A few minutes later, on the way back to the boat, Troy was again distracted, this time by young people at a hot dog stand. They were throwing him hamburgers and buns wrapped in paper, and he was loving it. But at that stand, there was a policeman who told Julie, "There are no dogs at Ontario Place!" We would have to find new dockage if we were to stay in Toronto.

The next day, at the suggestion of our new friend, John, we headed for National Yacht Club, where they would reciprocate with Henderson Harbor and let us stay.

John wasn't a member, but he was on the wait list and had a nearby slip. There was to be a race on Sunday. "Let's do it," said John.

"What do you mean?" I asked.

"The race!" he said. "Let's race your boat on Sunday morning. Pat and I will crew for you. We sailed with you from Trenton to Toronto. *Temerity* goes like a shot. I'm sure they would be happy to have you race at national. We'll crew. What do you say, eh?"

And so we did. We had a PHRF (Performance Handicap Racing Fleet) handicap, and we joined the race.

The race was surreal. Unlike at Henderson, where the fastest boats started first, here, the slower boats went first, and the faster boats had to work their way through the slower fleets. It was a foggy morning, impossible conditions for us in a huge industrial harbor with no visible landmarks, but John knew the course, and he and Julie figured out the headings and timing, and our plotting was right on. We found ourselves farther ahead of some of the fleet at each mark.

One memorable moment left a lasting impression. Two long sleek *R* boats, wooden boats from a previous era, slipped from the fog to our stern. They were in a spinnaker duel. The leeward boat was *taking the windward boat up into the wind.* The spinnaker of the upwind boat whipped ineffectively in the wind as the leeward boat slipped by and disappeared again into the mist. For a moment, we had slipped into an earlier time.

We had our spinnaker up too. We gushed through small waves as the finish loomed just ahead. Other boats had missed marks or couldn't find the finish, but we finished with gusto! At the end of the race, we were awarded a flag. It was for third place, but it was an honor to be proud of.

Afterward, I called home. My mother, in Lakewood, had bad news. My father had fallen and broken his leg. She didn't drive. They needed help.

We said our goodbyes to our new friends, John and Pat, and sailed out of Toronto Harbor straight for Port Weller, the northern end of the Welland Canal, between lakes Ontario and Erie. We arrived around midday, went to the blue phone, and called in.

"This is the sailing vessel *Temerity*," I said. "We are a twenty-seven-foot sailing vessel and need passage southbound."

The person on the other end of the phone had a list of questions for us. "Names of the crew, please."

"Henry Danielson, captain, and Julie Danielson, crew."

"We're sorry, but three able-bodied crew are required for passage upbound. There will be no exception to this rule due to the turbulence of the locks in the upbound direction."

What? We had never heard of such a rule. Hadn't we gone through the previous spring? Of course, that was downbound, the easy way. We would be going up. It was different. We were tied to the wall of the canal, and there were tourists walking by. A family with a twelve-year-old son looked admiringly at the boat. We started to chat.

"We've got to get back to Jamestown for a family emergency," I said. "We need a third person to get through the canal. Do you think your son would like to ride with us and be our crew?" I then added, "You could pick him up in Port Colborne, watch us along the way."

The boy was thrilled by the opportunity. His mom and dad seemed less enthusiastic, but they were just about to agree when it began to rain. That was it. The family darted for their car, and that was the end of that idea.

We tried using Troy Danielson, our dog's name, as the third crew member, but that really riled the lockmaster. We decided to wait for the next shift, but they had been warned. What would we do? Finally, we phoned a friend, Bob Hakel, in Ashville, who got his wife, Patty, to drive him to Port Weller. He would be our third crew member.

When he arrived at noon of the following day, we pushed off and motored through the huge locks up and up to the city of Port Colborne, where we tied to the wall and headed to a nearby restaurant for dinner. The upbound run had certainly been much more turbulent than our previous passage, and the third crew member was welcome indeed. As we were quite tired, we were hardly prepared for the topless waitress at a canal-side restaurant who took our order that night. We had not realized what a liberal and free place Canada could be. Bob had intended to sail across Lake Erie with us, but strong southwest winds with small-craft advisories kept us in port, and with only worsening conditions in the forecast, he called his wife, who came to pick him up. Two days later, Julie and I headed for Barcelona, but the southwest winds drove us twenty miles back to Dunkirk, where we tied up and spent the night before working our way west through, lessening winds and seas, to Barcelona, the following day.

Back at home, I could take Dad to his doctor's appointments and take Mom shopping. Things were okay. He was recovering nicely.

It had been a frustrating summer. Still, we had made new friends in Canada and learned much more about ourselves and our boat. In late October, Bill Sharp, a friend with a large Chevy station wagon hitched on a trailer, and he and I went to Chaumont to drag *Temerity*'s heavy iron cradle back to Barcelona, which would be her new home on Lake Erie. The Northern New York community of Henderson Harbor had changed from the rich green of summer to autumn, with blowing leaves, nearly bare trees, cold rain, and chilling wind. When we arrived back in Western New York with the cradle that Halloween night, our boat rolled and plunged with the waves in the man-made harbor at Barcelona. Before long, she would be snug in her barn over the long, cold winter.

CHAPTER 60

The North Channel

The following spring, we relished having just a twenty-minute drive to the boat rather than the five-hour ordeal of years before. *Temerity* was at her mooring by mid-May, and Julie and I enjoyed afternoon and evening sails out of Barcelona, even on school days. The evening offshore breezes offered exhilarating sailing with small waves. As we had in Henderson Harbor, we could drop the mooring with sails up, sail out of the harbor into the lake, and return without ever a thought of using the motor. That was real sailing, and we loved it.

The lure of the North Channel of Lake Huron had only grown stronger over the winter. When school let out for the summer, we were ready to go. There was a little very informal yacht club over the marina at Barcelona, and they had welcomed Julie and me as members. Our card from the Barcelona Lighthouse Yacht Club might give us reciprocal privileges with other yacht clubs around the lake. Even though they didn't belong to any organizations of yacht clubs, the card might give us an occasional free night.

Of course, we would be heading southwest along the Lake Erie shoreline, and southwesters were the predominant winds, so unlike sailing to Henderson Harbor to the east, this run was all upwind. *Temerity* loved sailing to windward. She was in her element. Along the way, we stopped at the Erie Yacht Club, Ashtabula, the Cleveland Yachting Club, Vermillion, South Bass Island, and finally, the Gross Isle Yacht Club at the foot of the Detroit River. It had been an exhilarating cruise so far. We had been welcomed everywhere we went. However, we were running short on supplies.

One of the things cruisers learn quickly is that convenient places to dock often aren't very near places to provision, like grocery stores. Also, small towns where it may be convenient to stop at often don't have public transportation, even taxis. So here we were at Gross Isle Yacht Club, basically out of food. We enjoyed dinner at the club, but we wanted to stock up. We walked around the yard to where a young man was swimming under a beautifully sleek race boat. He climbed out of the water, and as we visited, he asked if we needed anything. "Is there a grocery store around here?" I asked.

"Yeah, just down the street, a mile or so. Why don't you take my car and go get what you need?" He picked up his pants from a chair and handed me the keys. "You do drive a stick, right?" I nodded. "Right over there. I need a shower."

There it was, a brand-new Ford Cobra. Not the two-seater sports car, but a little hardtop. I couldn't believe the pedal pressure on the clutch. Julie and I rumbled down the road to the grocery, where we stocked up and returned to the club. Its huge engine begged to spin tires and misbehave, but this was a gift, not something to be abused.

We held her back and parked it right where we found it. "Can we take you to lunch?" I said to the young man when we returned his keys.

"Nope. Gotta get back to work. Oh, you heading upriver in that Morgan?"

"Yes."

"Look, when you get up to the Blue Water Bridge at the top of the Saint Clair River, just before Lake Huron, you'll be dealing with a really strong current. It's gonna be all that little seven-and-a-half can handle. Get really close to the Canadian shore when you go under the bridge. The back current will carry you through. It'll be all you can do to make it. Good luck."

With that, he was gone.

It took a full day to motor up the Detroit River and another day to get through Lake Saint Clair and the Saint Clair River to the Port Huron Yacht Club, near the imposing Blue Water Bridge, under which huge ships downbound raced by huge ships lumbering upbound as they plowed through the powerful current.

A young couple there had an Endeavor 32, a brand-new sail-boat, and we quickly became friends. They were clearly smitten by Troy, who somehow made friends with everyone. "Your friend is right," they assured us. "Stay close to the Canadian shore. You should be able to make it. But stay close and then go up the Canadian side for a while so you don't get sucked back down into the river. Oh yes, and don't go too far on the Canadian side. Kettle Rock looms there and has been the undoing of many a sailboat."

Light northerly winds prevailed when we set out the following day. We got as close to the Canadian side as we dared, and inch by inch, we moved under the bridge and into Lake Huron. They sug-gested they would go as far as Goodrich but that we should be able to make it to Bayfield by dark. Obviously, they didn't know the Morgan 27. With our motor in the raised position and our 160 percent jenny, we quickly passed the larger boat and moved easily up the eastern shore. We pulled into Goodrich that evening, but our newfound friends must have stopped at Bayfield. From there, the following day we sailed again north to Tobermory and the most southerly entrance to the North Channel.

We were in a land of shoals and shipwrecks, islands, and lovely coves. It was a real cruising ground, something that we had never before seen. We had a set of charts, and though new to us, they were old. One must remember that in the late 1970s, there were few aids to navigation. We would use a compass, which we carefully compen-sated, for direction. We knew to figure in deviation caused by mag-netic influences on the boat and variation caused by the difference between the magnetic and true north poles. For speed, we had a knot meter and log, but that was it. There was no loran or GPS for us. We would see an island or point of land and locate it on the chart. We would take bearings with a hand-bearing compass and mark the chart. We knew when we took bearings from two separate features, and the lines of position crossed, that was our location. Navigation was a full-time job. Especially for newbies like us. If we were lost, we were lost. That was it. We still didn't have a two-way marine radio.

We paid attention and referred to the islands and landforms we passed by their names. We constantly took bearings and marked our position on the chart.

We headed for Bay Finn. It was a fjord, the only one on the Great Lakes. I remember well the towering sides of the long inlet that led to the pool at the end. There, we dropped anchor off the stern and moved the bow to huge rocks, where, with a long painter, we could tie to trees. The water there was quiet. It was simply a lovely spot. After dinner that evening, the several cruisers there, along with their families, gathered for a campfire overlooking the boats and the pool. People brought wine and beer. It was a lovely setting. Of course, Troy made friends with everyone. He let little kids pet him and pull his ears. He would fetch sticks when kids threw them (not in the water, please!), and he was just his most agreeable self. Then someone suggested we have a talent show. Some of the kids said they could sing or dance. When it was our turn, we said we would have a dog show. There really wasn't much enthusiasm for the event until it was Troy's turn. He would come to whoever called him, sit, roll over, fetch, sit up, and stay until released. He loved the attention. Everybody agreed. Troy was the winner.

The next day, we walked to Cobalt Lake, a short distance from the pool, where, we were told, the sparkling, clear water held no fish because it was, according to the guidebook, radioactive.

We had a wonderful cruise. We anchored at Crocker Island and the Benjamin Islands and visited Little Current, where we bought a Hudson Bay Point blanket in red and black. Lake Huron offered us a magnificent downwind sail to Port Huron, where we sped downriver with the current behind us back to Lake Erie.

Finally, we had enjoyed a successful cruise in our new boat. We had visited and enjoyed travel in a foreign country. True, most of the people we cruised with were Americans, but we had found friends, navigated challenging waters, and learned a great deal about ourselves and our abilities.

CHAPTER 61

Creative Writing: A Class and Connie's Club

Over the years, some of the electives at the high school prospered, and others faded away. There was an opportunity for me to teach a creative writing class, and I jumped at it.

It had been taught by another teacher, but he grew tired of it. I was excited when I got the class, but it would be very hard work. Though the classes were small, it seemed there were papers for me to read and evaluate every night. That, along with other lesson plans, was challenging. Still, the youthful enthusiasm demonstrated by those in class made it more than worthwhile.

Mostly, the class revolved around writing poetry. I would bring in a sample of some form of poetry and have the students imitate the style, using their own material. We started with haiku, a Japanese form consisting of three lines of five, seven, and five syllables. It was everyone's job to create at least one example by the end of the class. The following day, we would copy our haikus on the board and discuss each piece. I would do one too. Interestingly, the ones I wrote were not always the best examples. I think, however, the fact that I would share my work with students made a big difference. They loved it when a student shared something better than my example. We talked about irony, about surprise.

The most technical writing we did was the sonnet. Students were asked to write a complete sonnet. We read sonnets by Shakespeare and John Donne as well as other, more contemporary writers. Still, we stuck to fourteen lines and iambic pentameter. We could have an octave and a sestet or end the sonnet in a couplet, Shakespearean-style. It was challenging, indeed, but I never ceased to be amazed at what these young people could fashion. I remember one young man the class nicknamed the Sonnet King. Somehow, he thought in iambic pentameter and pumped out amazing sonnets one after another.

Mostly, we focused on free verse poetry. Every Friday, we had a freewriting. Everyone had to write something, but the form was up to them. We looked at E. E. Cummings, a favorite, but free verse was truly free.

About the same time, the *Post-Journal*, our local paper, began the "A-Plus" page. It was a publication of student work in Southern Chautauqua County English classes. It proved to be a wonderful incentive for my creative writing students. I would type up the best work my students did and give it to a fellow teacher who was on the committee for A-Plus. These young people and their parents were so thrilled to see their work in print that it made all the work involved most worthwhile.

Eventually, I was asked to be the A-Plus representative from Jamestown High School. I got Thursday afternoon off once a month, which meant special lesson plans for the sub, lots of extra work, but no extra pay. Still, it was very rewarding.

We did other writing in the creative writing classes as well. We wrote dialogue, conversations between two characters, perhaps from different novels. We created stories and even plays. We rewrote and rewrote, trying to improve what we had done. Although this technique is endorsed by successful authors, it did not sit well with many of my students. They wanted to be done when they were finished.

There was one young lady who was very special. She loved to write poetry. She wrote about all kinds of things, but her sense of surprise, her imagery, and her use of words were, well, exceptional. She would show me work she had done on her own and ask me about it. She was attractive, always appropriate, one of those kids who is so special, a gift to a teacher. Her name was Connie Gould.

One day, Connie came in after school and asked whether I might sponsor a creative writing club after school. She said they had one at Lincoln, where she went to junior high. I said I thought we might be able to. "Can we meet on Tuesdays?" she wondered. I agreed, and that was how the script club got its start. *Scriptus Est* was the original name. "It is written," in Latin, said Connie.

I agreed to write up a notice for the morning announcements:

> *Anyone interested in forming a creative writing club, please come to Room 214, Mr. Danielson's room, after school on Tuesday.*

We got some recruits. We organized, elected officers, and decided our goals and aspirations for the club. We would write and share our writing, and we would publish a collection of our best work at the end of each school year. We would make copies of our book on the school duplicating machine, and sell it. Connie was the president. We met regularly, we wrote, we selected the best work, and we laboriously typed it on the manual Royal typewriter in my room. We typed it on mimeograph masters. There could be no errors. At the end of the year, we would compile the books, and every club member would get one. Extras could be sold for a quarter each. The club would have a treasury.

One Sunday afternoon, Julie and I had been skiing at Allegany State Park. There were groomed trails, miles of them, enough to exhaust and exhilarate the strongest skier. It had been a wonderful time. On the way home, we had the radio on. There was a news item about a hit-and-run accident on Orr Street in Jamestown. A woman had been killed. No further information was released. I knew two women who lived on Orr Street—one was a fellow English teacher, and the other was Connie. Orr Street was a long road with many houses. Why was I so uncomfortable?

Sure enough, later that evening, we learned it was Connie. She had been walking with her boyfriend on the wrong side of Orr Street on Saturday night when a car came up from behind, striking her and killing her instantly. The car sped away. A hit-and-run.

The school, the community, was devastated. I remember the funeral, the tears, the weeping parents. We collected some of Connie's work, and her parents added much more for a book in Connie's memory. The book was published locally, and it was an immediate success. She would have been very proud.

In spite of our loss, or perhaps because of it, the club continued. We changed the name to Script Club. It became official, and I was paid to be its sponsoring teacher. Every year, I agreed to take sailing the students who stayed with me the whole year and who worked to make our publication a success. By then, we had sold the Pearson 22 and had gotten a larger Morgan 27 sailboat, which we kept at Dunkirk Yacht Club on Lake Erie. Generally, there were only three or four students with us. They had to get permission slips signed by their parents, and they had to stick with me to the end of the school year. We had memorable sails.

I remember one young lady who never wrote for us but who diligently typed those mimeo masters. When we headed north toward Dunkirk and went over the escarpment with the vast expanse of Lake Erie below us, stretching out to blend with the blue sky, I said, "Well, there's Lake Erie."

That young lady looked at me and said, "What lake? I don't see no lake."

She had never seen a body of water she couldn't see across. I could hardly believe what I had heard. She had most likely spent her whole life in Jamestown. We all went sailing and enjoyed the rush of water on the hull, the wind in the sails. We kept heeling to a minimum, but we enjoyed what was left of the afternoon. On the way home, we stopped at Pizza Hut for dinner. It was always a good time. No one ever got seasick or was anything but polite and grateful.

But Script Club wasn't over yet.

Not by a long shot.

We kept at it until I retired.

CHAPTER 62

Nero's Fable

Years later, well into the eighties, our local Jamestown Community College sponsored a contest for anyone who could create an original dramatic production onstage at the college. There would be a cash prize for the winner. Script Club had grown by then. We had perhaps half a dozen strong writers, not so much from my creative writing class, but from the honors program at the school. They wanted to enter. As I remember, we had a little money in our treasury, and it would be enough to pay for our application. The application was a contract. Seats would be sold at the theater. By signing, I would guarantee that the group would perform. We had no play, not even an idea, but we did have time, and we had enthusiasm. I signed the document, and with several of our officers, we drove to the office at JCC and dropped it off with the required fee. That got the creative juices flowing.

What we came up with was a play called *Nero's Fable*. Nero, of course, was the emperor who played his fiddle while Rome burned. Our play was the story of a man who neglects his family and his children. He walks away from them when they need him most. He betrays their trust. I remember, when they first presented their outline to me, I was so impressed with the idea. I suggested they might have the father, the man, Nero, be seated onstage as an old man throughout the play. So the whole play would be a kind of flashback.

They liked the idea. "The old man," said Steph. "That can be you."

They wrote me into the play as well.

I would walk on, a sorry old man, sit in a chair in the corner, and watch my life unfold before me. At the end, I would walk off. I would have no speaking part, but I would be onstage, in costume. I was really moved. They worked so hard on writing the lines. One girl, Debbie, had to scream during the play. Her scream, I remember, was so convincing at practice I was concerned someone would call the police. Practice, we did. We practiced after school in the classroom, and then we signed out the stage at the theater, which was really a theater in the round, at JCC. We practiced evenings and even one Saturday morning. There was one girl with a very minor part who said she just couldn't make the practices. She stopped coming to meetings as well. Someone else took her part.

Finally, it was time for the production. We had costumes. We had makeup. Susanna had recorded theme music, "Blind Man," which we would play as I walked onto the stage at the beginning and walked off at the end. We had a dress rehearsal and, then, opening night.

Ours would be the first production of the night. Our director, Steph, decided I should be seated, in costume, in the lobby before the play started, an old man in a shabby suit with a sad face, a hat pulled down over my eyes. When our theme music started, I would stand and walk down the aisle and onto the stage, where I would take my seat for the rest of the play.

People were filing in, paying their admission, and moving to their seats. I sat there staring down. It was almost time. "Mr. Danielson," I heard an unfamiliar voice say. "Mr. Danielson!" The second time, the voice was a little too loud for me to ignore. I lifted my hat and my head only to be staring into the eyes of a clearly angry woman.

"Why won't you let my granddaughter be in your play? You said she couldn't be in your play, and I want to know why!"

People were gathering around us. There was a professor of English at the college there with his mouth open. I thought he was going to pass out. I tried to understand.

"Nellie?" I said. "She told us she couldn't come to practices. I said she had to come to practices to be in the play."

"That's not what she told me!" And with that, the angry woman stormed out of the theater.

I pulled the black hat back over my eyes and slumped back into my seat. We were definitely not off to a good start.

A few minutes later, the recorded music began. I stood and walked onstage. The rest of the production was perfection. I was so proud of those kids. They were wonderful!

There was a professional radio announcer who did a dramatic reading and another production. We won a cash prize.

Julie and I had a cast party at our house a few nights later. The kids made tacos. We all had a wonderful time.

Again, there was simply amazing learning going on here. There was self-imposed discipline; there was writing, memorizing, and acting. There was stagecraft, directing, costumes, makeup. They did it, not me. I was so proud of those young people I was beyond words.

It had all started with Connie's request for a creative writing club. The club was a success. It had offered hundreds of students the opportunity to express themselves in writing and see their work in print. Finally, we saw the results of our work onstage. What a thrill for all of us!

CHAPTER 63

The Marathon

As I mentioned earlier, winter weekends for Julie and me were always far different from weekends when I was growing up in Western New York. My father hated the cold and snow, and we would sit in front of the television on Sunday afternoons, watching football games or golf, building a fire in the fireplace, and he and Mom would enjoy a cocktail or two.

It was Julie that changed all that. She loved to ski, and she and I would go cross-country skiing anytime there was enough snow on the ground to do it. I remember one miserable, rainy winter afternoon, we were at my parents' house in Lakewood. There was a cross-country ski race on television, and Julie, sitting on the couch, announced, "I'm going to do that someday."

My father put down his paper, turned to her, and said, "Don't be silly! That takes years and years of practice. Very few people could ski like that for all those miles."

That was all it took.

There had been talk about possibly hosting a cross-country ski race from Panama to Westfield, across trails that had been set aside in Chautauqua County. When the formal announcement came out, Julie was one of the first to sign up. The race would be fifty-five kilometers, or about thirty-four miles in length, and it would be the first Saturday in February. The terrain was rough, and though there were bridges over streams, the race would take us into and out of

Chautauqua Gorge. It would be especially challenging. It was very unusual for Julie to do something I didn't do, but I volunteered to be a photographer for the race, not a participant. It was just more than I could imagine.

But Julie…she was used to challenges.

Julie had been stricken with polio when she was eight. She was paralyzed and suffered greatly as a child. When she was in eighth grade, she needed surgery, as her back had been so badly deformed by the disease. I knew her then. She sat in front of me in arithmetic class. She went away, had her operation, and came back to school months later in a full-body brace. One-third of her vertebrae had been fused in the operation. She could sit and walk and even run after the surgery. No one knew how it would work out in the long run.

Julie had finished high school, gone to college, where she competed on the swim team, married me, completed her Peace Corps assignment, and taught chemistry at Southwestern—why couldn't she compete in a fifty-five-kilometer ski marathon? She loved to ski. She simply glided over the snow, dipping into valleys, artfully slipping over narrow bridges. She would get far ahead of me and come back to see how I was doing. I didn't like that part. She was a natural.

We practiced and we practiced. We skied weekends at Allegany and drove to Panama to ski the trail after school. We had only an hour or so after school before dark. There was a lean-to a few miles down the trail. It became our goal to ski there and back before dark. A long descent made going in fun, but climbing the hill to get back out was another matter.

I remember the day I drove her to Westfield for the first marathon. It was very cold, below zero. We registered in the Westfield High School, and then the racers boarded buses to be taken to the start. My friend Ted and I drove there as we were volunteer photographers for the race, not participants. I remember, at the start, there were over a thousand racers in the field. Snow was coming down, and a helicopter hovered overhead. They fired a cannon, and the racers were off. There was a young man from Norway named Pere who sprung into the lead and never relinquished it. He was world-class. Ted and I followed the group, arriving at each road crossing just as the leaders plunged from the woods, crossed the road, and dived back into the forest. I got a photo of Julie as she burst into a clearing, her cheeks rosy, with a determined look on her face. How could she be expected to race with these people, a thirty-something high school chemistry teacher?

When the race was over, Pere, the Norwegian, had won, hands down. Julie finished first for women thirty to forty. She had won her age-group. I remember the applause when she picked up her trophy. It made me so proud.

Two years later, I entered along with Julie. The first time, I got a silver medal. That meant I made it two-thirds of the way. After that, until the marathon was discontinued for bad weather, I always managed to finish. Julie kept winning, finishing hours ahead of me. She was amazing!

I remember some of the things that happened along the way. Of course, I saw things farther back, unlike my wife, who was at the front. I remember one young man who had heavy old skis and who wore a down jacket. He explained to me that he was a runner. He thought if he could run a marathon, this should be a piece of cake. He exploded off the starting line, dashing off with the leaders. A few miles down the path, I saw him off to the side, red-faced and panting. He had overdressed with his down jacket. He was wringing wet, amazed that the rest of us were skiing by him.

Another time, I followed a group of men from out of state. When they came to the first log bridge, one of the men got his ski stuck between two of the logs that made up the structure. He pulled and pulled, but he couldn't get it free. People were backing up behind him. Someone suggested he release the ski and simply walk around and retrieve it from the ice on the creek below. He used his pole to release the binding, and the ski fell to the ice. He removed his other ski, ran to the far shore, and slogged through the snow to the ice and walked out to get his ski. Just as he picked it up, the ice broke, and he found himself waist-deep in freezing water.

There were falls and other injuries, but at every road crossing, there was an ambulance, fire truck, or police car with the motor running—a warm, safe place to be rescued.

Julie competed in all but one of the marathons. That unfortunate year, Julie and I had a Super Bowl party, as we always did, and we invited everyone to go skiing before the festivities. There were half a dozen or so of us gliding through the woods that Super Bowl Sunday afternoon. Julie had a fall. She said her leg hurt. We went home, and she cooked dinner for everyone and we enjoyed the game. It wasn't until the next morning, at the insistence of one of our friends, that she went to the hospital for an x-ray. She had broken her leg. There would be no marathon for her that year.

Still, the Chautauqua Overland Ski Marathons were an important part of our lives. They made living in the cold and snowy north so much more enjoyable compared to sitting in front of a blaring television, wishing you were somewhere else. Julie got a gold medal in each race she skied, finishing first in her age group two times, once in her thirties and once in her forties.

A highlight of those years was the year we competed in the Gatineau, a race near Montreal in Canada. That was a race on an international scale, with many top-notch competitors from all over the world. The trails were wide and well groomed, the hills steep. Even I finished, albeit with a broken pole and a broken ski. I'm sure I couldn't have gone another mile. Julie got a trophy for finishing in the top 20 percent of her age group. They called it the top 20 percent club. She was the only one to win an award in our group. We all enjoyed an unforgettable meal at a wonderful French restaurant. It was a never-to-be-forgotten weekend.

It was the experience skiing that gave us an opportunity to teach skiing at Chautauqua Institution, which we did with several friends for a number of years. A busload of people would arrive from Cleveland on a Saturday, and our students, older people, would stay in a heated lodge, Bellinger Hall, at the institution. Julie and I and our good friends Bill and Kathy would then teach them to ski. We would begin on the grounds of Chautauqua, teaching them to pole and kick and glide. We would also teach them to fall without hurting themselves and to get up after a fall. Then we would ski around the institution and, if the ice was suitable, onto Chautauqua Lake. The second day, we would take everyone to the Overland Trail, where they could ski in a prepared track. It was great fun. Everyone seemed to have a good time.

Skiing was indeed part of our lives. Sometimes we skied right from our house, out the back door, and up into the woods. Other times we would go down to frozen Chautauqua Lake and ski there. Most often, we would load the skis in the car and drive ten miles or so to the trail near Panama, or forty miles to Allegany. However we did it, it was good conditioning and good winter fun.

CHAPTER 64

Iceboats

Before I was born, my father was given an iceboat. It was a gift from a wealthy man who lived on the shores of Chautauqua Lake in summer and along the Hudson River in winter. It was a heavy wooden vessel, a sloop with jib and main. It was an aft steerer. There was a platform where several adults could lie down to avoid the low boom and a place for the helmsperson to sit aft. There was a reinforced crossways arch that supported the two outboard runners. The sails were canvas. It took several men to carry the parts onto the ice and most of a morning to assemble and rig. Once it was ready, helmsman and crew would push it along to get it moving and hop aboard. The wind took it from there. Unfortunately, on Chautauqua Lake, there was generally too much snow for much of an iceboating season. I sailed on it a time or two, but age, disuse, and a little vandalism led to its end.

In later years, several people at the Chautauqua Lake Yacht Club bought DN iceboats. My cousin Charlie Carlson was one. They were small and light, with a single sail. While I was in college, we would have informal races across the lake to the crib at Greenhurst and back. It was a new thrill. The crosspiece was aft, with a forward-steering runner. Goggles were needed along with a helmet and very warm clothing, as chips of ice flew from the forward runner as it sped over the crusty ice.

Pull on the sheet and feel the boat accelerate, accelerate sometimes to more than sixty miles per hour. The windward side would lift as the little boat all but flew over the rock-hard ice, one hand on the steering, one on the sheet. Watch out for skaters and ice fishermen! Head into the wind to come about, hear the runners roar as they skidded over the ice in a hail of ice crystals, the boom passed overhead, and the helmsperson set the new course. "Never sit on the sheet but let it drag behind" was a rule for us. In a gust, it must be eased to keep the sleek craft from capsizing, serious trouble at that speed.

After Julie and I were married, cousin Charlie gave us his DN. There were a few good years when cold and good ice came without snow, but they were few indeed. The DN was a one-man boat; others had to wait their turn, standing on the ice. It was probably the coldest sport in the world. A glass of scotch and water would freeze to slush if left for a few minutes on the ice. Our feet would do the same. Still, the adrenaline rush of such speed so close to the ice warmed us to the core.

Those were unforgettable times.

CHAPTER 65

Student Teachers

One of the many obligations that come with teaching is preparing others who have chosen the same profession. When one agreed to take a student teacher, he or she might be paid with a tuition waver for the graduate-level class of choice. It was understood that the student teacher successfully pass required teaching courses and be proficient in the field he or she was to teach. Student teaching would simply be practical experience for him or her and qualify that person to apply for a teaching position.

My first student teacher came with a very strong recommendation from her supervising professor. She was exceptionally bright, but she had a mild handicap. "She was very short," he said. I was not concerned at that time.

I met Ann the first time when she came to my room during exam week in January. She had a condition called dwarfism. She had very short legs and arms but a normal head and body. She was healthy and very bright. She was a strong speaker and was eager to take on the challenges of teaching school. I was a bit concerned, of course. How would she deal with high school students? They are not always the most sensitive people in the world. I had heard horror stories of young women student teachers bursting into tears at the hands of high school kids. Some students are very understanding, but others can be downright rude. How would she deal with classes? Would she be able to discipline unruly students? Would they do the homework she assigned? I just didn't know what to think.

Ann couldn't reach the blackboard in the classroom, so she carefully used a chair before the class to stand on to write topics she would cover in class on the board. She used a pointer during class. That worked fine. Her strength was, however, in her personality and wit. I had no idea. She knew everyone's name on day 1 of her student teaching career. She called students by name. She answered their questions and reacted to their comments with humor and intelligence. She had reasonable limits, but she could put unruly students in their place with a wry comment. No one fell asleep in her classes. They didn't dare. Even students who were easily distracted paid attention. There was a large powerful young man, a member of our winning football team, who took a particular liking to Ms. Johnson. I think, had anyone given her a really hard time, he or she might have had him to deal with as well.

One day, she told me that she was very disappointed in some of the students' inability or unwillingness to properly punctuate their work. We had done lessons on punctuation, but there seemed to be little enthusiasm and little measurable improvement.

The next day, Ann came to class with two stacks of signs. One was Mr. Comma, a profile of a man's face in the outline of a comma. The other was Ms. Period, a woman's face in a circle. She passed out one of each to each of the students and then went to the front of the class, where she explained that she would read a story and everyone would hold up either Mr. Comma or Ms. Period at the appropriate place in the narrative.

I would have expected something like this for an elementary school class, but high school? Was I wrong! She carried it off. The kids were eating out of her hand. They held up their signs, and either they got it right or they heard from her. There was energy in that classroom. Measurable improvement. I will never forget it.

She loved teaching literature and writing. *A natural teacher.* She corrected papers beautifully, wrote excellent exams, and did all I could ask of her. Unfortunately, assignments like study hall with over a hundred students, cafeteria duty, or any situation where she didn't know students by name was difficult for her. She eventually dropped out of teaching and became a successful attorney.

Another time, I had a young lady I found particularly smart and attractive. She worked hard at her lessons and developed the skill of walking toward disruptive students or situations rather than away from them. The English department had bought the novel *The Phantom of the Opera* to be taught in grade 10. The book was filled with details and lengthy description, and it left the students cold. This gal had seen the production of Andrew Lloyd Webber's musical in Toronto and somehow got a copy of the libretto, or manuscript of the play. I had a recording of the songs in the musical, which we played in class as the students read the various parts aloud. The story came to life. It was a teaching success. Afterward, she showed the black-and-white silent film of *Phantom* from the 1930s.

Students groaned. "Black-and-white?" they complained. "No sound?"

But silent movies are very hot media, meaning they require more personal involvement to follow than films with sound. Would they watch it at all?

She gave a test on the differences between the Lloyd Webber musical and the silent movie. The kids aced the test. They had indeed watched and absorbed the silent film. It was a win for all of us.

In my experience, student teachers were wonderful. They knew the music and literature of the day and often capitalized on that. I remember one young man who was able to direct the class to retell the story of *Romeo and Juliet* using contemporary, popular music. That was something I couldn't do. Student teachers sometimes had their weaknesses, often not understanding dress codes for teachers, but they were generally well versed and eager to teach the wonders of reading and writing to my students. I learned a great deal from them. Certainly, working with them made me a better teacher. I hope working with me helped them as well.

CHAPTER 66

Ashville

Back in Ashville, our lives became ever more interesting. We insulated and insulated the house. We added insulation to the attic and removed the wallboard on the inside of exterior walls, installed fiberglass insulation and, after having the old steel windows replaced, put up new wallboard. The price of oil, which had been nineteen cents when we bought the place, had risen to over a dollar a gallon, so there was method in our madness. Also, of course, we had installed a Jotul Combifire woodstove.

It was around New Year's the previous year when the furnace quit. I remember that night so well. The house grew cold really fast, but we built a big fire in the fireplace so we could keep warm. Forget that. All the heat streamed up the flue, leaving us cold. I slept on the couch by the fire so I could get up and add wood when the fire burned down. Of course, it was Julie in the bedroom who was really cold, so she would end up coming in to stoke the fire. When the repairman finally found time to come, he said it was an old-model furnace and they didn't make an ignitor for it anymore. He showed me how to light it with a propane torch.

Friends across the lake, Bill and Kathy, had bought a Jotul stove from Norway to help with heating their expansive home. We found a metalworker up the road who could build a shield for the front of the fireplace. We would install the new stove on a fabricated stone-covered slab just in front of the hearth. The stovepipe would go from the rear of the stove through the steel shield into the flue. The wood we had in the garage was, of course, too long to use in the Jotul, so we built a sawhorse and used a little Mini Mac chainsaw to cut it to ten-inch lengths, suitable for the small firebox. The results were magic. The stove was airtight and produced plenty of heat to warm the house on the coldest, stormy winter night, whether the power was on or not. We could burn it open and enjoy the ambiance of the fire or close it for serious heat, with no danger of sparks landing on the floor. We bought an iron pot so we could cook on top, and we grilled many a steak over burned-down coals. We made a contract with the conservation department, those in charge of local wood-lands, and they allowed us to harvest four standard cords of wood from the state forest near Panama. They marked trees they wanted removed. We would cut them down and haul them home in our little two-wheel-drive Subaru. A standard cord was four feet wide, four feet high, and eight feet long. It was a great deal of wood. Of course, after we brought it home, we would have to cut it to length, split it, stack it, dry it for a year, and then finally, burn it. It was serious work. But there was real satisfaction in providing for ourselves in that way. And it was enjoyable too. It kept us in shape. We would go into the woods on a Saturday when skiing wasn't the best, take down a tree, cut the limbs and trunk to manageable lengths, fill the back of the front-wheel-drive Subaru wagon to the roof, and then make the dash up the driveway to the house. After lunch, we might do a second run. After a while, we bought a snowmobile trailer with sides. That made for fewer trips.

Of course, there is a hazard in heating with wood. Chimney fires take many homes and even lives each year. There was a sweep in town who had a fine reputation. Her name was Annie Mae.

"Dirtiest flue in Ashville," she said after climbing down from the roof. "Your chimney is brick, not lined. Soot builds up in the corners, not good. Real fire hazard. Have to have it cleaned regular. Might think about having it inspected. Thank you very much."

He was from Cornell University, a pleasant young man, and he was doing research on wood heating in homes in Western New York. He removed the grills from over the vents in the walls on the sides of the fireplace and stuck his head inside. He climbed on the roof, looked down the flue, and went over the stove and the shield in front of the fireplace. Then he took photos, many photos.

"What do you think?" I asked him. "You're taking many pictures. You like this?"

"This is definitely one of the most dangerous installations I have ever seen," he said. "You can see the two-by-four studs right through the ducts. I'd have this whole thing torn out and fixed responsibly, if I were you."

With that, he got up, took a few more pictures, and left.

We had already had a basement dug under the house, which saved the floor joists from further decay. We had bought a new oil furnace. We had expanded the kitchen and added a forced-air solar wall to the south side of the house. We had replaced the windows and insulated. Why not combine a new roof with a new chimney? Even though we had insulated and reroofed, the roof still leaked. We negotiated with the contractor who had dug the basement, and he agreed to put a properly pitched six-by-twelve roof on the house and rebuild the fireplace. Rather than a traditional fireplace, we would have a stone wall with a hearth incorporated into it so that we could have a properly vented woodstove in the living room, with a separate flue for the furnace and a second stove in the basement to use when I wanted to do woodworking or relax downstairs.

I still remember the huge man that came to the house to help take down the old fireplace. After the dry wall was removed, he went after the brick structure with a sledgehammer. He hit it as hard as he could, but the hammer would bounce right off. Contrary to what the inspector had said, we found that the homemade fireplace structure was not flimsy at all, but three bricks thick on all sides. True, there was a two-by-four inside the vent, but far from the firebox and really not very likely to catch fire. With constant earthshaking pounding, the structure finally came down. The contractor went to the basement and found the foundation of the fireplace sufficient for much more than we had in mind. We used it for the new construction.

When it was finished, there was a whole wall of beautiful stone in the living room, complete with a mantle. The raised hearth would hold a new, efficient woodstove. The round, lined flues would carry smoke away without any corners for creosote to build up. There was a separate flue for the oil furnace as well as one for a basement woodstove. On the kitchen side, a small warming oven was built in. It was electric, with an ornate iron door, perfect for heating plates or keeping a main dish warm.

Unfortunately, there was a ragged hole in the ceiling where the stonework ended. The contractor insisted that wasn't his problem. He could fix it, but that would be another issue.

We paid him, and Julie and I fashioned a valance to surround the top of the fireplace with polished oak. When we were finished, we were very pleased. We had a stonemason do the heavy work, but we put on the finishing touches and made it our own.

We kept the driveway open, taught school, and skied, all the while having the inside of our house torn up and rebuilt. It was another adventure, and like so many others, it ended with a surprise. We ordered a new soapstone woodstove with a rear vent. I remember the night the owner of the shop where we bought it brought it to the house. He was by himself, and after driving up the driveway in the snow, he struggled to lug the crated stove up the front steps on its dolly and into the living room. When we opened the package, we discovered it was the wrong model. He had to get it out of the house, load it onto his truck, and go back to town for the one we had ordered. By the time he got back with the right stove, it was late at night. He was truly exhausted. However, the airtight stove held more wood and put out more heat. The rock wall absorbed the heat and helped keep the room at an even temperature.

The woodstove would hold a comfortable temperature in the house for a full day while we were in school. If there was sun, we needn't even light the fire. The solar wall would keep the place comfortable, even on the coldest sunny days. Our oil bill had gone from impossible to insignificant.

CHAPTER 67

Back to the North Channel

We had enjoyed such a wonderful time in the North Channel the previous year that we just had to do it again. In June, we loaded the boat and set out again for the North Channel. Erie, Ashtabula, and Mentor were all great yacht clubs, where we were welcomed. There was fine dining and atmosphere. At Vermillion, there was Casey's Restaurant, where we would find good food and entertainment.

I remember returning to the boat late at night from Casey's. We heard a mournful moan. It was Troy, tired of being left alone. Our old padlock had rusted shut, and we had replaced it with a combination one. Unfortunately, the flashlight I had left in the cockpit was dim, and I just couldn't see the numbers. Try as I did, I couldn't get the thing to work. I knocked on a nearby boat, and the companionway slit open. A hand came out with a working flashlight. Obviously, our dog had caught more than just our attention.

The Erie Islands were great fun. Usually, we stopped at South Bass, but if there was a regatta going on, we might visit the Lows Winery at Middle Bass or even check in to Canadian customs on Peele. The long pull up the rivers was always a challenge, but the Gross Isle Yacht Club made us welcome on the south end, and Port Huron Yacht Club was a special place at the north end of the Saint Clair River. There were other clubs along the way, including the Detroit Yacht Club and others that always made us feel welcome. We had been warned never to casually stop in Detroit, but our previous dealings with Africans and African Americans made us doubt those warnings.

Every year, there were new experiences waiting for us. One year, there was a warning of bad weather just as we arrived in Tobermory. Little Tub, the more downtown harbor, was full, so we headed for Big Tub, a harbor farther from town. We motored to a quay near a campground and found a spot between two other cruising boats. There were tents near the quay, and people were sitting in lawn chairs, looking out at the water. We were kind of blocking their view. No one said anything unkind—they were Canadians, after all—but we were obviously the uninvited guests.

I got to talking with the man in the boat ahead of us, and he suggested we go to dinner with him and his wife. He had an inflatable, he said, "with a proper outboard." Was he casting aspersions at our little Mercury? He knew this restaurant in town, and they had the best coconut cream pie he had ever tasted. We just had to join him and his wife. That was all there was to it. So we all four got in his rubber boat, he started the motor—a 9.9, which was bigger than the one on *Temerity*—and off we went. The wind had come up, and the pressure on one side of the inflatable was definitely going down. We would have to pass through a bit of exposed water on our way to Little Tub, and between the windblown waves and the deflating dinghy, Julie and I got soaked. When we got to the dock at the restaurant, we climbed out only to find a line of people out the door of the place. Cold and wet, we would have to wait outside in the cool wind for dinner. To top that off, it was a "family" restaurant. They didn't offer alcohol in any form, not even a beer. When we finally got seated and served a mediocre dinner, we learned they were all out of pie. Over the course of the evening, we found our host was a minister. He began to preach about his yachting skills and the importance of anchoring in building winds using his three-hundred-foot anchor line. We got back aboard his partially deflated dinghy and again got soaked on the ride back to Big Tub. While we were changing clothes and trying to warm up inside *Temerity*, our minister friend cast off and, with his wife at the helm, headed to the center of the bay, where he pulled a tangled mass of line through his forward hatch and attached it to his anchor. He struggled in surging wind and near darkness for half an hour to get things sorted but finally dropped his hook and anchored for the night.

The next morning, he was gone.

We spent several days in the Benjamin Islands that year, and two things of significance happened while we were there. The first was a campfire. One evening, a man rowed by in his dinghy, looked at Julie and me in the cockpit, and said, "Havin' a little campfire on that island over there. If you care to join us, bring something to drink and come on over." It turned out the man and his wife were sailors in Maine and had been invited to cruise with friends from Michigan on the North Channel.

We climbed into our tiny inflatable dinghy and paddled over. The conversation turned to the virtues of saltwater versus freshwater cruising. The man from Maine was not shy. He extolled the beauty of the Maine coast, the islands and the harbors, the fresh lobster and seafood. He went on and on about the hiss as the boat slid through the salty sea, the reliable winds, and the seamanship required to navigate in tides and currents. He started a little fire in Julie and me; the fire in front of us began to die down, but the fire inside would grow. We didn't realize it then, however.

A few days later, we were ready to leave that very protected harbor when the second thing of significance happened. We saw ripples, cat's-paws, on the water, but thought nothing of it. As we slipped out of the harbor, we passed the "sows and pigs," low rocks with waves washing over the tops. They were a serious hazard, and we had to avoid them. The waves were large, much larger than we had anticipated, and the wind was fresh. It was all I could do to hold our boat on course with our little seven-and-a-half Merc at full throttle, pushing *Temerity* through the building waves. The mainsail was still covered; we hadn't hanked on a jib. Still, we made little headway. As the boat bobbed in the waves, the motor lifted out of the water. It would scream as the propeller broke free and then slow when the prop was again immersed. The sows and pigs were getting closer! Julie ran forward to begin uncovering the mainsail, which made the movement even worse. I tried to contend with both the tiller and the throttle of the motor, slowing it when it broke free and applying full power when the prop was underwater. The effort was futile. In just a few minutes, Julie had the main raised, and we were able to shut down the motor, tilt it up, and beat into the waves. What justification for a boat that sailed well!

It wasn't until we prepared to slip into another anchorage that evening that we realized the gravity of the matter. The motor would not start. Squeeze the rubber ball in the fuel line, place the throttle on Start, be sure the gearshift is in neutral, pull the choke if the motor is cold, pull the recoil starter. Pull and pull, but nothing. No hopeful pop. *Nothing.* It was as though the fuel line was unplugged. Here we were in the North Channel of Lake Huron, miles and miles from a qualified Mercury mechanic, and our engine was deader than a doornail.

We sailed into the anchorage at Bear Drop Harbor that night. The guidebook warned us to approach "dead slow," but that was not possible. We made the entrance, dropped anchor, and drifted back to set the hook. What to do? I tried and tried until my arm was limp to start the motor, but with no results. Finally, I began experimenting with every variable I could think of until I finally found it. If the engine was in forward and the throttle was on fast, the motor would start, the prop would spin, and off we would go in a hurry. We had to do something more; this was not acceptable. Ease back on the throttle, and the engine would stall. To say our *sexy* broad was a fast woman was no exaggeration!

The next morning, we decided to leave the North Channel, sail across Lake Huron, and try to find help. We hauled up the anchor, I started the motor, and we circled the fleet on our way out of the harbor. When it was obvious we were just going too fast in areas of limited visibility, I shut it down. The boat would drift through that place, and I would pull the cord again and hope for the best. Fortunately, especially when warm, the engine would generally start again on the first pull.

We sailed across Lake Huron to a small Michigan town. We used the sails to take us into the harbor, and as a thunderstorm arrived at the same time we did, we anchored off a marina and waited for the winds to die before attempting a landing. Inside, a helpful mechanic took the motor off the boat and put it in his tank. He looked at plugs and timing and everything he could think of. "I just don't know what to do," said the mechanic. "What I think is that you may have caused a hairline crack in the crankcase somewhere when you over-revved. The motor is sucking air. That means there isn't enough draw to pull fuel from the carburetor except when the throttle is fully open. I think you need a new motor."

"Do you have one?" I heard myself asking.

The young man heaved a sigh. "No. I sold out my whole stock. I have a 9.9 in the back room, but it's next year's model. I can't sell it until after September 1. Company policy. I doubt I could even order a last year's model. Maybe you can find one around Detroit somewhere. I'm afraid that's the best I can do."

We paid the man for his services, and he lifted the motor back on *Temerity's* motor mount. Julie pushed us away from the dock, and I pulled the cord, and off we went in a roar of blue smoke. We got good at it. We raced down the Saint Clair River and found a place for the night in a bay in Lake Saint Clair. Julie had heard about the Black River as a place to cruise through in the evening. I wasn't sure, but we were getting better at this. I could keep the boat moving. We glided, starting and stopping our engine, with other boats through that neighborhood of lovely homes. It was later that evening, while we were anchored in a bay, that another boater, after noting our unusual engine management, suggested that there was an Evinrude dealer nearby offering last year's models at reduced prices. We got the address, and early the next morning, off we went.

We motored up a canal to the marina, shut down the engine, and glided to a perfect landing at his fuel dock. The man there was eager to sell motors. We picked out an Evinrude 9.9 with electric starting and an alternator to keep the battery up. He looked at the Merc. "Does it run?"

"Well, we've had some trouble. It is hard to start."

"Tell you what. You start it, and I'll give you two hundred for it."

I put the shift in neutral, pumped the fuel bulb, moved the throttle as far as I could toward fast, and pulled the starter. To Julie's and my amazement, the warm engine started but then quickly died.

"That's good enough for me," said the man.

We paid the sale price, and before long, the new motor was installed on the boat. We settled the bill with our Gulf Oil credit card and were ready to go.

"Oh, one more thing," said the dealer. He took the cover off the motor, grabbed a spark plug wrench from his bag, and removed the center-fire spark plugs that came with the engine. He then replaced them with traditional ones. "You can throw these in the lake. They're no damn good," he said.

I took the plugs he had removed and put them in the spare parts kit. With that, I touched the starter and listened to the quiet purr of the new engine on the stern of our boat. No more weak lights. No more dead batteries. No more pulling and pulling. More power to boot. Victory at last. What a joy! *Temerity*, our sleek broad, was finding character. We hummed quietly out of the harbor and down the Detroit River, and a huge weight lifted from our shoulders. Another season and another near failure turned to success.

The following year, right after launch on a run across Lake Erie, the new motor began to sputter and then die. It wouldn't start. While bobbing on the calm lake, I removed the replacement spark plugs and found them sooty and out of gap. I dug out the 'no-damn-good' center-fire ones, screwed them in, and reattached the wires. The engine fired right away, and they worked perfectly. They were still working perfectly ten years later, when we sold the boat.

CHAPTER 68

A Dash of Salt

It was important that the motor ran well that year because we had a long ride ahead of us. We were headed for Maine! Before we left, I asked the mechanic at our marina whether he should check out the new motor before we embarked on the journey.

"If it ain't broke, don't fix it" was all I could get out of him. We had read books on coastal cruising. We had ordered and studied tide and current tables. We understood that one doesn't just "get up in the morning and go" when sailing along the coast. He checks tides and currents first. We learned that one must compensate for currents when sailing across them. It is not an exact science, but it makes crossing possible. Also, currents often ran parallel to the coast. One can waste hours fighting the current or wait patiently until the current switched and fly to one's destination. We thought we were comfortable with it all, but we knew we had a great deal to learn.

We had upgraded the boat a bit. A radio direction finder, a primitive device that could home in on radio signals from towers marked on marine charts, enabled us to get bearings that, as long as there were two or more of them, let us locate our position on a chart. The position was approximate by modern standards, but it was certainly a help. We also had a marine radio, enabling us to acquire current weather information and communicate with other boats. We were ready.

We headed east on Lake Erie to Buffalo. We thought we would head under the Peace Bridge, as many of my Power Squadron friends had done, go down the Niagara River, and go through an old railroad bridge labeled *swing* on our chart. We would then continue to Tonawanda, where, at Wardell's Marina, we would have the mast lowered for the run down the Erie Canal.

The sail east was spectacular. We raised the spinnaker and gushed along at about six knots. We kept careful track of our position, noting visual bearings from shore. We used a hand-bearing compass to get lines of position, and finally the Peace Bridge drew into sight. We lowered the chute and sailed under just the main. We had never navigated in this part of the lake, but we were confident—that is, until a powerboat, an outboard-powered runabout, came alongside. A rather large man, alone at the helm, started screaming at us, "You can't go there!" His eyes were bulging, and his face was red. "You can't go there!" he screamed.

What was he talking about? We knew we had plenty of clearance under the bridge, which was approaching very rapidly. What could the problem be? We guessed he might be drunk. With that, the two boats were flushed under the huge bridge. We were impressed by the powerful current; it made the current under the Blue Water Bridge seem like child's play. The man was pointing downriver, where a much lower railroad bridge loomed. Meanwhile, I got on the radio and called the US Coast Guard. I told them I had sailed under the Peace Bridge and that I understood there was a problem with the "swing" railroad bridge. I needed advice. Should I continue?

The coast guard's reply was concise. "We don't give advice."

Meanwhile, the Canadian Coast Guard interrupted. "Go to the Canadian side and use the back current to head back into Lake Erie. Don't try to cross to the American side until you get well beyond Fort Erie."

We dropped the main and headed for the Canadian shore. Our friend in the other boat wanted to throw us a line and tow us. We tried, but our weight was just too much for him. We tossed the line back to him. Our motor was able to make way in the back current, but the pace was terribly slow. The 9.9 Evinrude worked tirelessly, and brick by brick, we inched our way back under the bridge and up the lake toward Fort Erie on the Canadian side. A friendly yachtsman in a power cruiser called on the radio and assured us that he was on his way upstream and could give us a tow if need be.

When we first thought we were clear of the current, we began to cross the lake, but again, we were being drawn into the powerful Niagara River. We headed back to the Canadian side and continued to crawl westward. A glance at the fuel tank gave us reason for some concern: our fuel was down to one-fourth tank. We had five gallons of spare fuel in a separate tank, but it was not mixed with oil. Could we safely mix and pour that fuel from the portable tank into the boat's tank with the engine still running? If we failed, we might catch fire or just wash again under the Peace Bridge, crash into the railroad bridge, and then drift downriver to the mighty Niagara Falls.

None of those were pleasant options.

Finally, we passed Fort Erie and began to cross the lake. We raised sail to help us, before long, we entered the Black Rock Canal in Buffalo, where we should have gone first! We fueled up at the marina there and entered the lock system. At the other end, we reentered the river below the bridges and the fast current. It was getting dark. Across the river was a small island with a restaurant on it. We found some lee behind it and dropped anchor for the night.

Dragging anchor is always a concern for the sailor. Can you imagine what it is like to try to sleep knowing a dragging anchor or a broken rode might lead to your boat being washed over Niagara Falls? It was sort of like sleeping with a green mamba in the house!

CHAPTER 69

The Erie Barge Canal

Early the next morning, we were up and heading downriver toward Tonawanda. Before long, we tied up at Wardell's Marina. We looked at an ancient crane near the dock that we assumed they would use to drop our mast. A man came out and introduced himself. He was the owner, and he told us that before we could get started, he would like us to join him in a little Sunday morning ceremony. Church? We followed him inside, where there were juice and coffee and sweet rolls. After a brief repast, a resounding march began, and we all paraded around the breakfast table with much laughter and merriment.

A short time later, Mr. Wardell appeared with a cup of gasoline he poured down the throat of the carburetor of an old Chevrolet six-cylinder engine. He replaced the air cleaner, and a moment later, the engine burst into life. Once we had removed *Temerity*'s shrouds that held the mast upright, he used the Chevy-powered crane to deftly lift the mast from its step on the keel, through the cabin roof, and, with our help, rested it on the bow and stern pulpits. We installed sawhorses on deck beneath the mast. When he saw the kit sawhorses we were using to support the mast, he disappeared and quickly returned with a handful of nails. After nailing the horses together, we lashed the mast in place, and we were ready to go. Because the mast was ten feet longer than the boat, it protruded both fore and aft. We were now a thirty-seven-footer.

We paid our toll for the Erie Barge Canal at the first lock and made our first mistake that night. There was free dockage at each lock—no need to pay for marinas or seek other shelter. So it was presumed that boats would simply tie up at the locks. Moving the boat through the locks was easy, so much easier than the Welland Canal, for example. There were vinyl-covered cables fastened to the canal walls at top and bottom. One simply ran a line behind the cable and watched to be sure that it didn't snag as the boat went up or down. These locks were a piece of cake.

The scenery, too, was magnificent. Most people think of New York as bustling city streets, tall buildings, and maybe a few parks. That, however, is New York City, not New York State. We found ourselves traveling through lush green valleys, through forests and small towns. Sometimes we looked down on farmhouses below us. It was the Fourth of July, Independence Day, and we had come to just such a setting. There was a farmhouse, there was a barn, and there were livestock and chickens milling about a short distance from the canal's edge. There were children outside, playing. It was dusk, and we had been moving since dawn. We were tired, and rather than going on to the next lock in darkness, we decided to just stop right there and tie up alongside. It was a still night. We tied the boat to some small saplings onshore, and an anchor held us off. We lit a fire in the grill and had dinner aboard, and later, we saw fireworks over some distant village or lake. It was beautiful, quiet, just what we longed for.

The next morning, we pushed off, started the motor, and a short time later, pulled up to a lock, but there was no activity. We tied to the wall, and Julie went to the lockmaster's office. There was no one there, but there was a phone number to call. She came back to the boat, and together, we walked across the street to a house and asked to use the phone. The man who answered the door disappeared for a moment and reappeared a short time later with a portable handset. Julie called the number, and the lockmaster answered. She explained that we were waiting at the lock.

"Yes, well, the lockmaster up the way called me last evening and said there was one more boat coming. I stayed here and waited for you. It was the Fourth of July. Do you understand? Finally, I got in my pickup and drove until I saw you tied to them trees. Please let the lockmaster know if you aren't planning to go to the next lock. I'll be down and take care of things as soon as I finish my breakfast."

A short time later, the lockmaster appeared, operated the lock, gave us a friendly wave, and we were on our way. We felt terrible. The poor guy had most likely been late for dinner, maybe even too late to take his kids to the fireworks. We had not realized that lockmasters were responsible for keeping track of boats in transit and that he had felt responsible for us, even on that beautiful Independence Day night.

On and on we went some 365 miles through magnificent countryside. We read a book along the way telling the history of many of the towns we passed through. It told the story of the building of the canal, from hand-shoveling and working with horses, sickness, and death to the cannon salute from Albany to Buffalo when the canal was finally finished in 1825. Small towns with neighborhood stores and friendly, inquisitive people made the trip ever more worthwhile.

Eventually, we found ourselves in the Mohawk River and then, at last, the Hudson River.

CHAPTER 70

The Hudson

There was a yacht club just down the Hudson River from where the Erie Canal entered the huge tidal flow. It was called Castleton on Hudson, and its reason for being was a place where yachtsmen could restep their masts, after transit of the canal, at a reasonable price. There was a hand-operated winch, so once the mast was secured, one could turn a wheel to lift it. When it was vertical, a member of the crew would guide the mast to the opening in the deck then reverse the winch and lower it into place, where it would be held while shrouds and stays were made fast and tightened. There was a clubhouse. Meals were served. *A delightful yacht club.*

Our second night on the Hudson, we stopped at Saugerties. We had no idea. We pulled into a little tributary and tied to some rather-run-down old docks. In front of us were some very old wooden buildings. They had porches, and they might have been boarding-houses or apartments, or even retirement homes—we didn't know. What we did notice was that there were many old people in straight chairs and rocking chairs on the porches. The paint was peeling, and the old people were wrinkled and unresponsive. There were signs: RAT POISON. It made us worry about our dog. It looked like a good setting for an Alfred Hitchcock movie.

A man came along to collect a docking fee, which, though, we felt was a bit excessive, we paid. He showed us the way to a museum, where there was, among many other things, an iceboat very similar to the one my dad had sailed on Lake Chautauqua. He then began to tell us a story about the history of Saugerties.

The chapter he told was about Prohibition. It seemed that this town was a place where people from New York City could come by train or boat, and boats from Canada could bring huge amounts of beer and booze, and they would all mix at Saugerties. There were huge parties and drunken orgies, and for years, it was the place to go. The hotels were prosperous and entertained famous people. The nightlife was first-class; it was all a boon to the local economy, and local officials just turned a blind eye. When Prohibition ended, that was it. It was over, and Saugerties became just another stop on the railroad. The hotels fell into disrepair, and that was the end of the story.

The next morning, we backed out of our seedy slip and headed south for West Point. We understood that the anchoring was challenging there. The water was deep, and the bottom was rocky. When we dropped anchor, we found two other boats nearby belonging to Canadians we had previously met on the Erie Canal. One couple had a young child with them; the other boat was sailed by an older couple. They had been traveling with a third boat that developed engine trouble and, rather than getting it repaired, bolted an outboard motor bracket on the stern, bought an outboard, and headed back to Canada. They felt the outboard would not offer sufficient power to propel them on the coast, their dream vacation.

We looked at our 9.9 Evinrude and wondered.

We had a pleasant get-together aboard *Temerity* that evening and explained that we would be leaving early, at six the following morning, so we could approach Hell Gate at slack. Everyone thought that was a bit extreme and laughed at our rather-compulsive behavior concerning tidal currents, but at six, when we hoisted anchor, the Canadians pulled their anchors up as well, and the three of us headed downstream. The current was with us, as we knew from our almanac it would be, and we slid through Hell Gate at slack. There were no waves, no muss, no fuss. There was nothing to it. We headed for Manhasset Bay Yacht Club, recommended by a friend who had grown up there, and the Canadians all went their separate ways.

The outboard seemed to like salt water as well as fresh. *Life was good.* We saw seaplanes lifting off and landing on the busy East River, and seaplane bases, and the huge city of New York up close. The number of tennis balls in the water confounded us.

It was all good.

CHAPTER 71

The North Atlantic

A few nights later, we found ourselves on Block Island. We sailed there and pulled into the harbor and anchored. Hundreds of boats greeted us in the harbor. We felt we had finally arrived. We went ashore and visited with some sailors around a campfire. We told them our dog, Tammy, was ill. Sadly, Troy, our loving springer, had died, and we replaced him with a Brittany named Tamoshantra of Ashville, or Tammy for short. She was a fine dog, but she was more reserved and, well, she didn't like the water. She wanted to come with us on the boat, of course, but if she had her druthers, she would have had us all stay home. Tammy was sick. She was listless and just didn't seem herself. We asked those around the campfire that night if they knew of a vet in the area we could trust to examine the dog. One man piped up and suggested a man in Jamestown, Rhode Island, just across from Newport.

We went back to the boat, dropped the dog off, and took a free launch to a bar on the island. We danced and had a few drinks and, around midnight, headed back to the boat. With all the boats in the harbor, we wondered if we could direct the launch to *Temerity.* As it turned out, it wasn't a big problem. When we entered the anchorage in that rumbling launch, there was one anchor light that shone out above all others. We had installed a new tricolor navigation light with strobe and anchor light, and this was our first opportunity to see it in all its glory. We were proud. The next morning, however, we had to start the outboard by hand—the battery was dead! A much-less-powerful bulb was first on the list of parts at our next marine facility. Our anchor light was simply too much of a good thing.

We headed for Jamestown, Rhode Island, across the harbor from Newport, where the 1980 America's Cup trials were happening. We found a spot in a crowded marina at Jamestown and found our way to the recommended vet. Tammy got a shot and some pills and a benign diagnosis. We were very relieved.

To celebrate, we left our slip and motored across to Newport, where slips were simply unavailable or sold at exorbitant rates. As we cruised along the shore, the radio suddenly burst into life.

"*Temerity*, *Temerity*, this is *Wind Dance*. Come in, come in. *Temerity*, this is *Wind Dance*, channel 16, please come in!"

Were we hearing things? People were waving frantically onshore. Was something the matter? Julie answered the radio, and it was the people we had stayed with at West Point. They wanted us to join them in a little cove there. We swung around and headed in.

Those onshore took our lines and secured them. They were so glad to see us. We could hardly believe it! They had left us without even saying goodbye. What was up?

When we got to shore, they took us to another Canadian in a CS 30. "Tell them about Hell Gate," they said.

"Well, I didn't know about the tides and currents," he began. "I just headed through as though it was a narrows in Toronto. Next thing I knew, I was going in circles, narrowly missing the wall. A telephone pole thrust itself up from the depths, barely missing the boat. I struggled and struggled and finally got control. It was frightening. I had no idea…"

"You saved us from that," our friends said. "We want you to stay here with us. The Canadian entry into the America's Cup has set aside this little cove for Canadian supporters. It isn't nearly full, and we want you to stay here and enjoy the trials with us. You can stay as long as you want."

We had thought visiting Newport was financially out of the question for us. We told them we had to return to Jamestown to settle up with the marina but that we would see them in the morning. Wow! What a thrill! What an unexpected surprise!

The next day, after securing the boat and removing the American flag, we found we were about a forty-five-minute walk from downtown Newport, where the heart of the action was found. The Australians, with their carefully shrouded and secret keel, and the Americans were there, along with the Canadians and others. The sleek hulls and fit crews paraded about behind locked fences. Very exciting! We asked about how to get to the course, and responses were varied but similar. "Follow the spectator fleet" was the most common answer. "Follow the blimp" was a close second.

So the next morning, we rose early, cast off, and headed for the harbor entrance. We could see the blimp overhead, and everything from runabouts to mega yachts was pouring out of Newport into the sea. We did our best to keep up, but our three-and-a-half-ton boat with its 9.9 Evinrude was little match for the mighty engines of the spectator fleet. We were washed in wakes and haze, but we found our way to the course, where we could get a ring-side view of the action.

We could see the sleek twelve-meter hulls slide past, raise spinnakers, and gush off into the haze. It was exciting. We didn't know what was happening—there was no play-by-play on the radio—but it was very exciting to see these lovely yachts race by. Then the fog set in. We had somehow drifted onto the course, and one of the competitors sped by very close to us. The trial had ended. We heard the spectator fleet start their engines and move away. Suddenly, we were alone on the sea. Where were we? We listened and heard the clang of a bell. We sailed toward the sound until we came to a bell buoy. We found its number, located it on the chart, and plotted a course for the harbor entrance. As we entered the harbor, the blimp passed right over us.

We had a wonderful few days with our Canadian friends, but unlike them, we hadn't come all this way to just watch some racing. We had to move on. There was a great cape ahead.

CHAPTER 72

Sandwich

"Don't try to round Cape Cod," they said.

Having discovered the value of a little local knowledge, we didn't. Besides, there were rumors of an approaching *system* that had us a bit worried. *A Cruising Guide to the New England Coast* suggested that there was a good harbor at Sandwich on the south side of the Cape Cod Canal. When we arrived, it was early in the day, generally too early for us to anchor. Still, we put down our trusty fifteen-pound CQR anchor and let out sufficient rode so we knew we would be fine.

As the day went on, numerous other boats arrived and dropped anchors. There were docks and a few slips along the shore, but no large marina, as there is today. By evening, the harbor was fairly buzzing with dinghies and filled with anchored boats. Curiously, many of the boats had fenders dangling from their sides. We were obviously foreigners, somewhat out of the conversation. Though the winds had picked up through the day, it wasn't until after midnight when the real storm started. We knew because of a crashing thud that terrified the dog and sent us both to the deck. Had we broken loose? Dragged anchor? What? It was an old Pearson 30. She had anchored beside us, and as the boats swung at anchor, we had bumped each other. Obviously, that explained the fenders. We got four fenders out and lashed two of them to each side of the boat. We kept watch, and it wasn't long before the two boats met again, though this time the result was less dramatic. The Pearson was crewed by a young couple who was full of apologies. He was trying to steer away from us, but as the boat wasn't moving through the water, it was futile.

"Let's lash the boats together," I suggested. "That way, we will be held by two anchors, and at least we will stop crashing into each other."

He looked at his young wife, she shrugged, and I tossed him a line. We pulled the boats together, and though the wind kept roaring, the movement eased a great deal. There were no other boats near enough to hit us, so we even went below and tried to sleep.

In the morning, the wind continued to howl. We learned that the young couple on the Pearson had just been married. She was quiet and reserved, and he, a little more talkative. They had been just a few days on their cruise and had already lost two of their three halyards up the mast. It looked like a motoring honeymoon for them. Julie found that totally unacceptable and insisted she go up their mast to retrieve the lost halyards.

I had a look at the remaining spinnaker halyard, and though it was clearly worn, it looked serviceable. We ran the halyard to a winch and attached our bosun's chair to the halyard, and after jumping a few times on the chair as a test, I began cranking my wife up the mast of this young couple's boat. Even though the boats were rocking and the wind was howling, Julie would not be put off. Up she went, clinging to the mast as I tailed and the owner cranked on the winch below. At the top of the mast, she grasped the two lost halyards firmly in her hand, and I lowered her back to the deck. Our newfound friends were so grateful. It was simply a joyous time for the four of us. Julie was hero of the day.

A little later, we had another drama. A brand-new Pearson 365 ketch that had been anchored on the other side of the harbor raised anchor and began to move out. They circled the inside of the harbor and were headed for the entrance before we realized what was happening. One of the yachts anchored near us had taken a long line ashore in his dinghy and lashed it to a post to dampen his swinging. The Pearson never saw it. The line caught in the vessel's bow pulpit and drove the new boat into the dock. The owner, a middle-aged man with two teenage daughters aboard, tried to cushion the blow but, in the crash, lost several fingers. People onshore helped secure the yacht while the young women attended to their father. An ambulance appeared on the scene, and the man was laid on a stretcher but got up and began milling about, to the horror of the ambulance attendants. It appeared he was searching for his missing fingers. Finally, he was taken away, seated in the ambulance. We were shocked by that unhappy experience.

A little later, the wind began to steadily abate. We let our new friends free to swing on their own anchor and took Tammy ashore for a badly needed walk. There was a man selling lobsters from a truck there. We went to a nearby hardware store and bought a large pot for boiling lobsters and a small pan for melting butter along with two pound-and-a-half live lobsters! We really were in New England. That evening, we feasted on delicious, freshly caught seafood.

The next morning, with the tide behind us, we continued east, through the canal, and back into the sea.

We had survived our first Atlantic storm. We learned that "any port in a storm" meant that people would come in to a safe harbor whether there was swing room for them or not. We had dealt with the situation, made some friends, and come out without embarrassment.

CHAPTER 73

The Coast of Maine

We continued toward Maine. Spending a night in Plymouth, in Situate, and farther along, we went through the canal at Cape Ann after spending a night in Gloucester. We sailed when we could, motored when winds were light, learned to manage tides and current, and felt more at home every day. Finally, at Kittery, we entered the state of Maine. I remember going ashore, buying groceries at Frisbee's store. Delightful!

In Portland, we stopped at Di Millo's restaurant, an old ferry converted to a restaurant. While we were in town, we met a man who was about to set off on an around-the-world cruise. That, in itself, was not so unusual, but he was going to do it in a seven-foot sailboat. He was a relatively large man himself, and we wondered how. He was being interviewed by the local press, and we were impressed, indeed, at the tiny craft. Where would he carry his water, his food? How would he exercise?

On that same dock was a middle-aged woman in a dinghy. The dinghy was powered by exactly the same outboard we had on the Morgan, a 9.9-horsepower Evinrude. Her blond hair was done up in a bun, and her white blouse and shorts were immaculate. I felt confident she belonged to a large motor yacht anchored in the harbor. She was buying gas for the dink and had lifted the six-gallon fuel can from the small boat onto the dock. "No damn good" was about all she could say. She poured a pint of oil mix into the tank and then filled it with gas. I noticed the tank only took three gallons. She had essentially doubled the oil to fuel ratio, and she thought there was something wrong with the motor!

"Hard to start, smokes like a chimney. I hate this thing."

"Gosh, we have a motor just like it on our Morgan 27 over there, and it brought us here from Lake Erie," I said.

"Feel sorry for ya. Must have been a terrible trip!"

"Well, we try hard to keep the fuel-oil ratio close to right," I said as I handed her the tank. She ignored my comment, pulled the heavy tank back into the boat, eased down onto the seat, and began to grind the starter until, in a cloud of blue smoke, it finally started.

The coast of Maine was lovely. We would enter a small cove and, without fail, a friendly lobsterman would insist we "pick up a mooring" rather than drop anchor. "All rock here," he would say. "Anchor not much good in a blow." So we would spend the night tied to a mooring. We would row our little dinghy to shore and buy groceries or visit a restaurant. We walked the dog.

That first year, we had no radar, no loran, no GPS. Careful navigation was our only way to keep from getting lost.

Then one afternoon, a wall of fog rolled right over us.

We tried not to panic but noted our position on the chart and plotted a course toward a bell buoy at the entrance to Tenant's Harbor. A short time later, we began to hear the chime of the bell. We found the buoy, confirmed its number with the chart, and followed the marked channel into port. We located a vacant mooring, and later that afternoon, we rowed ashore in fog and rain. There was a little fish market there, and fishermen were bringing fresh fish right off the boat, and those in the store were cleaning it and putting it in the cases. A nearby restaurant offered the same freshly caught fare. That first night, we had dinner in the restaurant. We had never tasted fish so fresh and delicious!

For the next two days, we gorged ourselves on sweet, succulent, fresh fish. It was a three-day blow, and what we thought might be a dismal port in a storm turned out to be a simple delight.

There were other adventures in Maine. We sailed into Stonington one bright morning while flying the spinnaker. Just as we entered the harbor, a gust caught the chute and nearly knocked us down. Julie eased the guy, and the power of it pulled the line from her hand. It flew free, neatly unfastening itself from the sail, landing in the water and sinking just ahead of us. Add one spinnaker sheet to the shopping list. While we were in Stonington, we noticed a building on pilings high over the water. There was a sign: FRESH LOBSTER. Several dinghies were attached to a float near a ladder. We used our long painter and tied the dinghy up to the float then climbed the ladder to the shop where the lobster was being sold. There was a short line of people ahead of us, so I went to the restroom. The room was a little bigger than a closet. The toilet was just a toilet seat on a kind of bench, as in an outhouse. Sure enough, right below me was the water, and floating in the water, right under the toilet, was *our dinghy!* Did I ever dash down that ladder and shorten the painter on the dink! No harm done. We got our lobster and an amusing anecdote to share as well.

We had been told by fellow yachtsmen that at South Freeport, there was a free shuttle to L.L.Bean, the famous Maine clothing store. We found a vacant mooring at the South Freeport Yacht Club, took our dinghy to shore, signed in at the register in the clubhouse, and called the number posted on the wall. There was no one around, but it was, after all, a weekday morning. A few minutes later, a young man appeared in a van, ready to take us to Bean's. We did our shopping and returned to the club. We loaded our few purchases into our dinghy and rowed back to *Temerity.* When we got to the mooring where we had left our boat, she was gone. Not only was the boat gone, but our dog, our clothes, everything was gone! We circled the buoy in disbelief. There was a launch from a marina that went by, and we flagged him down. I insisted that he call the coast guard right away as someone had stolen our boat. It was grand larceny, and I was ready to prosecute.

The young man at the helm of the launch was unimpressed. "Sometimes people complain if one of the yacht club boats swings too close to them. When that happens, they call the marina and they come to move it to a mooring with better swing room."

"Not our boat," I said defensively. "First, I used the painter attached to the float as my painter then backed it up with a line of my own. Second, there was no one on any of the boats nearby. I checked all of them to see if we were okay before we rowed ashore. No one answered my knock."

The young man picked up his radio. "What kind of boat was that?"

"A Morgan 27, named *Temerity*," I said.

Sure enough, just as the young man had suggested, the marina said they had moved the boat because it endangered other craft. He took us to our boat, where we climbed aboard. Tammy was sound asleep below. Everything appeared to be in order.

"There will be a fee for moving the boat and a mooring fee, of course," the young man said.

"You tell whoever told you that to come out here and collect that fee. I'm calling the coast guard and filing a complaint. I intend to have him arrested!"

"I'll tell him," he said.

With that, he pushed off and headed for shore. We spent the night at the marina mooring, and no one ever came to collect any fee.

Moving east, we stopped at Popham Beach, where a friend who taught English with me at Jamestown High School had a summer cottage. We pulled into the mouth of the bay and picked up a vacant mooring. There was a float at a dock near the shore, where we left the dinghy. "Think our boat will be okay at that buoy till morning?" I asked a fisherman.

"Be fine till tomorrow" was his terse answer. "After that, they'll be coming back."

We found a phone booth and made a call, and a few minutes later, Bill and his friend Chuck, our friends from home, picked us up in their car, and we headed to their place for drinks and dinner. The drinks started with manhattans and evolved to wine with dinner, and of course, we needed an after-dinner drink or two. Fresh fish was wonderful. Bill was an excellent cook. We savored the meal and the ambiance of their cottage on the Maine coast. We shared stories till the wee hours, when we finally borrowed their car and eased down the lane to the landing where *Temerity* swung at anchor. Julie and I climbed aboard the dink and rowed through the darkness and the current caused by the incoming tide to our boat. Once aboard, with the dinghy safely attached at the stern, we went into the cabin, closed the companionway, and exhausted, snuggled into bed.

It must have been an hour later when we heard it. It was a boat powered by a gurgling inboard engine, and it was getting nearer. Must be some fisherman coming in after fishing for the night, I thought. Then there was a *thump* and a knocking on the hull side.

"Hallo."

I climbed out of the warm bunk and stumbled aft and opened the companionway slide to be greeted by the cold, damp Maine night, face-to-face with a rather grizzled fisherman dressed in tattered foul weathers. "What can I do for you?" I asked. My heart was pounding. I was sure he was about to tell us we were on his mooring and we would have to leave now, at three in the morning, to find another place for our boat.

"Uh…*Nancy Jane*, you're on her mooring. She'll be comin' in tomorrow afternoon, 'bout three. Thought I ought to say somethin', lest you go back ashore tomorrow and leave the boat again."

"But it's three in the morning," I said. "That's eleven hours from now." I was still shaken from my rude awakening.

"We're headin' out, won't be back till afternoon, ourselves. Good night."

With that, he pushed off, and the small boat engine revved as the little "down-easter" slid off into the night. It wasn't easy to fall back asleep.

Our friends had suggested that, as we would be heading to Boothbay, we should go the *back way*. That meant heading upriver toward Bath and taking a shortcut across to Boothbay Harbor. They insisted that the scenery would make it worthwhile and it was miles shorter than the coastal route. We would have to use the engine, currents were strong and the route was narrow, so sailing would likely be difficult.

After a brief breakfast with our friends, we said goodbye and motored up the broad bay toward Bath and the Bath shipyards. We then headed east into the long, narrow winding strait. There was a bridge ahead of us, and as our chart lacked the detail to include the overhead clearance, we had to find it in an almanac. We had ample room for our thirty-seven-foot mast, and our little Evinrude purred smoothly as we passed under the bridge and wended our way among the lobster pots marked with colorful floats.

We were almost to Boothbay when it happened. There was a *clunk*, and the boat suddenly stopped. The motor still ran, but we were not moving. I stopped the engine, and the boat swung around. The current was pushing against the transom, or back of the boat, and a line trailed from underneath. There were no other boats in the area. What to do? I would have to cut us free.

The water surged by us. There was substantial current. I went below and found my bathing suit. There was a cool breeze, and wisps of fog were in the air. I was cold, sleep-deprived, and a little hungover. Not good. The water, Maine water, was like ice as I began my descent of the ladder Julie had hung over the side of the boat. She insisted that I wear a line around my waist so if the current carried me away, I could pull myself back to the boat. The downside of that was that if the line got tangled under the boat, held me there, and I couldn't surface, I would drown. At least I would have a sharp knife to cut things, including myself, free. The other worry was that after the boat was cut loose of whatever was holding it, I would have little time to climb back in before it continued with the current into whatever might be in its way—other boats, navigation markers, etc.

I knew there was no option. I lowered myself into the burning-cold water, and when my mask and snorkel were beneath the surface, I could see the problem. A float from a lobster pot had wedged itself between the top of the rudder and the bottom of the boat. The line was jammed solidly in place and was held there by the force of the current on the boat. I had a very sharp knife on a lanyard tied to my wrist. I sawed at the line, with my knife, but the cold and the current were strong adversaries. I had to come up several times for a breath. Finally, I cut through the line and was able to pull the wooden float free of the rudder. I grabbed the ladder and pulled myself into the cockpit, started the engine, and before any damage was done, we were back on our way toward Boothbay. I felt badly for the lobsterman who had lost his trap as a result of our running over his float, but at the same time, there were so many floats on the river it was difficult to avoid them all.

When we arrived in Boothbay, we enjoyed the lovely town. We inquired about winter storage and found several places that could accommodate us with either inside or outside storage. When I heard the price, I gasped. It was far more than we had budgeted.

"Out back," a man with a Greek fisherman's hat said to me, and we walked with him outside the office door. "Know a place called Webber's Cove in East Blue Hill," the man said to me once we were outside in the sun. "There's a yard there, nothin' fancy, but it's run by a good man. Might have room for your boat. Saw you grimace when Sam there gave you his price. This, here, is tourist country. They sock it to them tourists. Give 'em a call. Don't think you'll be sorry."

With that, he gave me a card with the name of the marina in East Blue Hill and a phone number.

"Thanks," I said. "I'll give it a try."

That night, after a succulent lobster dinner, we were walking through town when we came to large building right on the water. There were lights on inside. Obviously, a very large yacht was under construction in there, and we wanted a peek. We looked in the door and caught the eye of a young man.

"Want to come in and have a look around?" I was a bit shocked by his offer, but Julie and I nodded and walked through the door. "Name's Dan," he said. "I work the night shift. They saw and sand and cut and make dust all day, and at night, I clean and smooth and apply a little paint and varnish."

The yacht was a huge power yacht. She had diesel engines, a lovely salon, a beautiful galley, and several roomy cabins. The master cabin was aft. It had chests and a vanity and a large closet. There was an adjoining head. All this surrounded a king-size bed.

"Man who commissioned this yacht is over eighty years old," said Dan. "Imagine that, commissioning a million-dollar yacht at that age. Now watch this."

He grabbed two wires from the wall near the entrance of the opulent cabin and twisted them together. There was a humming sound, and suddenly, the ceiling over the bed separated, and two panels that looked like bomb bay doors slowly hinged down to reveal a polished mirror in the ceiling above. "Can you imagine that?" asked Dan. "This guy is over eighty. We didn't think he'd live long enough to see his yacht finished, and he had us build this into his stateroom so he could watch himself and his…well, you know what I mean."

With that, the tour was over. We thanked Dan for his kindness and headed back to *Temerity*, where Tammy was ready for an evening walk. We took her to shore, and then back on the boat, we all fell into a sound sleep.

CHAPTER 74

East Blue Hill

A phone call to the yard in East Blue Hill proved to be fruitful indeed. He did have room for us in his yard, and his price was in line with what we had paid in the Great Lakes. Good news.

The yard was small and simple. There was a forty-foot Swan sailboat on the hard having its teak decks replaced. We picked up a mooring and took the dinghy to shore. John would haul the mast and then store the boat outside, covered, next to one of his sheds. It sounded like a good deal to us.

Julie called her mother in Henderson Harbor, and she and Julie's sister, Betsy, and her two little boys, Toby and Zac, would come pick us up the following day. We made reservations for them at a motel in town. Life was good.

It was the following evening when things began to get a little difficult. We walked into town expecting to find Eleanor and family, but no one had arrived. It seemed the drive from Northern New York to Maine was much farther than they had expected. They had left word at the motel that they had gotten a late start and wouldn't arrive till after two in the morning. We walked back to the boat in the dark and were attacked and barked at by a very protective English springer spaniel along the way. The next morning, the family arrived, somewhat bedraggled. We took them sailing, the boys enjoyed playing along the shore, and we arranged to have the mast pulled and the boat hauled the following day.

"Be in the haul, our slip, at nine," said John. "We pull the mast and haul the boat then. Tidal area, you know. Dries out. We drop things, but we don't lose much."

We understood. If we were late, there might not be enough water in the slip to accommodate us. We would have to wait another day to be hauled. So the next morning, we had the boat in the slip promptly at nine. The mast came out of the cabin trunk smoothly and was promptly secured on the bow and stern pulpits. *Temerity* was then lifted free of the water and taken to an adjustable cradle onshore.

We loaded the six of us, our dog and luggage, into Eleanor's Malibu wagon and headed back to the motel, where we took Tammy into the shower to rinse off a little shore stink. Then, clean and ready, we began the long drive home. Of course, we would have to stop in Portland so Eleanor could have lobster at Boon's Restaurant. That was when the rain started. It became foggy, and the rain that began as light rain grew steadily. Then it poured. We stopped at L.L.Bean and drove all day, and as it began to get dark, we decided to pull into a motel and find a place for the night. Coincidentally, everyone else who was living in a tent in Maine that summer had the same idea. Motels were all full, especially for people like us who needed rooms for six people and a dog. Toby and Zac, aged three and six, were amazingly good, but there really wasn't much breathing room for any of us. It was four thirty in the morning when we finally pulled into the cottage at Henderson Harbor. Exhausted, we made popcorn for dinner and opened a beer. Betsy's husband, David, came downstairs in his pj's, wondering what the commotion was.

He had come back from a canoe trip in Canada at two that morning and had tiptoed around the empty house, hoping to not waken anyone. We all slept late the following day.

We had done it. We had taken our outboard-powered Morgan 27 over a thousand miles down the Erie Barge Canal, the Hudson River, and the North Atlantic to Maine, found a place for her, and gotten back home in time to teach school another year. We had managed 365 miles of canals and locks, navigated the Hudson River, including the bustling harbor of New York, sailed coastal New

England with its high tides and strong currents, met new people, and seen wonderful places. We had sailed through dense fog and enjoyed memorable vistas. We had done it without GPS or even loran. We used almanacs, parallel rules and dividers with good charts, and seat-of-our-pants navigation to find our way. We had reason to be proud.

CHAPTER 75

Tammy

It was fall in Western New York, and that meant hunting season. I had hunted with Troy, but he was just too enthusiastic. If there was a grouse or pheasant in the field, he would find it, but by the time it flew, it would be too far away for me to shoot. He was a wonderful pet but died of natural causes after seven years.

But Tammy, Tamoshantra of Ashville, her real name, was a pointer, not a flusher like Troy. With training, she could help me bring fresh game home to the table. We had done some preliminary work with her. We had gotten her to freeze at the scent of a pheasant wing. She would hold her point as well. We had taken her to a local gun club, where folks were shooting clay pigeons. She sat with Julie and me in the car as we watched the men shooting. We petted her and reinforced her. She remained calm. Then we opened the door and walked closer and closer to the loud noise and the action. Everyone fussed over her. She was wagging her tail. It was all good. She proved she was not gun-shy at all. Would she hunt? That was the question of the day.

Friends invited Tammy and me to hunt with them. Pheasants had just been released by the state in a nearby field. Both my friends had their dogs, a German Shorthair and an English Setter. They welcomed us but worried that young pup would scare the birds away. There were scores of men and dogs in the field that morning, and I feared it would be a washout for us with the new dog and all.

The way it is supposed to work is that as you advance through the field, the dog runs along in front of you. She wears a bell on her collar so you can always locate her in the heavy brush. When she catches the scent of a bird, she approaches the bird carefully. The instinct of the bird is to freeze when it senses the presence of the dog. When the dog is just a few feet from the bird, the dog freezes as well. This is called a point. A good dog will hold his or her point until the hunter approaches. The hunter hears the bell on the collar of the dog stop ringing when the dog is on point, and then advances. When the hunter gets close to the dog, the bird panics and leaps to the air. That is the moment the hunter has to shoot. If the bird is hit, the dog watches and dashes to retrieve the bird, bringing it back to the hunter without damaging it. If all this happens, it is a wonderful accomplishment for the two of you.

On this particular day, the three of us got a total of six birds. Tammy pointed all of them, much to the surprise of everyone. She wasn't good at the retrieving part, but she would locate a downed bird and hold it down until I got there to pick it up. I was very proud of her.

Unfortunately, she was a little spoiled by the pheasants. They had been raised in cages and weren't terribly savvy. When we went out in the woods for grouse or woodcock, she could locate the birds all right, but she would be frustrated with me if I didn't get there right away. She would quiver with excitement, and then, sometimes, just at the wrong moment, she would bark and the bird would break and fly into the air, and that would be it. I wouldn't even get a shot. In that case, I would be frustrated and mad at her. How could I train her not to do that?

Sometimes, however, I was close enough so when I approached her on point, the bird would fly and I would get a shot. If the bird went down, good, but heaven help me if I missed. In that case, the dog would look at me sadly, as if to say, "You jerk!" It was as if she wanted to know how she could train me to be a better shot.

We didn't kill enough birds to upset the balance of nature much, and Julie and I always enjoyed cleaning and cooking and eating the birds we did shoot. We had many adventures together.

At one point, Tammy just wouldn't come when I blew the whistle. I had trained her to do that, but after we had been hunting for a while on any particular day, when she got too far away, she just wouldn't come back. I was frustrated. Finally, Julie agreed to come along to see if she could help. She figured it out right away. After we had been hunting for a bit and Tam barked at the wrong time, or I missed an easy shot, we would both get frustrated. She would begin to hunt for herself, and I would find it difficult to keep up. I would blow the whistle harder and harder. Julie saw this right away. The very loud whistle was a warning to the dog. "He's mad, watch out!" I learned to take it easy on the whistle, and things were better.

One evening, on the way home after an unsuccessful hunt, when both of us blamed the other, a deer dashed out of the woods and struck the side of our little Subaru. It broke its neck and died instantly. I didn't know what to do. I knew I was supposed to report an accident, and there was some damage to the car. I knew it was legal to take a deer home after an accident. An old pickup came by and stopped, and I asked the guy about the procedure. Did I have to call the police first?

"Don't worry about it. Just take the deer home, clean it, and eat it. Look at the damage it did to your car," he said as he helped me lift it into the back of our little Subaru station wagon. Our Brittany looked at me as if to say, "That deer must have been really bad!"

As soon as I got home, I dutifully called the police to tell them that I had hit a deer.

"So where is the deer located?" asked the lady at the station.

"In my garage," I told her. "I hit it up on Butts Road, and there are no houses there. Of course I brought it home before I called you."

"You know it is a mandatory thousand-dollar fine for moving an untagged deer? You are supposed to call the police so they can come and tag the animal, and then you can move it. I'll talk to the sheriff and see if he can waive the fine."

After what seemed an interminable time, the lady came back on and told me that an officer would be by shortly with the tag. "Show him the deer and the damage to your car, and if everything fits, you won't be fined. Don't ever do that again."

I assured her I hoped never to strike another deer and that, if I did, I would be sure to follow the rules. In the meantime, Julie had gotten down one of my hunting books that talked about dressing deer. We knew it was important to gut them right away, but we also knew it would be a good idea to wait for the sheriff before we did anything.

We waited and we waited. The deer was bleeding in the back of the car, so we dragged it into the garage and suspended it from the rafters on a rope. Julie got plastic bags ready so we could cut the meat into appropriate-sized pieces and freeze it.

Finally, a sheriff's car pulled into the driveway, and a young man stepped out. He was freshly shaven and smelled of Old Spice. Obviously, he was beginning his night shift. He looked sleepy, as if he had just gotten out of bed. He looked at me and frowned. "I understand you have moved an untagged deer. You know there is a major fine for doing that!" he said. He was trying to be stern.

"I am sorry, Officer," I said. "I didn't know that technicality of the law. I explained that to the lady when I called."

The young officer, in his clean uniform, walked to the deer dangling from the rafter on a rope, its neck obviously broken, and examined it carefully. Then he stooped down and looked at the dent in the fender of the Subaru, right behind the front wheel, where the deer had struck the car. He got up, still perturbed, and handed me the tag. At that moment, he turned and walked right into the canoe suspended from the ceiling of the garage. It caught him in the forehead, and he went down on his back on the dirty garage floor. I offered him a hand to help him up, but obviously humiliated, he said, "Get your hands off me!" He got up with his cap askew and brushed garage dirt from his clean uniform. Then, without saying goodbye, he stormed out of the garage, headed for his car, and zoomed off into the night. Julie and I smiled, and after I gutted the deer, she skinned it, and we began cutting it up and making it ready for the freezer. It was a long night, but many tasty meals of venison in the coming months would justify the effort. One thought lingered, however. I sure was sorry for anyone that young officer arrested that night. He certainly was not in a happy mood when he left our house.

Tammy and I hunted together for years, and during the season on a Friday or Saturday night, should the phone ring, Tammy would be very attentive. If I so much as looked at my gun or hunting clothes or checked the ammunition in my hunting vest, she would simply be out of control. Julie and I would go to bed at the usual time, and in the middle of the night, I would hear heavy breathing. It was the dog. "Is it time yet?" She would pant and all but bark as she woke me, eyes wide. Her paw would scratch the mattress. Such enthusiasm was wonderful, but it did have its downside.

One time, I took her to the vet. I had taught her to heel so she would walk beside me without a leash. She loved to please. Unfortunately, she didn't like the vet. We walked together, and I looked down as I opened the door to the office. Gone! Once she realized where she was headed, she bolted, leaped into the open window of a Chevy station wagon parked at the office entrance, over the lady at the wheel with a sick cat in her lap, and landed in the passenger seat. The young woman at the wheel stared straight ahead, frozen in place. I apologized and ran around the car to retrieve my dog. Tammy was not interested in visiting the doctor's office. I had to drag her from the car, snap a leash on her, and pull her into the waiting room.

CHAPTER 76

Back to Blue Hill

In June of that year, my cousin Charlie offered to take us back to the boat in Maine. He borrowed a motor home from his friend so his wife (Barbara), his mother, and mine could travel with Julie and me and our dog to East Blue Hill Maine, where we found *Temerity* safely resting near a barn, still in her cradle, after the long winter. It was a lovely trip. Everyone enjoyed seeing the boat, and we all had a memorable dinner at a fine Blue Hill restaurant.

It wasn't until everyone had left and Julie and I began preparing *Temerity* for her trip to New Brunswick that things got interesting. We had to sand the bottom and clean and polish the topsides then tape the waterline and paint the bottom. It was while we were doing that that we discovered the dog was not as in love with exploring by sailboat as we were.

"You got a brown-and-white dog?" a man with a distinctive down east accent asked.

"Yes," I answered.

"In my truck and won't get out," said the man.

Sure enough, Tammy was curled up in the seat of his old black pickup truck, and it was all I could do to drag her out. Wherever the truck was going was fine, as long as its owner wasn't spending another summer on the water.

We launched the boat, and reluctantly, Tammy jumped aboard and sniffed the air as we motored off into the sea.

Our destination was Jonesport, where, on the Fourth of July, the community sponsors the annual Lobster Boat Races. As we headed out into the sea, we found ourselves engulfed in deep fog. This time, however, things were different. We had bought a loran receiver that would give us precise information on our position and would enable us to navigate safely through fog and know our exact position. We had paid dearly for the device, but we understood that we needed more than our dead reckoning skills to navigate safely in such treacherous waters.

We had wonderful sailing as we moved eastward. One evening, we anchored off Hurricane Island. There was an Outward Bound school there, where young people learned to gain confidence living in the out of doors. We took Tammy toward shore in the dinghy, and when we reached the float, she leaped off and charged up the long ramp to shore and disappeared into the woods. We followed her up, but when we got to the top of the ramp, probably twenty-five feet above the level of the sea, she was gone. We visited with some of the people there, who told us about their experiences on the island. They climbed and camped and rowed and made the most of their primitive surroundings. Just then, Tammy reappeared. She ran toward the ramp at full speed and then, to our amazement, appeared to dive off the land, where she plunged a full twenty-five feet into the cold water below. There was nothing but bubbles from where she had landed, but then her little head bobbed to the surface. A young man standing on the float reached down and grabbed her collar and helped her onto the dock. She shook wildly. If she was hunting and other dogs splashed through puddles, Tammy would go around. She would never think of swimming on her own, so why would she have dived off the cliff? The only thing we could think of was that there were three posts where the ramp touched the land. Between two of them was the safety of the ramp, but between the other two, there was the twenty-five-foot drop to the sea. Must be she just wasn't paying attention.

"Did she do that on purpose?" the young man who had pulled her from the water said to me.

I assured him it was a mistake. "She hates to swim," I said.

307

"Hmm. They make us do that, jump into that cold water. I sure wouldn't do it if I didn't have to."

With that, the two of us and our wet and somewhat-humiliated dog climbed into our dinghy and rowed back to the boat.

We sailed to Isle au Haut on that trip as well. It was far out to sea, and because it was so remote, it was said to be a breeding ground for the puffin, a colorful seabird. We sailed along the shore of the island but saw none of the rare birds. We came to a small cove, where we dropped anchor for the night. Then we noticed something very strange. There was a man in a rowboat moving along the shore. He was very dark skinned, and he was rowing the boat very badly. His oars would sometimes skim across the top of the water, and from time to time, he would appear to lose control completely. How odd. We didn't know what to think. Were we prejudiced? Did we think he was doing something wrong simply because he had a dark complexion and was rowing poorly in this remote part of Maine?

After a bit, I waved to him, and he began to row toward the boat. I hailed him, and right away, I felt a warm sense of relief. His two-word reply revealed a strong African accent. We visited for a few minutes, and when I learned that he was, indeed, from West Africa, being hosted here by his American Peace Corps teachers, I tossed him a line (rather than have him try to row up to the boat) and pulled him over to us. He climbed aboard, and we showed him around. He had never seen the inside of a small sailing boat before, and he shared a sense of wonder. When we told him that we, too, had taught in Africa in the Peace Corps, he was simply incredulous. We just had to come ashore and meet his hosts.

As she was a bird dog and we didn't want to hurt any puffins, we put Tammy on her lead, launched the dinghy, and followed our African friend to the dock of a rather-large cottage onshore. There we enjoyed sharing experiences with two Americans who had taken the unusual step of bringing one of their students home so he could see for himself the world where we Americans live. Unexpected guests that we were, they insisted we stay for a meal. It was a lovely time, and when we got back to the boat later that evening, we were amazed at our good fortune. What a coincidence! There, on that remote island of Isle au Haut, we met people with experiences so like our own. It was wonderful, and the next morning, it was difficult to raise anchor and leave.

CHAPTER 77

The Races

All the while, we were headed for Jonesport and the Lobster Boat Races. It would have been possible to slink along the coastline and get there, but there was a bridge in the way. The Jonesport Beals bridge had a clearance of thirty-nine feet, and with our thirty-seven foot mast and three foot antenna, we knew we couldn't make it…so we had to go around. That meant heading around a large island, an extra forty miles.

No sooner had we left than the fog set in. It wasn't fog like we were accustomed to in Western New York, but thick, heavy fog that left us little more than a few hundred feet of visibility. There was current, but little wind. We were under power from our trusty outboard, and for the first time, we had to rely on our new loran C. Between carefully plotting our position on the chart with the aid of the loran, we made our way ahead. At one point, we had to find a sounding buoy. We heard a fog signal from an anchored ship, but no bell. We knew it was near, but instead of the bell, we heard people talking. Then we heard what sounded like someone dumping tin cans into a garbage can. It was eerie. The fog signal from the anchored ship ahead grew louder, and as we approached, it seemed very near. Ahead of us, out of the haze, a slanted orange line somehow rose from the sea toward the sky. As it drew nearer, it became clear that the orange stripe was on the side of an anchored white coast guard cutter. The ship had obscured the buoy from us, but its signal had led us right to where we needed to be. We rounded the end of the island, and before long, the fog had lifted and we found ourselves in Jonesport, just a few miles from where we had started, but on the other side of that thirty-nine-foot bridge. Of course, we could never have gotten under that bridge in the Great Lakes, but here, with seventeen-foot tides, as bridge heights are measured from mean high water, we would have had plenty of room at low tide. It is one thing to learn things from a book and quite another to be able to apply them.

The following day, we rose early and motored to the channel where the races would be held. We had no idea what to expect, but that was what we were there for, an adventure. We anchored among a fleet of spectator boats in clearing weather. There was still some fog, but splashes of sun broke through. Excitement was in the air. A powerboat anchored next to us, and the owner, looking at the beautiful Morgan with our trusty Evirude 9.9 on the stern, leaned over the side and called out, "You come all the way from New York in that boat? You got a real engine down below, don't cha?" When I assured him the outboard was our only engine, he simply shook his head and turned away. These were powerboaters, after all.

Before long, the sun came out, and the water was sparkling blue. The races were against the clock as the boats roared over the course. Each boat had to have both a helmsman and a second person near the stern. There were single- and multiple-outboard lobster boats, gasoline-powered inboard lobster boats, and diesel lobster boats. Their skippers piloted them through the course skillfully, earning applause from the crowd. Though it was not the most exciting racing ever, it was unique, and the crowd was into it.

Later, in a little restaurant, we overheard a spirited debate about whether *nitro* should be allowed. Nitro, in lobster boat races, really? "Damn shame!" said one wrinkled face under a Greek fisherman's hat. "Be somethin' to see with a little nitro in those engines."

From Jonesport, we snaked up the coast to Eastport, the most easterly city in the United States. Powerful Bay of Fundy currents buffeted us and pushed us along as we moved between islands and visited the small city. In Saint Andrews, we cleared Canadian customs. Our dog was sick, but a friendly vet gave her a shot that cured her ills.

On we went to our final destination, the Reversing Falls at Saint John.

CHAPTER 78

Saint John

The Cruising Guide to the New England Coast had guided us safely this far, and now it was up to us to finish our voyage by traversing the falls. The Reversing Falls are an aptly named phenomenon. What happens at Saint John is that water from the Grand River flows to the coast, where it enters the Bay of Fundy, a coastal area with some of the highest tides in the world. At low tide, the water rushes down the river, tumbles over the rocky bottom, and gushes into the sea. At high tide, as the sea is higher than the river entrance, the water from the sea rushes into the river while the water from the river continues to try to get to the sea. This creates huge standing waves and turbulence. At both high and low tides, the river is not navigable. It is wildly rough. However, at midtide, for a short period, the river is calm and deep enough for yachts and small ships to navigate. Having navigated the Reversing Falls would be something to be proud of.

Julie and I carefully studied the tide tables and headed for the mouth of the river. We knew that we had a short window, roughly twenty minutes, to make the entrance and continue upriver to the Royal Kennebecasis Yacht Club, beyond the tidal flow. In our navigation plan, we had to compensate for the wild effects of the Bay of Fundy tidal currents, not to mention wind and, of course, reduced visibility. We had to be just right. When we broke out of the fog and saw the opening ahead, we were greeted by calm water. Our mighty 9.9 Evinrude pushed us smoothly upriver through the shoals and tall cliffs. We went under a bridge, where the guidebook suggested we head for a buttress and let the current push us off. We did as suggested and ended up right where we belonged in midchannel. At the yacht club, we found a place to moor and were warmly welcomed by the membership. There would be a party that night. We were welcome to attend.

After lunch, we went for a walk along the cliffs where we had so recently taken *Temerity.* Arrogant courage, indeed. There below us was a raging river with white water and standing waves. What outboard-powered-sailboat owner would ever imagine taking his vessel through that rapids? Bleachers! There were bleachers there so tourists could sit and view the wild water and any boat that dared traverse the river mouth.

We stared with wonder at what we had just come through. For us, it was like a passage on the Hudson, calm and smooth, and now, a short time later, it was wild!

Later that evening, after a delightful dinner at the club, we visited with local sailors. They told a story of the New York Yacht Club that ran a race up to Saint John. At just the right time, when the water was smooth, the participants moved their boats upriver through the calm water. Everyone knew the rules, and all was fine. Later that evening, a large power yacht recently bought by a very rich New York Yacht Club member appeared at the club. The owner had navigated up the coast and headed upriver as a surprise to his sailing friends. They greeted him at the dock, and when they congratulated him on his navigation skills, he was surprised. He hadn't known anything about the Reversing Falls; he was just lucky to have hit the river mouth at slack. We heard that story several times. Club members loved to tell it.

We learned a great deal about tides and currents from those we met at RKYC. Stories of races in the Bay of Fundy where sailors would anchor at the start of a race and wait six hours for the tide to change before venturing forth had amazed us. We had a wonderful time visiting with them and sharing experiences.

Unfortunately, bad weather was approaching. A powerful system was heading our way, and rain was forecast for the next several days. What would we do? One can only spend so much time holed up in a sailboat on a rainy day.

Our new friends were quick to suggest, "Get out of Dodge!"

"The Grand River is very navigable," they insisted, "and beautiful besides. First thing tomorrow, head up the river. That will get you away from the coast and the bad weather. After fifty miles, you will come to Grand Lake. There you can drop anchor in a quiet cove, jump over the side, and swim in warm, freshwater. Imagine that. Swimming from a yacht!"

As we were from the Great Lakes, not the frigid North Atlantic, we had no trouble imagining swimming from the boat in freshwater. However, cruising upriver to avoid a storm sounded like an enjoyable and wise thing to do. Besides, it would really flush the salt from the engine, and that seemed wise as well.

CHAPTER 79

Grand Lake

As we motored up the river away from the foul weather on the coast, we appreciated the lovely rural countryside. There was minimal current, no fog or rain. The boat moved easily. It was delightful. It was evening when we arrived at the lake, and there was a small cove nearby with a Marionette aluminum cruiser anchored there. We moved in just outside the other boat, and before we could get the anchor down, the bow lifted and we heeled slightly. For the first time since we had left Lake Erie, we were hard aground. The good news was, we weren't on rocks, just a sandy bottom. There was an older couple in the Marionette, and they got right up when they saw what had happened. Perhaps they would come to our aid. Wrong! They both grabbed folding chairs and moved to the foredeck, where, cocktail in hand, they could more easily watch us struggle.

Meanwhile, I revved the engine in reverse, to no avail. Then we let out a bit of the mainsail on the boom so Julie could slide out a ways and help heel the boat over. I moved as far to leeward as I could, and again, I revved the engine. Ever so slowly, we began to slide back to deep water. Once clear of the shallow spot, we deployed our fifteen-pound CQR anchor, and we spent the evening in flat, calm conditions. We suffered no damage, except to our egos.

With a clearing forecast on the coast, we wasted no time on Grand Lake but headed back downriver. About halfway, we found a gas dock with a little bar-restaurant nearby. We filled our tanks at the marina and walked into the restaurant for lunch. It was a delightful place with a huge fireplace, beautiful woodwork, and several lovely young waitresses along with a man who was bartender and cook. We had a beer and ordered another and fresh fish sandwiches. The place was empty but for us, and so the waitresses were fussing over us. The beer was cold. It was wonderful!

Suddenly, one of the waitresses looked at me and blew a wisp of blond hair from her face. Her features darkened, and she said, "Oh no! Oh my god! Not now."

"Easy, Carrie," said the bartender, whose face also grew stern.

The other girl wiped her hands on her apron. "We just have to do this," she said.

And then they turned to us.

"You might want to go. At least you might want to eat out on the porch or on a picnic table over there under those trees. We're so sorry."

I was about to ask what was happening that could be so bad when it became clear. There was a roar in the air, and the first of perhaps fifty motorcycles shattered the peaceful afternoon. Bandannas and Harleys, black leather and tattoos came with the noise as a large group of riders began parking their bikes and revving their engines before they shut them down and then noisily paraded into the bar. Finally, a Chevy conversion van pulled into the only space left. The rear side door slid open, revealing a very large woman in a purple dress who nearly filled the rear seat.

We understood completely. Grabbing our sandwich plates and beers, we moved toward the picnic tables as more bikes pulled in. I pushed a generous tip into the hand of the harried waitresses as we walked back to the boat, touched the starter on our quiet little outboard engine, and glided off downriver.

317

CHAPTER 80

Heading South

Somehow, the image of leaving through the Reversing Falls is as fresh in my mind as arriving. It was much less challenging when we left RKYC, as the time of slack tide was clearly posted at the club. Members had been wonderful to us, and it was a bit sad when it came time to leave. We pushed off, motored under the bridge and through the narrows, and then fairly plunged into a wall of fog as we hit the cold seawater. The warmer freshwater stays on top of the cold seawater for a bit, but once we had gone past the coast, visibility quickly dropped, and we were again navigating by loran-C.

Of course, there were many things that happened on the way home, far too many to mention, but there were some that stick in mind even after all these years. Certainly, our visits to Northeast and Southwest were two of them.

Northeast Harbor, Maine, is a convenient stopping place along the coast. There is a marina and several fine restaurants in town. After we secured the boat in the marina, we took Tammy for a well-deserved walk. Along the way, we passed a small group of people going in our direction. Tammy, on a lead, strained to get acquainted with those we walked by. The man in the center said something innocent, like, "Nice dog," but I was immediately struck by something. I knew him. I knew his voice. He looked at me and nodded, and I could hardly believe my eyes. It was Walter Cronkite, the *CBS Evening News* commentator. He smiled and nodded, and well, that was it.

Later that evening, at a restaurant called the Popplestone, Julie and I were enjoying our dinner when we noticed a bit of commotion in another part of the restaurant. We thought nothing of it until our waitress pointed out that it was, indeed, Walter Cronkite. She said he was in town, picking up a new Hinkley from nearby Southwest Harbor, where those luxury yachts were built. As we were preparing to leave, we had a drink at the bar when a waitress hurried over and spoke to the bartender. "Grand Marnier," she said, "for Walter!" His party was leaving as we were when he stopped, turned, looked away thoughtfully for a moment, and went into the men's room. How odd that such a chance meeting of someone who read the news each night should make such a large impression on me, but I shall never forget it. At the same time, how difficult it must be to be recognized by every passerby, to be unable to go anywhere without being recognized, and perhaps to be followed or fussed over. I had to envy him for his luxurious yachts, but the stir he caused in passing seemed hardly worth it.

Southwest was not far away, and people seemed to think it was a place worth visiting. So we did. We went to the marina there and toured the Hinkley facility. Beautiful sailing yachts were being built to the very highest standards. In the background, however, were several sheds where older boats were being refitted. Their hulls were being filled and sanded and then painted in magnificent colors, and their interiors were refurbished like new. Could they take our Morgan and perhaps repaint it in that magnificent dark red on the topsides of some Hinkleys? They could, but the price was far out of reach of a teacher's budget. We went through the store where sport coats and bags and lovely jewelry emblazoned with the Hinkley emblem were for sale at prices reflecting the prices of the yachts.

Back on board, we started our little engine and headed for Somes Sound, a fjord, the only one on the Maine coast, not far from Southwest. There was a warning in the cruising guide that because there were *snags*—what I took to mean old trees—on the bottom, it was important to rig a trip line on one's anchor so, should it get caught in debris on the bottom, it could be retrieved by the trip line, which was attached to the back of the anchor. We had an old water ski line with a small float on the line. It was black, as was the float. I remember, the water was deep where we anchored, at least twenty feet. We would need about seven times that in anchor rode to be safe. The ski line would not have to hold the boat, so it could just float to the surface. We let out 150 feet of anchor line, and about a hundred feet away, the little float bobbed on the surface, with a bit of excess *floating* water ski line marking the anchor. As it was a Saturday, there were numerous boats looking for a place to drop the hook. It was frustrating because these sailors would motor right over the little float marking the position of our anchor. Should they catch the line in their prop, it might cut the trip line or at least dislodge the anchor; it could even wrap up around the shaft, and who knew what would happen then? I pointed and even yelled at people, but they seemed totally unaware. Finally, in frustration, we motored ahead, grabbed the trip line, and attached a large white fender to it. That did it. From then on, boats were more respectful and kept away from our anchor.

It was about four thirty in the morning when it happened. Tammy was in the companionway, and she was barking anxiously. They were little squealy barks. Suddenly, there was a *thud*, and then another *thud*. I sprang from bed in my nightshirt and dashed up the companionway to find myself nose to nose with a man standing in his underwear, in the companionway of a red Hinkley sailboat right alongside. "You dragged your anchor!" I said.

The man looked at me, calmly, and said, "I don't think so. I think you dragged your anchor."

With that, he pointed his hand at the anchor line stretching from the bow of his boat. There was our fender, looking like a half-sunk bobber, going up and down with the small waves. Obviously, it was supporting the anchor, which was dangling like an oversize fishhook below it. He had moved a fender between our boats so they no longer bumped. He was surprisingly good-natured, which was a huge relief to me.

He looked at me. "Do you know what happened?"

I stared at him, openmouthed. "I...no, I had plenty of scope...I..."

"When the tide came up last night around one, the float marking your anchor, that fender there, lifted your anchor, then the current took you upstream in Somes Sound. Your boat might have gone four or five miles. Fortunately, you didn't hit anything, or it would have wakened you. As the tide receded and the direction of the current reversed, you came back. On the way back, your anchor snagged my anchor line, and here we are. You banging against the side of my boat! I don't think you did much damage. Do you?"

I didn't know what to say.

"The tide goes up nearly twenty feet here. That fender would have had no problem lifting your anchor. What is it, twenty pounds? What do you think?"

"Fifteen pounds," I said. "I can't believe it!"

What the man had said was completely reasonable, though the thought of our swirling five miles up Somes Sound and back in the middle of the night with an anchor dangling from a fender and not ever touching bottom, shore, or another boat completely mystified me. What would there have been to wake us? It was a quiet night. There was only the gentle rocking of the waves.

I agreed that we had not damaged each other's boats and thanked the man for his explanation. I certainly would never use a fender to mark an anchor in tidal waters again. Julie went forward in the dinghy, and we untangled our anchor lines and reset our anchor. What an experience! Just when you think you've got this sailing thing down...

By then, the sun was rising. It was time to get up and plot our course for the following day.

CHAPTER 81

Sailing West

The sail down the coast was uneventful, but several things come to mind. One time, while sailing near Vinalhaven Island, we found a golf course with a dock. There was a black hose lying on the dock. *Temerity* had such a small water tank, about ten gallons, and as we were running low, we thought we might just land there and take on a little water. We tied to the float, and right away, we realized our good fortune. Not only was there ample water available, but because the black hose that ran all the way to shore had been lying in the sun, the water was also hot! After we secured the boat, we went below to don our bathing suits and gather soap, shampoo, and towels. We really needed a wash. What a find!

It wasn't until we returned to the dock that we realized it. Two golfers had walked out on the dock while we were changing and opened the tap. They were thirsty and wanted a drink, so they let all the hot water run out so they could each have a sip of cool water before they returned to their game. I'm sure they wondered why these crazy sailors would be dressed in bathing suits. There were NO SWIMMING signs clearly posted on the dock. We went ahead and filled the water tank and the tiny solar shower attached to the base of the mast.

One day, we stopped in Portland in thick fog, but we hugged the edge of the channel as a huge ship overtook us in the entrance. It was unnerving to hear the gush of water made by her bow moving nearby and not be able to see her at all. Still, we were clear of the ship and safe. Inside the harbor, we found ourselves very disoriented in the fog, but we picked up a mooring and no one came to collect a fee. The next morning, we continued our sail up the coast.

At one point, we saw a small dark island ahead and to port. As we approached, it appeared to be moving! It was moving, and it was an island. It was the island of a partially submerged submarine. Officers on the "island," or conning tower, gave us a friendly wave as we passed by.

There was, however, one event that stands out more than any of the others. Years before, in the early seventies, Julie and I were on a camping trip in New England when we stopped at a place called Rockport Harbor. There we had seen and bought a painting of *Motif One*, a lobster house that had been used as a subject for artists for years and years. It had burned and been rebuilt. We thought it would be fun to revisit that site from our boat. We eased into the harbor at Rockport and found a slip very near the famous landmark. After enjoying the ambiance of the little community, Julie and I went for a walk. We found an ice cream stand and enjoyed a cone. Then, as evening approached, we headed back toward the boat, looking in along the way at the artists' studios that lined the street.

Temerity sat quietly in her slip as we approached. She was beautiful there in the afternoon light. I noticed that I had neglected to tilt the engine out of the water, which I always did when stopping for the night. Then I saw it.

The Evinrude had a six-gallon aluminum fuel tank that we kept at the aft end of the cockpit floor. Behind that, just in front of the engine, were two plastic five-gallon fuel tanks filled with raw gasoline. Someone had tossed a lighted cigarette between the tanks. It had burned out, but it left a brown mark on the white fiberglass. Had that cigarette ignited the fumes from those tanks, there would have been a terrible inferno. No doubt we would have lost the boat, and Motif One might have been lost again!

I was simply beside myself. Who would do such a thing? It obviously wasn't an accident. No one accidentally tosses a lighted cigarette at fuel containers aboard a boat by accident! What would we do? Should we call the police? Leave?

I was fuming, and Julie had gone below to make dinner when a woman and a man came by. They were an attractive young couple. He smiled and looked at me and began asking simple questions about the boat. I was in no mood to visit, but I somehow couldn't help myself. We fell into conversation, and before long, he and his wife came aboard for a look around. I noticed he had a "whale watch" sticker on his shirt. He said he and his wife had been on a whale watch that day and that they had enjoyed watching hundreds of whales. When I asked him where the whales were, he gave me the expected answer. "We just went out of the harbor for a while, and there they were." Then he tilted his head and looked right at me. "You know," he said, "if you were at the mouth of the harbor at seven tomorrow morning and watched the whale watch ships go out and you could get a compass bearing on them, I'll bet you could follow them to the whales. I gather they send spotter planes out early, and then all the boats just head for the pod, wherever the plane locates it. Anyway, the whales are great."

With that, he and his wife left the boat and headed for a nearby restaurant.

"Remember what I said about those whales!" He smiled at me and shook my hand as he left the boat. We had never seen a whale. What an idea!

It was difficult getting to sleep that night, knowing that there was someone around with a very distorted sense of humor. Would he come back and try to blow us up in the night? But Tammy, though she was a timid dog, would warn us if someone tried any mischief, I told myself, and the next thing I knew, there was an alarm bell ringing and it was time to get up.

After a quick breakfast, we untied the boat and pushed off into the quiet morning. Sure enough, just after seven, with mist hanging over the water, several boats loaded with tourist whale watchers headed out of the harbor, and all of them took the same course from the harbor mouth. We followed, but soon we found ourselves to be quite alone. The whale watch boats, much faster than us, were gone, and we were motoring along in the calm, hazy morning. We shut down the engine and raised sail. We were on course but otherwise alone on the quiet sea. Naturally, we had no idea how far we had to go, if the pod had moved or what.

It was around ten when it happened. There was a swirl on the water on the starboard side of the boat, and a huge head appeared off the bow and then dived beneath the waves. We gawked in awe as the water seemed to darken beneath us. Had he or she swum under the boat? Should we be afraid? I rushed down the companionway to find the camera. Telephoto lens? Would they be too close? Maybe I'd need the wide angle. Would we see any other whales? There were whales on our right, our left. They would look at us with an intelligent eye, arch their backs, and plunge into the sea, often showing us their huge horizontal tails as they sounded. They never breached, but we lowered our sails, and they stayed with us. They were nonthreatening, seemed gentle, and were somehow curious. We kept our distance, but they stayed near. As the pod began to move, we raised sail and moved along. They didn't seem to mind. The thrill we felt was hard to describe. It was the tingling thrill of childhood. We were giddy with delight. Julie made lunch, and we enjoyed it on deck, watching these magnificent beasts. Tammy watched but never made a sound. She had no interest in taking on these mammoths.

It wasn't until late in the afternoon that we realized we had a ways to go before we could anchor for the night. We set a course for Marblehead, raised sail, and reluctantly left our gentle friends. They were humpbacks, and neither Julie nor I will ever forget that amazing day. It was nearly dark when we pulled into the mooring field at Corinthian Yacht Club at Marblehead. We had picked up a guest mooring and were on the foredeck, about to lower the dinghy, when a young man approached in a yacht club launch. "Please don't take your dinghy to shore," he said. "I will be happy to take you to shore at no charge for any reason. We have no place for dinghies onshore. You can reach me on channel 9."

We quickly closed the boat, and the launch took us and the dog ashore for a walk. It was a lovely area, and people at the club were warm and welcoming. We returned to the boat for dinner but came back later to visit the bar. There were Olympic games on the TV, and we enjoyed several beers. When we were ready to return to the boat, the bartender asked to see our yacht club card. I showed him my Barcelona Lighthouse Yacht Club card, and he looked at me strangely. "You've come all the way from Lake Erie?" he asked. I confirmed that we had. "In that case," he said, "drinks are on the house!"

The launch took us swiftly back to *Temerity*. Tammy was not particularly happy to see us after our having left her in the boat, but the young man at the helm was happy to take the dog and me back for a short evening walk and then back to the boat. Afterward, we sat in the cockpit and enjoyed the beautiful evening. Tammy curled up beside us, head on Julie's lap. All was well. As we sat there, a young couple in a beautiful Soling sailboat slid silently between the moored yachts. Back and forth, in and out they glided, just missing the moored boats with insolent skill. It was mesmerizing and beautiful in the moonlit night.

The anger and frustration of the previous day had been replaced with a sense of utter bliss. We had enjoyed perhaps the most naturally rewarding day of our lives after enduring the uncaring malevolence of a total stranger the day before. Somehow, the magic of the whole cruise settled in on us.

Long Island Sound carried us to the city of New York. We timed Hell Gate perfectly and again bowed to the majesty of that magnificent city. The Erie Canal and the Niagara River were old hat. I will never forget Lake Erie opening up before us when we got out of the Black Rock Canal. Favorable winds and sunshine carried us to our new home at the Dunkirk Yacht Club in Dunkirk, New York. *Temerity* fairly surged through the freshwater in a moderate southerly breeze as she sailed up the shore.

It was a beautiful early afternoon when we headed into the harbor at Dunkirk. We passed the huge power plant at the harbor entrance and followed the buoys to the main pier, where we swung to starboard toward the club. We found a vacant slip on the west side of the docks and pulled in. After securing *Temerity*, we entered the clubhouse, where we found a large drawing of docking assignments. Inadvertently, we had taken the slip assigned to us. It was another magic moment.

CHAPTER 82

Back Home

We had enjoyed a wonderful two summers sailing the boat in the great North Atlantic Ocean. We had learned about salt water, marine life, tides, and currents. We had learned to navigate in fog. Mostly, we had learned that the world is filled to a large part with caring, loving people. It was as simple as that. We had enjoyed our trip to the sea, and we were ready to somehow do it again.

On the home front, things were not so rosy. My dad, who had been diagnosed with lung cancer years before, was not doing well. We drove him to Roswell Park in Buffalo, where he stayed for a while, and we visited him often. His cancer had metastasized, and even though he had had part of his lung removed, it had spread to other parts of his body. Sadly, he died in October of that year, leaving my mother alone. We became closer than ever to her and traveled to Florida with her each year at spring break.

Teaching school, hunting, cross-country skiing, and sailing continued to occupy our time. We became more active at the Dunkirk Yacht Club, where we raced *Temerity* every Sunday during the summer. Parties and sailing at the club became a larger part of our lives other than cruising. I was made chairman of the race committee, and that kept me closer to home.

When word got out about our cruise to New England, Julie and I were asked to speak about our cruise to the Chautauqua Power Squadron at their Change of Watch celebration in Jamestown. I had been an apprentice member of the squadron as a boy with my dad and had successfully passed the boating, seamanship, piloting, and weather classes with the older men. We rejoined the squadron, and before long, I found myself teaching the Safe Boating course each spring and fall. Sometimes it was in Barcelona, New York, at a marina, sometimes in my classroom at Jamestown High School, and several times at a school in Dunkirk. One day each week for several months, I would teach kids all day at school, go home and have dinner, and then drive, perhaps sixty miles round trip to teach adults for a few hours in the evening. I really enjoyed the experience.

It is interesting to me that most people quickly assume that teaching the adults is easy compared to the kids. That is true, to a point. The adults are more like the kids than different, though they don't like to admit it.

In my English classes, I would ask the students to read something, and then, to keep them honest, from day to day, I would give them a quiz to see who was really doing their homework. In the boating classes, I would also assign a chapter to be read by my students. From years of experience, I knew that unless they read and digested the material, it was unlikely that they would pass the test at the end if they just relied on classroom discussions for their information. So I gave tests, little quizzes, to keep everyone honest.

These people were doctors and lawyers and judges. They were busy folks who were pillars in the community. People with boats—big expensive boats often—who wanted the insurance savings that came with passing the Safe Boating course. Naturally, they expected they would pass the course, a boating course, after all. As an experienced teacher, I could tell right away when they weren't doing their homework. We had some speed, time, and distance problems in the book. We called them 60D Street, along with exercises in charting and converting true headings to compass headings using the TVMDC method and ESAW. That is, true, variation, magnetic, deviation, compass; east, subtract, add west, going down. Right? It wasn't all that easy, and they didn't get it either unless they studied the material. So I would throw them a quiz every week or so. Failing a quiz was not all right. These people did their homework. The classes were fun and very productive. The adults, much like the kids, did homework only when they knew they would be held accountable for the material.

Chautauqua County is in the snowbelt south of Lake Erie, and driving to the lakeshore was often challenging for me on cold winter nights, but teaching safe boating to eager adults made it all worthwhile.

With our master's degrees and tenure, we continued to be thrilled teaching young people. We continued to take graduate courses. We skied in winter and sailed in summer. We taught and took more boating courses. We raced our boat and became more deeply involved in the Dunkirk Yacht Club. We cut and split wood to heat the house, going so far as to install a solar wall heater that heated and circulated air through the house whenever the sun was shining. That was not what most people did in those days, but it was what we did, and we found that on a zero-degree day, when the sun was shining, the solar heater could hold the house at seventy degrees. Of course, we had an oil furnace for backup. We found we loved living close to the bone, close to the earth. The boat, however, was a little small. Hmmm.

CHAPTER 83

Trilogy

Temerity, our beautiful Morgan 27, had certainly served us well. She had taken us cruising in the North Channel of Lake Huron, and she had challenged the New England coast. She had endured storms and wild weather in Lakes Erie and Ontario along with the North Atlantic. She was a true friend. She sailed beautifully.

One time, I remember leaving Rochester, New York, for Sodus at the same time as a much larger cruising boat. We both arrived at Sodus that evening. They complained of no wind and having to motor the whole way. We took a nearer shore route and raised our 170 percent genoa; much to their amazement, we had enjoyed a lovely sail.

But she did have shortcomings. Her outboard motor provided no hot water and very little electricity. She was not at her best pounding through heavy seas under power. Storage was limited.

We started looking. Like the last time, we wanted inboard diesel power and wheel steering. We wanted standing headroom below, with offshore capability. We also wanted a fin keel and spade rudder. We wanted a fast cruiser that we could race.

There was a C&C 33 in Rochester that captured our imagination. It had an Atomic 4 gas engine, and when I looked it over, it seemed one couldn't get a spark plug wrench in the space over the aft spark plug on its four-cylinder engine. "Well, we just don't change that one," said the owner. So much for that.

There was a magnificent Niagara 30 in Niagara on the lake. We made an appointment and drove a hundred miles to get up there to look at it, but the owner never showed.

Finally, in Henderson Harbor, we found the boat of our dreams. It was a Saber 33. We had read about it, and it seemed just right. It would be expensive, but we both were working, and we felt we could finance it and make the payments. There had been a Saber 28 at Henderson Harbor Yacht Club, and it was a wonderful boat. We sailed the Morgan to the dealership at Henderson Harbor while we were staying at the cottage and asked if we could take a look at the Saber. The salesperson there was busy and asked us to wait. He said the boat was being cleaned and that a serious couple would be looking at it later in the day. He explained that it was quite expensive. I wondered if he would take a look at the Morgan and give us an estimate of her worth. He glanced out the window and chuckled. Finally, he came out of his office and frowned. "Okay," he said, condescendingly, "you kids can go out and have a look at the Saber, but please don't get it dirty! I have to take a couple sailing this afternoon, and I want the boat pristine."

With that, Julie and I got back into our sailboat and headed for the cottage. We definitely didn't want to do business with him!

The previous year, at the Cleveland boat show, we had looked at a Tartan 34. She was everything we wanted, from her opening ports to her shallow draft and fast design. She was beautiful, but we dismissed her because we felt she was just far too expensive. It was 1987, and it was August. We got in our Subaru and headed west. We knew we were headed for Grand River, Ohio, the home of Tartan Yachts.

We pulled into the driveway and walked up to the office. We told the lady there that we were interested in a Tartan and that there wasn't a dealer near where we lived, which was true. She said that the regular sales representative had the day off but that we could talk to the accountant. His name was Howard.

Howard appeared dressed in business clothes, hardly what we had expected. He was personable and showed a real interest in us and what we wanted. We toured the plant, where some of the boats were made, and eventually, he introduced us to Tim Jackett, the new designer for Tartan. Tim showed us a new boat that he had designed. All previous Tartans had been designed by Sparkman and Stephens, but this one was his own design. It had the sleek look of the 34, with opening ports and a Scheel keel, drawing only four feet, eleven inches, perfect for shallow Lake Erie. What was more, it was a 31. It was smaller and less expensive than the 34, but it had all the amenities of the larger boat.

Hull number 1 was there, waiting for us to take her for a sail. We climbed aboard with Howard, started the two-cylinder diesel engine, backed away from the dock, and glided out into Lake Erie. We hoisted the main and pulled out the roller furling jib. It was as though she had been built just for us. Behind the helm, I fell off the wind a bit, the sails filled, and we moved ahead easily through the calm water. She pointed well, and the wheel steering was smooth and effortless. She had pressure water and carried forty gallons of water and twenty of fuel; there was a water heater that would heat water when the engine was running or dockside, when she was plugged in. There was a stove that ran on compressed natural gas. Natural gas is lighter than propane and thus would not collect in the bilge and be a fire hazard should there be a leak. There was a head with a holding tank. The rig was grounded for lightning protection. What was there not to like?

Hull number 1, the one we had sailed, was already sold to a couple in Detroit, but production would begin soon in Tartan's North Carolina plant. Howard assured us that we could take delivery before winter. The boat would be stored inside over the winter, and the company would include sails of our choosing in the deal.

By then, the plant was closing. We hadn't sealed the deal, but we had a list of available options, and they said they would send someone to look at *Temerity* and make an offer. We were so excited we grinned like kids all the way home.

Back in Ashville, I decided to sell the life insurance policy my parents had bought for me as a child. It grew much more slowly than stocks we had invested in, so that made some sense. My mother agreed to give us a loan at a modest rate of interest. We would use our cash savings. After Tartan called and offered us $16,000 for the

Morgan, we knew we had to buy the boat. We had only paid $14,875, and that was ten years before. We made an offer, it was accepted, and we headed back to Grand River, where we handed over part of the money, and they provided paperwork that promised the boat would be built in their Hamlet, North Carolina, plant. We would get hull number 24; it would be shoal draft with a Scheel keel, have wheel steering, and have an eighteen-horsepower Yanmar diesel engine. We wanted no roller furling, no "chicken jib" for us. We wanted hank on sails, 125, 150, and 175 percent. They agreed to supply those along with a racing spinnaker and self-tailing winches. It seemed impossible we could be doing this, but the deal was done.

Temerity pulled away from her slip at Dunkirk Yacht Club for the last time on a cool September morning in 1987. We sailed her west in favorable winds to Erie and then on to Grand River. We had the large jib up on the Morgan, with the full main, and as we were on a broad reach, we were flying. I remember, as we approached Grand River, an older Tartan 34 fell in alongside. He tried to pass us to leeward and dropped back and, then, tried to pass us to weather. No luck. We had stripped the Morgan before we left, and perhaps for the first time since we bought her, she was in true racing trim. We beat the Tartan to Grand River, and he pulled up alongside once we were past the harbor entrance. "Nice boat," said the Tartan owner.

"Tradin' her in on a new 31," I replied.

"What you doing that for?" he answered with a grin.

After the boat was secure at the yard, we talked with Tim, the designer, who thought we might want to see the boat while it was under construction. He suggested coming to North Carolina just before the hull was attached to the deck. That way, we would be able to view the engine installation, wiring, and the furniture that was being installed. I wondered whether we wanted to be there when the hull was pulled from the mold. Friends suggested that was the most important part of construction. Tim said he didn't think that was important. "Sometimes the hull comes out smoothly, sometimes it doesn't. If it doesn't come out easily, we will make complete repairs. In any case, it's your boat."

We decided we would drive to Hamlet.

It was a full day's drive to Hamlet, North Carolina, so we scheduled a full day to be there, found a motel room, and stayed two nights. At the plant, we were given a tour and then introduced to our boat. Her hull was glistening white above and below the waterline. The transition from the fiberglass hull to the lead keel was, in our eyes, perfect. The propeller and shaft were strong, straight, and firm, just as I had hoped they would be. I looked at the Martec folding prop and wondered where it would take us, folded smooth as we rushed along under sail or expanded and driving the boat through the water when the engine was powered. I brushed my hand under the keel and thought about the ground it might touch and fish and great animals of the sea that it might glide by.

Inside we could see the galley and the placement of the stove and sink. The nav station, in beautiful, dark teak, with its comfortable seat, was an amazing little desk. I could imagine it with the loran system installed, working on plotting problems with the chart before us and no horizon in sight. Of course, there were no cushions, but we could see the v-berths forward and the double berth aft on the port side. There was dust from construction everywhere, but we were thrilled. She was just what we had hoped for. It was a wonderful day, and we had a chance to discuss with the builder placement of winches and other items. Everyone was helpful, and we hung around until the plant closed in the afternoon. What a wonderful day!

D-day was in November. Julie and I drove to Grand River to see the finished product in her cradle at the Tartan Yard. She was complete, ready to launch, except for bottom paint, which would come later. Sadly, we would have to wait until spring to christen her; wind-driven rain and snow made a launch out of the question. She would be stored in a heated part of the plant until then.

"Could we, um, come and see her and do a little work on her over the winter?" I heard myself asking.

"Don't know why not," said the manager. "We'll be open on Saturdays, and as long as it's nothing major, you're most welcome."

We both beamed.

We got to know Route 90 between Westfield and Grand River really well that winter. Saturday after Saturday, we would have a project planned, drive to Grand River, and carry it out. First, it was the loran-C, then the VHF radio. Wiring had to be concealed, and the instruments had to be located in just the right place. I was under strict orders from Julie not to drill any extra holes! These were all things that hadn't been part of the original deal. We really got to know the boat well.

When spring finally arrived, Julie and I drove to Grand River one afternoon after school so we could be there and break a bottle of champagne over the bow when she was launched for the first time. Tartan wanted to do sea trials with the engine, and we wanted to be there, even though the mast was not yet in place.

"May she always take us to sea, and may she always bring us back," said Julie as she smashed the carefully netted champagne bottle over the anchor roller. Once she was launched, we shared a second bottle with the launch crew and set out for our first ride. The engine started right up, and we glided around the small harbor, testing and getting used to the steering, shifting and speed controls, and the electronics. The Tartan representative who was with us took careful notes, but we were very pleased. Everything seemed to work perfectly! We enjoyed Tartan sandwiches at the local pub in Grand River that evening before the long drive home. Julie and I returned for a test sail with the designer the following Saturday, and finally, when everything was perfect, we sailed our baby back to Dunkirk for a memorable summer of sailing.

We named her *Trilogy*. Unlike the "arrogant courage" *Temerity* reflected, *Trilogy* was simply a story in three parts. She was our third boat, after all, and as our other two boats had names that began with *T*, *Twiga* and *Temerity*, along with our two dogs, Troy and Tammy, why not continue the tradition? We had enjoyed good luck with our *T* things, that was for sure, so the new boat was *Trilogy*. We ordered a decal and carefully applied it to her transom, with Ashville, New York, our home. She would be documented, a true ship of the sea. She was ours. She was just what we had wanted. We felt really good about that.

So we raced her, and we bought a second spinnaker, a small one, from a used sailmaker. We didn't win, but we had the thrill of sailing a beautiful new boat. She flew under spinnaker and seemed to sail to her handicap. We took her to Henderson Harbor that first year and sailed in the Thousand Islands, a good place to try out a diesel engine, and though we sailed, mostly we motored. We sailed home to Dunkirk, where we were in for a letdown.

CHAPTER 84

Bad News

It was the end of that year, sometime in August 1987, when we found it. It was a small lump in Julie's breast. There were doctor's appointments, lumpectomy surgery, a biopsy, and then confirmation that it was cancer. It was "nicely encapsulated," said the doc who removed it, but it was cancer. There was a painful operation to remove and check lymph nodes under Julie's armpit. There would be chemo and radiation. We were more deeply in debt than we had ever been, and Julie had cancer. There was sympathy all around, but cancer had always been a death sentence, and though the doctor was "optimistic" and we had "found it early," there was a dark cloud hanging over us. Julie took no time off school. She missed one day after the nodes were removed, but she kept on teaching chemistry. Every Friday afternoon, we went for chemo. She donned a frozen cap to help her keep from losing her hair. She never lost her hair, and she never threw up. She wasn't going to let this beat her.

This was Julie, after all, who, at eight, had been diagnosed with infantile paralysis—polio. This was Julie, who was paralyzed by the disease, whose spine was weakened to the point surgery was required to fuse it back together. This was Julie, who, after surgery, remembers waking up in a tub of ice water, freezing cold. This was a girl whom the docs thought might live to be thirty or so, if she were lucky. Here was a girl who, when urged to move her wheelchair through the halls of the hospital, wanted to race the other recovering children.

Here was Julie, my wife, and we weren't going to let this beat us. She had, after all, competed in and won cross-country ski marathons in Chautauqua County among women her age. She even finished a running marathon in Cleveland when the odds were piled against her. Julie was an *odds beater*.

I was commander of the Chautauqua Power Squadron that year, and we had our one and only district conference in Jamestown. Julie, still undergoing treatment, and I, along with the rest of the squadron, worked tirelessly to carry it off, and we did. It was a huge effort and a smashing success.

We had a long, cold winter, but we knew spring would follow. There were more treatments, trips to Roswell Park in Buffalo, examinations, and when Julie finally endured her last chemo treatment in July of 1989, at the age of forty-four, she wondered if we could take *Trilogy* to Lake Superior for a real cruise.

CHAPTER 85

Superior

We didn't have a great deal of time. I remember pushing off from the dock at Dunkirk and setting sail that first evening. A bat had taken up temporary residence in the top of the mainmast and dived at us as we raised sail just outside of Dunkirk. A bad omen? How would we know? We sailed night and day, without stopping, the length of Lake Erie and through the islands at the western end of the lake. We passed South Bass, Middle Bass, and Pelee Islands and continued to the Gross Isle Yacht Club at the mouth of the Detroit River, where we spent a night as reciprocal guests of the club. Early the next day, we began laboriously motoring up the Detroit River to Lake Saint Clair. Our diesel supply was running low, so after motoring through the large still Lake Saint Clair, we found a fuel dock with DIESEL printed on a sign over the pumps. The attendant, looking at our lovely boat, was impressed. He explained to us, however, that his tank had failed inspection and there was no other fuel stop for miles up the river. Obviously touched by our disappointment, he suggested that we get whatever containers we had and follow him to his truck. We didn't have a separate tank, so he grabbed a tank from his shelf, and we all three climbed into his pickup, where he drove us to a fuel station up the road. The tank he had grabbed was more like a wastebasket with a snap-on lid, and after we filled it, I held the lid tightly in place as we drove back to the marina. He wouldn't take any money for his help, and he provided us with a big funnel so we could dump the fuel from the tub into our tank. He told us just how far we would have to go to the next fuel stop. That was no problem, though it was against a rather-strong current. We made it, and there we filled up completely before we left the Saint Clair River.

Fair weather held, and we sailed north under the Blue Water Bridge into Lake Huron. We sailed past Goodrich and Bayfield and Tobermory, with no intention of stopping until we reached the entrance to the Saint Mary's River. We sailed in three-hour shifts through the night, carefully watching for ships, sailing when there was sufficient wind, and motoring when there wasn't.

In Saint Mary's, we did some clothes shopping in a wool outlet, buying things like earmuffs, scarves, and warm socks. Superior has a reputation of being cold. We had heard about storms, winds from the north that could be cold and mean. The Soo Locks at Sault Saint Marie were not impressive, except for the constant drone of the "Ballad of the Edmund Fitzgerald" that played over the loudspeakers to entertain those watching ships and boats locking through. Our first stop on Superior was at Whitefish Bay, where we had a chance to visit with other sailors. "Shorten down early" and "Be prepared for cold and wet" was the heart of their advice. We took them seriously. We had installed a Force 10 diesel heater in the boat, and there was comfort in knowing it was there if we needed it. Our goal was to sail to the Apostle Islands at the western end of the lake. It would be a long haul, but we were determined.

There are two things I remember most about that cruise. The first was sailing along the south shore with forest and trees as far as one could see. There was often no sign of roads or buildings or any human activity. It was beautiful, and as we gushed along, pushed by the wind, we felt close to and part of nature. It was later, after we had passed through the canal on the Keweenaw Peninsula, that we experienced something truly unique to us.

We had been sailing all day in moderate breezes when it began. The lake became glassy calm. Still, there was wind. Somehow, it had separated itself from the water. The waves diminished, but the boat continued to glide along. A high wind, perhaps fifteen feet above the water, filled the sails. The phenomena continued until evening. I began to work with tightening the brake on the helm and adjusting the sails to see if *Trilogy* would track and stay on course without my touching the helm. After a bit, I found the boat would stay on course for minutes at a time. Julie made dinner, and instead of serving it in the cockpit as she normally would, she set the table up in the cabin. I ducked below to see if shifting my weight would affect the helm, but we stayed on course. There were no other boats in sight, but still, I had to peek every few minutes. It was exhilarating to think our boat could sail by herself without an autopilot. I actually ate my dinner below.

It was night, there was no moon, but millions of stars overhead were reflected on the glassy water. Far ahead, we began to see the flash on the light on Outer Island. Still, there was wind. Somehow, the wind filled *Trilogy*'s sails, pushing us along on a close reach. The boat gurgled through the water, but there was no wave action. The stars were reflected on the water. It was stunning. That was not all. Northern lights flashed and glowed in the sky. They were green and purple and red. We sat in the cockpit and watched in awe. The winds were so steady we were able to secure the wheel, and the boat stayed on course with only minimal adjustments. Hour after hour we continued, and then there was more flashing. First to the south and then to the north, flashes, definitely distant flashes of lightning, appeared on both shores. Sleep was simply not an option. There was a never-to-be-forgotten light show surrounding us and filling sky and water with a brilliance like we had never seen. We might be the last people on earth but for the regular flashes of Outer Light. There were no ships, no pleasure boats, just us knifing our way through the smooth, calm water in the middle of the night.

Was this a warning? Was there an approaching front that would explode overhead and turn smooth Superior into a raging storm we could not endure? The VHF radio had predicted no dangerous weather. Julie brought a portable radio from the cabin, and we found quiet classical music from Canada added a bit more magic to the moment, a moment words cannot properly describe.

The light on Outer Island grew nearer, and finally, the outline of the island appeared above the water. We found our way into the harbor and, at first light, to a dock maintained by the National Park Service. Invigorated rather than exhausted by our night's sail, we secured the boat and headed off on a trail through thick woods toward the western side of the island. We were glad for the exercise as we walked along and followed the narrow path outlined on a pamphlet we found outside the ranger's office.

It wasn't until we reached the western shore that we began to put together what should have been obvious. To the west were thick black clouds. It began to rain. It was cold rain pushed by a building wind. Rain splashed on our faces, and we turned and headed back. Quickly the trail turned to mud. My boat shoes and Julie's sandals weren't made for running in mud, and we hadn't brought wet-weather gear. Our clothing quickly became soaked through. We had not noticed several divides on the trail that were only obvious while heading east. Which way? Julie got out the map, but where were we? Memories came to mind of my Power Squadron classes, where I discussed the dangers of hypothermia. People in the mountainous west would start out to climb a mountain trail in the morning in shorts and Ts and an unexpected storm with cold wind and rain would chill them, sometimes killing them before they could get back to base camp. Then there was the fifty-fifty rule. An adult in fifty-degree water for fifty minutes has a fifty-fifty chance of survival. Would we suffer from hypothermia?

We were shivering and exhausted when we got back to the boat, but there was still hot water for a shower, and we lit our diesel heater and soon warmed up. The park ranger paid us a visit and invited us to a nature study later that evening. With the wind whistling through the rigging, we soon fell asleep.

Later, we enjoyed a nature talk, one of several we would hear on the islands. The park ranger, a delightful woman, caught sight of our Power Squadron flag and had to share a story with us. She said there was a local squadron from a nearby city that took an annual cruise to the islands. They tied their cruisers to the docks, washed their boats every day, and drank a lot. They were never any trouble, just pleasant families. One year, they did have a problem. There was a bear on the island. It would frighten tourists, and it made everyone uneasy. They trapped it, loaded it in a truck, and took it into the forest on the mainland and released it. A week later, it was back. It must have walked back to the shore and then swum to the island. The bear made its way to the marina in the night and found the fleet of pristine Power Squadron yachts tied to the docks. With its muddy paws, it walked back and forth on the clean white decks, leaving bear tracks wherever it went. It was gone by morning, but the squadron members were thrilled. Suddenly, their summer cruise in comfortable yachts had become a first-class adventure. They had a story to tell! What couldn't they do? They couldn't wash their boats! What if it rained? What would they do then? They took lots of photographs and left a day ahead of schedule so they could show their friends back home.

We explored several other islands over the next few days, made a trip to Bayfield on the mainland, and finally set sail for home.

We sailed into the canal at the Keweenaw Peninsula. It was in the very early morning, and at Coppermine, we tied to a slip in front of a small restaurant. It had been cool in the night, and we were wearing warm sweaters and our wet-weather jackets. Tired and hungry, we walked from the boat, around the building, to the front door, where we entered. "Those are the people from the boat," someone muttered. A friendly waitress seated us, and before long, a steaming breakfast was in front of us. Everyone there seemed to be a tourist, we thought. We wandered to a museum in town and soon found ourselves fitting right in with all the other tourists in the place. The museum was informative and interesting. We spent the night there, and the next morning, we again headed east.

Again, images of our boat gushing through the water come to mind, but one that I will never forget was simply a middle-of-the-night sail under a full moon. Julie was asleep, and *Trilogy*, with the wind behind her, moved easily through the waves. I scanned the channels on the VHF until I happened upon a conversation between two friends on different ships discussing their late-night snacks. They described the sandwiches they were eating and talked about what was happening in their private lives. There was nothing particularly personal or embarrassing, but they were both on ships in this huge cold sea and they thought they were so isolated that no one could be listening to what they were saying. Marine radio is intended for formal conversation only, not idle chatter. But here I was, listening in on them as they discussed the sandwiches they were eating. I suppose it was rude of me, but it underscored the vastness of Lake Superior. It was also a kind of alarm. Because they assumed they were so alone, would whoever was at the helm of those ships expect a thirty-one-foot sailboat to be in their path? I checked the lights on the mast and at the bow. They were on, but not very reassuring. I scanned the horizon but found no ships in sight. I called below, and a light clicked on. It was Julie's turn. She zipped her jacket and, with a broad smile, climbed into the cockpit. My turn for a snooze.

The sail home was unremarkable. There were a few squalls on Lake Huron, but nothing noteworthy. We literally seemed to fly down the Saint Clair and Detroit Rivers with both wind and current behind us. Lake Erie, too, was a breeze. We stopped at Grand River, where we visited with our friends at Tartan. A kind man there lent us his van so we could pick up some groceries. He had worked for Tartan in years past, and he pointed out his current boat, a Nauticat. It had been built in Finland, had a pilothouse, and could be steered from inside in bad weather. He liked it a lot.

Back in Ashville, life was good. Julie was healthy. We had sailed from Erie to Superior and back in August. We endured no wild storms. Perhaps that bat in the rigging was a harbinger of good things to come, not an evil omen, after all. Sadly, Tammy, our friendly Brittany spaniel, had become ill and died, of cancer.

CHAPTER 86

Saint Lawrence

So what next? Our boat was still new and had proven herself able. What else could we do? What about the Maritime provinces of Canada? We hadn't done that. Winter found Julie and me, but especially Julie, poring over charts of the Saint Lawrence River and the Maritime provinces. We read about the powerful currents in the Bay of Fundy, the beautiful Bras d'Or Lakes, the Strait of Canso, Nova Scotia, and New Brunswick. Could we do it all in one summer? Could we sail across Lake Erie, through the Welland Canal, the length of Lake Ontario, out the Saint Lawrence, past Ottawa and Montreal to the Gaspé, south to Nova Scotia, Prince Edward's Island, and then cross back to Maine, sail west to New York, and finally return via the Hudson River and Erie Canal to the south shore of Lake Erie, all in one two-month-long summer vacation?

We thought we could.

One afternoon, while at a luncheon at a friend's house in nearby Lakewood, I sat across the table from a man named Jack. During lunch, he reached into his pocket and pulled out a little rectangular device. He clicked some buttons and began talking as though he was on the phone. As cell phones were not yet widely available, I was impressed. "Anyone you'd like to call?" he asked. He went on to explain that what he was using was a two-meter ham radio, connected to a relay so it could be used as a phone. Julie and I were intrigued! If we wanted to learn more, Jack was teaching a course on ham radio in Jamestown, and there was room in his class. Before long, we found ourselves practicing code and listening to him speak about talking to folks all over the world using voice and, sometimes, code. We learned radio theory, and we learned Morse code. We practiced on our computer using a program called Morse Man Plus. We bought radios, first a handheld two-meter and then a high-frequency rig. We installed a G5RV antenna in the backyard and sunk a copper rod by the house foundation for a ground.

We took the "novice" and then "technician" tests, and we passed. We could transmit and receive across the bands in code, and we could talk on ten meters when conditions in the ionosphere made it viable. I remember my first ten-meter voice QSO with a man who lived on the White Cliffs of Dover, England. I was nervously calling: CQ, CQ, CQ, KB2JFN. The man responded with his call, and when I realized I was talking across the Atlantic, I could hardly think of anything to say.

More frequently, Julie or I made the call-in code on eighty meters. One never knew who would answer, but it was usually someone in a several hundred-mile radius. One time, a man from Flint, Michigan, picked up. He slowed to my rather-pathetic speed, and we continued to chat for some time. Turned out he was a photographer for the Buick Motor Division of General Motors. He sent me a card with an advertising photo of a ten-year-old Buick Electra. I was really fascinated with this new toy.

We mounted the radio aboard *Trilogy*, installed an antenna tuner, added a portable antenna to the rail, and we agreed to have a daily QSO with Jack as we headed out the Saint Lawrence. It would be in code. He thought we might be impressed with the reliability of the system.

So along with our springer spaniel pup, Tudor, we left. It was the day after school let out when we closed the Ashville house and arranged for a ride with Julie's sister to Dunkirk so we wouldn't have to leave our car on the street all summer. We started the engine, cast off our lines, and headed across the lake on a magnificent summer morning. The Welland Canal, our old friend, had no surprises for us, and the loran-C set us on a course directly for Galloo Island on the eastern end of Lake Ontario. From there we would head for the cottage, where some rotted wood had been replaced on the floor of the swim room.

We fairly gushed through the night. The autopilot worked flawlessly, and we slept in shifts as one kept watch and carefully ticked off landmarks on the chart while the other rested. The lights on Main Duck and Galloo Islands were reassuring, and bearings from the nuclear facility at Oswego combined with them to show us we were right where the loran said we were. From there it was an easy sail in familiar waters to the cottage at Henderson Harbor. Sure enough, the floor in the swim room had been repaired, but not painted. That wouldn't do. Dirty feet would soon soil the pine boards and make painting more difficult and less effective. Julie dug out a can of gray paint from storage, and before long, the job was done. Some leaky plumbing was revealed when we turned on the water. It smeared the paint, but once the plumbing was resolved, an old Coulter family adage kicked in: "Two coats are three times as good as one." So we painted the floor again.

Finally, we locked the doors behind us, hauled the dinghy onto the deck, raised anchor, and headed north. From there we sailed to Kingston, Ontario, across the lake, where we checked into customs and received our cruising permit to allow us to proceed on our journey. We sailed down the Saint Lawrence, past Cape Vincent, to the Thousand Islands and Clayton and Alexandria Bay. The river was busy with huge freighters and container ships, ferries, and commercial vessels of all kinds along with recreational traffic. At night, we anchored out whenever possible, but often we would find accommodation at a pier or marina. Tudor, our young English springer spaniel, made friends easily. There were several places that made an impression on us.

The first was the Eisenhower Locks, the locking system that made the Saint Lawrence navigable to ships of the sea. It wasn't a terribly impressive set of locks, but the lock tenders insisted that we don life jackets while locking through. We complied, of course, and it no doubt added a level of drama for the spectators in the bleachers. We anchored out in Montreal as fish jumped all around the boat.

In Quebec, we entered a lock that took us to the community marina. With the rising and falling tides of the river, it was the only way to provide safe dockage. We walked the beautiful city for hours and had a delightful dinner in the Chateau Frontenac. It was a night to be remembered.

One evening, we came to a marina where only French was spoken. Those in charge couldn't seem to understand any of our questions regarding services of the marina but had no difficulty telling us the cost of a slip, which we felt was very high. Rather than pay his price, we decided to anchor overnight in a small cove just across the marina. That seemed a good idea at that time, but the next morning, while trying to leave the little cove on our way to the main channel, we ran hard aground. Finally, the wake of a passing freighter lifted us just long enough for me to haul us off with the help of a line made fast to an anchor. I remember Julie and me scrambling to get the anchor up and the boat away before wind and wave washed us back aground.

At the confluence of the Saguenay River, near Tadoussac, we saw our first whales. They were belugas, small white whales, and they came quite near the boat. We were really excited about seeing them and snapped pictures. Tourists, in small inflatables, motored right up to them to get very near. They showed little respect for the magnificent creatures, interested only in their close-up photographs. Farther off, we saw the spout of what we thought might have been a gray or perhaps a sperm whale. Whatever it was, the magic of these huge mammals impressed us greatly. We were awed by their size and their gentle nature.

As we sailed farther out the river, we noted how the current and wind moved us as far as it did each day. Following seas and winds carried us along. Often, we would change jibs from a substantial 150 percent to a smaller 125, or even 100, which, along with a reefed mainsail, would still get us to our intended destination hours ahead of schedule. I have a clear memory of Julie lowering one sail and raising the other on the foredeck. We would then fold the sail brought down and stuff it into its bag. We were flying down the Saint Lawrence, and with our limited schedule, that was fine with us. At Rimouski, we were amazed how early we arrived. We had a favorable tide, wind, and current. Every night, we communicated with our friend Jack back in Jamestown via code. We told him our position and a little about what was happening as we sailed. We were amazed at the reliability and power of the radio. One night, while we were tied to a huge iron barge, with our antenna just a few feet from the side of that ship, we thought we would have little chance to pick up signal. But we were wrong. It all worked like magic. "KB2JFN, KB2JFN, AC2D." Loud and clear, Jack's signal came in. Wonderful!

On and on we went, always with the wind at our backs as we slid through whitecaps to the next port. Finally, we rounded the Gaspé Peninsula and went into the harbor at Gaspé. There we received a warm welcome from local people we met, but of course, we were on our way before long. It was a seafaring town with a fishing fleet as well as recreational vessels. Local restaurants served us delicious meals. At Prince Edward Island, we visited the yacht club at Charlottetown. What I remember most about that was a conversation we had there with other coastal sailors.

We had used the loran-C for navigation in the United States for several years, and it had never let us down. We would routinely convert the *time differences*, which loran received, to latitude and longitude so they would be easier to plot on the chart. The receiver would do it automatically. At PEI, however, the Canadian sailors there insisted that, on the coast, it was essential that the time differences received by the loran be used to plot your position on the chart directly. They believed that too much accuracy was lost by converting to latitude and longitude and that one might find himself compromised by dangerous shoals in very limited visibility if the shortcut conversion was used. We had used the latitude-and-longitude method in the United States and had never found a problem. How could it be so different here? I wondered. They were sure, however, and before long we would learn the importance of their advice.

In the Bras d'Or Lake, we explored beautiful saltwater lakes that looked every bit like the freshwater lakes we had grown up on. There were excellent anchorages and deep water that made for great sailing for yachts of all sizes. One night, at a local fish diner, we met an attractive young couple who was delivering an eighty-foot mega yacht to the Caribbean. Her nine-foot draft limited where she could run for cover in the event that a tropical storm or hurricane should confront them. Because the boat had powerful winches and was designed to be sailed shorthanded, they were able to sail her in all but the most challenging conditions. The boat had just been completed, and the couple was delivering it to her new owners.

CHAPTER 87

The Straits of Canso

After a pleasant time in this lovely fog-free part of the Maritimes, we ventured back into the North Atlantic. We would travel through the Straits of Canso. *Trilogy* was on top of her game as we eased toward the straits. She was beautiful and received compliments wherever she went. We stopped and bought fresh fish from a local fisherman, and then when the tides were right, we ventured forth into a dense bank of fog. How dense? Let's just say that it was nearly opaque. Julie, from the chart table below, called up a heading, and that was where we sailed, or should I say, motored. The water was calm, and with the currents around the straits, one wouldn't want to linger. We motored for the better part of an hour. Julie would confirm our position on the loran below, and it was clear we were making good headway. Ahead of us was just a white blanket in all directions. I could see perhaps a hundred feet ahead of the boat, but that was all.

Then I thought I saw something ahead and to the side. First, I thought it might have been a large mammal, a dolphin or a whale, but no, it was a rock. I pulled back on the throttle, pushed the shift into reverse, and we stopped. Julie's puzzled face appeared in the companionway. "What?"

"I think I saw a rock. Look, over there!"

Sure enough, the small waves on that calm morning were breaking on the top of a brown rock. I peered over the side, and there was bottom; the depth meter read just ten feet. Julie disappeared back in the cabin and refigured our position using the *time differences* the Canadians had insisted we use along the coast.

"We're in the middle of a shoal," she said. "Be careful and head east."

I eased the boat into forward, and ever so gently, with Julie on the bow, we moved ahead to get us out of the troubled waters. Before long, the depth began to increase. We were again in deep water, but we were still moving through a blanket of fog. Julie used the time differences, and we tracked our way as we moved along the coast toward the south. For several days, we sailed and motored carefully to the south. Constant vigilance was essential as we moved without the piercing eyes of radar. At night, we would seek shelter in a harbor on the chart. Visibility was so low it is difficult to describe.

One evening, we approached a small harbor and found a navigation buoy in the fog. We circled the marker, trying to find it on our chart. In the meantime, there was a break in the fog, revealing a man standing on a wall within shouting distance. I hollered to him, "Which way to the harbor entrance?"

"Follow me!" he shouted back.

With that, the young man scrambled down a ladder on the wall to a little aluminum boat, started the outboard with a pull of the cord, and continued into the fog, which parted ahead of him, revealing a perfectly clear opening in the wall. We entered and secured the boat, and a minute or so later, we were again completely engulfed in the fog. Later that evening, we visited with a man who told us of going out in fishing boats and, when storms came up, "jamming their boats into the ice" for protection. They stored fuel and food and water to enable them to survive in the cold Nova Scotia winter, often for days and weeks at a time. Life there seemed cold and lonely and miserable to us.

CHAPTER 88

White Haven

After another day sailing in the fog, we followed a trawler into a place called White Haven. It was a delightful cove with just a few fishing boats. We anchored and looked at the colorful houses of a small town built right on the water. We launched the dinghy and, with our friendly springer spaniel, Tudor, rowed for shore. The dinghy crunched on the little beach, and Julie and I carefully carried it above the high watermark while Tudor explored the smells of the neighborhood, her tail wagging enthusiastically. Where was she, anyway? We called and scanned the area, and there she was, up on the porch of a little house, enthusiastically emptying a bowl of cat food and then slurping water from another bowl next to it. Her tail was wagging her whole body so enthusiastically that she looked as if she were acting in a television commercial. Only the cat, retired to the porch swing, was unsure about the situation.

After corralling the dog, I knocked timidly on the front door, and when a lady in a neat dress and apron appeared, I did my best to apologize for the inappropriate behavior of our dog.

"You must be the people on the yacht," she said.

Unaccustomed to having our boat referred to as a yacht, I hesitated as I said, "Yes, it's our boat in the harbor. We just came in to anchor and spend the night, on our way south toward Halifax."

"Well," she said. "And your dog ate the cat's food. In that case, I think you'll just have to come in and meet my husband." She smiled broadly and opened the door so we could enter her warm home. Inside we met her husband and several young children, who were bouncing around. They were gracious and fun. However, our apology simply wouldn't do. We would have to go to the local Hoop La Days in White Haven. That was all there was to it. There was to be a dinner that night at the local fire hall, and we would go with them. There would be dancing with a one-man band. We would leave the dog aboard the boat and row back in at around six in the evening. The party would be over around midnight. Would we come?

Of course! So Julie and I rowed back to *Trilogy*, changed our clothes, and left Tudor, who wasn't altogether happy about that part of the arrangement, and we rowed back to shore. The family had a small Chevy II, and it took two trips to get everyone from the house to the community center.

It seemed the whole town was there. There were drinks and food and a great deal of laughter. Many of the people in town were related, and everyone seemed to know everyone else. They were so kind and gracious to us that we could hardly believe it. Such warmth and kindness in this foggy, cold world. Then the band began to play. He was, indeed, a one-man band. There on a stand were a trumpet and a sax, a harmonica, and a guitar. There was a set of drums. The musician slipped into his seat and began to entertain us by playing on multiple instruments popular music that we knew and loved. He could sing too. This wasn't the keyboard player with recorded backup; this guy was for real, and whether he was strumming the guitar or playing the sax or singing, the music was wonderful. We danced. Julie and I danced with each other, and we danced with people we didn't know at all. It was wonderful fun. The beer flowed, and the music played. It was a night to be remembered. Finally, like everything else, it ended.

It was around midnight when we piled into the Chevy II and drove back to the little house near the harbor. Our hostess made tea as we relaxed in the cool evening. There was an older man there who wanted to visit with us. We told him about our trip and where we were headed. He said he had been a fisherman and that he understood that Hurricane Bertha had formed in the tropics and was heading north. He thought that we would be well to get to Halifax, where we could find good protection, promptly. He explained that the storm was just a possibility but that hurricanes cause very rough seas along the coast in Nova Scotia.

CHAPTER 89

Halifax

So it was with that grim news that we rowed back to the boat to pick up Tudor for her evening walk. Above the little village, *Trilogy* looked so peaceful as she tugged gently on her anchor in the still harbor. Her anchor light glowed from the masthead. Somehow the fog had mostly lifted, and the calm sea looked friendly and beckoning.

The next morning, we rose early, raised anchor, and with some difficulty, broke our ties to the little haven that had been so kind to us. There was a fair breeze, and we headed for Halifax. We knew we would have to sail through the night to make it, but we both agreed it sounded like the right thing to do. We knew we would have to check in with harbor control when we got there, and they would guide us into the harbor through the rather-heavy ship traffic visiting and departing from the busy port.

The sail was again through dense fog. We grew tired of staring into the endless white, but even more difficult was the dense darkness. Was there a ship out there bearing down on us? We charted our course with the aid of the loran, carefully using the time differences to verify our position, but we constantly peered into darkness, aware that we had only our eyes and ears to protect us from danger that might lie ahead. Of course, mariners had sailed for years without electronics, and we, too, noted our time and position regularly, so we at least had that to fall back on. We used sound signals, too, then listened carefully for a reply. We had done it before, but the fog and the currents made it all the more challenging.

Only one thing of note happened on that sail, and it was far into the night. We used the masthead lights for navigation while under sail, so there was no illumination ahead, important for seeing nav lights on other vessels. There it was. Just a glimmer of white ahead of me. I quickly moved the wheel, and we slid past a lobster boat, the crew hauling traps with an electric winch. They waved as we glided past, silent, with our large dripping sails sucking energy from the wet wind. In a moment, they were gone, not a sound or a glimmer in the dark Nova Scotia night. A tragedy averted? Yes, a collision of two vessels at night is a very dangerous thing. But it didn't happen.

I picked up harbor control at Halifax on the VHF the following morning, and they guided us safely to the docks at the Royal Nova Scotia Yacht Squadron, where we were welcomed warmly.

We expressed our concern about the approaching storm, but no one there seemed terribly concerned. "Your slip is secure, and you may keep it for the duration of the bad weather or longer, if you wish," the dockmaster told us. He smiled reassuringly at me.

Back aboard, we secured the boat and then went about what we thought would be appropriate storm preparations. There were warnings on the radio. The storm was real, and it was coming. We removed the mainsail and dodger and doubled the mooring lines. We added crossed spring lines and ran additional lines to pilings in adjacent slips. We would wait to run lines across the docks to pilings on the other side. Might be a hazard to dock walkers if we did it ahead.

Hmmm. No one else seemed to be preparing with our enthusiasm. The boat next to us had a furling jib, the sheets hanging loosely. Other folks came and looked over their boats but seemed to shrug and walk away. Dodgers, even Bimini's, were left up to weather the storm. I ventured into the clubhouse, where I found the manager. I mentioned to him that I had ham radio aboard should there be a breakdown of communications. He wasn't impressed. "I appreciate all that you two are doing," he said. A hurricane here isn't as it is in the tropics. It is usually a big rainstorm. I expect this one will be the same. But thank you for your offer, anyway."

A man and his wife in a nearby boat introduced themselves and reassured us that we would likely weather the storm easily in the boat and there was no need to find a hotel or other accommodation. They wondered whether we would join them in the club for dinner that evening.

It was a lovely time. Rain was coming down outside, and the storm was on its way, but the food and the company were excellent. He was an active member of the racing fleet at the club, and he knew local waters quite well. During our conversation, the ham radio came up. We mentioned that we had used it throughout the cruise but that somehow the tuner wasn't working properly. We wondered whether he knew anyone who might fix it.

Our new friend thought for a moment and then mentioned someone who worked on offshore oil rigs. He maintained radios, and he would know how to get ours fixed. He suggested we make a general call on our two-meter rig and someone would know how to get in touch with him. I thanked him for his suggestion. This whole field was really new to me. I wasn't sure.

Back on the boat that night, we endured wild winds, and rain roared on the decks. We rolled a bit in our slip, but there was no damage to the boat, and Julie and I, with the dog snuggled between us, slept well.

The next morning in the rain, I tried the two-meter to contact this radio person, and magically, someone gave me his call, and I tried it and he came on. He said he was familiar with the 735 Icom radio and he would pick ours up later that afternoon to have a look at it. Meanwhile, the brunt of the storm had passed. Several people had been washed off an overlook at Peggy's Cove and had been rescued by others who attached ropes to lawn chairs and threw them to those in the water. A ship had foundered not far from Halifax. Obviously, though our preparations might have been a bit overdone, it had been well we had found shelter when we did.

There was a young man there, big and strong, who had sailed single-handedly from the UK in a single-handed race. A rubber seal that cost less than a dollar had failed, and as a result, his boom vang had failed and he had gone from first to last place in the race.

Disappointed, he made repairs and set sail for England. He told us that he expected to set his sails and sleep on the downwind run back home. Next thing he knew, he found himself in the midst of a hurricane. He had to be rescued. His boat was for sale, cheap. So though it might not have done catastrophic damage, it was a major storm. We had done the right thing.

The following day, we toured the city. When we got back to the boat, we had a surprise. The man who had taken the radio on the previous day returned it, repaired. It worked perfectly. When I asked him if he could take a check or a credit card, his reply astounded me. "Ham radio operators work together and help others. They don't charge for their services." Suddenly, Halifax had become a very special place. This man made his living repairing radios on offshore oil rigs, but he wouldn't take money for fixing ours because Julie and I were hams!

We reinstalled the main and dodger. We thanked the people at the yacht club for their hospitality, and we pushed off.

One of the places we sailed by was Peggy's Cove, where the storm had swept people into the water, fortunately with no loss of life. We could hardly believe it. The weather was so fair as we glided by. The sun was shining. Imagine that! At the club, someone had suggested Pirate's Cove as the perfect place for us to spend a night. It came with a warning: "The place is so small there is really just room for one boat. If someone is there when you arrive, you will find protection outside."

We followed our chart carefully and wended our way into the tiny hurricane hole. It was a tight fit, but it was magical, indeed. We took the dinghy to shore and climbed nearby hills to look down on *Trilogy*. There she was in a tiny cove just her size, protected on all sides by steep hills. We were truly alone that night. No one ventured near. It was a bit of magic.

CHAPTER 90

Crossing the Bay of Fundy

But there was another challenge ahead. At the southern end of Nova Scotia, the Bay of Fundy lies. There, the great Atlantic Ocean moves in and out regularly and creates some of the highest tides in the world. With those tides are currents that will carry a small boat or a giant ship up into the bay and then back out into the sea without mercy. If the wind is blowing against the current, huge waves are formed. If the wind is with the current, boats can be propelled over the bottom at great speed. Everyone agreed that we would need to "shorten down early" in case of bad weather, maintain a lookout, and keep the boat closed up tightly. Oh, and seasick medicine. "Don't forget your Bonine!"

"How would we steer toward our destination with such contrary currents?" I found myself asking.

"Just set your course for your destination. Over the twelve hours or so, the tides compensate."

"Really?"

"Well, more or less."

So that was it. We found ourselves rounding the southern end of Nova Scotia and heading for the coast of Maine. Northeast Harbor? That was what we had in the loran. We had lowered the dodger and secured it, we had the boards for the companionway close at hand along with life lines attached to the boat and life jackets, but the weather was fair. We sailed easily, and then, off Yarmouth, the boat somehow slowed and became unresponsive to the wheel. What could that be? Stray current?

No. A huge piece of kelp had somehow attached itself to the rudder. With the help of a boathook and a little reverse from the engine, we managed to disentangle ourselves from the underwater menace, and the boat took off again on a smooth, comfortable reach. Afternoon turned to evening, and we enjoyed dinner in the cockpit. We were sailing on an easy reach as the full moon appeared overhead. It was a beautiful night.

"You don't think we could…" Julie began

"Set the spinnaker?" I finished her sentence.

In a flash, my agile wife dropped into the cabin and returned with the smaller of our two spinnakers. She went to the foredeck and hoisted the *sock* to the masthead and brought the two sheets aft to the cockpit. In a moment, we had led the sheet and guy through the blocks near the stern, and she was lifting the long spinnaker pole to the mast and attaching the topping lift and downhaul. With the guy, the windward sheet, led through the end of the pole, we were ready. Julie pulled on the line attached to the spinnaker sock, and the large sail began to appear behind the jib. I released the halyard from the cockpit, and she gathered the jib as it dropped to the deck. With that, the blue-and-white sail filled, and after a little adjustment, we found ourselves gushing over the waves with eased main and full spinnaker on a glorious, moonlit night.

Who would believe it? I took pictures. The autopilot was steering, the spinnaker was set, and Julie and I were basking in the moonlight on a magical sail. We were making five to six knots crossing the Bay of Fundy. There were no monstrous waves. Although it appeared we were right on course, one check of the loran showed that we were indeed being sucked up the bay. Would we end up in Canada and miss Maine altogether? The barometer was steady, the sky was clear, and the forecast was promising. The tide shifted right on time, and we continued under spinnaker across the mighty bay. It wasn't until well after midnight that the wind shifted slightly and we again raised the jib, collapsed the chute, returned the spinnaker pole to the deck, and continued toward our destination. The weather held, and by the afternoon of the following day, we had checked into US Customs in Northeast Maine.

We sailed south toward New York, and as the end of summer was approaching, we found ourselves making long steps. Through the Cape Cod Canal, south to Long Island Sound, the mouth of the Hudson, and New York City we sailed. We sailed up the Hudson River to Castleton on Hudson, where we used their hoist to lower *Trilogy's* mast to the deck. From there, under power, we found our way to the Erie Canal and on to Buffalo, where we reset the mast at Wardell's Marina in Tonawanda. It was almost Labor Day when we retied to the dock at Dunkirk Yacht Club. We had been gone two months, had sailed thousands of miles, and there she was, our beautiful, almost-new boat, *Trilogy*, at the dock, looking every bit as she did before we had started.

CHAPTER 91

Bermuda

The summer of 1991 was different for us. We took the boat, as before, but this time, we just sailed up to Henderson Harbor and anchored her out front. Julie's dad had died years before, and her mother was left alone to tend to the cottage. The three girls had bought it from her. It needed to be painted. We spent the summer at the cottage with Julie's two other sisters and their families scraping and painting and fixing up the hundred-year-old cottage. When we were done, we sailed back to the Welland Canal and back across Lake Erie to Dunkirk. That was it. Done deal.

But somehow, after exploring the Maritimes and the New England coast, our summer at the cottage didn't seem very satisfying. While we had been in Halifax during that stormy weather the previous year, we recalled being in a marine store while several men were there busy selecting charts for an offshore cruise they were planning. They would sail to Bermuda. They were so excited about the prospect of the voyage and so enthusiastic about the chart selection that we were impressed. We dismissed them at that time, but the memory stuck.

There was an article about cruising to Bermuda in *Cruising World* that winter. It had to do with a first offshore adventure. Were we ready to truly take the boat offshore? Was our boat built for such a voyage?

It was the fall of 1991 when we found ourselves on the way back to Grand River. We talked with the designer of the boat, who assured us that she was, indeed, designed to be safe offshore. He affirmed that sailing to Bermuda at the right time of the year was a reasonable idea. He suggested we carry a life raft and an EPIRB, an emergency position locating beacon, along with single sideband high-frequency radio. We would need storm sails too. There would have to be a separate track for a storm trysail on the mast and a separate very small storm jib.

We were ecstatic! We did have a world cruiser! Well, sort of.

We couldn't wait for spring! We ordered the life raft first. It was a Plastimo, four-man, double-floor raft, self-inflating, with a canopy. It came in a valise rather than a hard case. When it arrived in Ashville, we felt our enthusiasm grow. We signed up for the JN, Junior Navigation class from the Power Squadron being taught in Warren, a forty-minute drive from our home in Ashville. We had gotten a used sextant while we were in Florida the previous year. It was a beautiful brass model that had no *error*, meaning it had never been dropped or abused. It was still in the original case and, as far as we could tell, had never been used. I remember lying on the gravelly beach on cool October evenings on Chautauqua Lake and managing to see an ever-so-slight curvature, a distant horizon, just enough to take a sight. I would then follow the instructions, and as Julie marked the time, we would record the sextant readings on planets, stars, and the moon. Amazingly, when the sights had been reduced, we were generally able to pinpoint our location, usually to within a mile of where we were. What geniuses they must have been who figured all this out! What a thrill! We passed the class and found we had both passed all the courses the Squadron had to offer except N, or navigation. Unfortunately, that course was not available in our area.

Meanwhile, we continued with our ham radio classes. We practiced our code and studied radio theory. Julie, a science teacher, after all, learned the theory quickly. She was also a code natural. She would listen to code on tape until she could decode complex sentences with words and numbers at ever-faster speeds. For me, it was much more difficult. Julie passed the general, advanced, and extra exams with ease, so she could access all the bands and use voice at any time. I struggled with the code. I could do the code, but I would become frustrated and lose my place. I couldn't seem to pass the test. I took the general exam in Jamestown several times, but I would come up just short time after time. I really wanted the access it would grant me to the ham bands. Finally, I began to drive to Erie, Pennsylvania, on Saturdays to take the test there. I remember, the second time I made the drive, there was a woman there supervising the test who recognized me. "Oh, you poor man!" she said. That did it. I passed, and with the award of the general certificate, I had the radio privileges I needed. It was May, and it was just before we were ready to leave.

We contacted our Erie sailmaker, and he built a tiny storm jib and storm trysail for our boat. We got sail track to attach to the mast so we could hoist the trysail at any time without having to remove the mainsail, a time-consuming task. We ordered an emergency position-indicating and reporting beacon, or EPIRB, a device that would, when switched on, transmit a distress signal and give our position to all passing aircraft and ships. We registered it, complete with phone numbers of whom to call to verify that we were indeed at sea and possibly in need of assistance. Finally, we joined the Waterway Cruising Club, a ham radio organization one would contact daily and report our position and any difficulty we might be having. Should we not contact them, they would send an alert. They would expect a call from us every day on our passage. We also bought a Global Positioning System, GPS, to help us on our way. It would be important as loran would not work that far offshore. We paid a thousand dollars but were assured such a fine instrument would never be cheaper.

Adding to our enthusiasm, we learned that the five-hundred-year anniversary of Columbus's voyage to America would be celebrated in New York Harbor at just the time we planned to arrive there, around the first of July. Wow! We were fired up!

On top of all that, it was our twenty-fifth wedding anniversary, and my mother threw us a big party at the Chautauqua Lake Yacht Club in Lakewood. My dad had been a charter member of the club, and all our friends and relatives were invited. Julie's aunt and uncle from Los Angeles came. I remember, my cousin Charlie's wife, Barbara, gave us T-shirts with "Happy 25th, Bermuda or Bust" printed on them. It was a very happy send-off.

So finally, we were ready to go. We said our goodbyes to our friends and family, left Tudor, our beautiful springer spaniel with Julie's sister, and the day after school let out, set out from Dunkirk Yacht Club for the Niagara River. This time we remembered to use the Black Rock Canal, navigated the Niagara River without difficulty, and arrived at Wardell's Marina before dark. We lowered the mast early the next morning and were on our way. By now, the Erie Barge Canal was old fun. We were moving in June, and traffic was light. There was, however, one small incident. I opened my contact lens case one morning, and the right lens was somehow missing. I searched the boat, with no results. Had it slipped from my finger the night before when I was taking it out and gone down the drain? It simply was not in the head. What to do? Could we sail all the way to Bermuda with me a Cyclops, a one-eyed monster? I went ashore at one of the locks outside Rochester and called my mother. I knew there was a spare lens in a case in the drawer to the left of the bathroom sink in our Ashville house. Would she please go to the house, go to the bathroom drawer, retrieve the lens, and send it overnight to Julie's niece Kimberly, who lived in Jersey City, right across the Hudson River from New York?

She said she would do her best.

We reset the mast at Castleton-on-Hudson, and after spending another night at West Point, we headed south. It was a rainy day, and the nearer the city of New York we got, the harder it rained.

We had arranged to meet Kimberly, Julie's niece, at a marina near the Colgate Clock on the New Jersey side of the Hudson, right across from New York City. Winds were gusty. It was an ugly afternoon. There was a great deal of boat traffic in the area in spite of the weather, and we motored into the little cove, hoping for the best. Boats were milling about, and just as we arrived, we saw a boat pull away from the dock in front of a little restaurant. As he pulled out, we slipped into his space. Magic. We tied to the pier and expected to be approached to pay, but no one came by. Julie phoned Kimberly, who said she had received the lens and would bring it right over. So we waited. Rain poured down, and clad in our yellow foul-weather gear, we walked about. There was an odd odor in the air, and we had heard fire sirens when we first arrived. Was something amiss? We waited and we waited.

Finally, Kimberly appeared. She seemed terribly distressed, clad in a white rain jacket, with tears streaming down her red face. Her long blond hair soaked. She clutched a small packet in her hand. We went into the restaurant there and sat down, dripping wet. She said her husband, James, had agreed to drive her to meet us, but on the way, they found the street to where we were was barricaded. No traffic could get through. When Kimberly asked to be allowed to pass, she was told by a firefighter on the scene that there was a chemical fire and that the fumes might be hazardous.

No one was allowed on the street. She returned to the car, got the package with the contact lens, and raised the package over her head and, calling "Medical emergency," dashed under the tape and ran down the street through the smoke to the little restaurant where we had agreed to meet. No one had pursued her, but she was terribly shaken by the whole affair. She dashed into our open arms and gave us a powerful hug.

Julie and I did our best to calm her, and before long, we had ordered dinner for the three of us. I had the replacement contact, and finally, the barricades had been lifted and James appeared to drive his still-shaking bride back to their nearby home.

Obviously, she had taken my lost lens very seriously, and her determination had seen her through the ordeal. I got my lens, and she got to the meeting place in spite of all the odds. What a wonderful girl to go so far for her aunt and uncle. Thank God nothing bad had happened to her.

After dinner, we returned to the boat in the rain and snuggled in for a well-deserved night's sleep.

Next morning, at first light, we pushed off and motored into New York Harbor. Pleasure boats would be able to anchor in the harbor that day and night to view the parade of tall ships that would pass by, along with the fireworks display to follow. A local radio station would announce the event so we would know something of the history of each vessel and where it was from. There were thousands of pleasure boats trying to obey vague orders of where we could and could not anchor. The coast guard and local police boats made their presence known but tried hard to not be obtrusive. The anchor splashed down, and we set it and fell back on the rode. It was a beautiful midsummer morning. We would have a splendid view of the ships, with the city of New York and the Statue of Liberty in full view.

Square-rigged sailing ships from all over the world entertained us that day as they passed by *Trilogy*. Many of them had men standing on the yardarms and in the rigging. All motored by, but several had a few sails set for the display. It was an amazing glimpse at the sailing history of the world. Of course, the *Constitution* wasn't there, nor was Nelson's *Victory*, but there were brigantines and schooners along with full-rigged ships. It was a wonderful, unforgettable day. Our galley was well stocked, so Julie made a delicious lunch and dinner. The day sparkled as the sun reflected off the wavelets in the calm harbor. There was a lovely sunset, and when it was finally dark, two barges were towed into the harbor, and the most amazing fireworks display I had ever seen took place. It lasted more than an hour. We were aghast! Our ears were ringing. Outside us, a lovely Constellation yacht had anchored, its classic lines just outlined in the city lights. Magnificent!

The harbor was officially closed. We were in a mass anchor zone. Our masthead lights twinkled. We were all one, protected from passing ships and ferries. How fortunate we were to be there on that special night!

It was almost as though the city of New York was throwing a big party because Julie and I were sailing to Bermuda! Absurd, of course, but one has the right to dream! We went to bed happy. Around 3:00 a.m., it happened. There was a *thump*.

I leaped from bed, and once again, we were side by side with another boat, which turned out to be the Constellation I had so admired earlier. The captain appeared, sleepy-eyed and disgruntled.

"How much scope do you have out?" I asked him.

"All of it!" was his terse reply. "It's deep here!"

In fact, it wasn't so deep where we were anchored, and when I explained to him that I had about five to one scope, five times the depth of the water, which is minimal, he looked at me with a sheepish glance. "Oh," he said. He explained he had over ten to one. Therefore, when the current switched and the boats had swung, he swung into us.

I saw the light come to his eyes. He wasn't used to apologizing, but he did. He pushed off, moved forward, and started pulling chain up on his windlass. Before long, we were several boat lengths apart. He waved a friendly wave, and we both retired to our cabins.

The next morning, we hauled anchor and headed past the Statue of Liberty, under the Verrazano–Narrows Bridge, to Atlantic Highlands, where we could anchor and supply the boat for the week-long voyage to Bermuda. We took the cart from the boat in the dinghy to shore and made several trips to a small market. We really stocked up with both fresh and canned goods, filling the refrigerator. We were ready to go.

Along the way, we stopped at a large yacht. She was well over forty feet, and her sleek lines and tall bridge deck isolating the cockpit from the cabin told us she was a serious racer/cruiser. There was a gentleman in the cockpit, and I asked him if he had sailed to Bermuda. "Many times!" he replied enthusiastically. "We've done the Newport Bermuda race numerous times over the years."

"Well," I said, "I wonder if I could ask you a few questions. My wife and I are about to set out for Bermuda, and I wondered what you monitor on your SSB radio. Where do you get your weather updates while offshore?"

"Oh, I'd have to ask my radioman," he replied.

"And about the barometer. You see, we are from the Great Lakes, and well, Lake Erie is a thousand feet above sea level, so we have a different standard. We will reset the barometer to sea level. I just wonder whether you have suggestions about what to watch for."

He wasn't ready for my questions, but his answer, again, surprised me. "I'd have to talk to my weatherman," he said. "If you are around this evening, stop back and I'll tell you what he said."

I thanked him, and we went on our way. That evening, we stopped back. The same man was there in the cockpit, a cocktail in his hand.

"Oh, hi," he said. "I talked to the crew about you two going to Bermuda in your thirty-one-footer. We came to the conclusion, ah. We don't think you should go!"

We thanked him and returned to the boat.

Other people had been more helpful in the harbor. The next morning, we got up as usual, checked the weather on SSB and VHF, marked down the barometric pressure, started the engine, raised the anchor, and moved easily out of the small cove where we had anchored. We checked into the Waterway Net and declared our destination, assuring them that we would check in each day until we reached Bermuda. And that was it. There were a few casual waves from folks in other boats, but there was no band playing; no one was jumping up and down. We were embarking on the cruise of our lives, and these people were just sitting there, sipping their coffee. Obviously, they didn't know or care. Why should they?

Julie hanked on the 150 percent jib, I raised the main, and we shut down the engine. We were off. The GPS marked our position and gave a countdown to the roughly six-hundred-mile-away islands of Bermuda. There was no turning back for us. We had installed a solar panel on the stern. The battery was charging. Bermuda bound!

That first day at sea was memorable only because it was fair and winds were moderate. We saw a few dolphins and many seabirds. Toward evening, we heard a deafening roar. We believed it was the SST Concorde leaving New York and heading to Europe. By then, the shore had completely disappeared. There was no land anywhere in sight. Our tricolor light on the masthead alerted ships of our presence, but that was all. It was us and nature.

We hoped to make about a hundred miles each day and arrive in about six days. The weather was fair. Stars made a dome over us. We had never seen stars so brilliantly shine down. They went from horizon to horizon. We took turns on the helm and slept in three-hour shifts through the night. We pledged never to venture into the cockpit at night without first *snapping on*, or clipping the lines on our harnesses to the lifeline that ran around the cabin. That way, we could move about. But should we fall overboard, we would still be attached to the boat, not lost in the wake. The first night was gentle. The autopilot, an auto-helm belt-drive model, kept us on course when the person on watch was charting or doing other things. We made sure the batteries were fully charged before nightfall, and the starting battery was reserved for just that, starting the diesel engine. The house battery would run all appliances. Of course, there could be no music in the boat at night—one of us had to sleep!

But there was plenty to do. We marked the chart regularly and kept a careful watch for ships, making sure to do a visual 360 every fifteen minutes. When we saw a ship, we would call it on the radio. One time, the ship was a tanker carrying oil to Israel. I remember remarking to the captain that it seemed unusual that we would ship oil to the Middle East. His reply astounded me. "None of Israel's neighbors will sell it to them."

The next morning, the sun came up in a stunning red sunrise. "Red sky in the morning, sailor take warning" was an old adage. Again, the day was fair. We expected to hit the Gulf Stream that day, and we knew that the temperature of the water in the stream was ten degrees warmer than in the rest of the Atlantic. We had a thermometer made just for measuring seawater temperature. Of course, with the Gulf Stream comes a substantial current to the north, not our friend, as we were heading a bit south. But the Gulf Stream also brought wonderful wildlife. There were many dolphins, and unlike the day before, they were leaping into the air, breaching, as it is called. They were big mammals, and it was great fun to watch them. "When the sea pig jumps, mind the pumps," another old seafarer's saying. Were they trying to tell us something?

We listened to the weather forecasts on the SSB, and they came in static-filled bursts with latitude and longitude and then the forecast. There were many different areas covered, and it was a bit confusing. One area simply listed *gales*. It wasn't where we were, but somehow it was worrying. That evening, the winds began to increase. We found ourselves heeling way over in gusts. It was noisy, and things were falling about below. We dropped the 150 and raised the 125 percent jib. We reefed the main. Still, the winds howled. We made the second reef. Waves were growing, and though we were okay, we understood the importance of "Shorten down early" or "Reef the first time you think of it," old sayings that smart sailors live by.

We had a tiny jib we had had made for the Morgan years before. It had a long lead on the luff, so it rode higher on the forestay and would be clear of breaking waves. We had never used it. With spray dashing over the foredeck, we put it up just before dark, right after we had tied in the third reef on the main.

We had the storm trysail attached to its own halyard and lying on the cabin top, ready to launch in an emergency. Even with the third reef tied in the large mainsail, it was clearly too much. We pulled down what was left of the main and, with the help of a halyard winch, hoisted the tiny sail from its bag. The sheets were attached aft, and before we knew it, we were again under control. Even though winds were well over thirty knots, the boat sailed more upright. Our speed didn't diminish markedly, but we felt we and not the wind had the upper hand. No more violent lunges in gusts. No more rounding up into the wind. Even though the waves were huge, larger than we had ever seen, they were well spaced. Neither of us had any sensation of seasickness, perhaps due to our adrenaline flow. It began to rain, first lightly, then hard. Visibility was diminished. With reduced sails, the autopilot was able to control the boat, and we could make corrections with the remote from the navigation station in the cabin. Nevertheless, every few minutes, one of us would scan the horizon.

One time, Julie saw a light astern. It was a ship, and though they shared our heading, when we spoke to the radioman, he claimed he could not see us on the radar. He would warn the captain, and they would avoid us.

We were alone on the sea, just the two of us on our thirty-one-foot Tartan sailboat. The wind screamed through the rigging, the rain pounded on the decks, and the boat rushed through mounting waves. Still, we were okay. Julie had made sandwiches ahead, and we ate them when we were hungry. We even slept in short naps in spite of being tossed about on the berth. The wind screamed, the rigging hummed, the boat lunged through the seas, but we were okay.

The next morning, we called the Waterway Net and made our report. We were just another boat calling in in bad weather. With daylight, things looked better, and we dropped the trysail and again raised the triple-reefed main. Toward evening, to be on the safe side, we raised the trysail again. The winds were falling, and by morning, we found ourselves at sea under more normal conditions. The storm was over.

It was then that I covered my mouth and raced for the head. I vomited wildly. I'll never know why. Perhaps it was the pent-up emotions I couldn't release earlier. Anyway, it was a one-time event. I never suffered motion sickness before or after. If there was momentary relief, it was only momentary.

When I tried to contact the Waterway Net that morning, they simply couldn't hear me. I called and called, but with no success. Perhaps the storm of the previous day was interfering with reception. Whatever the reason, I could not pick up their signal. If I didn't call in, they might report a problem. I had to do something, so I scanned the bands until I found a ham radio club having a QSO in Virginia. I was able to reach them, I told them of my plight, and they agreed to contact the Waterway Net and tell them of our position and that all was well. Finally, a bit of real relief.

With that good news, the sun peeked from behind a cloud, the sea returned to its beautiful blue, and we found ourselves speeding through the leftover waves under only a single reef and a small jib. Life was good.

There was a pod of whales in the distance that morning, but that was it. Winds were fair, and *Trilogy* gushed along on her way to Saint George's on the island of Bermuda. Our destination was the navigation buoy off the harbor entrance, and it was entered into our GPS

On the morning of the sixth day, according to the new GPS, we had nearly arrived. We scanned the horizon, looking for Bermuda, but there was only white haze. Then we saw several Bermuda longtails, beautiful white birds famous for greeting visitors to the islands. We knew we had arrived!

Finally, we came to the entrance buoy. From there we changed course for the harbor entrance. Still, however, there was no sign of an island. Because it was upwind, we motored. We had heard stories that said much of the population of Bermuda had come from shipwrecks. We didn't want to be another shipwreck, so we motored straight and true toward what we believed to be the entrance to Saint George's. First, there were little white spots in the haze. They proved to be the roofs of houses. Little by little, the hillsides came into view and, finally, the entrance to the harbor itself. We had indeed arrived!

I called Bermuda Harbor Control on the VHF, and the answer was prompt. "Are you in need of medical help, food, water, or fuel?" When I assured them that we were fine, we were directed to a dock, where we could sign in to Bermuda Customs. We were so excited to be there we could hardly contain ourselves. Nearby, there was a small shop where motorbikes were for rent. We picked one out and got the keys, and after a very brief introduction, we were off on our scooter. We had a map, and Julie shot a little video as we bumped along. Of course, we had to stay left, but we had done that in Malawi. It was no big deal. How wonderful it was to see the stone walls and fields! The houses and buildings were lovely. "Beware of road rash" were the last words we heard from the man at the store, but we were careful to avoid all hazards.

We had been warned that restaurants were expensive in Bermuda but that food in markets was just slightly more costly than in the States. We shopped in stores and ate suppers on the boat. We found that Hamilton could be a quiet little town until a cruise ship or two came in, flooding it with bustling tourists.

One evening, in a quiet time, we found ourselves in a little park. There was a chirping noise. At a nearby gift shop, a delightful woman took the time to introduce us to tree frogs, little creatures that live in trees and chirp in the night. Wonderful!

Another afternoon, we were on the boat, tied next to a beautiful Swan cruiser. The couple aboard was from Sweden, and we enjoyed visiting with them. They were Swedes, world cruisers, and they assured us that *Trilogy* was indeed built to sail the world. We were amazed. We thought we had stretched our boat to her limits sailing her to Bermuda, but these folks said there really was no limit.

They had inherited some money when his mother passed away, and they spent it all on this boat. It was all they had. He would work odd jobs at marinas from time to time, and she would publish articles in yachting magazines. They didn't have insurance. They fished and lived close to the sea in their lovely yacht. She taught Julie to make a trolling lure to pull behind the boat while we were offshore and then how to rig it to the backstay. What friendly, lovely people! What courage to invest everything in a boat and sail off, literally into the sunset, a citizen of the world! Could we do that? Perhaps we could.

After about a week, we were anchored off Hamilton one evening when an older man in a dinghy came up to the boat. He had a white beard and was wearing dark clothes and a Greek fisherman's cap. "Come on over for a Dark and Stormy," he said as he slowed his outboard and putted by. "I'd like to talk with you two." His boat was a Cape Dory 28, a boat we had dreamed of having when we bought the Morgan some twelve years before. The evening was cool and breezy, and we joined him in the cabin as he poured dark rum in ice-filled glasses and added ginger beer to make the drinks Bermuda is known for. We learned he lived on the island and, like us, he had sailed his boat from the States. He listened to our story. We told him about the gale and our difficulty forecasting it.

"You know about Herb?" he asked me.

"Herb?"

"Herb lives here in Bermuda in a place called Secret Garden. You can contact him on SSB, and he will help guide you. He does it all for free. He keeps track of boats all over the Atlantic and guides them safely to their destinations. I'm going to contact him and alert him that you might be calling when you head back. By the way, when do you plan to return?"

I thought a moment about the rather-direct question, and then I said, "I think in about another week. We are really having a very nice time here and—"

"How about tomorrow?" I heard him say.

We were stunned. We hadn't planned to leave for at least a few more days. But he didn't relent.

"We are well into hurricane season, you know. Tropical waves are forming already and racing across the sea. I know you think your boat is a world cruiser, capable of anything, but you don't want to find yourself in a hurricane. You know, out there, there is no rescue. I suggest you contact customs in the morning and set sail. The races are over. The racers are back in the States by now. The hurricane season is the reason. I'll call Herb and find out if there are any problems. If you don't hear from me, you know the coast is clear. Please be on your way."

With that, we said our goodbyes, and we motored our tiny inflatable dinghy back to *Trilogy*. It was the second week in July, and perhaps our friend was right. We packed the dinghy away and decided to provision and check out of Bermuda the following day.

Checking out of Bermuda proved to be remarkably easy. Our passports were stamped, and that was about it. We understood that we would listen for Herb each evening and that he would give us weather information and direct us regarding the best headings for our destination. We loaded the last of our provisions aboard, Julie bought a T-shirt, we pushed off the pier, and away we went.

As before, our departure was terribly routine. We sailed off on a clear day with a fine forecast. Just as Bermuda began to fall out of sight, several Bermuda longtails flew by to say goodbye. Amazing!

Julie and I were accustomed to our watch schedule. We slept in three-hour shifts and enjoyed breakfast together early each morning. There were no gales. We reefed the main a time or two, but the weather was in no way threatening. Herb suggested a heading for us, and we followed the heading. We were always moving in the direction of New York Harbor, so what was the big deal?

One evening, he said that we would encounter a weakening cold front that might contain some thunderstorms. Sure enough, on my watch that night, the sky was lit up with lightning to the north and south of us. We shortened sail dramatically, but aside from drenching rain and some distant lightning and thunder, we passed between the worst of the squalls, and there were no problems.

On the third day out, he said that a tropical wave was approaching from Africa. We overheard him telling boats to the south of us that it would be wise for them to head for shore and seek shelter. When it was our turn, he simply said that we should hold our course for New York. It wasn't until we called him when we first saw the outline of the Verrazano–Narrows Bridge that we had a bit of a shock.

"Oh, *Trilogy*," he said. "We have been so concerned about you. Had that tropical wave turned to the north instead of the south and become a hurricane, there would have been nothing that you could have done to escape it. We are so relieved that things worked out for you."

We thanked him for his efforts and heaved a sigh as we headed back to Atlantic Highlands, where we would spend what was left of the night at anchor.

The next day, we checked into customs, and on our way to the grocery store, we found the same man who was sure we shouldn't have gone in the first place. When I told him that we were back and that everything had gone well, he just shook his head.

We had done it. We had taken our thirty-one-foot sailboat from Lake Erie to Bermuda and back. We had endured a gale. We had demonstrated our seamanship! Were we ready for bigger things to come? We thought we were.

The city of New York is always impressive to sail by. We continued up the Hudson to the Erie Canal and on to Oswego, where we were fortunate enough to be able to restep the mast without a wait. As it was early afternoon and there was a fair breeze, we set out for Henderson Harbor, where we would secure the boat to her mooring. Winds increased through the night, and when we rounded Six Town Island and headed into Henderson Bay, it was well past midnight. We beat into the harbor and picked up the mooring under sail. It was calm at the anchorage, but as we were about to lower the main, a gust of wind came over the hill and caught the mainsail, tossing it to one side and striking Julie on the side of the head. She was momentarily knocked unconscious but fortunately fell into, not out of, the boat. Once the bleeding had stopped, she assured me she would be okay as we settled in for the night. We had no car. There was no one at the cottage. We slept on the boat and headed for shore first thing in the morning.

When we told the neighbors our tale, they insisted we take their car and take Julie to the hospital to be checked out. They suggested Mercy Short Wait was a good alternative to a much longer wait at the local ER. The professionals there took one look at the cut on her head and examined her right away. She needed numerous stitches. They determined that she avoided a concussion and, after the stitches were removed, would likely be all right, but they wanted to talk with her further.

"You say you were struck on the head by the boom of your sailboat at one this morning and that you or your husband had not been drinking. Is that right?"

It was obvious that the people at the emergency center were skeptical of Julie's story, and to their credit, they wanted to make sure that the injury wasn't the result of a domestic dispute.

Julie was able to convince them that I indeed had not beaten her up, and after what I felt had been an interminable wait, she appeared, smiling and ready to return to the cottage.

Later that day, Julie's sister and her mother and our faithful dog, Tudor, appeared to welcome us back. We hugged our loved ones, and though she was a little miffed at being left behind, even Tudor was thrilled at our presence. Our dog had lived with Julie's sister while we were gone and had even made friends with Betsy's cat, a former foe, while we were away.

So we were back. We stayed a few days at the cottage and then sailed Lake Ontario south and west to our old haunts, Sodus, Oak Orchard, Rochester, Wilson, and the yacht club at Youngstown, where we were sure we could find help transiting the Welland Canal to Lake Erie. Though the club was friendly and helpful as always, there didn't seem to be anyone going our way. Perhaps we would find someone at the north end of the Welland, at Port Weller, who could help us.

The next morning, I called on the radio for any boat transiting the Welland Canal from the north. We would need a hand on our thirty-one-foot sailboat.

There was, to our amazement, a response: a boat from Ashtabula, Ohio, was going to make the passage, and the owner's son, Grey, would be happy to help us out. They wanted to know where we were and how soon we could make it. The canal would be opening for them soon!

"We are just outside the canal," I lied. We could see the canal entrance, but it was miles ahead of us, a good half-hour away.

"So how long do we have to wait?"

"Oh, we could round the point into the canal in ten minutes or so," I said rather unconvincingly.

But they waited, and fully half an hour later, we rounded the point. We pulled up alongside a beautiful forty-foot yacht where a young man of about eleven waited at his mother's side. He was all smiles until our dog, Tudor, bounded onto the deck. Suddenly, there was some uncertainty. Something about a black lab that had given the lad some trouble on another boat. Tudor, however, was all tail wagging and tongue, and her enthusiasm quickly quelled the young man's fears.

We were a team.

The upward run through the Welland can be a bit of a challenge much more so than the descent. The currents caused by inrushing water are significant and, especially if the vessel is moored near a vent, where water floods the lock, it can be a rough ride to the top. But the two of us, with young Grey, were able to control *Trilogy* with no problem.

That evening, when we were released from the locks to the wall at Port Colborne, we learned what wonderful people Grey and his family were. They included us for dinner on their boat with their friends. There must have been a dozen of us, and we all gathered on their boat for an unforgettable feast. They had been traveling in Lake Ontario with several other boats, and well, we just had a wonderful time. There were cocktails and wine and appetizers and delicious entrees. It was simply a beautiful evening. We partied late into the night, sharing our stories, enjoying our newfound friends. They followed us to Dunkirk Yacht Club, where we celebrated again the following night and on and off for years thereafter.

So we were home. We had sailed to Bermuda and back, six hundred miles offshore, and we had made it. We had been to Superior. What was left? What would we do to really show the world?

Well, there was the Lake Michigan trip and the Lake Superior trip. Hmmm.

CHAPTER 92

Threes

It was a year or so after the Bermuda trip that Julie and I decided to take our boat to Lake Michigan. It wasn't a big deal, but it would be a long sail. We would go to Chicago, maybe even Milwaukee, and explore Lake Michigan! We would go to Mackinac Island, under the Blue Water Bridge, and head south. There would be Lake Charlevoix, Harbor Springs. What an adventure! On the way back was Green Bay. Imagine, Green Bay!

Nothing great was ever accomplished without enthusiasm!

So we went. We packed the boat, loaded fresh food, took Tudor, our English springer spaniel, and just after dusk on a delightful July night, pushed off the dock at Dunkirk, heading for points west.

Sailing was majestic. The moon was full. Visibility was reasonable, and the instruments guided us along. Textbook. It wasn't until we reached the head of the Saint Clair River that things got interesting. We intended to stay at the Port Huron Yacht Club, but as they were hosting the Lake Huron Mackinac race, the docks were full. Still, the club dockmaster guided us to a nearby lagoon, where he said, "It might be possible to tie to trees for the overnight. We could still use the club facilities. So we did. Indeed, there was deep water right up to the shore and saplings nearby. We carefully set fenders and a fender board to keep us off the rocks then made the boat secure to the young trees. It was deep enough, and we were reasonably protected, so we felt all right about leaving the boat. We walked to the club to socialize a bit, and I visited the men's room, where a line extended out the door. While I was waiting my turn, I was surprised when a rather-large man dressed in white shorts and a T-shirt barged the line. He pushed the head door open and walked right in the men's room. A few seconds later, he emerged and looked at those of us waiting in line with a broad smile on his face. "You guys are such good sports. You're all invited to *Heritage* for a drink this evening," he said.

In spite of the fact that Julie and I really didn't know anyone in the club and we definitely weren't going on the Port Huron Mackinac race, we took the fellow up on his offer. *Heritage* was a twelve-meter America's Cup yacht, built of wood, that was designed by Charlie Morgan, the designer of our Morgan 27, *Temerity*. She was built to compete for the America's Cup in 1970, but *Intrepid* beat her in the trials, and she never got to race. When we saw her at the club, her varnished hull stood out. She was beautiful in gleaming hardwood. The captain, the man I had seen in the clubhouse, waved us aboard. After a quick tour of the deck, we ventured below, where we were in for a surprise. The interior was sparse, with pole berths for the crew and a device for dispensing ice-cold cans of beer to visitors. The surprise was that there were a number of physically and mentally handicapped adolescent children aboard. These kids would have the thrill of sailing on a world-class yacht in a world-famous yacht race. What an experience! There was a wonderful woman who took care of them, and it was obvious that they all were thrilled at what was about to take place.

We sipped our beer, simply amazed at the fact that this person, who had appeared so gruff and insensitive by crashing the line, was providing an opportunity of a lifetime to these young people so physically and mentally challenged. It was a telling and sensitive moment that made one feel very good and almost shed a tear at the same time. We drank our beers, learned about the magnificent yacht and her designer, and found our way to a little restaurant in town for a bite to eat. The club dining room was filled beyond capacity.

Tudor, our friendly spaniel, was glad to see us when we got back to the boat. We went for an evening walk and then returned to *Trilogy*. We hoped for an early departure the next morning.

CHAPTER 93

One

Even though we pushed off early, the top of the river was crowded with boats of all sizes as we ventured forth. The Blue Water Bridge loomed ahead of us, the diesel engine in *Trilogy's* bilge roared, and we headed for the Canadian side, where we glided against strong current under the giant span very near the northern shore. People on the nearby piers cheered for us. Even though our two-person crew, dinghy on the foredeck, and dog virtually disqualified us as contenders for the Mackinac race, they cheered anyway. Once we were out of the current, we set sail and headed into the huge lake while the rest of the fleet stayed behind the starting line, waiting their turn to vie for position at the starts for the various classes.

All day we sailed in very light winds, and gradually, we were overtaken by the racers. There is something absolutely magical about a large sleek yacht slicing through the water in what appears to be very little wind. There was one particular vessel that came very close to us as she glided by. Because she was so long, her hull speed was several times ours. Her mast reached high into the sky, capturing zephyrs our sagging sails never saw. She was beautiful, as were the young women gracing her decks. She was so close, so lovely, so silent that we watched in awe as she ghosted by.

But morning turned to afternoon, and then to evening, and the winds somehow went from not much to nothing, the lake became glassy, and the fleet was reflected in the water far behind us. They were behind us, of course, because we, not racing, could start our engine and get on with things. So that was what we did. Evening turned to night, and with our autopilot, nicknamed Nigel, doing the steering, we droned on. Julie went to bed, and I took my turn on watch. I checked the navigation and scanned for obstacles in our path. There are few things more beautiful than a calm Great Lake on a summer night. It was warm and still, utterly peaceful.

As I looked aft, I noticed something new; the aft starboard quarter of the cockpit seemed to have a red glow to it. I climbed the steps into the cockpit, and sure enough, one of the engine warning lights was glowing red. I crouched down and tried to read the instrument, but the red light was just too bright. I got a flashlight. "ALT." It was the alternator. At least it wasn't oil pressure. Apparently, the alternator wasn't performing as it should. If that was true, the autopilot and the running lights would soon take their toll on the battery. The engine, being a diesel, should run without a battery, but everything else would quit. What to do? Shutting down the engine did not sound like a good idea as we would waste electricity starting it again.

My commotion had wakened my wife. We decided to first remove the engine cover and make a visual check. Sure enough, the belt turning the alternator was in place and turning smoothly. A quick check with a voltage meter confirmed the diagnosis. The alternator was producing no voltage.

We replaced the cover and clamped it in place. The Lake Huron chart showed Harbor Beach, Michigan, to be the nearest harbor. We plotted a course then turned off the autopilot, the GPS, and everything electrical except for the running lights. I took the helm, and we headed for Harbor Beach. It wasn't long before we spotted the harbor lights. Our running lights were glowing dimly when we arrived a few hours later. We eased into the harbor and motored slowly to a marina, where we secured the boat to the fuel dock. The marina was closed, but the docks were full of boats. Someone would surely be there in the morning. We shut down the engine, closed the boat, and went to sleep.

Next morning, there was a woman who greeted us. We told her our problem, a failed alternator, and she frowned. We couldn't stay at the fuel dock. She was sure of that. She pointed out a slip partway down the dock. I switched the battery switch from 1 to 2 and crossed my fingers, and as I touched the starter, the engine roared to life. We moved the boat and secured it to the appointed slip. I unbolted the alternator from its mount, and we carried it to the marina store, where we were told there was no one local who could repair it. It would have to be sent to a nearby town.

"I'll call Mort over in Bad Axe. He does these things," said the woman.

"Bad Axe?" I said.

"Yeah. Mort does electrical. Maybe he'll drive over 'n pick it up. I'll call 'em and see."

Before long, an old Ford pickup appeared at the marina, and alternator in hand, I walked over to introduce myself to Mort. He was an older man with a white beard, long hair, and very worn ball cap. I opened the passenger door to his truck, and there was a jagged hole rusted through the passenger-side floor. I put the alternator on the seat.

"Doesn't produce any voltage," I said over the rumble of his engine. "The alternator light comes on."

"Hope it ain't one of them foreign ones," said Mort. "I'll bring it back tomorrow."

I glanced down at the alternator, and the word Hitachi was neatly lettered across the side. With that, I closed the truck door, and Mort shifted to reverse, turned around, and in a cloud of blue smoke, roared off. Something told me I would never see my friendly alternator again. Bad Axe. He was taking it to Bad Axe! Are you kidding?

We spent the afternoon walking around the marina. There wasn't a great deal of interest there except there was one sailboat that caught our eye. It was a Cabo Rico 34, and it was brand-new. The boat was simply beautiful. A Perry design, with her full keel, she was made for distance cruising. The owner came by, and after we introduced ourselves, he gave us a tour of his boat. She was outfitted with the latest electronics, even a chart plotter, something we had never seen. It showed a chart on its screen and the position of the boat on the chart. The owner, however, was not pleased.

"Look," he said as he pointed to the screen. "The boat is not where it should be in the harbor. It appears to be on the wall there. I can't navigate with this. What if I were in the fog?"

We didn't know what to say. It was obvious he was using a small error in the GPS positioning to justify never going anywhere at all. Obviously, his boat wasn't a day sailor. It looked as though it had never left the dock. He was still working and complained that his work wouldn't let him get away. It made us think how fortunate we were to have the time to do serious cruising. At the same time, it made clear that there are plenty of little things that can get in the way. If one is looking for reasons not to go cruising, there are loads of reasons out there.

The following day, Mort from Bad Ax left word with the marina that he had been able to repair our alternator and that he would deliver it after lunch. Sure enough, the fix had been made, and when I bolted it back in place, plugged it in, and started the engine, the trouble light went out. All was well.

CHAPTER 94

Two

We paid for the repair, paid our marina fees, and pushed off. It was as if nothing had happened. We sailed north toward Mackinac, but this time there were no racing boats on the horizon. We were again alone on the vast expanse of water. Toward evening, the wind began to die. We started the engine, and the trouble light was off, as it should be. All was good as we glided over the still water. Suddenly, everything changed! The motor groaned and stopped. The boat stopped abruptly. Obviously, something had caught in the propeller. I donned my bathing suit and dropped over the side into the cool water. Sure enough, a massive amount of netting and rope had entangled around the prop. The propeller itself was obscured by the mesh. Julie handed me a very sharp serrated knife we kept aboard for just such an occasion. She attached a lanyard, and I tied it to my wrist. If we lost the knife, the job would be very difficult. So I went to work.

I began by cutting away the line and netting that descended from the prop and shaft to the deep blue below. Of course, I was holding my breath, and each time I went down, I was able to work a shorter time. To add to the challenge, several fishing lures and their sharp hooks were also entangled in the netting. Should one snag me, I would be unable to get to the surface for a very important breath of air. Similarly, should the line from my wrist to the knife be tangled in the mess, I would suffer the same fate. Add to this the fact that the sun was setting and it would soon be dark. It was a somewhat stressful situation.

I cut and cut, gasping for breath each time I surfaced, and finally, I cut away the last of the debris from our folding Martec propeller. We had gathered much of the material, including the fishing lures, and hauled it aboard the boat for disposal ashore. I climbed the stern ladder and toweled off. The real question, of course, remained. Was there damage to the shaft or other parts of the drivetrain caused by the sudden stopping of the diesel? I turned the ignition switch and pressed the starter, and the engine roared to life. That was good. When I put her in gear, there was a swirl of water behind the transom, and the boat began to move forward. To our great relief, there was no vibration. Everything seemed to be working fine. Julie and I both remembered one time, while sailing with friends in Miami, an anchor rode had been caught in the prop. That ended in a bent shaft, the boat's taking on water, and a very expensive repair. Not this time, thank goodness!

CHAPTER 95

Three

So we again set our course for Mackinac, and on we went. The next morning, the island was near, and we ventured into the harbor, where we found little space. There were no open slips, but we did find a place where we could drop anchor and have ample swing room. I backed down on the hook, and everything was fine. We launched the dinghy and headed for shore. The race had ended several days before, and many of the yachts had left. Mackinac is a beautiful island with no automobiles, only horse-drawn vehicles. It is a special place indeed. Of course, we wanted to see the island, and what better way to view it than by bicycle. We found a shop with a sign, BIKES FOR RENT, and we stepped inside. Sure enough, they had bicycles of all sorts, but it was a tandem that caught our eye. We reserved our ride, took the dog, Tudor, back to the boat, and hurried to the shop.

Our ride around the island was majestic indeed. We had both ridden bicycles for years, but this experience on a tandem was new to us. We might have weaved a little at first, but soon the ride was second nature. Other bicycles rode by, and soon we found ourselves overtaking those ahead of us. It was exhilarating! The beautiful Grand Hotel came into view, and we enjoyed its majesty. We rode around much of the island, but soon our time was up for the rental, and we headed back to the shop. We paid our fee and walked toward the harbor. Along the way, there was an ice cream shop. We ventured in and bought two cones, which dripped a bit on our hands as we walked along.

"Look at that boat!" Julie said as we walked toward the shore. "It looks like another Tartan 31."

"Yes," I said. "If I didn't know better, I'd think...my god! It is our boat. It's being towed! Oh no!"

Trilogy was clearly visible, her painter tied on the transom of a powerboat, and being hauled toward a vacant slip several docks away. Julie and I both broke into a run. When we finally reached the dock, the towing company was just tying her up. There was a man standing by the boat who was clearly distraught. He was wide-eyed and eager to apologize.

"I'm so sorry," he said over and over. His agitation made us feel for him. "My wife. My wife had never run our boat before, and I was giving her lessons on driving a powerboat and she was doing pretty well, and then she turned in front of your boat, but much too close, and the outboard hit your anchor line, and all of a sudden, our boat stopped. I thought everything was all right at first, but by the time I got the anchor line away from the outboard, your boat was right on the rocks of the wall. I pulled up your anchor and put it on the deck, and I used the anchor line to try to pull your boat off, but it was stuck. I waved to a cruiser going by. He helped me, but he couldn't get the boat off either. He called the towing company, and they came, and finally they were able to pull the boat free. They towed it here. I think it is okay. I have insurance. I'm so sorry."

I was simply aghast. I didn't know what to say. Julie had opened the companionway boards, and Tudor hopped out, wagging her tail, happy to see all the friendly people.

"My wife," the man continued. "She's still out there, in our boat. I got on your boat to steer it to the dock and told her to just move around. I don't think she even knows how to stop it. Oh dear. Let me give you my name and number, and yes, I have the name and phone of my insurance company."

After the brief scribbling of numbers, the man began waving both arms in the air toward a small boat moving in circles in the harbor. The last we saw of him, he was running toward another dock farther down the harbor.

A man from a nearby boat donned his mask and snorkel and lowered himself into the water to survey the damage. When he emerged after several dives, he said the bottom had been ripped off the rudder. Apparently, it had been trapped between rocks, and the pounding from the waves along with the powerful boats pulling it had pounded and broken the bottom few inches clean off. There was a jagged stump where the smooth bottom of the foil used to be. We checked and found that the helm still turned smoothly and there was no leak around the rudder post. He was simply amazed that the rudder post had not been bent.

The man who had caused the problem had taken full responsibility in view of several witnesses, whose names we recorded. We had all the info. What more could we do? Julie and I looked away and saw the other man still waving frantically at a small boat circling nearby.

We talked to the generous fellow who had surveyed the damage. "I've really looked," he said, "and I don't see anything else. There are a few good-size dings in the keel, but nothing serious. I think you can just continue on your cruise and deal with the problem when you get back. Take her out. See how she handles. That's what I'd do."

With that, another man came forward. "This is Jack's slip," he said. He's gone cruising for a week or so. You can stay here as long as you need to."

Perhaps you've heard the old adage that bad things come in threes? So that was it. Three bad things had happened: the alternator, the net around the prop, and now this! We hoped our luck would change.

Early the next morning, we motored back out into the lake and headed south on Lake Michigan. The boat was okay. She wouldn't point as high as she should, and she seemed a bit slower, which was understandable with her damaged rudder. Still, she was fine. We continued south to Chicago, where we found ourselves welcomed warmly at the Chicago Yacht Club. We enjoyed a Cubs game at Wrigley Field, where a new player, Sammy Sousa, hit a grand slam home run and won the game against the Montreal Canadians for the Cubs. We went to the Museum of Science and Industry, where we explored a coal mine and examined firsthand a WWII German submarine, and we sailed home. We stopped in Milwaukee on the way, enjoying warm fellowship at the yacht club there. We stopped in Green Bay. Our bad luck had run out. There were no more problems.

In Dunkirk, when the boat was hauled that year, we examined the damage. We contacted our friends at Tartan, who assured us that even if the entire fiberglass section of the rudder had been smashed, there was a stainless rudder inside the fiberglass that would have allowed us to keep going. We followed the company's suggestion to allow the broken section to dry out over the winter and to repair it in the spring. They sent us a pattern of how the bottom of the rudder should look when finished. We bought the materials, and when we were done, it looked brand-new. A little Marine Tex in the keel smoothed that out too. What had seemed like a huge problem at the time was gone. We were ready for another year.

CHAPTER 96

And On

There were more sails both west and east. One of the most memorable was when we met Julie's sister and her son Toby at Whitefish Bay on Superior. We listened to the "Ballad of the Edmond Fitzgerald" as we watched ships lock through into Superior. Up the eastern shore, we visited Brule Harbor, on the Canadian east end of the lake. We anchored in the completely protected bay and were the only vessel there. Thick moss covered the ground, and rich forest overgrew what was once a lumbering port. We were so isolated in such a beautiful setting it was truly heartwarming. Words can hardly describe it. Toby took the dinghy and explored, and we rested on the boat.

Next morning, we ventured back into the lake, and as we headed for Whitefish Bay, a clear squall enveloped the boat. Gusty winds caused us to shorten down to the second reef and partially furl the jib. We were fine, but I noticed on the chart there was the image of a shipwreck right where we were. The words *Edmond Fitzgerald* were written underneath. I mentioned it to Toby, and his eyes grew large. Somehow, the ghost of the ship and myriad others that had gone down in that mighty inland sea haunted us for the rest of the day. The winds calmed, but the memory and the feeling of that ghostly squall lingered.

Sailing the Great Lakes in the fair winds of summer was a challenge, no doubt, but it was a challenge in which we had succeeded.

We had navigated all five lakes, many of them several times. We had raced and cruised, and we had learned. We had been successful. We had ventured several times to the coast, sailed to Nova Scotia, and went offshore to Bermuda. What was left for us to explore?

CHAPTER 97

Grade 9 Advanced

The 1999–2000 school year would be our last year of teaching after thirty years with our respective school systems. For us, it was a very special year. At fifty-five, we didn't feel we were used up, but with our master's degrees and the extra credits we had earned from supplemental study, we were expensive employees for our local school boards. They offered us free health insurance for ten years if we agreed to retire. It was simply an offer too good to refuse.

The last year was wonderful, as were all the years before. As a kind of reward, our English department chair offered me ninth grade advanced students. As I had never taught either ninth graders or advanced students, I found myself with a special challenge.

Somehow, teachers who taught the advanced classes got them for life; there was seldom an opening. It was that year I learned why.

These were simply amazing kids. They were smart and eager to be challenged. They had loads of support from home. They expected to do well, and their parents expected them to do well. They had spirit, and they were creative. I liked to encourage writing, and they loved to write. I liked to ask difficult questions, and somehow, I couldn't seem to challenge them too much. Some of their families were movers and shakers in the community. They were wonderful kids. Though it was not easy to prepare for them each day, it was a joy. They challenged me every bit as much as I challenged them.

As it was 2000, the turn of the century, the State Education Department had a statewide contest for an essay having to do with "the most significant decision made in the twentieth century." The essay would be documented and supported with facts and opinions. I made it an assignment for the class.

I remember students discussing Truman's decision to drop the atomic bomb and his decision to drop the second bomb. There were decisions about wars and about a women's right to vote. There were American decisions and foreign decisions that were considered and defended. Still, there was one decision that I would not soon forget. That was Eleanor Roosevelt's decision to resign from the DAR. The Daughters of the American Revolution had refused to attend a meeting where Marion Anderson, a black woman, had been invited to perform. Because of that, Eleanor Roosevelt, wife of President Roosevelt, had resigned. It was well before the civil rights confrontations of the sixties, but it was a strong statement about African Americans and women. It showed the wife of a powerful president taking on prejudice and intolerance in spite of the political consequences it might cause her husband.

We discussed our progress from time to time in class, and I never failed to be amazed at the creative talents of these young people. I was so impressed with the efforts of these amazing kids I suggested we enter all the papers in the state contest. We did.

We didn't win, but several made honorable mention. Also, I got a note from the organizer of the contest asking whether I would be interested in taking the contest over for the following year!

I told him I would wave to him in Albany as Julie and I moved the boat south on the Erie Canal to begin our retirement.

Another time, I borrowed an idea from a former teacher. I had everyone pick a significant event from the past century and, after dressing for the part, present a commentary or skit representing that moment. One girl, whose father was a community leader and a prominent attorney, decided to do something with Rosa Parks, the African American woman who, in a segregated community, refused to give up her seat to a white patron in a crowded bus. Her presentation was moving and filled with detail. When I asked her where she got her information, her answer was straightforward. "I wrote her a letter," she said. Sure enough, she showed us a letter addressed to her and signed by the famous Rosa Parks.

As I remember, she was a tall attractive young woman, friendly and smart. She was a delight to have in class. She was agreeable and always ready to contribute. One particular Monday, she came to class in a bit of a huff. It seemed she had been out later than usual on Saturday night and her parents had been concerned. She announced that she would be grounded the following weekend. She wouldn't be confined to her room, but rather, the family would travel to a park in Pennsylvania, where they would view elk. No, she wouldn't be going to any parties; she would be viewing elk! We were all amused at her punishment, but it showed to me a kind of caring by her family that showed concern and an attempt to change behavior with honey rather than vinegar. It truly impressed me.

CHAPTER 98

Retirement

So that was it. Our teaching life was over. I remember saying farewell to the kids on the last day. There was a nice picture of me in the yearbook, a few dinners, and that was it. No more lectures, no more quotes of the day, no more spelling and vocabulary quizzes. I would be an English teacher no more.

It was May of that year when a dear friend, Sylvia, at the Dunkirk Yacht Club wondered whether I had any old neckties left over from my teaching career that I might give to her to weave into a chair frame she was making for her grandson. She would weave them to make a colorful seat and back. I eagerly obliged with fifty or so ties I was sure I would never need again.

Four years before, in 1996, Julie and I had bought a condominium in Englewood, Florida. We would leave Dunkirk the day after Labor Day in the year 2000 and sail our beloved *Trilogy* to Buffalo and the Black Rock Canal, down the Niagara River, to the Erie Canal, the Hudson, and then we would wend our way south via the Intracoastal Waterway to Florida and our new home. Florida, the Bahamas, and the Caribbean would be our new cruising grounds.

It was the night before we left, at the annual Labor Day party, when the commodore asked everyone to step to the rear deck of the club for a ceremonial toast to Hank and Julie on their cruise south. There, on that warm September evening, were fifty of our closest friends raising a glass to us, each of them with one of my old neckties neatly tied over his T-shirt or blouse. It was a fond farewell and a signal of many more adventures to come!

CHAPTER 99

Sailing South

So that was it. The party was over, and there was nothing to do but snuggle in bed and then get up in the morning and leave. Well, there was one more thing. We had sold our Subaru, and we had a rental car that Julie's sister had agreed to pick up and return to the dealer for us. We would simply leave the keys in the glove box. Simple. Everyone had left the party, so we took the keys and went through the gate, crossed the park, and put the keys in the glove box, closed the door, and headed back for the club. Not the most secure arrangement, but for one night, it would have to do. Back at the club gate, there was a sign. "Sept. Combo." By tradition, the combination to the clubhouse gate changed monthly, and it changed after the nearest holiday, Labor Day in this case. What was the September combo? We hadn't recorded it as we expected to be gone by then. Here we were on the night before our celebrated departure, and we had locked ourselves out of the club, away from our boat, our bed, our home for the next few months. Fortunately, Julie had our phone. She made a call to friends and managed to get the new number so we could open the gate. Whew.

The lake level had dropped a bit overnight, and the next morning, *Trilogy*, loaded for the cruise, backed from her slip and bumped a few times on the bottom, and we were off. The sail to Buffalo, the Black Rock Canal, the Niagara River, and the Erie Canal was old by now, this being our sixth transit from Dunkirk to the Atlantic.

The Intracoastal Waterway was interesting as we moved south, but there were few surprises. We were made welcome by communities along the way. I remember anchoring in Annapolis, where we enjoyed the Annapolis Sailboat Show in early October. We stopped at Wilmington, North Carolina, where we visited Julie's mom, who lived in a retirement community there. After Wilmington, we sailed offshore to Northern Florida. Winds were northerly and strong, and because of large waves, jibing was a concern, but we rigged a preventer, a line from the end of the boom to the deck forward of the mast on the leeward side, and the sailing was no big deal.

We mostly motored down the Intracoastal in Florida until we got to Stewart, where we stopped to visit a good friend. There we took the Saint Lucie Canal to Lake Okeechobee and then the Caloosahatchee River from the lake to Fort Meyers on the West Coast of Florida. On that route, we were introduced to alligators sunning themselves on the banks of the waterway and beautiful birds, egrets, herons, ospreys, and eagles, all watching us pass without the least concern. Along the way, there was one bridge that made us wonder. It was a lift bridge for a railroad, and when it was at its top, it was just a foot or so short of our mast height. Local Indians could be hired to lash fifty-gallon drums of water to the decks of passing yachts, causing them to heel sufficiently to pass under the bridge even if they were substantially taller than the clearance should allow. We figured we could just move weight, including our own bodies, to leeward and heel our girl enough for clearance. Our approach was a rather tense moment, and though the radio antenna did scratch along on the underside of the bridge overhead, we made it without damage. Evenings we stopped at small towns along the way and generally enjoyed dinner in local restaurants. Charlotte Harbor opened before us as we passed under the bridge from Port Charlotte to Punta Gorda. From there it was just a short sail north on the Intracoastal to Englewood, where halfway between Marker 22 and the Tom Adams Bridge, we swung *Trilogy* to port and headed for our dock at Sandpiper Cove. Dolphins rolled ahead of us, pelicans dived into the water, and our lovely condo lay ahead of us on that beautiful November afternoon. The secondhand Pontiac we had bought and moved south was snug in its parking space, waiting to help us begin the Florida life.

Before long, we were headed by car back to Western New York for Christmas, and then, back in Florida, we pushed off for an exploration of the Keys and the Bahamas. The condo was rented. We were committed.

We sailed south, where we first stopped in Fort Myers Beach. We anchored in the harbor and took our dinghy ashore to a dock owned by an elderly gentleman, who accommodated visiting sailors for tips. Walking through the packed streets of the island community, we finally found a place to eat at a rooftop restaurant within sight of the bridge to the mainland. Traffic on the island and the beach was near gridlock, and we laughed at how we could walk faster than traffic moved. It was during dinner that an emergency vehicle with screaming siren on the bridge found itself locked in traffic. Despite its flashing lights and sirens, there was no place for it to go. Suddenly, dinner didn't taste so good. How could we keep Manasota Key, our Florida home, from becoming so overdeveloped? We knew at that moment that we would not want to live in such a place.

Naples had an anchorage and a public marina, where we could dock. We contacted friends and had a quiet day there. From Naples, we headed out to sea. We set sail across Florida Bay to Marathon Key, where we anchored in a beautifully protected harbor. We would take the dinghy to shore, where, for a modest fee, we could leave it. Restaurants catered to us, offering showers as well as meals. Other sailors amazed us with their stories and cruising adventures. A lady who lived on a twenty-four-footer, a very small sailboat near us, said that she was from Buffalo, not far from our home in Ashville in Western New York. Every day she donned her pristine nursing outfit and rowed her dinghy ashore, where she drove to the local hospital to practice her profession. She told us she was a nurse, and years before, she had worked in the emergency room at a major hospital in Buffalo. She said that they had a serious increase in heart attacks on Sunday afternoons in Buffalo. She wondered how that could be. She couldn't understand it until a physician friend took her to her first Buffalo Bills game. That was in the early nineties, when the Bills were going to, but not winning, Super Bowls. She, too, got caught up in Bills fever and ended up with a season ticket herself. But it was her story about collecting medical supplies from local providers and sailing to Cuba to donate them that really caught our attention. "You what?" Yes, she made the trip in her twenty-four-foot boat, flying the American flag, was welcomed in Cuba, and then sailed back to Florida. She had to stay in Havana Harbor while she was there, but she felt she was warmly welcomed. Here she was anchored in Marathon, living in a small boat, and basically ignored by everyone. It was 2000. Wasn't she the definition of a *hero*? Wasn't that a courageous thing to do?

Key West is known as a party haven, so when Julie and I anchored in town, we expected little less than heavy drinking and partying. We took a tram ride around the city, and the tour director pointed out several sites we might visit. Hemingway's house was one; the *Atocha* museum was another. Hemingway had cats with six toes, and some of their offspring still roam the island. We didn't see any. One of his wives replaced the boxing ring at his place with a swimming pool while he was away. Our tour guide told us that when the great author returned home, he took one look at the pool, pulled a penny from his pocket, and hurled the cent into some still-wet concrete. She then showed us the penny, still visible in the concrete pool deck. He apparently valued the boxing ring much more than the pool.

The Atocha museum featured a gold bar worth a million dollars, recovered from the wreck. Each of us could reach through a narrow slit in the vault and hoist the million-dollar ingot but not, of course, take it home. There was jewelry made from gold found on the wreck one could purchase. The wreck was beautifully documented by the museum. It was well worth the visit.

Mallory Square beckoned at sunset, and a man balancing a shopping cart on his forehead, along with jugglers and acrobats, captivated us until we came to a magician from the UK. He wore short sleeves, unlike most magicians, and began his act with simple disappearing-coin tricks. Julie, who had studied magic, was captivated. The more she challenged him, the more convincing he was.

He would turn around, perform more slowly, but his sleight of hand was…well, magic! We stayed with him for a while, amazed by his skill. Later, when the sun set in the west, we were a little surprised when everyone applauded. It was a wonderful evening, but the sun sets quickly in Key West and full darkness follows soon. As the crowd at Mallory Square began to dissipate, we realized it was past time for us to return to *Trilogy*.

We found the dinghy easily enough, still tied where we had paid to leave her, but *Trilogy* was simply one of the many boats swaying at anchor across the bay. We had a small flashlight, hardly adequate illumination, but we made our way, rowing across the current toward what we thought to be our boat in nearly total darkness. Fortunately, there was little traffic and next to no wind. Our boat was right where we thought she should be, and we climbed aboard, tired but exhilarated by our day's adventures.

The Dry Tortugas, named for turtles, was our next destination. We sailed to the islands without difficulty and anchored in the lee of the island. The attraction is a huge prison. It was built before the Civil War, and certainly, its most famous prisoner was a man named Mudd, who treated John Wilkes Booth, the man who shot President Abraham Lincoln. Our tour of the prison was at night. We carried kerosene lanterns and walked the place in darkness. Iron used to reinforce concrete in the walls of the prison had rusted and expanded and had caused deterioration of the prison walls. We heard stories of Dr. Mudd and his attempts to escape. On the other side, we learned that he had courageously helped save the prison population from an epidemic that sprung up during his stay there. The prison was actually a Union fortress during the Civil War, in spite of its being so far south.

On the way back to Key West in the late afternoon, *Trilogy* abruptly stopped as she was sailing along. A telltale line descended deep into the water at her transom. We had obviously snagged a trap of some kind. I would have to cut us free. I donned my bathing suit, mask, and flippers and slid over the side. Sure enough, the line from a small buoy had lodged itself between the forward edge of the balanced rudder and the hull. It was jammed solidly in place. It took just a moment for me to draw my sharp knife, cut through the line, and free the boat. While doing so, I made a little cut in my finger. Ouch! There was a little brown cloud around my hand. Meantime, a song kept going through my head. *Dum dum, dum dum, dum...* It was the music from *Jaws.* This wasn't the Great Lakes, after all. How far can a shark smell blood underwater? I was glad I had my flippers. The boat was free, and I quickly kicked my way to the ladder. I climbed up over the side and onto the boat as the sails refilled and we once again headed for Key West.

Sailing the Keys is a delight, and island by island we continued toward Miami, where we were to wait for the ideal time to make the crossing to the Bahamas. It was important that no winds with north in them were in the forecast. North winds, contrary to the Gulf Stream, which flows north, can cause large waves, which challenge the navigation of small boats. We stopped in a Miami marina and did some shopping on a nearby street. We were amazed that some of the salesclerks spoke no English. Julie tried on some clothing, and when she asked the clerk if it needed to be dry-cleaned, the lady fled in search of an interpreter. On a darker side, we priced a camera in one shop, and then when we went down the street to another, the salesclerk followed us and, frowning, watched us as we made our purchase next door.

Back on the boat, we anchored in a part of the harbor called the Stadium, where water ski shows had been held in the past. There was a couple in a twenty-eight-footer anchored nearby, and we had a chat. He had been waiting for weeks for just the right forecast. It was clear to us that the perfect day would never come for him. It was either too cloudy or too windy or whatever, but he wanted to be on the safe side, and he wasn't about to hoist anchor and sail into unknown waters.

The following morning, we got up with the sun, checked the forecast, and headed out into the Gulf Stream. Though there wasn't much wind, we could sail easily. We headed for Cat Cay, but the northerly current was much stronger than we had anticipated, and when we arrived at Bimini, miles north of or intended destination, we were surprised at the power of the stream. True, we could have started the engine and powered against the current, but we were sailors, and we loved to use the wind.

Cruising the Bahamas was rewarding and somewhat challenging. One can almost always see the bottom while sailing the Bahamas bank, and that white sand sliding by just below the keel is not terribly reassuring. Occasionally, a large fish would dart from under the boat as we sailed along. It takes a while to accustom oneself to sailing in shallow waters with an iron keel dangling below, but after a bit, we got used to it.

Highborn Cay was one of our first stops. There was a Hunter 34 named *Irie* there that somehow looked familiar to me. We met the captain and his wife and struck up a conversation. They were from the Detroit area originally and kept their boat at the Port Huron Yacht Club before they moved to Florida. In Florida, they lived in El Galleon condominium on Manasota Key. What? They were our neighbors. That was where I'd seen their boat. They lived right next door. From that moment on, we became fast friends.

One of the attractions of Highborn Cay is the spring. There is a sign on the shore that points to the trail that goes to the spring. I grabbed a five-gallon water container, and Julie and I followed the trail. It went up a rather steep hill, which seemed a bit unusual, but after a few minutes, the trail rounded a bend, and there, dangling from the branch of a small tree, was a coil spring for a car suspended from a rope. It may sound like a cruel joke, but the spring teaches an important lesson to those sailing in the Bahamas. Water is not easily available, and if it is available, one may have to tote it a fair distance. Carrying five gallons back to the boat from that spring would have been daunting. The lesson here: turn off the water when brushing one's teeth. Water is precious, indeed.

There was a national sea park at Wardrick Wells Cay. Buildings were under construction, and free dockage was available if one was willing to work. Julie and I tied up and took the challenge. I remember nailing down flooring in a building. The work was manual labor, but the workers were more than worth the day. There was an old man who had sailed for years on his small boat, *Blew by You.* Attractive young couples pitched in and earned their keep. Everyone did his part willingly. It was an amazing day. Construction progressed at a rapid pace.

And so it went. Island after island greeted us. We anchored, we swam, we enjoyed restaurants, and we slept on our boat night after night. We met interesting people. We fell into the cruising lifestyle. At Staniel Cay, we swam in caves where a James Bond film had been made. We learned where to get water and fuel, and we continued south until we reached Georgetown, where a great flock of cruisers gathered for the winter. On the way to Georgetown, Julie decided it would be a good idea to fish while leaving a small harbor in a roaring current. "I can't help you if you catch a big one," I said. She caught a big one while I was navigating the treacherous harbor mouth and fighting a vicious current at the helm. The fish that Julie landed was delicious! It was in Georgetown where I learned the difference between plantains and bananas. It was also in Georgetown where we decided to turn around. We had explored the Exumas, and it was time to come about and head back for Englewood.

We had tasted the cruising life, and it was sweet.

Back in Englewood, we found the couple to whom we had rented the condo had taken beautiful care of the place. They wanted to come back. What good news! We raced the boat a few times in Venice and then found a marina in Port Charlotte where we could store her for the summer. They would prop her hull up on jack stands, and that would be it. No need to cover her. She would be supported, and her mast would be left standing. Unlike Western New York, there would not be feet of snow. There was no need for antifreeze. After a coat of bottom paint and a little wax, she would be ready to launch in the fall. Should a hurricane hit, well, we were insured.

Still snowbirds, we drove back to Western New York, where we visited the cottage, sailed our fourteen-foot West Wight Potter, and took care of the house.

CHAPTER 100

2001

Two thousand and one was a bit more difficult. Of course, there was the terror of 9/11. We had sailed by the towers and, we had taken the subway from New Jersey and landed at the base of the World Trade Center. How sad. What a senseless loss.

We headed for Florida in October but returned for a wedding in November. That was when we discovered that my mother, living alone and in her late eighties, was not doing well. She had fallen and hurt her back, was not taking her medications, and was not eating well. We wanted her to come to Florida to be with us, but she insisted that we had our own lives to live and that she didn't want to interfere. We found an assisted-living community where she could go. She could afford it, and they would provide a nice room and meals. Several of her old bridge club friends lived there. Why not? She finally agreed, and we moved her in before we returned to Florida. We came home at Christmas, and she seemed much better and even liked the place. We celebrated the holidays together with family. When we returned to Florida, we were off to the Abacos, the northern Bahamas Islands.

CHAPTER 101

Abacos

It was an easy sail, really. We left Miami as we had the previous year, and we headed for the Abacos. One of our first nights, we found ourselves talking with a man on an OE 34, a boat I had long dreamed of owning. He had been an officer on the *Nautilus*, the first American nuclear submarine. He was fascinating, one of the unusual people one finds in the cruising community. Fun.

We moved on to Marsh Harbor, where we ran into Ed and Joan Will, old friends from the Dunkirk Yacht Club. They were in their trawler, *Willem*. What a wonderful time we had with them. That was when we heard from Julie's sister. My mother had been taken to the hospital with heart problems. She thought we should come home. We made arrangements to store the boat and bought air tickets. Sure enough, Mother was found to have multiple myeloma. She elected to have palliative care and hospice, not to be treated for the disease. She died two weeks later, still in the hospital. What a sad time it was for us. Still, life goes on.

Back on the boat, we found ourselves more and more at home on the sea. We decided to head back to the United States. We checked out and then noticed a Nauticat 35 sailboat docked nearby at customs. That had been the boat of my dreams. Her long waterline, fin keel, and spade rudder, a Sparkman and Stevens design, indicated that she would sail well. Her pilothouse, two heads, and two double cabins indicated she would provide ample space for four and a dry place to navigate in foul weather. What was more, we learned she was for sale. She was beautiful as she sat by the dock. The owner was engaged in a card game belowdecks and wasn't about to come out and sell us his boat, but he did pass along his card.

Bad weather was approaching, forecasts for the following day included northerlies, and the next several days looked unsettled. If we were going to cross the stream, this was the time. Just before sunset, we cast off and headed west. Winds were favorable as *Trilogy* passed through the harbor mouth and headed into the Gulf Stream. Ship traffic was light that night, and we slid along on autopilot, sure that we didn't want to get caught up in the approaching cold front.

We came in to Fernandina Beach and checked in with customs. From there we sailed down the Intracoastal to Miami and the Keys, eventually finding our way back to Englewood. Mother's estate was settled.

Still, that Nauticat 35 haunted us. We looked it up on the Internet, and sure enough, she was for sale. We talked about it. Finally, we made arrangements to go and check it out. Destin was a full day's drive from us. We really were fond of the boat. It was well equipped with air-conditioning and all the navigation instruments we could imagine. It even had a diesel generator, a 110-volt model mounted on the port side. Wow! I knew that having a survey done by a competent surveyor was very important, but I had never hired a surveyor, and so we were a bit uneasy.

Later in the summer, from Ashville we booked a flight to Destin, Florida, her home port, and hired the local marine surveyor. The owner graciously allowed us to sleep on the boat the night before and the night of the survey so we wouldn't need a motel. What an adventure!

We rented a car and got there on the eve of the survey. Everything went just as planned. We met the owner, who showed us around the boat. We slept well that night, and early the following morning, the surveyor arrived with his bag of tools. He went right to work, examining every inch of the boat, bow to stern. He used the anchor windlass to hoist him up the mast, trusting me to keep tension on the halyard as he ascended. He removed the inflatable dinghy and found some decay in the transom. He unscrewed gussets around the chain plates that anchored the halyards or mast supports and checked that they hadn't been corroded by saltwater leakage. He checked every instrument and made notes on every piece of equipment aboard. He was thorough and took pains to miss nothing. After lunch, we started her up and moved under the bridge to a large marina, where the boat slipped into a haul-out slip and was raised out of the water.

The surveyor shook his head. "Blisters," he said. "It may take a year or more to dry out this hull before you can make repairs. I suggest you not buy this boat."

The owner, who had come with us, was shocked. "I think a little Marine Tex will take care of it," he said sheepishly.

"If your girlfriend had pimples, wouldn't you marry her anyway?" said a grisly yard attendant.

But that was exactly why we had hired the surveyor. We were amazed at his candor. We had paid him for his opinion, and he gave it. "Don't buy this boat."

The deal was off.

The owner told us we could still sleep aboard that night. The next morning, we drove our little rental car back to the airport and took off for Western New York and then Ashville.

What next?

CHAPTER 102

Brokers

There was an ad in one of the boating magazines that mentioned several Nauticat 35s. We talked to a broker, and after a while, we decided to head to Annapolis and have a look. One boat was weighted down with stuff and, though comfortable, not well equipped for cruising. But there was another that captured our imagination. She was called *Cloud Nine.* Interestingly, she had only 425 hours on her hour meter, and she was sparsely equipped. She had electric, self-tailing winches, something we didn't think we needed, an expensive feathering propeller, roller furling jib, and in-boom furling main, but that was about it. There were three 4D twelve-volt batteries, but no generator or water maker. There was a third bunk in the forward cabin. It appeared to us that the boat had been ordered in Finland but then shipped to the United States at the last minute. Its propane system had no electric solenoid. That was an established requirement in the United States. There was no generator aboard, and the Yanmar fifty-horsepower engine had just a fifty-five-watt alternator, hardly enough to support electric winches and the refrigeration system aboard. There were no solar panels. There were basic navigation instruments, depth, wind, speed, and direction, as well as boat speed, and they were double, one on the bridge and the other in the pilothouse. There were two compasses. The windlass on the bow was hand-powered. A winch handle on the windless allowed the crew to hoist chain and anchor.

We learned that the first owner had lived north of the I-95 bridge in Washington, DC. He lived aboard and seldom ventured under the bridge, which opened only after midnight on weekends, to travel or cruise. He obviously had a girlfriend who wore high-heeled shoes. She had left her impression on the polished wood pilot-house floor. The current owner kept the boat on a lift in front of his condo in the Annapolis area. He was retired navy and told us he had been aboard the *Nautilus* on its first cruise. What a coincidence! He was an elderly man. It seemed to us this boat was a little used-dock ornament.

We had promised my mother we would not cross an ocean while she was still alive. But she was gone now. This boat held one hundred gallons of fuel and two hundred gallons of water, enough for serious cruising. True, it was not well fitted to cross an ocean, but we would want to fit our boat out ourselves if we were going to use it for long-range travel.

We hired a surveyor, and his report was filled with issues. As before, we took the boat to a nearby marina to be hauled out. This time, however, there was no problem with the bottom. The boat had been stored on a lift out of the water, after all. The surveyor didn't like the copper gas lines or a propane system without an electric sole-noid to shut down the system should there be a fire or gas leak. He thought the manual gas valves in the system were a dangerous liabil-ity. He thought the bottom paint needed to be removed and a sealer be applied to prevent osmotic blistering. He was sure the cutlass bearing in the propeller shaft needed to be replaced. Still, this was a little used Naucticat 35. With some careful preparation, she could be made ready for serious cruising. We made an offer, and she was ours.

We took her to a yard suggested by the broker. They would remove layers of bottom paint and add sealer and new paint. Then they would remove the folding prop and replace the worn cutlass bearing before replacing the prop. They would also add two insula-tors to the backstay so we could use the insulated portion as a sin-gle-sideband antenna for the ham and single-sideband marine radio. In the meantime, Julie and I would do what we could to refine and update the navigation system. We would add the solenoid to the gas system, thoroughly clean the engine compartment, install our ham radio equipment, and be sure she was ready to go. We would sleep aboard while she was being refitted in the yard. The only stipulation the owner had made was that, as we would purchase the boat on a Friday, we would have to take her away on Saturday, and we could not sleep aboard on Friday night.

To do that, we would have to reregister her in our names. We were warned that registration was an important step. Even though we intended to document the vessel, we would need temporary registration. Without it, we could be arrested and fined. Unfortunately, or fortunately, by the time we had gotten the paperwork from the seller, the Department of Motor Vehicles in Maryland was closed. What to do? The broker suggested Delaware. "There is no sales tax in Delaware," he said. With that, we headed across the border, where we drove to the nearest DMV. The registration process was straightforward even though we were not Delaware residents. We paid our fees, bought decals of the numbers, and attached them to plywood boards we had already fashioned and painted. My cousin lived nearby, and we arranged to have dinner and spend the night with her.

The launch was simple. The salesman flipped the switch, and the boat was lowered into the water. Julie and I climbed aboard, I started the engine, and we backed out into the river. It was a quiet Saturday morning in early October, but it wasn't quiet for long. As we moved through busy Annapolis harbor, we heard a racket below. Cupboard doors were opening and slamming shut as the boat rocked on the wakes of passing vessels. Julie ran below, grabbed a screwdriver, and went to work adjusting the latches so that the doors shut and stayed shut, while I steered from the cockpit. By the time we reached the haul out at the marina where the work was to be done, my capable wife was exhausted, but our new friend had settled in. She was already much more fit than when she had started just a few hours before.

We thought the men at the yard were wonderful. Once she was on her stand, they began working on the nasty business of scraping many layers of bottom paint from the hull. They wore masks and eye protection and suits to protect them from the noxious dust, but it was nasty work, and it took several days. While the men were working on the hull, Julie and I went into town to purchase needed items for the boat. One day, we picked up a coffeepot and some pots and pans for the galley. A tradition of boat buying is that when one has a boat surveyed, there is an understanding that whatever is aboard the boat when it is surveyed goes with it. When we had this girl surveyed, however, there was liquor in a cabinet and a full complement of cookware in the galley. When we returned to claim her, however, all that was gone. It wasn't a big deal, so we just bought new. Well, all of a sudden, the credit card said, "No." We had exceeded our credit limit. We contacted the company. We had the money, but it would take some time to correct. Whatever.

Back on board that night, we managed to cook a light dinner in the one pot we did have, and we ate from two plates we had brought with us. It wasn't elegant, but it worked. After dinner, it began to rain hard. It grew cold, and the wind whistled through the rigging. We had electricity, as the boat was plugged into the yard's power, but there was only a small propane heater in the forward cabin. It was a Monday night, rain pounded on the cabin top, and we lighted the Force 10 propane heater. We had brought a six-inch TV from the other boat, and we were able to get *Monday Night Football* with our "rabbit ears" on the TV. The heater was warm, and as it was vented overboard, it was safe. The dorade vents admitted fresh air. After dinner, we found ourselves warm and dry and somehow very comfortable in our little cabin. The game was fun to watch, but it was the warm ambiance of the cabin with the rain pounding overhead and the wind screaming through the rigging that made us think of the challenging times we might face in our new friend. Whatever lay ahead, we felt ready for it.

Several days later, we took the car and again headed for town. We settled our finances and did some more shopping. When we got back, several men were working on the cutlass bearing that had to be replaced to satisfy the survey. They were taking the feathering propeller off the shaft and throwing the parts in a bucket. As they were doing it, they were visiting with one another and laughing.

"Ah, did you record the settings on the prop?" I heard myself saying as I watched them casually take the rather-complicated propeller apart.

"No. Not a big deal. After we change the bearing, we'll reassemble it just like that one over there." He pointed to a racing boat about the same size as ours. "We've done lots of these. Don't worry."

With that, there was a bang as another part dropped into the bucket. He told us that the man who had removed the backstay had been bitten in the hand by his dog. He couldn't work until his hand healed. Unfortunately, he had taken the clevis pin that attached the backstay to the mast. We had tried our best to get a similar clevis pin, and later that evening I hoisted Julie with the heavy wire/radio antenna up the mast. She fastened the new backstay in place at the masthead and we connected the lower end to the chain plates on deck. The hull had been sealed with epoxy sealer, primed, and the first black coat of paint had been applied. Blue paint would be applied later.

The following afternoon, when we came back to the boat, she looked ready. The yard foreman assured us that all the work had been done. We were to inspect her and let them know if there was anything more we wanted done. We should understand that if we were dissatisfied after launch, it would cost $150 should we need to haul her again. Then it would cost $150 to relaunch her after the work was completed. If we were satisfied with the work as it was, we would launch at eight the following morning. We looked her over and agreed that everything looked fine. With that, the crew went home, and we were left to another quiet night on the boat.

Still, something about those men working on the propeller the previous day bothered me. Julie found the book for the prop, and we began to study it. Within the handbook, a letter and a number were circled, indicating the settings that had been used when the prop was installed originally. I went aft and had a look at the prop. I had read that the engine turned the prop clockwise to move the boat forward. When I looked at the prop, however, it was plain that if the prop was turned clockwise, water would be moved forward and the boat would go astern. Something was very wrong! We got an Allen wrench and began to disassemble the prop. It was growing dark, but with the aid of our flashlight, we could see that the numbers and letters did not agree at all with the settings marked in the manual. We took the pieces into the pilothouse and figured out how the prop should be correctly reassembled. We had had a folding prop on our Tartan sailboat. This feathering prop was more complex, but still, we understood how it should be. Early the next morning, we finished breakfast, and in the dawn's early light, we carefully reassembled the prop on the shaft. We used the settings in the manual and locked the settings in place so when the boat was in forward, it would indeed go forward. We greased it and hoped it was ready to go. We finished just before the foreman arrived. We went into his office and made our final payment, but we never mentioned the prop.

With that, Julie and I walked to the launch slip and watched as the travel lift picked our boat up, moved it over the water, and lowered it gently into the sea. We stepped aboard, and I went below to start and warm up the engine.

"Now, gently back her out of the slip," said the man running the travel lift. "Take her out and do a big circle in the bay here. Speed her up, slow her down. If you need any further adjustments, bring her back, and we'll see what we can do."

The man who had serviced the prop was there too. Both men smiled. I shifted the engine into reverse, and we slowly backed from the slip. I nodded, and the men looked at each other and then tossed the lines they were holding on deck. Out of the slip, I shifted to forward, and the boat obediently moved ahead. We sped up and made a large circle, and I gave them a thumbs-up. When I glanced at the two men left behind, I saw them, hands on hips, their mouths open in apparent disbelief.

We had reserved a place at a dock in Davis Creek, not far from Annapolis. The dock was at a vacant lot owned by a gentleman who had been a noted television cameraman. Our broker had made the arrangements. It was remote, indeed. We would leave the boat there while we drove our car back to Florida, picked up our cooking utensils and other boat gear, loaded it all in a rental car, and drove back to the boat. We would then have to return the rental to BWI Airport and spend a few days installing radios and making the boat ready for offshore work. Interestingly, we would be in a very rural setting, with no car, no access to hardware stores or marine shops. In fact, there would not even be a restaurant or market nearby. We loved challenges, and this was a challenge indeed. My Delaware cousin picked us up at the airport and brought us to the boat. She took us to a store for groceries, and we all went for a short sail when she said goodbye and headed home. We worked hard on the installations and, a few days later, motored back to Annapolis just in time to meet friends Joe and Betsy, who were there for the Columbus Day weekend boat show.

We filled her tanks with water and fuel, and we headed south. The first night, in a small creek, we anchored. In the middle of the night, there was a *thump*. Sure enough, the wind had come up. We had dragged our anchor and had bumped into another nearby boat. The reason was obvious. We had not put out enough scope. The anchor line was too short. Not good. But things got better as we moved along. We would call her *Tapestry*, we decided. We hoped she would present us with a carefully woven picture of our world, a tapestry etched in fabric with feelings and smells and real-life adventures carefully melded into tactile memories. The cruise went very smoothly as we moved south. We stopped in Wilmington and gave Julie's ninety-year-old mom an afternoon cruise on the new boat. We moved offshore as we sailed to Florida and eased our way down the east side to the keys. It was at Marathon Key that things got interesting. I remember we were taking on diesel at a fuel dock. What I remember most, though, was that there were manatees under the dock and the attendant had dropped a hose over the side. The manatees were drinking freshwater from the hose. Wow!

That was when we got the news. There was a rather major cold front approaching from the west predicted to arrive at the Florida coast early the following morning. We decided on the spot to push off and head for Englewood. We were sure we could beat the storm. Off we went. The afternoon sailing was easy over Florida Bay, and it wasn't until nightfall that things began to get really interesting. After 3:00 a.m., distant flashes of lightning illuminated the night sky, and winds began to increase. The forecasts were ominous. We had intended to make landfall at Boca Grande, but sailing up a lee shore in possible gale-force winds did not seem wise, so we headed for Fort Myers Beach instead. We got there at first light, just before the storm hit. I called the bridge tender on VHF, and when I asked for an opening, his reply was that he was not allowed to open the bridge in winds in excess of forty knots.

I was stunned! But then he backed off and said it wasn't quite that windy yet. "Come on in, sailor, I've got an opening for you." Whew!

It was pouring rain when we arrived in Englewood, our Florida home. A few days later, we had a christening party on the dock at the condo, and Julie smashed another bottle of champagne over her bow. This time, we christened her with her new name, the one so carefully added to her transom. We worked on her. We added davits so we could hoist our dinghy up over her stern for easy access and out-of-the-way storage. Julie made a cover for the dinghy to keep the water out. We added our solar panels from *Trilogy* and integrated them into the electrical system. We set up our ham radios, carefully grounded them, and connected them to the backstay antenna. One problem we couldn't handle, however, was the autopilot. It had died on the way south, and we needed to have it replaced. As the steering system on the new boat was hydraulic rather than mechanical, we felt we needed professional help with that part of the job. After a phone call, a smiling young man from a Sarasota business that specialized in such work appeared at our door. He had a replacement and, after a morning's work, had the replacement working. Beautiful. I'll never forget the bill either. It was for $1,500.39. I know the part cost less than $400, but when one is dealing with yachts, if you have to ask…

We got mail! The state of Maryland thought, as we had pur-chased our boat in Maryland, that we owed them sales tax. As we had used our New York State address when we registered the boat in Delaware, New York thought we owed it sales tax. Finally, as we had passed under bridges in Florida with our Delaware license, Florida thought we owed them sales tax. This was not good. But things began to fall into place. As the boat had never been to New York, it was tax exempt. As it had not been registered in Maryland, it was exempt there too. A call to a local Florida State senator informed us that we had ninety days to get the boat out of Florida before sales tax would be collected. Good news. Our federal documentation and Delaware registration would keep us legal for at least ninety days.

CHAPTER 103

Away

Leaving Englewood was bittersweet. After packing the boat with our personal belongings and loading the boat fridge and storage areas with food, we packed all our leftover clothes from the condo into the trunk of the car, parked our Pontiac in our spare parking space, said goodbye to the renters, and left. We untied the boat, started the engine, backed from the slip, and headed south on the ICW. It was the third of January 2002, well before our ninety days would have run out. We visited friends in Naples and then headed for Key West via Marathon and the Keys.

Our goal was to sail first to the Bahamas and then to the Caribbean via what was called the Thorny Passage. That route would take us to the Turks and Caicos Islands and then to Haiti, the Dominican Republic, and finally, the US Virgin Islands. The route was fraught with shallow water, and we were warned to be wary of desperate pickpockets who might use razor blades to slit our pockets and take our wallets. Hmmm.

It was in Key West on the sixteenth of January, my birthday, that we found ourselves anchored next to a lovely Canadian sailing yacht named *Red Wine*. The owners were having a party that night, and they asked us if we would like to join them. We did. There was plenty of red wine and a delightful dinner. But the highlight of the evening was a discussion of our intended cruise. "Why not take I-64?" said one of the guests. I told him that I didn't understand,

and he explained. "Go to the Bahamas, as you plan to do anyway, and then head east to sixty-four degrees west. Then head south. You will be roughly on a line between Bermuda and Saint John in the US Virgin Islands. By heading east, wind and current will be favorable. When you reach sixty-four degrees, head south to the islands. Winds and seas will increase greatly as you progress, but you will be on a reach, and they will be manageable. Best of all, you will avoid all the perils of the Thorny Passage."

"So have you done this?" I asked.

"No, but I know people who have," he replied. "Believe me, it is the better way."

That night, after we motored the dinghy back to *Tapestry*, I pulled an old book, *Ocean Passages of the World,* from our little library. I remember looking for the route sailing ships used when traveling from Florida to the Virgin Islands. Sure enough, they followed a path similar to what the man on *Red Wine* had described. Hmm.

We left Key West the following day and headed back toward Marathon, where we met our friends Bob and Carol. They would accompany us in their small-diesel lobster boat from Marathon to the Bahamas. We had been told that traveling with the Gulf Stream from Marathon to the islands was much easier than crossing from Miami, as we had done in the past. It was while we were in Marathon that I found myself standing in line to use a pay phone for PocketMail, a trendy device used to record and send e-mails from telephones. While waiting, I visited with a man who had actually sailed the very route we had heard discussed on *Red Wine*. He assured me the passage would likely take more than a week, but it was a reasonable way to go. We would, of course, be truly offshore the whole way, but for a well-found vessel, it was the safest route.

CHAPTER 104

Bahamas

Once again, we headed for the beautiful islands we had so enjoyed the two previous years. But this time, we had another goal. We would leave the Bahamas and sail offshore to the Caribbean, where new adventures would await us.

We worked our way promptly toward the islands and checked in. A customs and immigration officer came aboard and examined our papers. He looked around and, apparently satisfied, signed our paperwork and wished us well.

We were on Staniel Cay in the Bahamas when things got interesting. We swam in the underwater caves where part of *Thunderball*, a James Bond picture, had been filmed, enjoyed the ambiance of the place, and endured several powerful fronts that passed through. That was when I saw him. He was a retired Canadian police officer who had once been part of a Toronto SWAT team, and he was traveling with his wife on their boat. He had been aboard *Red Wine* in Key West several weeks before when we had discussed our plans on my birthday.

"What are you waiting for?" he said when he saw me.

"I'm sorry," I said. I couldn't remember his name.

"Well, I thought you were heading for the Caribbean?"

"There is another front approaching," I said, somewhat unconvincingly.

"Yes, Henry, there always will be. Why not go today? They've got the fuel pumps running at the marina. It's early yet. You could be off and away from the islands before dark."

I suddenly remembered the couple on that Newport 28 in Miami Harbor that had been waiting all year for the right day to cross to the Bahamas.

I said goodbye and headed for the boat and Julie. "Why not?" I said, and my wife, who never says no to adventure, was eager to go. We hauled up the anchor and headed for the marina, where the fuel pump had indeed been repaired. We filled the tanks with diesel and water. While we were there, we said our goodbyes to Bob and Carol, who had come with us on that part of the journey. When Bob shook my hand, I thought I saw a tear in his eye. I gave Carol a hug as she handed us a loaf of fresh bread, and we pushed off. We were on our own in our new boat, headed toward new horizons.

Around six that evening, we contacted Herb Hildenberg, who regularly helped boaters move about using his computers and communication facilities located in his home in Saint Catherins, Ontario.

The call was routine. He was on the air, and we contacted him. We told him of our plans. He agreed it was a good time to make the passage, and he suggested a heading that was north of where we were planning to go, more toward Bermuda. The one thing we knew from working with Herb on our way home from Bermuda years before was that the one condition he had was that you do what he recommended if you wanted his continued help. He suggested what our position would be the following day, and we agreed to head for it. Before we signed off, the skipper of a large sport fisherman called in. Herb suggested that he, too, should head north to avoid rough weather between us and the Virgins. The skipper insisted he had to get south and heading north and east didn't make sense. It was the very next evening that he again called Herb. This time, his tone was different. He talked of huge waves, difficulty making progress, very rough going.

It was beautiful sailing for us that evening. Julie prepared dinner, and we were able to eat in the pilothouse while the boat sailed herself through gentle seas. We slept in three-hour shifts at night as our boat gushed silently along. Every fifteen minutes or so, one of us would stick our head out the companionway and explore the horizon for ships. The stars on moonless nights were simply amazing. Words cannot describe them. Though we used the autopilot from time to time, we spent most of our waking hours at the helm, steering from the comfortable seat, looking out the windshield at the stars and sea ahead. Three hours on, three hours off. It was remarkable how easy it was to fall asleep and to rouse oneself when one knew the safety of the ship depended on it. Came morning, the gurgling percolator and the rich smell of coffee filled the pilothouse. There were naps in the afternoons, there was fishing, but mostly, there was us and the sea. Every afternoon, we talked with Herb and made our best effort to be where he had asked us to be the day before.

After seven days of sailing east, we came about and headed south. We began to estimate our arrival time at Saint John. Of course, it was only important that we arrive in daylight to help us navigate in those unfamiliar waters. Everything looked good. We should arrive in the daytime, we thought.

Each day we called into the ham radio Waterway Net and reported our position. We had a regular routine, and soon the cruising life became easier. As we ventured south, we were impressed by how long it had been since we had seen a ship or even an airplane. At night, the stars and planets shone down on us, and truly, we felt we could see farther into the night sky than we ever had. Still, planes and ships were few. From time to time, we would have to run the engine to keep the batteries charged or, when the wind was too light, to let us make three knots. But when we were sailing, there were just the sounds of the boat moving through the water and the wind in the rigging.

One night, as we ghosted along, we had the VHF marine radio on channel 16, as we always did, when we heard an emergency call between an aircraft and a boat in distress. The aircraft called itself Coast Guard San Diego, but how could that be? We listened intensely. They were apparently participating in the rescue of crew members from a boat in distress. But San Diego? The conversation went on for a while, and we were mesmerized. How could this have happened? VHF marine radio is line of sight. Fifty miles is the absolute maximum distance a signal can travel. But sometimes there are weird atmospheric conditions and there is a skip where the signal bounces off the ionosphere and magically travels thousands of miles. Indeed, this signal had traveled several thousand miles to reach us en route to the Caribbean all the way from the Pacific Ocean, near San Diego. Of course, as this was an emergency at sea, we didn't interrupt, but a friend familiar with such phenomena later said he thought it might have been possible to have a two-way conversation. Imagine that!

As we approached the Virgin Islands, the winds began to increase markedly, and the waves grew and grew. Large waves at sea are widely separated, and it wasn't until we spotted a container ship that we realized how large they were. The ship would appear and disappear as we were lifted and dropped between the waves. We reefed the sails as we realized that, at our present speed, we would arrive in the early morning rather than in broad daylight. We shortened sail further, but the wind continued to increase, and we went ever faster. The course Herb had selected for us had made it easy for us to make good time, but it was clear we should make landfall in the middle of the night.

Sure enough, it was 2:00 a.m. when we saw the first lights of the Virgin Islands. We hove to. In other words, we tacked the boat but did not move the jib to the leeward side. That way, Tapestry basically held her ground and didn't move. We maintained our watches and kept a careful eye out for ships. At first light, Julie made coffee, and by the time the sun broke over the horizon, we were again moving through magnificent tall islands toward Saint John, where we would check in with customs and begin our Caribbean adventure.

CHAPTER 105

Saint John

The island of Saint John was mostly a national park. We anchored the boat in Cruz Bay and walked to the customs office. We checked in with customs easily and then returned to the boat. I remember we visited a nearby sugar mill while we were there. The apparatus that had been used for making sugar was prominent. Its chimney rose in the air, and the mill itself was s symbol of the Virgin Islands. One of the byproducts of the sugar industry was the making of rum, certainly an important product then and today. Schoolchildren were touring the site with their teacher while we were there. It was a beautiful moment watching the kids scamper over the sugar mill and learn about this important part of Virgin Islands history.

But there were places to go and things to see. We enjoyed Saint John and Saint Thomas for a while. In Saint Thomas, we climbed the hundred steps to Blackbeard's castle and enjoyed the island's tourist attractions.

The British Virgin Islands were tantalizing as well. They were exciting to visit, but the charter industry had filled them with sailboats and bars tended to cater to Americans who came there to sail, much as we did. I remember Norman's Island, where we anchored and went to an old ship anchored in the harbor. I believe its name was the *Willie T.* Something like that. The ship was actually a bar and a small restaurant. The attraction was that after a few drinks, young female patrons might be bribed to go to the upper decks, remove their clothes, and jump off, falling nude past the open deck containing the bar and its many wide-eyed patrons on their way down. It was a thrilling spectacle indeed. Unfortunately, a young lady hurt herself in the fall while we were there, and though it was not serious, there was nothing beautiful or fun about that.

CHAPTER 106

Saint Barts, Nevis and Saint Kitts, and Montserrat

Saint Barts, or Saint Barthélemy, as it is more formally known, was a real adventure for us. We sailed into the harbor at Gustavia, named during its Swedish occupation, and checked in with customs. Then we anchored off some restaurants in the harbor and took the dinghy to shore. The city was lovely. Some of the shops had high-quality goods that were very expensive. I remember a place specializing in men's dress shirts. The walls were lined with shelves of shirts in every shade imaginable. All of them were expensive by my standards. What a surprise that was! That evening, we walked by a lovely restaurant right on the water. We looked at the menu posted out front. There was *Tapestry*, swinging on her anchor, framed by the lovely glass windows of the eatery. "Wallpaper, isn't *tapestry* another word for *wallpaper?*" a friend had once said when we mentioned her name. Sure enough, *Tapestry* was indeed providing wallpaper for this lovely restaurant.

It turned out we so liked the island that we rented a car. It wasn't just any car, but a Moke, a mini with no doors or windows, just a convertible top and windshield. What a joy it was to move through the warm tropical air in that little car! We stopped at a restaurant and enjoyed lunch with true French flair. A wonderful salad filled our plate as we looked over a pool and the sea. It was a new world.

Later, we decided to visit a beach. It had been recommended by the car rental people. Why not?

The beach was lovely too. It was another introduction to a culture quite new to us. We walked onto the beach in our street clothes to be greeted by people in all manner of dress. There were men and women who were completely nude lying on towels on the sand, exposing themselves to the sun and anyone who wanted to look. There were others in bathing suits. Sometimes, men and women, some clothed and some nude, sat together and shared a picnic. People swam together, some in bathing suits, some without. There were old people and young people, and everyone seemed to be enjoying himself or herself. In spite of all the beautiful and not-so-beautiful bodies to look at, there was no erotic behavior displayed by anyone. People were friendly and open and pleasant. What a wonderful spot!

We returned the car and got back on the boat, and the next morning, it was off to Saint Kitts and Nevis.

Saint Kitts and Nevis are two separate islands that are located quite close to each other. When Columbus saw them, he thought they were so high they touched the clouds. Still, they have very different governments, and one must check in to customs in each. Neither is easy. I remember long dinghy rides from the anchored boat, taxi rides from customs to immigration, and loads of hassle. I remember, in one of the offices in Nevis, there was a young black woman. It was during the Iraq war. I remember she took my US passport and looked at me and said, "You Americans, have you killed Saddam Hussein yet?" as she handed me my passport. With that rather-cool greeting, I wasn't sure we wanted to spend a lot of time there. Back on the boat, we motored down the coast to a quiet bay where we dropped anchor. Onshore, a large yacht had washed up, apparently in a storm. We went to the beach and examined the hulk. It had been stripped of all electronic and most metal gear. Later, as we were relaxing in the cockpit, two boats came by, both flying French flags. We had heard about the French. Other cruisers had said they wouldn't leave you alone. If you were the only boat in a secluded cove, a Frenchman would feel comfortable coming in and anchoring right next to you. Sure enough, they came very near us, dropped anchor, and began to enjoy the anchorage just a few hundred feet away. Whatever their reputation, they certainly hadn't intruded on us. We had a pleasant evening and, early the next morning, continued south.

From there we sailed to Montserrat. We pulled in and again visited customs. There was a museum in town that told the story of the comparatively recent eruption of the volcano on the island. Death and destruction resulted from rocks and boulders hurled from far under the earth as the volcano erupted. Lava and ash covered much of the island, and rocks rained down, smashing homes. Damaged homes were still visible to passing yachts. To this day, clouds of smoke and ash pour from fissures on the island. We were warned to keep our distance as we sailed by. Another violent eruption was always possible, and many of the former residents had been relocated in the UK. The island had been home of a recording studio for popular music, but no more. It was a smoldering reminder of the potential hazard caused by volcanic activity.

CHAPTER 107

Heading Home

It was there we turned around and headed back. We stopped at Antigua, where we found a comfortable English island. There were lovely pubs built of stone. A comfortable village. From there we headed back toward the Virgins, where we would store the boat for the summer. We stopped on the Dutch side of Sint Maarten, where we found a delightful town with competent repair people and fine restaurants.

Finally, we came back to the BVIs. We met our friends Ed and Joan, who had rented a place on Tortola. I remember leaving the boat in Soper's Hole, anchored behind a wrecked tugboat in a picturesque cove. We took the dinghy to shore, where Ed and Joan met us. We went to their lovely home and enjoyed several days with them, exploring restaurants and magnificent vistas on the island. We arranged for the boat to be hauled for the summer at a nearby marina. While we were there, we met Hastings, Ed and Joan's friend, who was a boat mechanic and a delightful man who lent real insight into the islands. During that stay in Soper's Hole, we met another gentleman who would have a profound influence on our later life.

I took Julie to shore one morning so she could do her morning run. As I was about to return to the boat, I noticed a man who was working in a French sailboat near where I dropped Julie off. I said hello. He told me he had just bought his boat, a used charter boat, and that he was about to pick up his life raft and sail across the Atlantic to Europe. I expressed interest, and he paused. "Have a computer?" he asked.

"Of course," I replied.

"Look up *World Cruising*," he said. "That'll tell you about the ARC. They go every year in May, before the hurricane season and after the winter storms. Costs about a grand. Been doing it for years. Amazing safety record. They pay for slip fees, and you get terrific meals along the way. Print the whole site. 'Bout twenty-five pages. Last page is the application. They tell you how your boat has to be prepared, what you need, the works."

"I suppose you need three people."

"Nope, any boat twenty-seven to sixty feet can go. Two people is all that's needed. My dad told me Croatia was the most beautiful place he had ever seen. Was there in WWII. That's why I'm going. Hey, do it, and good luck!"

And that was it. I picked up Julie an hour later, and we talked about it. Could we? Would we?

Finally, reservations to Florida were made, and *Tapestry* was hauled, placed in a cradle, and made ready for summer in the Virgins. Other sailors had warned us about storage. "Remove all food," they had said. "Rats can smell tuna even through the can. Spread rat poison throughout the boat. Roach poison is important as well. Remember to put bleach in the water system. Put crumpled-up screen in the dorade vents. Push it in hard and secure the vents from the outside." Finally, they said, "Make sure they don't store your boat under a tree, especially a tree that doesn't have a rat shield around the trunk."

That was a big order, but we did all we could. We didn't have to antifreeze anything, of course, but we did remove all sails and covers and the bimini. We sealed her up and crossed our fingers. When we left, she was in the middle of the yard, but there was no question she would be moved. Would she be under a tree? We asked that she not be. How would she do with tropical rains? Could she survive a hurricane?

We hoped for the best, took the ferry back to Saint Thomas, boarded an airplane, and flew, via Puerto Rico, back to Florida.

We rented a car at the Tampa airport and drove home to Englewood late at night. We stopped for a bite to eat on the way. Our renters, Roger and Sandy, had left the condo spotless, as they always had. After a few weeks, we climbed in our used Pontiac and headed for Western New York.

And there we were. We, two white people, had married, joined the Peace Corps, and gone to learn to teach in Macon County, Alabama, in all-black schools when segregation was the law of the land. After that, we had gone to Africa and taught on Likoma Island, a place with no civil authority and five thousand Africans. We loved those people, and we felt the feeling mutual. On the way home, we had gone around the world.

People had told us how dangerous such things were, but we found that most people were loving and kind, and more than once, we had been rescued by those we had gone to help.

Back home, we taught in separate high schools. Again, we found the students there smart, kind, and hardworking. We had retired and sailed to the Caribbean. Again, everyone was better than advertised. People were helpful and seemed to be trustworthy.

Would we join the ARC and sail to Europe? It was there in front of us. When Jimmy Buffett had wanted to learn to fly, he bought an airplane. We had a proper yacht. The application was before us. Would we fill it out, write the check, make the commitment?

We found we were having deepwater dreams.

ABOUT THE AUTHOR

Hank Danielson has enjoyed life from many perspectives. He was born near Jamestown, New York, where he and his father boated and fished and even built a seventeen-foot boat together in the family garage. He mowed lawns, delivered papers, saved his money, and with help from his family, graduated from Grove City College in 1967. He married his high school sweetheart, Julie, and they joined the Peace Corps, where they taught school in Malawi, Central Africa. After Peace Corps, the Danielsons earned master's degrees while teaching high school in Western New York. Hank started the Script Club, a creative writing club focusing on poetry, drama, and prose, while teaching English at Jamestown High School.

Sailing was his summer passion, and he and Julie explored the Great Lakes and the Eastern Seaboard in several small cruising sailboats. Hank taught safe boating classes with the United States Power Squadrons in Chautauqua County for over twenty years. Winters found them cross-country skiing.

In retirement, Hank and Julie travel to Southwest Florida in winter, where they are active cyclists, riding as much as one hundred miles each week with their club, the Coastal Cruisers. They are still active sailors and teach sailing to teens at Dunkirk Yacht Club on Lake Erie in summer. They have explored the Caribbean and sailed transatlantic and through the Mediterranean in their thirty-five-foot sailboat, *Tapestry*. Wherever they went, they found a wonderful world that greeted them with welcoming, open arms.